T0329597

NEW SOUTH AFRICAN REVIEW 4

A FRAGILE DEMOCRACY – TWENTY YEARS ON

NEW SOUTH AFRICAN REVIEW 4

EDITED BY GILBERT M KHADIAGALA, PRISHANI NAIDOO, DEVAN PILLAY AND ROGER SOUTHALL.

WITS UNIVERSITY PRESS

Published in South Africa by:

Wits University Press
1 Jan Smuts Avenue
Johannesburg

www.witspress.co.za

Published edition © Wits University Press 2014
Compilation © Edition editors 2014
Chapters © Individual contributors 2014

First published 2014
978-1-86814-763-2 (print)
978-1-86814-764-9 (digital)

All rights reserved. No part of this publication may be reproduced, stored in a retrieval system, or transmitted in any form or by any means, electronic, mechanical, photocopying, recording or otherwise, without the written permission of the publisher, except in accordance with the provisions of the Copyright Act, Act 98 of 1978.

Project managed by Monica Seeber
Cover photograph © Claire McNulty
Cover design and layout by Hothouse South Africa
Printed and bound by Paarl Media, Paarl

Contents

Preface

A Fragile Democracy – Twenty Years On, the fourth *New South African Review,* is one of doubtless numerous attempts to characterise the state of South Africa some two decades after those magnificent days in late April 1994 when South Africans of all colours voted for the first time in a democratic election. As we write this, we are approaching the country's fourth such election, a significant indicator of the overall success of our democratic transition – for although there may prove to be wrinkles there is every expectation that the forthcoming contest will again be 'free and fair'. Nonetheless, there are likely to be changes in the electoral landscape, there being significant prospect at time of writing that the ruling African National Congress's (ANC's) proportion of the vote will fall below 60 per cent, the level of electoral dominance it has consistently achieved hitherto. While the ANC can claim many triumphs, and can convincingly claim to have transformed South Africa for the better (materially and spiritually), there is nonetheless widespread discontent abroad. The ANC itself displays many divisions. The Tripartite Alliance (which links it to the South African Communist Party (SACP) and the Congress of South African Trade Unions (Cosatu)), is creaking; it is threatened by new opposition parties which appeal to disaffection – especially among the poor and those who feel excluded from the benefits of democracy – and even the established opposition party, the Democratic Alliance (DA) today seeks to cloak itself in the mantle of Mandela. Even while the ANC boasts about steady growth, more jobs, improved service delivery and better standards of living for the majority, critics point out that the economy is stagnating, unemployment remains stubbornly high, corruption flourishes, popular protest abounds, and government and many public services (notably the intelligence agencies and the police) have earned an alarming reputation for unaccountability. So we could go on – but we won't, as we would rather encourage our readers to engage with the wide-ranging set of original essays provided by our authors. All we will say here is that there can be no one narrative of the achievements, disappointments and – yes – outright disasters of the last twenty years, but we are confident that, as ever, the *New South African Review* will add constructively and critically to the debate about where South Africa has come from and in what direction it is going.

The *New South African Review* remains centred in the Sociology Department at the University of the Witwatersrand, although this year the editorial team has been joined by Professor Gilbert M Khadiagala of the University's Department of International Relations. Apart from being indebted to our many contributors, we would like to record our thanks to both the Dean of Humanities, Professor Ruksana Osman, and the Head of the School of Social Sciences, Professor Shahid Vawda, for their encouragement and provision of financial support. Ingrid Chunilall and Laura Bloem, administrators within the Department of Sociology, undertook numerous unglamorous and demanding tasks associated with the organisation of the volume with their usual good humour and efficiency. Last but not least, we owe a huge debt to the team at Wits University Press, notably Veronica Klipp, Roshan Cader and our technical editor Monica Seeber, who not only remained enthusiastic about the project but evinced enormous patience when we as editors failed to toe the line and meet deadlines.

Gilbert M Khadiagala, Prishani Naidoo, Devan Pillay and Roger Southall.
January 2014

South Africa's fragile democracy:
Twenty years on

Devan Pillay and Roger Southall

South Africa's fifth democratic general election takes place a few months after the passing away of the pre-eminent icon of national liberation, Nelson Mandela. His death on 5 December 2013 was greeted with a massive outpouring of grief, as millions from all sections of society – black and white, workers and capitalists, rural traditionalists and modern suburbanites, young and old, socialists and liberals – paid tribute during the week-long proceedings leading up to his funeral. It was a time of reflection and of celebration, of tears and of joy, remembering a life that embodied the hopes and dreams of millions, not only in this country, but throughout the world. Indeed, in an unprecedented show of international solidarity, world leaders from almost every nation descended on South Africa last December to hail one of the true heroes of the modern era. In keeping with his legacy of reconciliation, the leader of the capitalist West, the US president Barack Obama, shook hands with the leader of socialist Cuba, Raul Castro.

But what was Mandela's true legacy? In many senses (as Mao Tse Tung once said in relation to the French Revolution) it's too early to tell. The country is caught between celebrating the achievements of our democracy, and bemoaning the abject failure to eradicate poverty, unemployment and widening social inequality. Were the 'balance of forces' in 1994 such that a political settlement was only possible if the essentials of (predominantly white) corporate economic power and white land ownership remained intact? Or was there space to use the 'Madiba magic' to demand much more, if not the promise of 'socialism' then at least the inclusive development path envisaged by the Freedom Charter? Historians will be debating this for decades to come.

Whatever the strengths and weaknesses of Mandela's political legacy, his personal attributes shine through, and resonate with the best in humanity – the combination of humility and steely determination to achieve one's goals; personal integrity; the willingness to introspect, admit failures and learn from others; kindness towards other living beings and a generosity of spirit. These are the qualities towards which South Africans aspire, that oblige most people – except the lunatic fringes – to forgive whatever shortcomings this icon may have had, and to dwell on the gifts he has bestowed on the nation and the world.

With this in mind, many South Africans judge the shortcomings of those who came after Mandela as leader of the African National Congress (ANC), and of the country. Thabo Mbeki was judged too aloof and arrogant, refusing to listen to the ANC's alliance partners and forging ahead with a disastrous HIV/AIDs policy. He was ousted by Jacob Zuma who, genial and cuddly, clearly does not have his predecessor's grasp of policy issues and is severely tainted by his personal failings – including his social conservatism – and strong allegations of corruption. It is no wonder that members of the ANC booed whenever his face appeared on screens during the memorial service for Mandela last December. Many believe that had Mandela been younger and fitter, and served a second term as the country's president, he would have recognised that the country's orthodox economic path was exacerbating poverty and inequality, and corrected its course (unlike Zuma, who came to power on that promise but failed to deliver).

Nevertheless, despite the shortcomings of the ruling party and its leader it is generally accepted that the ANC, as the historic liberation movement, will win a renewed mandate. It is also widely expected that it will lose some ground electorally, with many predicting that it will receive less than 60 per cent of the vote (compared with a high of just under 70 per cent in the election of 2004). The ANC will, however, undoubtedly triumph again, and celebrate its victory as a victory for democracy – which, in broad-brush comparative terms, it will be. No transition to democracy is ever 'an easy walk to freedom'. Two decades after the collapse of the Soviet Union, Russia under Putin has lapsed back into authoritarianism; within a few years of independence numerous African countries fell prey to dictatorships, coups or civil war; more recently, the 'Arab spring' in country after country has reverted to winter. So, despite the fact that for many South Africa is a 'dominant party democracy' – that is, one in which a ruling party dominates the electoral and political arena under a rubric of formal political competition but faces no apparent threat of losing power – it remains a country where the classic political freedoms (of assembly, movement, association and speech) which were denied to the majority under apartheid remain largely intact, even while various indicators suggest that the quality of democracy is declining.

Any attempt to assess the state of democracy in South Africa after twenty years is obviously a perilous enterprise and, unsurprisingly, there are competing narratives. On the one hand, the ANC government and its supporters claim that while much remains to be done it has brought about significant changes for the better; South Africa is a robust and noisy democracy, and while alarmingly high levels of inequality, poverty and employment persist, major strides have been made in improving the material lives of the majority. On the other hand, critics from both left and right aver that the ANC has proved arrogant and unaccountable, has undermined (or threatened to undermine) key aspects of democracy, and has pursued an agenda of racial transformation which, while promoting the rise of a party-connected elite, has rendered it hugely inefficient and unable to tackle the challenges of reversing the ravages of apartheid. Those on the right want to see more free-market reforms and the leashing of labour, whereas those on the left want more aggressive state intervention to oversee rapid industrialisation, and greater protection for labour. A growing voice is nervous of both excessive state bureaucracy and expanding market domination – and prefers a society-led holistic development path that balances economic growth with environmental sustainability and social equity.

These narratives can scarcely be reconciled – indeed, their debate constitutes a welcome characteristic of South African democracy. In any case, whether we choose to consider that South Africa's glass is half full or half empty will reflect political and ideological positions alongside the particular location of actors and observers (a black mineworker being unlikely to agree about rights and wrongs with a white corporate executive). Nonetheless, it can be argued that the virulence of the debate reflects a deepening sense of crisis and disillusion, a sense that the discord which today characterises South African society is so extreme that it threatens any prospect of social coherence; that it continues to reflect racial divisions and disharmonies; and that a greater sense of national unity is vital if South Africa is to face up to its massive problems. It is fear that South Africa is on a dangerously downward spiral that explains the centrality of Nelson Mandela in the public imagination.

Concerns about South Africa's developmental and democratic trajectory are shared by all contributors to the present volume. What follows is an assessment of the achievements and failures of the democratic transition, within a historical and comparative context.

THE FOUNDATIONS OF DEMOCRACY

The negotiations which culminated in South Africa's transition to democracy in 1994 had proceeded along two tracks. Most famously, the political actors involved, led principally by the ANC and the National Party (NP), reached an agreement (albeit after tortuous contestations) which saw the 'new South Africa' emerge as a constitutional state – one whereby the government and people would ultimately be subject to the values and procedures laid down by a constitution. Equally significant, however, were related discussions between business and the ANC (recognised as the incoming government) which linked the transition from white minority to black majority rule to *de facto* acceptance of free-market capitalism. Although the terminology was to be downplayed – for many within the liberation movement looked forward to a rapid transition to socialism – South

Africa from 1994 was to become a *capitalist* democracy – one in which the ANC would be enabled to hold political power whilst, in the beginning at least, the existing white elite retained economic power. Yet in recognition of the popular forces in play – notably as represented by the Congress of South African Trade Unions (Cosatu) – this capitalist democracy was to be characterised by a social compact between business, the state and labour which embodied hopes that the conflicted economy of the past, characterised by bitter struggles between capital and labour, could be replaced by one founded upon mutual cooperation. Although the resulting deals are often depicted as an 'elite compromise', implying cynical backroom, self-interested bargains struck between old and new elites to limit the extent to which the ANC would be able to democratise (and socialise) the economy, they were arguably necessary. Without them it is unlikely that the political settlement would have been secured at that point; with them, the productive capacity of large-scale capital could hopefully be mobilised and re-oriented to serve the needs of all South Africa's people.

The settlement was intended to provide the basis for democracy. How should we assess its success?

SOUTH AFRICA AS A CONSTITUTIONAL STATE

In 1996 the founding constitution of 1994 gave way to a 'final' constitution, promulgated by a democratic parliament acting as a constituent assembly. Its key features centred around a constitution which made its own supremacy, and that of the rule of law, the cornerstones of democracy; a separation of powers between the executive, the legislature and the judiciary; an independent judiciary whose judgements were to bind all organs of state and all to whom they were to apply; and the creation of independent state institutions to support multiparty democracy. The Constitution incorporated a Bill of Rights enshrining a multiplicity of liberal and social freedoms (rights to life, property, equality before the law, dignity and so on) as well as an obligation on government to promote the interests of persons historically disadvantaged by unfair discrimination (socioeconomic rights). It also required that public administration should be governed by the democratic values and principles enshrined in the Constitution. Institutionally, it established three levels of governance which allocated prime responsibility for policy making and financial administration to the national government, but devolved major policy implementation responsibilities to nine new provinces and local authorities (whose racially segmented predecessors were to be rationalised into a more coherent and united system of local government later confirmed by the first democratic elections in 2000). In essence, the political settlement laid down that the government should be held accountable to the Constitution, the guardianship of which was to be entrusted to a Constitutional Court which would have the authority to rule whether any official conduct or legislation was valid, and whether the government was meeting the obligations imposed upon it under the Constitution (Hoffman 2011).

Under the Act of Union of 1909, South Africa had been governed in an essentially Westminster style which, when push came to shove, enabled governments of the day to enact any legislation they chose. As a result, white minority dictatorship was largely exercised in ways which were fully legal. Under democratic constitutional rule, in contrast, governments are bound by the constitution, and the constitutionality of the laws they enact and the actions they take can ultimately be challenged. The foundation for this was laid down by the requirement of the 'interim' constitution of 1994 that the final constitution, as approved by a constituent assembly, should secure the concurrence of the Constitutional Court that it was in line with agreed constitutional values. This is a constraint that the various ANC governments have had to take seriously, for on different occasions the Constitutional Court has ruled against the constitutionality of actions or ordered the government to fulfill its obligations.

In a recent contribution, Theunis Roux (2012) has argued that the success of constitutional courts is bound up with their capacity to negotiate a tension between politics and law. From this perspective, he has proposed that the Constitutional Court in South Africa has managed to balance its concerns to maintain its independence (its ability to act as the arbiter of the Constitution) by carefully assessing the political risks of its ruling against the government. His approach emphasises the importance of the Constitutional Court's ensuring its legitimacy among citizens, thereby undercutting any tendency of an elected government to equate majoritarianism with democracy. Indeed, a key part of this strategy was the Court's depiction of its role as tantamount to holding the ANC in government to its own longstanding human rights commitments. In other words, it has sought to ensure that although its decisions may go against the government they are not directed specifically at the ANC. Nonetheless, Roux fears that the political threat to the Court (and hence to the Constitution) is increasing. On the one hand, the slow rate of economic growth and the continuing failure to redistribute wealth is exhausting the patience of poor South Africans and 'the time for gradualist, rule-of-law-respecting social reform is running out' (Roux 2012). On the other hand, the ANC's descent into factionalism is encouraging a drift towards populism, and a tendency of both left and right factions of the party to ascribe the country's developmental shortcomings to constraints imposed by the Constitution.

The threats to constitutionalism are real. At one level, they are philosophical. The ANC's liberation movement heritage is clearly emancipatory, yet it is simultaneously authoritarian (Southall 2013). The ANC demonstrated by its leading role in the struggle for freedom that it embodies liberal and human rights values, and it was hugely instrumental in seeing these placed at the centre of the Constitution. Against this, however, the ANC evinces marked tendencies to view itself as the embodiment of the nation, a monopolistic perspective which encourages a majoritarian persuasion, designates opposition as counter-revolutionary – if not illegitimate – and is impatient of minority rights and legal restrictions. Its essentially Leninist conception of state power, and its projected need to capture the commanding heights of society and the economy, proclaims not only its right to rule (based upon its understanding of its role in history as much as upon its electoral pre-eminence), but is also fundamentally at odds with the separation of powers as laid down in the Constitution. Consequently, while ANC governments (under four different presidents) have remained wary of challenging the Constitution head-on, they have often pursued a strategy which has sought to undermine it. Most notoriously, presidential powers of appointment have been used to bend state prosecutorial and intelligence services to the advantage of dominant factions in the party, stripping them of their independence and involving them in intra-party factional battles (as illustrated most vividly by their being drawn into the long-running bitter contest between Thabo Mbeki and Jacob Zuma, culminating in the latter's eventual ejection from office). At all levels of government, too many appointments have been based upon political criteria rather than professional merit, with resultant developmental failure, not least because ANC elites regularly use their positions in party and state to further their personal material interests and to block attempts to probe and prosecute corruption. The fundamental argument is that, in line certainly with numerous other ruling elites, those who run the ANC's party-state seek to make it largely unaccountable (as explored in detail by Dale McKinley in his analysis of 'secrecy and power', below).

Roux and others point out how the initial Constitutional Court was composed of judges who were in philosophical agreement with the ANC's culture of human rights, which in many ways was way ahead of the values of the party's large constituency – indeed, it was left to the Court to rule that capital punishment was unconstitutional. Yet there are legitimate fears that as time wears on, and as political challenges to its dominance mount, the ANC elite is becoming increasingly willing to pander to illiberal aspects of its culturally conservative political base with, for instance, its encouragement of patriarchal practices and values which challenge the right to nondiscrimination on the grounds of sexual orientation enshrined in the Constitution (see Zethu Matebeni, below). Even more worrying is the alliance the ANC has struck up with traditional leaders, which at present is evidenced by attempts by the party leadership to enact a bill which many lawyers, civil society activists, academics and others fear will systematically deprive millions of rural dwellers who live in the former homelands, and are thereby subject to chiefly rule, of their rights as citizens under the Constitution (explored here by Aninka Claassens and Boitumelo Matlala). In this, and other affairs where the government seems intent on avoiding or circumventing constitutional requirements for popular consultation (for which see John Clarke's chapter on how local Pondo interests stand in danger of being overridden by a deal struck between mining interests and political elites), civil society as much as opposition political parties have a major role to play in using the Constitution to hold the government to account. To succeed they will need a Constitutional Court which continues to protect its independence through a shrewd balancing of the often conflicting pressures of politics and the law. It looms as a concern, therefore, that under the Zuma presidency there have been apparent efforts to leverage the executive's ability to influence recruitment to the judiciary, usually justified by reference to the need for (demographic) 'transformation'. The independence of the judiciary remains at the heart of South Africa's consolidation of constitutional democracy.

THE SOCIAL AND ECONOMIC COMPACT

The political settlement of 1994 was underwritten by agreements concluded between the incoming ANC elite and large-scale capital. Successive developments (the Durban strike wave of 1973, the independence of Angola and Mozambique in 1974, the Soweto uprising of 1976, the final defeat of the Smith regime in Zimbabwe in 1980) had increasingly persuaded key elements in business that democracy in South Africa was on the way, and distanced them from an NP government which pursued a militarised strategy of reform from above and was adamant that it would not concede majority rule. Unsurprisingly, business was to be more organised than the government when, following the collapse of the Soviet Union, the then president, FW de Klerk, con Development Programme ceded the need to engage in open-ended negotiations with the ANC if a radical outcome to the liberation struggle was to be avoided.

Since the late 1970s, the more progressive and far-sighted elements of business had begun to engage in strategies which were ultimately to become formalised in ANC policies of black economic empowerment (BEE). Slowly but surely, partly in response to a growing shortage of appropriately skilled whites, partly with a political eye to the future, the large corporations began to recruit blacks into managerial positions. From the early 1980s, such moves were complemented by a succession of meetings with the ANC in exile, on occasion held in defiance of government wishes, at which personal connections were forged and in which common interest in maintaining the productive capacity of the economy were stressed. From the early 1990s, business was joined by international financial institutions in urging the ANC to abandon its liberationist commitments to socialism in favour of market-oriented policies, their persuasiveness reinforced by the ANC's lack of experience in, and appropriately trained personnel for, running an advanced economy (see, for example, Bond 2000). Mandela's personal and political commitment to forging racial reconciliation was to be matched by his growing conviction that pursuit of radical economic policies would result in an outflow of domestic rather than an inflow of much needed foreign investment if necessary rates of economic growth were to be realised. Once the 1994 election was over, the ANC's collectivist commitments, embodied in its Reconstruction and Development Programme, were to be swiftly replaced by a Growth, Employment and Redistribution (GEAR) policy which, although proclaiming similar objectives, adopted market-oriented and unambiguously capitalist means. GEAR was soon to be complemented by the legislative formalisation of BEE which, by the extension of share deals and corporate appointments to chosen members of the ANC elite, enabled business to secure and further its interests through 'political connectivity' and deracialised the apex of the economy by the creation of a class of 'patriotic capitalists' beholden to the ruling party.

For what Scott Taylor (2007) has termed the emergent, pro-market 'reform coalition' to be realised it needed to be underpinned by a wider social compact. There were two dimensions to this. The first outcome was the creation of the National Economic Development and Labour Council (Nedlac), whose purpose was to seek consensus on social and economic policy among government, business, labour and civil society before they were discussed in parliament. The principal achievement of Nedlac was to be the passage of key statutes which restructured the framework of industrial relations. Pride of place was enjoyed by the Labour Relations Act of 1995 (LRA) which sought to replace the existing adversarial culture that had characterised industrial relations with 'codetermination' (on the post-war German model) between employers and employees. It brought together all employees (hitherto treated differentially by the law along largely racial lines) together within a single system of industrial relations, also guaranteeing organisational rights to trade unions, overhauling dispute resolution procedures, and establishing clear rules on dismissal. The LRA was later to be supplemented by the passage of three other measures, the Basic Conditions of Employment Act of 1997 (designed to ensure fair labour practices); the Employment Equity Act of 1998 (designed to promote equal opportunity in the workplace); and the Skills Development Act of 1998 (which aimed to promote investment in training). Although the passage of these Acts recorded the ANC's intent to pay its debts to Cosatu, at the same time they constituted an attempt to bring the order and predictability to industrial relations which business had long desired. Indeed, if strike statistics are anything to go by, they seem to have worked, at least until the mid-2000s.[1] The broader effort to promote social dialogue was, however, to be undermined by the second dimension of the social compact.

During the latter years of apartheid, large-scale capital had undergone a major process of consolidation into huge conglomerates as international companies disinvested in response to political turbulence and sold their assets to local buyers. From the early 1980s, South African large-scale capital had increasingly come to appreciate that only a democratic settlement could provide the opportunity for kick-starting an economy whose steadily worsening performance had its roots in the enormous costs of maintaining a repressive political apparatus based on white minority rule. Further, by the late 1980s it was recognised that, apart from locking up capital within the country, the protectionist regime which apartheid had fostered had rendered South African companies inefficient and uncompetitive. Consequently, when democratisation came, with GEAR in its wake, it offered not only the challenges presented by international competition, but also major opportunities. Large-scale capital underwent a restructuring. Major conglomerates such as the Anglo-American Corporation, Sanlam and Old Mutual 'unbundled', choosing to focus on their 'core' businesses, their 'non-core' assets being snapped up by a mix of public and private investors, domestic and foreign. Meanwhile, a parallel process involved a number of major South African corporations (Billiton, South African Breweries, Anglo-American, Old Mutual and Liberty Life) being allowed by government to migrate to the London stock exchange and to become truly multinational. And as foreign investment flowed in the economy became increasingly internationalised and financialised, developments which were matched by the growth of the service sectors and changes in the composition of manufacturing. In particular, key employment sectors within manufacturing – such as clothing and textiles – were to find themselves placed under threat by imports from low-wage competitors based in, notably, China, while, in contrast, the mining sector – albeit shifting away from gold to minerals such as platinum – was to be boosted by the rising global demand for commodities (Mahomed 2010).

These structural changes were accompanied by an increase in capital intensity in major industries, notably mining, associated industries and agriculture. In part an adjustment to technological advances, this was also a response by private employers to the perceived costs of the new framework of industrial relations. The result was a restructuring of the labour market which saw full-time work steadily giving way to an increasing informalisation of employment. Whereas, on the whole, 'standard employment relationships' were extended in the public sector (which became increasingly unionised), private employers sought to reduce costs by replacing labour with machinery; by outsourcing their supply chain to smaller employers; shifts to part-time work; and so on. Overall, the proportion of the workforce in full-time employment (and hence protected by trade unions) began to decline,[2] as the proportion of workers employed in an essentially deregulated labour market, into which the government's new labour dispensation did in fact extend (or if so, very unevenly), increased (Webster 2006; see also Nicholas Pons-Vignon's and Miriam Di Paola's chapter in this volume).

The outcome of these and other changes is that the post-1994 'reform coalition' and the associated social compact have begun to unravel, as relations between government, business and labour have become increasingly fractious and contested. Nedlac's importance and effectiveness declined significantly following the government's adoption of GEAR, as large-scale business acquired greater influence. This in turn led to increasing strains between the Mandela and Mbeki governments and Cosatu, culminating in the role of the organised left (Cosatu and the South African Communist Party) in unseating Mbeki at Polokwane in 2007 and securing his ejection from the presidency in 2008.

The arrival of Jacob Zuma to power was projected by his supporters as heralding a move to the left in government economic policy, versed principally in terms adopting strategies characteristic of a 'developmental state' in which the state would assume a greater role in directly promoting public sector – and guiding private sector – investment. A major outcome has been the formulation by government (in association with an inclusive set of advisors from industry, unions, academia and civil society) of a National Development Plan (NDP). Winning the broad support of business, this envisages the government's heavy engagement with private capital over coming decades in the expansion of the infrastructure needed to fuel the economy's development. In practice, however, little appears to have changed. Significant sections of Cosatu now reject the NDP as an extension of GEAR; business complains bitterly and regularly that official rhetoric favouring a developmental state is contradicted by policies across different government departments (notably the ministries overseeing mining and trade and industry) which deter investment and impose red tape; and employers complain that the passage of a Labour Relations Amendment Act will serve only the interests of Cosatu, and increase the costs of employment in what they deem to be an already highly 'inflexible' labour market. Meanwhile, faced by the difficult financial conditions since the onset of the global financial crisis in 2008, the government has retained its conservative macroeconomic

framework, prioritising the containment of official expenditure and the control of inflation over the stimulation of the economy to promote investment and employment. South
Africa, laments Sampie Terreblanche (2012), has become 'lost in transformation'.

As the second decade of democracy draws to a close, South Africa seems at war with
itself, veering off course rather than staying on track. Yet such a judgement needs to be
cautious, as the following comparative perspective indicates.

SOUTH AFRICA AT TWENTY: A COMPARATIVE AND INTERNATIONAL PERSPECTIVE

The ANC in 1994 promised 'a better life for all'. In retrospect, the outcome of the democratic era has been mixed. If we assume that 'a better life' means a longer, healthier
and wealthier life for the majority, then the evidence, as recorded by the South African
Institute of Race Relations (2012), is very ambiguous.

- Life expectancy for South Africans has actually declined from 62.9 in 1990 to an
  expected 58.6 in 2015).
- South Africans' well-being, as summarised by the United Nations Development
  Programme Human Development Index, has managed to improve, but at a
  dismally slow rate (from 0.615 in 1990 to 0.619 in 2011, whereas the corresponding
  figures over the same period for Ghana, for instance, have seen a much greater
  improvement, from 0.418 to 0.541).

While these indicators are depressing, those regarding the number of people living in
poverty are only faintly more encouraging (although definitions of poverty are highly
contentious). According to one measure, for instance, whereas some 49 per cent of Africans
lived in 'relative poverty' in 1996,[3] this figure had fallen to 45 per cent in 2011 (having
risen to a high of nearly 59 per cent in 2002); average household income for Africans
having increased by some 210 per cent between 1996 and 2011 (at current prices).

Official statistics show that the proportion of households with access to free basic
water increased from 59 per cent in 2001 to 85 per cent in 2010/11; functioning sanitation facilities increased from some 5 million in 1993/94 to 10.9 million in 2010/11; and
electricity increased from 51 per cent to 74 per cent, and so on, over the same period.

Similarly, there has been an overall improvement in the standard of housing, the number
of formal dwellings having increased from 5.8 million in 1996 to 11.3 million in 2011.

All such indicators are inevitably selective and patchy, varying markedly along racial
lines, across province, and between town and country, and so on, with life expectancy
having been severely affected by HIV/AIDS. Yet the general message is that the standard
of living of people at the bottom of society has been rising – the result of the government's
expansion of the number of recipients of social grants, which leapt from 3.4 million in
2001 to over 15.5 million in 2011/12.

Nonetheless, for all that the ANC in government can claim major credit from such indicators, a widespread response is that although such general indicators are well and good,

the overall performance could and should have been a lot better, and that poorer people's expectations remain hugely unsatisfied, not least because inequality remains so vast, albeit somewhat deracialised since 1994. To many at the bottom of the heap, inequality may have in reality become more visible (and hence more politically salient), as at all levels of society ANC-connected elites appear the major beneficiaries of programmes such as BEE and access to jobs in government and other wealth-making opportunities. Nor does it help that the rich display a penchant for highly visible consumption, with those at the top of the corporate pile raking in vast salaries. Meanwhile, although white poverty is beginning to make an appearance, the overwhelming proportion of senior jobs in the corporate sector continue to go to whites and, overall, whites have done very well (in income terms, educational access and jobs) under ANC rule. In consequence, while the ANC can validly claim that much has changed for the better since 1994, the response from its own constituency is that change has not been fast enough, and that far too many continuities with apartheid South Africa remain. The result is a disconcerting lack of social coherence, with the post-1994 glow of national reconciliation increasingly assaulted by class and racial divisions.

Present trends point to a worrying trajectory, with accompanying dangers for democracy. While the relationship between democracy and development is extremely difficult to disentangle, general perceptions are that the quality of democracy in South Africa is declining.[4] From a comparative perspective, this is not unusual. Brief reference to the experiences of Zimbabwe and India, two countries which have faced not dissimilar challenges to South Africa, may be instructive.

Zimbabwe's record is particularly relevant to that of South Africa because it has played out against a similar background of liberation struggle fought against settler colonialism. The independence election in 1980 brought Robert Mugabe's ruling Zimbabwe African National Union-Patriotic Front (Zanu PF) to power, ruling in coalition with its rival Zimbabwe African People's Union (Zapu) as the junior partner. The coalition soon collapsed, however, when Mugabe found reason for a brutal crackdown on Zapu, which eventually sued for peace and dissolved itself into the ruling party in 1987. The resultant political calm did not last for long, for democracy then came under assault in the early 2000s with the rise of the opposition Movement for Democratic Change (MDC). Formed out of the trade union movement and civil society in response to the economy's plunging into a severe downturn, the MDC posed a major challenge to Zanu PF hegemony which was marked by the government's defeat in a constitutional referendum in 2000.

Shaken to its core, Zanu PF resorted to increasingly authoritarian behaviour. In a bid to win back popular support, Mugabe now threw government support behind a campaign of seizure of white farms, launched independently by 'war veterans', regardless of the cost. As the economic crisis (and inflation) spiralled out of control, the MDC continued to grow, despite facing mounting repression and Zanu PF's skewing of elections. Its moment of triumph arrived when, with the economy in tatters, it won a narrow majority in the National Assembly elections in 2008, with its leader, Morgan Tsvangirai, only denied a victory in the presidential election by official rigging, which forced him into a run-off with Mugabe. However, this proved to be a step too far, for Zanu PF now launched into full war mode, inflicting such brutality upon MDC supporters that Tsvangirai ultimately opted to withdraw.

Effectively backed by South Africa and its most powerful partners in the regional body, the Southern African Development Community, Zanu PF now clung on, not only to the presidency but also the most powerful positions in a regionally-negotiated coalition government. Although the MDC played a significant role in the years that followed in pulling the economy back from the brink, its leaders were themselves to fall victim to many of the sins of incumbency (translating political office into wealth), and were never able to challenge the grip which Zanu PF, backed by the military, maintained on state power. The culmination was a victory for Zanu PF in an election in 2013 which, while owing much to its manipulation of the electoral machinery, also reflected its putting on an election campaign (centred around populist themes of indigenisation and empowerment) to which the MDC had no effective answer.

If democracy has been effectively subverted in Zimbabwe, it has survived severe challenges in India. India's colonial history of direct domination by Britain is contrasted with that of South Africa's domination by settler colonialism, but there are strong connections between the two countries. Notably, the ANC initially modelled itself on the Indian National Congress and, once independent in 1947, India was a major source of strength to the anti-apartheid movement. India, like South Africa, was a highly diverse country (despite the breach with Pakistan) demanding that Congress preach national reconciliation under Pandit Nehru just as the ANC was later to do under Nelson Mandela. Although its electoral majorities were never as large as were later to be secured by the ANC, Congress was politically dominant for the first twenty years of democracy. As the party of liberation, it won major victories in the first three national elections until, in the late 1960s, it began to experience internal splits and contestations (similar to those experienced by the ANC today). The outcome was a lurch to political authoritarianism under Indira Ghandi and populist nationalisation of key sectors of the economy, only for a divided party to then be defeated in the late 1970s when Congress stood down from power nationally. Subsequently, formerly-dominant Congress has variously been in opposition, or a majority or minority player in coalition governments. In short, India has survived as a democracy, but only as a very messy one, even marred at times by sectarian (notably Hindu-nationalist) extremism and intolerance.

Twenty years after its own liberation, South Africa – like Zimbabwe – is facing a mounting economic crisis and increasing social and political strains. This crisis is not as extreme as that faced by Zanu PF in the early 2000s, yet the ANC is similarly faced by stagnating growth, worsening unemployment, acute inequality, widening mistrust between government and large-scale capital, and associated divisions within its own ranks. Its response is in many ways similar to the line pursued by Zanu PF: consolidation of a 'party-state'; stress upon the right of the party elite to rule on behalf of the people; a determination to subordinate wayward elements within Cosatu to Alliance discipline; a militarisation of the police, and so on. Ambiguities about the virtues of constitutionalism combine with populist initiatives to counter challenges by the opposition, whether the Democratic Alliance to the right or the populist Economic Freedom Front (EFF) (formed by Julius Malema, formerly president of the ANC Youth League after his expulsion from the ruling party) to the (quasi-)left. However, although it may well be argued that the ANC shares many liberation movement pathologies with Zanu PF, and while many within the ANC lionise Mugabe for his anti-imperialist and forceful Africanist rhetoric, the foundations for democracy in South Africa appear more firmly rooted. The ANC has remained committed to free elections; although under considerable political pressure to 'transform' the judiciary remains independent; and, perhaps above all, civil society remains robust (a lively media, widespread social protest, emergent social movements and rowdy political debate), despite ANC attempts to clamp down upon trade union independence and to encroach upon wider freedoms. Just as the immensely diverse nature of Indian politics and society appears to dictate the continuance of democracy, so the diverse nature of South Africa appears to strain against the long-term political dominance of the ANC.

Yet the Indian developmental trajectory presents its own huge challenges. The rise of the socially conservative Bharatiya Janata Party (BJP) from the late 1970s was to see the triumph of market-oriented policies, which were also rapidly adopted by Congress. The outcome was period of remarkable economic growth, with Congress statist policies largely reversed, and with India now featuring as an 'emerging market' based upon the development of a new industrial economy. This has been accompanied by the growth of a middle class, which many observers view as laying a foundation for further development and entrepreneurial energy (although others claim that it is fragile and precarious). However, as in South Africa under the ANC, India's capitalist growth continues to foster gross social inequality, and does little to address deeply-entrenched levels of poverty and pervasive underemployment and unemployment. This is highlighted, notably, by the successes in combating such social ills by the very different strategies pursued at state level in Kerala, where competing political parties pursue some form of developmental-statism by whatever the political party that comes to power (for a South Africa/Kerala contrast see Williams 2008).

Although such broad-brush comparisons are dangerous, they may be suggestive. Ultimately, the ANC will make its own future and will, one hopes, learn from the experiences of other ruling parties in the global South in order to avoid the worst of their mistakes and to emulate the best of their policies. However, for all that the ANC puts forward as its desired goal that of the pursuit of a 'democratic developmental state', disturbing trends point to the dangers of its increasingly resorting to authoritarian and populist measures. After twenty years of democracy, things in South Africa may well get worse before they get better.

The ANC's new deputy president, Cyril Ramaphosa, a key drafter of the country's Constitution (and former leader of the National Union of Mineworkers) embodies in many ways the tensions inherent in South Africa's body politic. While Zuma continues to blemish the image of the ANC with his gaffes and at times incomprehensible public utterances (causing his spokeperson in January to plead with the media to stop asking him to decipher his president's remarks), Ramaphosa by contrast is urbane, erudite and highly knowledgeable about ANC policy. After the launch of the ANC elections manifesto in January, it was Rampahosa and not Zuma who was thrust into the media spotlight, to conduct lengthy interviews with television stations, explaining the intricacies of ANC policy. He effortlessly addressed many piercing questions, admitting to 'shortcomings' and the need to continuously improve, coming across as convincing, affable and believable. He harks back to the Mandela era of hope and reconciliation

Of course, you would have to forget that it is the same Ramaphosa that represents much that is wrong about black empowerment – he became an instant billionaire after he left politics in 1994, and is the darling of big business. In other words, he represents the conversion of black working class empowerment to black elite enrichment, a chief characteristic of twenty years of democracy. Along with Trevor Manuel, he is the main champion of the orthodox economic trajectory now embedded in the National Development Plan, skilfully brushing aside objections from Cosatu ('their issues are being dealt with by a special tripartite commission,' he told the television channel ANN7's Hajra Omarjee on 12 January – omitting to mention that this commission had not yet met six months after it was formed). It is, however, his role in the massacre of Marikana mineworkers in August 2012, as a board member of Lonmin, that rankles critics most. Lawyer Dali Mpofu, now a member of the EFF, accused him of being part of a 'toxic collusion' between the state and business, in that he urged 'concomitant action' by government against the striking mineworkers, who he described as 'criminals'. On the next day, thirty-two mineworkers were mowed down by police (see Pillay 2013).

That, in essence, is the ruling party of South Africa, which has presided over the country's still fragile democracy over the past twenty years. As a key component, alongside business, of a fractuous but coherent power elite, it simultaneously embodies the hopes and fears of South Africans. However, the state of the ANC and government is only one aspect of an assessment of where we are as a country. To quote Max Du Preez (2013):

> My lefty friends in New York moaned and bitched about George W Bush when he was president and called him names ... But they didn't say America was rotten and start making plans to emigrate – we might have a weak and ineffectual government and a rather embarrasing president right now, but our country and our people are as vibrant and strong as we were when we negotiated that unlikely settlement in 1994 ... There is a lot more to South Africa and South Africans than Jacob Zuma and his present crop of ANC leaders. In fact, there is a lot more to the ANC than Zuma and Co.

NOTES

1   Workdays lost to strikes during the period 1989-1994 ranged from a low of 3.09 million to 4.2 million. Between 1995 and 2006, they ranged between 650 000 and 3.1 million (SAIRR 2010-2011: 417).

2   Gross labour market figures need careful dissection, but some indication is given by the reduction of non-agricultural private sector employment from 3.9 million in 1990 to 3.08 million in 2001(SAIRR 2002/2003: 149).

3   The term 'relative poverty' refers to 'people in poverty … defined as those living in households with incomes less than the poverty income', which varies according to household size (SAIRR 2012: 322-3).

4   'The South Africa chapter of Human Rights Watch's *2012 World Report* states that the country 'continues to grapple with corruption, growing social and economic inequalities, and the weakening of state institutions by partisan appointments and one-party dominance.' The 2011 Mo Ibrahim Index of African Governance shows that although South Africa ranks fifth overall among African governments, its scores have consistently declined over the past five years, with a significant reduction in scores for rule of law, accountability, and participation. Freedom House's *Freedom of the Press* report downgraded South Africa from 'free' to 'partly free' status in 2010 (Beck 2012).

REFERENCES

Beck K (2012) South Africa: Democracy, Rule of Law, and the Future. www.freedomhouse.org/blog/SouthAfrica-democracy-rule-law-and-future.

Bond P (2000) *Elite Transition: From Apartheid to Neoliberalism in South Africa.* Scottsville: University of Natal Press.

Hoffman P (2011) Democracy and accountability: Quo vadis South Africa? In Daniel J, P Naidoo, D Pillay and R Southall (eds) *New South African Review 2: New Paths, Old Compromises?* Johannesburg: Wits University Press.

Du Preez M (2013) *A Rumour of Spring: South Africa After 20 Years of Democracy.* Cape Town: Zebra Press.

Mohamed S (2010) The state of the economy. In Daniel J, P Naidoo, D Pillay and R

Southall (eds) *New South African Review 1: Development or Decline?*Johannesburg: Wits University Press.

Pillay D (2013) The second phase: Tragedy or farce? In Daniel J, P Naidoo, D Pillay and R Southall (eds) *New South African Review 3. The Second Phase – Tragedy or Farce?* Johannesburg: Wits University Press.

Roux T (2012) *The Politics of Principle: The First South African Constitutional Court, 1995-2005.* Cambridge, Cambridge University Press.

SAIRR (South African Institute of Race Relations) (2012) *South Africa Survey 2012.* Johannesburg: SAIRR.

Southall R (2013) *Liberation Movements in Power: Party and State in Southern Africa.* Woodbrige and Scottsville: James Currey and UKZN Press.

Taylor S (2007) *Business and the State in Southern Africa: The Politics of Economic Reform.* Boulder, CO: Lynne Rienner.

Terreblanche S (2012) *Lost in Transformation: South Africa's Search for a New Future Since 1986.* Johannesburg: KMMR Publishing.

Webster E (2006) Trade unions and the challenge of the informalisation of work. In Buhlungu S (ed.) *Trade Unions and Democracy: COSATU Workers' Political Attitudes in South Africa.* Cape Town: HSRC Press.

Williams M (2008) *The Roots of Particpatory Democracy: Democratic Communists in South Africa and Kerala, India.* New York: Palgrave.

ECOLOGY, ECONOMY AND LABOUR

1

Economy, ecology and labour

Devan Pillay

Twenty years after the start of democracy, the labour movement in South Africa, which has always sought to re-embed the economy into society, is now realising that this is insufficient – it also has to be re-embedded into the natural environment from which it draws its sustenance. This has long been realised by social theorists such as Karl Marx, who understood that both land (that is, nature) and labour are the sources of value (something both Marxists and non-Marxists in the twentieth century have completely misunderstood). In the 1930s the social democrat Karl Polanyi saw the dangers in the commodification of land and labour (through the so-called 'self-regulated' market) leading society to the edge of a precipice.

In other words, instead of what Ben Fine calls 'economics imperialism' – where the dismal science holds sway over all else – the economy has to be subordinated to society and the natural environment. The Congress of South African Trade Unions (Cosatu), and in particular its largest affiliate, the National Union of Metalworkers of South Africa (Numsa), have produced policy papers over the past year that begin this journey of realisation. Jobs in the future have to be decent green jobs in industries that use renewable energy. Indeed, Numsa goes further and calls for a socially owned renewable energy sector, in recognition of the dangers that the 'green economy' embraced by our government – in keeping with the dominant global discourse – is little more than green neoliberalism, where large corporations seek to make huge profits out of the 'sustainable development' industry.

The National Development Plan (NDP), which impressively examines the full dimensions of climate change and ecological destruction brought on by incessant economic growth and consumption, ends up with policy proposals that effectively negate this insight. It gives primacy to the minerals-energy-financial complex – indeed, Cosatu views the economics chapter in the NDP as a leap backwards to the orthodox economics of the much reviled Growth, Employment and Redistribution (GEAR) policy, which has brought massive inequality, rising unemployment and persistent poverty. On labour issues the NDP mainly envisages the creation of low-paid informal jobs, and has no ambition to tackle social inequality. It is what the social analyst Jeff Rudin calls 'symbolic policy': pretending to understand the massive problems created by our economic trajectory, using the language of critics, but actually adopting a business-as-usual approach (with a few minor concessions here and there to labour, the poor and the environment). It is the classic art of paradigm maintenance.

In this section Nicolas Pons-Vignon and Miriam Di Paola examine the labour market during the democratic period, and conclude that labour market restructuring has failed workers. Instead, it has strengthened the gains made by white capital under colonialism and apartheid which the labour movement, they argue, has on the whole not countered. What is needed, they say, is a political economy tactic that takes class struggle seriously, instead of the timid approach that sees fixing education or promoting informal activities as a solution to poverty. Such a tactic requires a strong, united and militant trade union movement to put pressure on government (or, indeed, to help change the composition of government).

Ian Macun provides an overview of the state of organised labour since 1994, and asks whether unions have been significantly weakened in recent years or whether they still exercise influence over the ANC and government, and over employers through, for example, the extension of collective agreements such as in the clothing sector. He argues that it is necessary to look at different dimensions of power in the unions, including not only absolute membership but also union density, especially in specific sectors. For example, unions are very powerful in the energy, mining and public sectors, and overall retain a relatively high union density of around 30 per cent. Despite splits in some unions, Macun argues that unions remain very resilient, with deep organisational power, buttressed by a supportive legal and policy environment. As such they still exercise institutional power in the workplace and within national politics through the alliance with the ruling party.

Nevertheless, the Marikana massacre in 2012 highlighted the degree of social distance that has emerged between union leaders and the membership – including the critical interface between shop stewards and members. As some unions lose membership the key issues have become ensuring democratic workers' control in unions and representing their members' interests effectively.

Bridget Kenny looks at the case of Wal-Mart and the South African Commercial Catering and Allied Workers' Union (Saccawu). The American retailer is well known for its low prices, which come at the cost of anti-union behaviour, low wages and minimal worker security. This leads to a form of 'reverse Fordism' where low incomes (as wages to workers, or squeezed prices paid to smallholder suppliers) feed the demand for lower food prices, leading to a downward spiral of working-class impoverishment. Saccawu played a major role in challenging Wal-Mart's entry into South Africa, and received the backing of sections of government such as the departments of Trade and Industry, and Economic Development. The eventual settlement at the Competition Tribunal obliges Wal-Mart to support supplier development and to accept union organisation in its various retail outlets.

However, Kenny argues, the loud public debate around the Tribunal has no bearing on the real issues: huge inequalities within the food system, characterised by a low-wage, racist labour system. It avoids the critical questions about our developmental trajectory, based on the logic of food production for profit, which excludes the vast majority from active participation in a system of sustainable food security – an issue recently taken up by Numsa and the Food and Allied Workers' Union (Fawu).

Jeremy Wakeford and Keith Gottschalk take us into other issues of sustainability, namely oil dependency and electricity generation respectively. Wakeford considers the risks inherent in the country's dependence on imported oil within the context of general resource depletion and environmental degradation, the global production and consumption of oil, and the implications for oil prices. South Africa, he argues, has vulnerabilities in its liquid fuel-related industries, and should consider alternatives such as domestic liquid fuel production and a massive shift of bulk freight from roads to railways – and an overall shift towards public transit in cities and to electrified transport systems.

Gottschalk asks why the democratic government has been so enamoured with the atomic energy lobby. He argues against the easy explanation of corruption and clientilism and builds a case for highly skilful foreign and domestic nuclear energy lobbies, composed of bureaucrats, engineers and politicians, which have seduced successive administrations by appealing to atomic power as the ultimate political symbol and an aura of state power. The state has consequently ignored or downplayed cost-effectiveness, complexity and the potential for catastrophe. Gottschalk says that the focus should be on a mix of imported hydropower and gas, and solar power, which requires a major revision of the 2010 Integrated Resource Plan.

The power of the corporate lobby runs through all these chapters, illustrating yet again the manner in which the state has become enmeshed with the interests of corporate capital and not those of the people (despite the revolutionary rhetoric at party and union events). Indeed, as Marx argued, the state is increasingly becoming the executive to manage the interests of big capital, in the first instance, and of the people only when they make their voice heard. After twenty years of elite democracy, the workers, the poor and society in general are re-asserting Nelson Mandela's deeper legacy: reconciliation *with* social justice.

CHAPTER 1

The South African labour market after eighteen years: It's class struggle, stupid!

Nicolas Pons-Vignon and Miriam Di Paola[1]

INTRODUCTION

The liberation from apartheid generated great expectations of change in the workplace and the labour market (Pons-Vignon and Anseeuw 2009). This was due to the key role of trade unions – both as a political force and through successful undermining of the racist order which had been established in workplaces – in overthrowing the system of minority rule, (Von Holdt 2003). Apartheid geography had ensured the racial separation of dwellings. Encounters (often brutal) between people considered to belong to different racial groups took place, mostly in what Marx calls 'the hidden abode of production'. The history of 'forcible commodification' (Bernstein 1994) of southern African peasants into wage labourers, one of extreme violence, was followed by the imposition of a migrant labour system and of colour bars (limiting the promotion of blacks) across workplaces, with the active support of the state and capital. In the absence of alternative sources of income, wage employment came to occupy a central place in the daily life (or reproduction, in Marxist parlance) of most South Africans; but with a record-breaking unemployment rate (standing close to 40 per cent), more and more research points to the *restoration* of employer power post-1994 through the widespread use of outsourcing and an explosion in casual and informal employment (Buhlungu and Bezuidenhout 2008;

Pons-Vignon, forthcoming; Von Holdt and Webster 2005). The economically liberating stable employment to which most South Africans aspire has therefore not materialised but remains the overarching objective of progressive forces in which unions continue to play a leading role (Barchiesi 2011).

And yet, reading the media or the reports produced by the International Monetary Fund (IMF), one could believe that the South African government has yielded to the dreaded sirens of populism, at least in the labour market. Rigid rules have allegedly been established, killing flexibility by over-protecting workers who are poorly skilled and over-unionised; a deadly mix which lies at the root of high unemployment and poverty (Klein 2012). Such arguments follow the South African (neo)liberal tradition (Knight 1982; Hofmeyr and Lucas 2001; Kingdon and Knight 2007) according to which the key to unlocking growth and reducing poverty in South Africa would be to reform the labour market (making it 'flexible') and equip poor people with useful skills. Similar arguments were used in the early 1990s to dismiss the report of the Macro-Economic Research Group (MERG, see Freund, forthcoming), and debunked by Sender (1994) who exposed their weakness. The new claims associated with this neoliberal perspective on the labour market suffer from serious empirical limitations, whether in attempts to point to 'high' wages as the cause of unemployment (Forslund 2013; Strauss 2013), or to claim that South Africa's labour market is rigid (Bhorat and Cheadle 2007). This position is, however, reflected in sections of government, notably the National Treasury, which champions a 'youth subsidy' ensuring a transfer of taxpayer money to employers to facilitate the creation of casual jobs, and in the recently endorsed National Development Plan (NDP).

Such a perspective corresponds to a residual view of poverty (Oya 2009), according to which poverty alleviation requires a combination of free markets and improved human capital, and meaning that the poor ought to be equipped with what they lack, whether it is education or capital. The intrinsic inconsistency of such an approach has been captured by Amsden (2010) when she noted that Say's law (supply creates demand) does not hold: increasing the supply of skilled workers will not alone generate sufficient appropriate jobs for them. Moreover, and crucially, the flawed characterisation of the South African labour market as 'rigid' has diverted attention away from a more grounded assessment of its performance. This chapter thus offers a critical review of post-apartheid labour market restructuring, showing that it has not failed for lack of flexibility, but rather because it has not protected poor workers. The changes which have taken place in the labour market have indeed reproduced, rather than challenged, the unequal relationship between capital and labour.

THE DISMAL PERFORMANCE OF THE POST-APARTHEID LABOUR MARKET

The new democratic regime carried expectations for millions of South Africans to find good jobs, with some security as well as wages and benefits, allowing them to live decently.

Most of them have been disappointed. Because jobs are the main source of direct and indirect income for most South Africans, high unemployment and growing casualisation have made their reproduction extremely difficult.

Unemployment: Discouraging and structural

Unemployment in South Africa is amongst the highest in the world and represents the most significant expression of the country's deep and lingering socioeconomic crisis. According to the Quarterly Labour Force Survey for January to March 2013 (StatsSa 2013), the official unemployment rate stands at 25.2 per cent; this figure climbs to 36.7 per cent if discouraged jobseekers are included. Unemployment still bears an unceremonious racial stamp with the black population being the most affected (28.8 per cent in the first quarter of 2013), closely followed by the coloured population, while white unemployment stood at only 7.2 per cent.

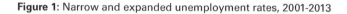

Figure 1: Narrow and expanded unemployment rates, 2001-2013

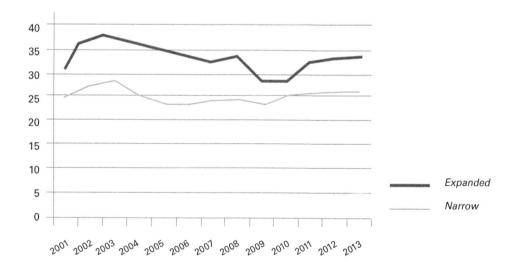

Source: StatsSA (2008 and 2013), authors' calculations for expanded rate

Note: The methodology of the labour force surveys changed in 2008, with the introduction of the Quarterly Labour Force Survey. For the period 2001-2007 we draw on the Historical Revision March Series, published in 2008, to facilitate comparison with the new series. For 2008-2013, we use the Quarter 1 figure for each year in order to ensure coherence with the previous period.

While government's 'official' rate (excluding discouraged job-seekers) downplays the extent of the unemployment crisis, the 'expanded' rate appears to be a better reflection of the situation of the labour market. Indeed, the reason for excluding discouraged job-seekers from the unemployed is that they are allegedly less motivated (therefore less likely) to find work. While this may be true in certain countries, recent research shows that in South Africa 'there is little to distinguish the searchers from the non-searchers in terms of their commitment to finding work' (Posel et al. 2013).[1] As a result, 'the non-searching unemployed form a legitimate part of the labour force and their exclusion from the official rate should be reconsidered'. As shown in Figure 1, the 'strict' or narrow rate has entailed a substantial underestimation of the number of unemployed people. Yet, even when only active job searchers were considered, the incidence of long-term unemployment in South Africa stood at close to 70 per cent of total unemployment in 2011 – meaning that two-thirds of those officially unemployed had been so for a year or more (OECD 2011). As a result, 59 per cent of the unemployed had never been in employment in 2008 (Leibbrandt et al. 2010).

In spite of the depth of the unemployment problem in South Africa, many economists have sought to explain it as an abnormality rather than engage with the dynamics that (re)produce it. This started in the early 2000s, with Bhorat emphasising 'the simultaneous existence of a skilled labour shortage and unskilled labour surplus' (2004: 976) to argue that skills development would be the key to reducing unemployment. This argument was profoundly flawed for, as pointed out by Makgetla and Van Meelis (2003): 'Even if more jobs were created for skilled than for unskilled people, it does not follow that increasing skill levels would in turn generate more jobs.'[2] In the following years, drawing on dual labour market theories (which posit that there are two distinct labour markets, a formal and an informal), some economists have argued that 'insider' formal workers were forcing many 'outsiders' to either remain unemployed or to work informally (Kingdon and Knight 2007). Informal employment in South Africa is very low, however, especially by comparison with other African or middle-income countries, and much of its growth has been related to the informalisation of work rather than to new opportunities in the informal economy. Why can't informal activities 'soak up' more of the excess labour in South Africa? Valodia (2013) suggests that:

> Unlike most developing countries where small-scale, informal producers are able to capture a significant proportion of domestic consumption, the South African economy is dominated by large-scale, monopolistic producers with reach deep into the consumption basket of the South Africans of all income classes. Even in the most remote, rural and low-income communities, the basic consumption basket is dominated by goods produced in the formal economy, with very little – if any – capacity for local, informal producers to capture a sizeable proportion of local demand.

It is furthermore important to discard the notion that unemployment is high because informal wage employment is not captured by labour statistics; if anything, informal sector (especially *self*) employment is exaggerated by the Quarterly Labour Force Survey (Pons-Vignon, forthcoming).[3] Following Pollin et al. (2006), our contention is that South Africa's unemployment is a product of its structural economic features, with the three immediate reasons accounting for the very high unemployment rates being historically high unemployment, sluggish growth, and declining labour intensity of growth. Growth has overall been sluggish in South Africa since the late 1960s, with the exception of the period 2003 to 2007. Mohamed (2010) argues however that economic growth, during the latter period, far from being associated with long-term investment in the real economy, was linked to increased debt-driven consumption and speculation in financial and real estate markets and much of the growth in services employment was related to the outsourcing of low-pay services from manufacturing, in particular cleaning and security (Tregenna 2008). While the official unemployment rate had slowly declined during the 2000s, unemployment went up again after the economy recorded a million job losses in the wake of the global crisis. Last but not least, the continued dominance of sectors associated with the minerals-energy complex means that the most dynamic sectors are capital- rather than labour-intensive, with limited capacity to increase employment significantly even when they grow (Ashman et al. 2011).These structural features suggest that it will be necessary to change fundamentally the economic structure in order to tackle unemployment and poverty.

Largely ignoring these structural dynamics, debates about unemployment in South Africa have been dominated by calls for more labour market flexibility as the sustained unemployment crisis means that the national focus is primarily on job creation, often couched in 'any job is better than no job' terms. However, Bhorat and Cheadle (2007) have shown that the South African labour market was not rigid at all when compared to that of other countries:

> Classified as an upper-middle income country, the comparisons across the regulatory indices are surprising. In the first instance, it is evident that South Africa's measures of labour regulation compare quite favourably with those found in the rest of the world. In almost all of the individual regulatory sub-indices, South Africa yields a level of regulation that is lower than both the mean for upper-middle income countries, and for the sample of countries as a whole. For example, in the case of alternative employment contracts – the legislative regime governing part-time work, contractual employment and so on – South Africa yields an extremely low measure of labour regulation.

It is furthermore evident that if the roots of unemployment are structural, they cannot be reduced to a mere 'frictional' dimension related to a neoclassical understanding of the labour market as the place where supply and demand for labour meet. The focus on an imaginary 'rigid' labour market (and elusive 'overpaid' unskilled workers) is therefore little more than a diversion from a serious engagement with unemployment. It is all the more so that the South African labour market is in fact extremely flexible (and probably too flexible). Employers can do pretty much whatever they please in practice.

Casualisation: When no job is better than many jobs

The quality of jobs in South Africa has declined dramatically over the past twenty years. The implication is that working poverty, which was a structural feature of segregation and apartheid (Wolpe 1972), has all but disappeared. Many South Africans work long hours, but for miserable pay and in insecure, often hazardous conditions. Is any job really better than no job?

Non-standard forms of employment are increasingly common throughout the South African labour market, in line with the global restructuring of work which has led, through a great diversification of employment arrangements, to widespread *precariousness*. Contrary to what is often assumed, this is not restricted to the 'margins' of the labour market, but is increasingly a feature of its core (Chang 2009). In South Africa, restructuring started ahead of the transition to democracy and has since become a wide-ranging phenomenon in sectors as diverse as healthcare, mining and forestry (see Pons-Vignon and Anseeuw 2009; and Von Holdt and Webster 2005 for a broad range of case studies). In mining in 2008, one out of three workers was employed by a contractor or a sub-contractor (Bezuidenhout 2008), a figure which has probably increased in the wake of the 2012 violence across platinum and other mines. The forms taken by work-restructuring have been varied, and include the growth of third-party employers such as labour brokers and contractors, alongside a sharp rise in casualisation, documented in a vast range of sectoral case studies but poorly captured by labour force surveys (for a methodological discussion, see Sender and Pontara, 2010). Casualisation, for instance, entails work arrangements such as homework (Godfrey et al. 2005) or the hiring of gangs of workers by the day to perform certain tasks. With a few exceptions, for instance in transport (Barrett 2003) or metals and engineering, trade unions have not been able to counter employer strategies and prevent casualisation.

Labour casualisation has entailed a marked deterioration in levels of pay and security. In terms of pay, this is visible in the consistently low wages received by workers covered by sectoral determinations (see section 2), two-thirds of whom were classified as 'poor' in 2007 – with an *increase* in the number of poor workers in certain sectors since the adoption of a determination (DPRU 2010). In terms of employment security, out of a workforce of 13 million in 2008, 5.8 million workers were not covered by unemploy-ment insurance; 2.7 million did not have written contracts; and 4.1 million did not have paid leave entitlements (Marais 2011). Workers have suffered most where employers have adopted task-based payment, which often leads workers to super-exploit themselves to meet unrealistic production targets (Pons-Vignon, forthcoming).

It is therefore unsurprising that the problems associated with the labour market have contributed to a sharp crisis of reproduction experienced by many poor people in South Africa.

The crisis of reproduction

South African workers are confronted with a particularly difficult socioeconomic situation, rendering their reproduction costly and difficult. Combined with the casualisation and unemployment crises which they experience in the labour market is an increasing commodification of essential services, from transport to healthcare (Barchiesi 2011). The upshot is that workers require more cash – at the same time as the incomes of many are declining. The ensuing reproduction squeeze often precipitates workers into the arms of very costly providers of consumption credit (Bateman 2012; James 2012). South African wage levels must therefore be understood in the context of a very expensive cost of reproduction due to commodified and often poorly managed services.[4] Although some of the poor in South Africa have benefited from increasing conditional cash transfers, the latter typically contribute to entrenching neoliberalism when they are associated with the private provision of services (Ghosh 2011). Moreover, grants are, like micro credits, primarily channelled to purchasing goods provided by large-scale oligopolistic producers (Valodia op.cit.), able to fix prices for certain basic foodstuffs such as bread or poultry (Competition Commission 2010).

A crucial consequence of labour casualisation has been to exacerbate poverty, as the ability of workers to support dependants has been adversely affected.[5] In poor households, it is common that workers' wages are 'the main safety net … [hence] even the limited income available to low paid workers is eroded through support for the unemployed' (Coleman forthcoming). The weight of interpersonal solidarity imposed on the poor in South Africa is not limited to wage transfers, but also includes care. Many companies have thus managed, thanks to outsourcing and casualisation, not to bear the costs associated with HIV and AIDS. The economic burden of the disease has been shifted from business onto government, households and individuals, with women paying the highest price of caregiving (Marais 2005). Where contract and casual labour is extensively used, workers' benefits are nearly absent and the entire cost of healthcare is displaced onto formal and informal caregivers (nurses and especially women of the family of the affected persons). In the context of insufficient investment in public health, access to health services is skewed not only in terms of race and class, but also against rural dwellers. This may explain why South Africa's labour force participation rate is so low (54.8 per cent in the first quarter of 2013); indeed, many women are prevented from entering the labour market because they are looking after ill family members. Some are supported by NGOs or by new government schemes, but they are paid way below other healthcare professionals. Moreover – and crucially – sick workers who do not have permanent contracts cannot benefit from company-supported medical aid or sick pay.

Deepening inequality

With such poor records in employment creation and growth, it is not surprising that the unequal distribution of wealth has not altered. The country has the unfortunate record of being the most unequal in the world, ahead of Brazil, with a Gini coefficient rising from about 0.56 in 1995 to about 0.63 in 2009.

In a country where, despite the low rate of employment, low labour force participation and pervasive casualisation, wages remain by far the most significant share of income, particularly for the poorest, it is hardly surprising that poverty remains a critical issue in spite of a relatively large social grant programme. Inequality among wage earners has increased (Strauss 2013). When measured in racial terms, inequality dynamics are also surprising: racial inequality decreased dramatically during the last twenty-five years of apartheid while it did not fall between 1996 and 2001 (Leibbrandt et al. 2010)

If workers, and in particular poor workers, have lost since 1994, who has won? Like other countries, South Africa has experienced a rapid rise in the income of the super-rich, with the share of total income earned by the top 1 per cent jumping from about 10 per cent in the 1980s and early 90s to 18.1 per cent in 2007 (Unctad 2012). This trend has been supported by an unflinching commitment to 'orthodox' macropolicies and is closely related to the rise of the financial sector and of its ability to absorb resources at the expense of other sectors (Fine and Ashman 2013).

The failure of the post-apartheid labour market is therefore visible in the deepening of inequality, in particular between classes. Functional inequality between capital and labour has thus been increasing steadily, as Forslund (2013) notes:

> On average, real wages have been increasing less than labour productivity, at about 2 per cent per year, with labour productivity averaging about 3 per cent in annual increases since 1994 … The wage share of GDP has therefore been falling … [from 50.1 per cent in 1995] to 44.5 per cent [in 2010]. (pp. 108-109, see Figure 4 as well).

The process of work restructuring described above has been an instrument of 'authoritarian restoration' of employer power over workers (Von Holdt 2003). But how could such a strategy be successful, and workers be so undermined, in the context of an allegedly progressive (or rigid, for some) labour market legal framework, based on worker-employer cooperation, and by a historically strong labour movement?

THE EMPEROR IS NAKED: UNPACKING THE MYTH OF 'PROGRESSIVE' LABOUR LAW IN SOUTH AFRICA

The first section of this chapter has painted a bleak picture of the South African labour market, pointing to the terrible difficulties many South Africans face in their daily lives. The combined high unemployment, low pay and widespread casualisation, however, appear to be a paradox, given the often criticised 'rigidity' (understand: protectiveness for workers) of the post-1994 labour law architecture. But how can the South African labour market be rigid, preventing employment creation, and at the same time unable to protect workers? The evidence supporting the claim that the labour market is 'rigid' is actually very thin, as shown by Bhorat and Cheadle's aforementioned comparative survey of hiring and firing regimes (2007). It is therefore inaccurate to argue that rigidity or 'high wages' are responsible for unemployment (Strauss 2013). Recent research making such claims, for instance by Klein (2012), amounts to little more than an unsophisticated rehash of the 'reactionary rhetoric' dismissed by Sender (1994). Building on Forslund's critique, we will therefore not engage such unconvincing arguments but, rather, attempt to account for the failure of the post-apartheid labour law framework to protect workers.

The failure is noteworthy when one considers that the new framework was characterised by progressive intentions and informed by a participatory, Northern European model (Donnelly and Dunn 2006). The new government, supported by a strong labour movement, carried out what was presented as a radical restructuring of the workplace aimed at ensuring racial equity, improving working conditions and democratising firm level decision-making. It built on the reforms which had followed industrial (and political) action by the black trade union movement since the early 1970s. It could be said with hindsight that the Labour Relations Act (LRA) of 1995 walked in the footsteps of the 1981 LRA in the sense that it established institutions in which unions could participate, thus asserting the legitimacy of majority black unions while continuing 'the ongoing effort to divert union power away from the shop floor' (Lichtenstein 2013). The crucial decision which was made in the new labour law regime was to leave most of the regulation of labour and pay (including minimum wage) conditions to sectorial bargaining councils, and to leave the establishment of the latter to unions and employers. In sectors where unions were too weak to bargain, sectoral determinations would be adopted by the minister of labour, on the recommendation of a five-member employment conditions commission (ECC), in order to regulate conditions of pay and work.[6]

This architecture goes a long way towards explaining why so many workers are poor and unprotected in South Africa. It would, however, be naive to think that industrial relations frameworks are the sole, or even the main, reason for labour market outcomes. The restructuring of the labour market has reflected the restructuring of the South African economy. In this section we explore how the new industrial relations system has entrenched the power of capital, first through the inability of collective bargaining (and unions by extension) to protect many workers and then through the very limited effect of direct state intervention in the labour market. Thirdly, the weakening of trade unions is discussed.

Collective bargaining

Until the end of apartheid in 1994 (and since long before its start), South Africa had been characterised by institutionalised racism in the labour market. The large migrant, badly-paid and tightly controlled black workforce was a central feature of the mining economy (Moodie 1994). Whites benefited from institutionalised racism, for instance in the form of job reservations or of the rule that they should always be in a hierarchically superior position. Black trade unions, which developed from the 1970s, first focused on eliminating the most humiliating practices of daily racism in the workplace, such as the blurring between racial and technical lines of hierarchy.[7] Their success later provided an essential foundation for the mounting economic and social contestation which would lead to the fall of the apartheid regime. The largest confederation that emerged from this movement, the Congress of South African Trade Unions (Cosatu), has become a member of the Tripartite Alliance which has ruled South Africa since 1994. Since tense (to use a euphemism) labour relations were a key feature of apartheid, a progressive workplace regime was a crucial expectation associated with the democratic transition.

The legislative framework of industrial relations adopted by the new government was based on the Northern European model which entails, firstly, strong social partners including trade unions deeply rooted in workplaces and, secondly, high levels of collaboration between capital and labour. Such a progressive regime has, however, not materialised in South Africa out of the potential contained in the new legislation. The belief that unions would grow stronger in workplaces in the post-apartheid period turned out to be unfounded in most cases. It was expected that social 'partners' would collaborate at the national, sectoral and firm levels to agree on policies and pay levels whereas class struggle has-proved more visible than class collaboration at all levels, in particular in workplaces.

The cornerstone of the new labour market structure is the Labour Relations Act (LRA) adopted in 1995, which encouraged (or relied on) what Todd (2004) calls 'process voluntarism' – effectively leaving most of the regulation of labour relations in the hands of unions and employers. Bargaining councils (BCs, formerly industrial councils) were retained as the primary forum for collective bargaining, and bargaining at sectoral level was preferred. The Act also provided a mechanism whereby unions (or employers' associations) which were not sufficiently representative to form a BC could seek to establish a statutory council, with limited powers to bargain. There was also provision for a plant-level structure, the workplace forum, influenced by the German work councils.

The number of BCs has declined, after a peak at ninety-nine in 1996. There were forty-seven bargaining councils in 2009. This can be attributed to councils collapsing in some industries, or mergers of regional councils into national councils in others. Councils can have their collective agreement extended to all employers and employees within the scope of the council and not only the members of the party organisations. Companies can (and often do) apply to the BC for an exemption from some or all provisions in the agreement(s); about 80 per cent of applications for exemptions are granted – confirming that the system does not lack 'flexibility' (Bhorat and Cheadle 2007).

This seemingly progressive legal regime, however, has been constantly degraded in the past twenty years (Pons-Vignon and Anseeuw 2009). First, the National Economic Development and Labour Council (Nedlac) is hardly the forum for democratic policy consultation which it was intended to be, largely because government has not taken it seriously in many important instances, in particular not when the landmark Growth, Employment and Redistribution (GEAR) programme was adopted in 1996. Beyond Nedlac, and in spite of its continuing participation in the Alliance, Cosatu has been consistently frustrated with the policy options chosen by the ANC and, crucially, the latter's refusal to have an open debate on decisive policy choices (Cosatu 2002).

In practice, the new architecture has not produced the intended dense web of negoti-ated conditions. BCs have not extended their scope to any significant extent in the post-1994 period – and in some sectors have declined. The tendency has been away from centralised bargaining (which is typically associated with the best outcomes for workers) to more local, fragmented bargaining. Coleman (forthcoming) thus argues that:

> While centralised bargaining is critical for the labour movement … it is not in its current voluntaristic form able to drive the transformation demanded by the South African situation. Indeed the fragility of collective bargaining institutions can be used by employers to attack wage levels.

This is particularly visible in wage agreements, with low wages inherited from apart-heid being perpetuated in many cases. The implication is that wages vary greatly across sectors, reflecting the strength (or weakness) of unions: in 2005, the minimum wage for unskilled electrical workers was R185 per week, whereas it was R647 for the same category of workers in metals and engineering (Budlender 2009). Ironically, some of the most favourable wages and conditions have been achieved by the National Union of Metalworkers of South Africa (Numsa) without a bargaining council! (In the auto assembly sector, a national bargaining forum, governed by rules agreed upon between employers and the union, has thus allowed for flexible and effective bargaining.)

Other institutional forms supposed to promote collective bargaining have had even less success. Workplace forums were supposed to be consulted about the restructuring and reorganisation of production, training, pay schemes and disciplinary procedures – but only a handful have been established. Employers were reluctant about co-determina-tion and joint problem solving, while unions 'feared that (workplace forums) could serve to co-opt workers and reduce their willingness to oppose employer proposals' (Budlender 2009: 10). Similarly, very few statutory councils have been established – meaning that workers not covered by a BC have to hope for a sectoral determination.

The main driving force behind this hollowing-out of the collective bargaining frame-work has been the organisational restructuring to which many companies have resorted. The increase in the contracting-out of core and non-core activities in many sectors has resulted in the growing casualisation of jobs discussed in Section 1. The resulting precari-ousness in which many workers find themselves has negatively affected their ability to join unions and engage employers in the many forums established by the LRA. Crucially, it has allowed employers to replace 'extra-economic' coercion with economic coercion (Pons-Vignon, forthcoming); this is a stark reminder that relations between labour and capital are more often characterised by conflict than by collaboration.

One of the more surprising outcomes of the failure of collective bargaining to protect workers in post-apartheid South Africa has been its inefficiency in promoting employ-ment equity. Given that most low-skilled workers are black, the increase in within-wage earners inequality has been associated with increasing racial inequality. There have been exceptions, however, not least in the one sector which, according to Budlender (2009), corresponds, to some extent, to the intent of the post-apartheid labour law: the public service. Improved representation (trade unions were hardly tolerated before 1994 in the state) and the hiring and promotion of black professionals (Von Holdt 2010) have allowed state employment to play a classic role of class formation. As a result, the state seems to be the only 'sector' where the objectives of employment equity of the broad-based black economic empowerment (BB-BEE) policy have been met. Elsewhere in the labour market, BB-BEE has been primarily geared towards the creation of a black bour-geoisie, rather than towards undoing the racialised (and racist) wage structure preva-lent in South Africa. This is reflected in the division of tasks between the ECC and the Commission on Employment Equity (CEE); while the latter is in charge of monitoring progress in terms of (racial) employment equity, the former is supposed to monitor wage differentials. But because the ECC has been absorbed by its advisory work related to sectoral determinations (see below), while the CEE has 'focused primarily on advance-ment into the top levels of the hierarchy' there has been 'serious neglect of monitoring of wage differentials' (Budlender 2009).

Ineffective direct state intervention in the labour market

Although collective bargaining is the cornerstone of the South African system of labour law, there are residual provisions for direct state intervention, in particular in relation to 'vulnerable' workers. This sub-section focuses on sectoral determinations, which offer very limited protection to workers, and on the weak enforcement capacity of the Department of Labour. Not only is protection minimal, it is often elusive.

Sectoral determinations set minimum conditions of work and pay for sectors where there are no bargaining councils, usually reflecting the weakness of unions, as well as documented exploitation; they have concerned sectors such as forestry, agriculture, domestic work and security.[8] The establishment of minimum wages seems to have helped increase sometimes extremely low nominal wages, but case studies suggest that employers have found ways to counter wage increases by shifting to hourly or task payment, or reducing other benefits (Murray and Van Walbeek 2007). Sectoral determinations have thus resulted in increased casualisation because they are not monitored by trade unions, and also because of poor enforcement mechanisms (see below).

As Coleman (forthcoming) puts it: '(t)he system of sectoral determinations … is both partial (only covering some low paid sectors), uncoordinated, with big variations in the minima, and without any coherent rationale in terms of the basic subsistence needs of workers.' Indeed, as illustrated in Figure 2 below, the minimum wages set in this way tend to be very low, with an average of just above R2 000 per month. Increasingly, the minimum becomes the benchmark, with wages hoarding around the regulated minimum wage. In other words, even if it was implemented rigorously, direct state intervention in the labour market would hardly manage to uplift poor workers.

There is, moreover, a severe lack of enforcement of labour regulations. It is striking that in 2007, four years after the adoption of a sectoral determination for agriculture,

Figure 2: Minimum wage levels in sectoral determinations in rands per month, 2013-14

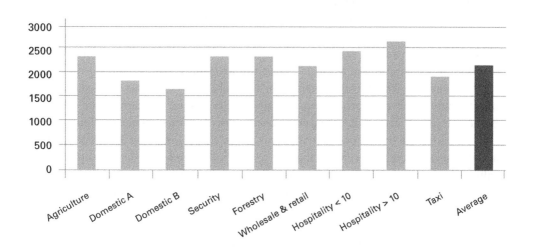

Source: Department of Labour, various documents available at http://www.labour.gov.za/DOL/legislation/sectoral-determinations.

Note: Domestic A & B correspond to different geographical areas; Hospitality >10 & <10 refer to enterprise size. For Security, the minimum wage indicated is for the category 'general worker', applicable after six months of service; for Wholesale it is for a 'general assistant'; and for Taxi it is for 'workers not elsewhere specified'.

28 per cent of workers were paid *below* the minimum wage, and that 36 per cent still did not have written contracts (Bhorat et al. 2012). In a recent study of Gauteng horticulture, Nkosi (2013) finds that most workers are unregistered immigrants who 'do not have rights'. This poor compliance on the part of employers is related to the weak enforcement (inspection) capacity of the Department of Labour. As Stanwix (2013) argues: '[in] agriculture, the risks [associated with non-compliance] have been low and the penalties light.' Inspectors are tasked with monitoring and enforcing compliance with the Basic Conditions of Employment Act and sectoral determinations, as the state does not monitor agreements emerging from collective bargaining (which are supposedly monitored by BCs themselves). While the violence inherent in some sectors probably deters inspections (as in the collective taxi sector), there are many suggestions that the South African labour inspectorate is slow and ineffective. Research into why this is the case, and how the deficiencies of such an essential function can be fixed, is urgently warranted, for many South African and foreign workers have no one else (hence, often, no one) to turn to in case of abuse.

As a result of the limited scope of bargaining councils, as well as the limited coverage of sectoral determinations, the extent to which minimum conditions are in fact regulated is at best uneven. Combined with poor enforcement capacity, this produces a striking picture of an inefficient legal framework at odds with the widespread perception. Overall, state intervention in the labour market mirrors the inefficiency of collective bargaining in defending workers against employers.

The new labour law regime in South Africa was inspired by 'corporatism'. The central idea was that it was going to protect workers thanks to strong trade unions negotiating conditions in centralised bargaining councils. This was consistent with demands by Cosatu unions dreaming of a 'mixed' economy based on co-determination – but capital wanted none of it. The pervasive increase in atypical employment has entailed an erosion of trade union ability to protect workers and take advantage of many of the provisions of the new legal framework.[9] The *workplace* strength of unions has been seriously dented with the transition to democracy, with many union cadres taking up jobs in government and the private sector, thus enhancing unions' *political* influence – what Buhlungu (2010) calls the 'paradox of victory'. This happened at the very moment when workers needed to be defended in the context of widespread restructuring; thus, while unions retain power in certain sectors, they have not prevented widespread casualisation, even in the public service (Hassen 2005).

The weakening of trade unions in post-apartheid South Africa has to a large extent been masked by two phenomena: the participation of unions in the ruling Tripartite Alliance, and the massive unionisation of workers in the public sector which has prevented a collapse in the number of unionised workers (standing close to 3.1 million out of a total workforce of 13.5 million – see Macun, in this volume) while accelerating sociological and political evolution in Cosatu. This may explain why unions have failed to respond to capital's systematic dodging of the new labour relations regime which they promoted. Rather than 'co-determine' anything with their workers, most employers have turned (often starting in the 1980s) to externalisation and casualisation.

CONCLUSION

This chapter has highlighted two trends in the post-apartheid labour market: its failure to address major socioeconomic challenges and the inefficiency of collective bargaining for protecting workers, combined with the weakness of direct state intervention in the labour market. The progressive restructuring of labour relations, starting with the creation of decent work opportunities for the majority of South Africans, has turned out to be a pipedream. Instead, the labour market has, like the economy and the state, been restructured in a neoliberal way which has entrenched the structural inequality between capital and labour (Segatti and Pons-Vignon 2013). Under apartheid, state power had been mobilised to advance the interests of capital. 'Liberalisation' – actively supported by the state before and after 1994 – has generated an even more unequal relationship by allowing capital to leave the country and leverage high unemployment to undermine the workplace strength of labour. The protection promised by post-apartheid labour law hinged on the existence of strong trade unions, which would have been able to advance the interests of workers through bargaining councils, but even if workers have benefited from the new legislation in some sectors, the increase in atypical employment has eroded trade union power and their ability to take advantage of it.

Our contention, therefore, is that labour market restructuring in a context of economic liberalisation has benefited capital. The failure of a strong and militant trade union movement (with a few exceptions) to counter these moves is an uneasy reality for many. Macun (in this volume) suggests that unions' organisational power and democratic control have been undermined in the post-apartheid era. This lies at the heart of the broader failure of trade unions to advance the interests of labour as a class – an unexpected outcome after twenty years of democracy – and yet the mobilisation of mine and farmworkers signals that many workers, including those whose power may seem very limited, are willing to take up the struggle against capital. The re-building of labour's power in South Africa will pivot on the ability of progressive forces to (re)connect with workplace activism.

Such outcomes are however all but unavoidable. In Brazil, after a brutal setback driven by neoliberal forces in the 1990s (with the Real Plan of 1994 mirroring GEAR), a labour-supported government has achieved an impressive reduction in poverty and inequality. This, according to Baltar et al. (2010), can be attributed to 'minimum wage revaluation policy, social security, income transfers and improved wage bargaining'. The authors show that from 2004 onwards bargaining outcomes improved, entailing an increase in the wage share of value added. This is not surprising, and coherent with a 'relational' understanding of poverty (Oya op.cit.): when labour as a class reaps more benefits from growth than capital, inequality and poverty decrease. The Brazilian experience shows the need for state intervention to limit casualisation and increase minimum wages (and ensure they are applied), supported by trade unions strongly rooted in workplaces and able to bargain for better wages.

The South African labour market presents a major analytical challenge. Why does employment intensity remain so low, in spite of very high unemployment (surplus labour) and evidence of a very flexible (or casual) labour market? In other words, why do employers not employ more people, especially in unskilled jobs, since cheap workers are widely available? It is unlikely that such questions can be answered with the limited tools of neoclassical economics; they will require a political economy approach which takes class (and class struggle) seriously. We hope that this chapter will help discard some of the myths surrounding the labour market, and encourage research which explores the heart of the matter, away from simplistic suggestions that 'fixing education' or making the labour market even *more* flexible than it is could be solutions to poverty.

REFERENCES

Amsden AH (2010) Say's Law, poverty persistence, and employment neglect, *Journal of Human Development and Capabilities*, Vol. 11, No. 1: 57-66.

Ashman S and B Fine (forthcoming) Neo-liberalism, varieties of capitalism, and the shifting contours of South Africa's financial system. *Transformation* 81-82: 144-178.

Baltar P et al. (2010) Moving towards decent work. Labour in the Lula government: Reflections on recent Brazilian experience. GLU Working Paper No. 9.

Barchiesi F (2011) *Precarious Liberation: Workers, the State, and Contested Social Citizenship in Postapartheid South Africa*. Albany, NY: SUNY Press.

Barrett J (2003) Organising in the informal economy: A case study of the minibus taxi industry in South Africa. SEED Working Paper, 39.

Bateman M (2012) 'From magic bullet to the Marikana massacre: The rise and fall of microcredit in post-apartheid South Africa', Le Monde diplomatique, November.

Bezuidenhout A (2008) New patterns of exclusion in the South African mining industry. In Bentley K and A Habib (eds) *Racial Redress and Citizenship in South Africa*. Cape Town: HSRC Press.

Bhorat H (2004) Labour market challenges in the post-apartheid South Africa. *South African Journal of Economics*, 72(5): 940-977.

Bhorat H and H Cheadle (2007) Labour reform in South Africa: Measuring regulation and a synthesis of policy suggestions. DPRU Working Paper, University of Cape Town.

Budlender D (2009) Industrial relations and collective bargaining: Trends and developments in South Africa. Industrial and Employment Relations Department (Dialogue) Working Paper No. 2, ILO.

Buhlungu S (2010) *A Paradox of Victory. Cosatu and the Democratic Transformation in South Africa*. Scottsville: UKZN Press.

Buhlungu S and A Bezuidenhout (2008) Union solidarity under stress: The case of NUM in South Africa. *Labor Studies Journal* 33: 262-287.

Chang DO (2009) Informalising labour in Asia's global factory. *Journal of Contemporary Asia* 39(2): 161-179.

Coleman N (2013) Towards new collective bargaining, wage and social protection strategies in South Africa – Learning from the Brazilian experience. GLU Working paper.

Competition Commission (2010) Competition Commission settles with Pioneer Foods, media release, 2 November, available from www.compcom.co.za.

Cosatu (2002) Theory of the Transition. Cosatu paper prepared for the Cosatu/ANC bilateral, 9/10 February.

Donnelly E and S Dunn (2006) Ten years after: South African employment relations since the negotiated revolution. *British Journal of Industrial Relations* 44(1): 1-29.

DPRU (Development Policy Research Unit) (2010) Addressing the plight of vulnerable workers: the role of sectoral determinations. Report to the Department of Labour.

Dugard, J (2013) Urban basic services in South Africa: Rights, reality and resistance. In Langford M, B Cousins, J Dugard and T Madlingozi (eds) *Symbols or Substance: The Role and Impact of Socio-Economic Rights Strategies in South Africa*. Cambridge: Cambridge University Press.

Forslund D (2013) Mass unemployment and the low-wage regime in South Africa. In Daniel J, P Naidoo, D Pillay and R Southall (eds) *New South African Review 3*. Johannesburg: Wits University Press.

Freund B (2013) Swimming against the tide: The Macroeconomic Research Group in the South African transition 1991-94. Review of African Political Economy.

Ghosh J (2011) Dealing with the poor. *Development and Change* 42(3): 849-858.

Godfrey S, M Clarke and J Theron (2005) On the Outskirts but Still in Fashion. Homeworking in the South African Clothing Industry: The Challenge to Organisation and Regulation. Development and Labour Monograph 2/2005, University of Cape Town.

Hassen EK (2005) The power behind the desk: Democracy, collective bargaining and the public service in South Africa. *South African Labour Bulletin* 29(1): 10-14.

Hofmeyr J and R Lucas (2001) The rise in union wage premiums in South Africa. *Labour* 15(4): 685-719.

James D (2012) Money-Go-Round: Personal economies of wealth, aspiration and indebtedness. *Africa* 82, Special Issue 1: 20- 40.

Kingdon G and J Knight (2007) Unemployment in South Africa, 1995-2003: causes, problems and policies. *Journal of African Economies* 16(5): 813-848.

Knight J (1982) The nature of unemployment in South Africa *South African Journal of Economics* 50 (1): 1-12.

Klein N (2012) Real wage, labour productivity, and employment trends in South Africa: A closer look. Working Paper 12/92.

Leibbrandt M, I Woolard, H McEwen and C Koep (2010) Employment and inequality outcomes in South Africa: What role for labour market and social policies? Report to the OECD.

Lichtenstein A (2013) From Durban to Wiehahn: Black workers, employers, and the state in South Africa during the 1970s. Paper presented at Wits Institute for Social and Economic Research (Wiser), University of the Witwatersrand, 25 February.

Makgetla N and T van Meelis (2003) Unpacking unemployment. *New Agenda* 10: 87-107.

Marais H (2005) Buckling. The impact of AIDS in South Africa. Centre for the Study of AIDS, University of Pretoria.

Marais H (2011) *South Africa Pushed to the Limit: the Political Economy of Change.* London: Zed Books.

Maree J (2011) Trends in the South African collective bargaining system in comparative perspective. *South African Journal of Labour Relations* 35(1): 7-37.

MERG (Macro-Economic Research Group) (1993) *Making Democracy Work: A Framework for Macroeconomic Policy in South Africa.* Cape Town: Centre for Development Studies and Uppsala: Scandinavian Institute of African Studies.

Meth C (2008) The (lame) duck unchained tries to count the poor. School of Development Studies Working Paper No 49, University of KwaZulu-Natal.

Mohamed S (2010) The state of the South African economy. In Daniel J, P Naidoo, D Pillay and R Southall (eds) *New South African Review 2010: Development or Decline?* Johannesburg: Wits University Press.

Moodie TD (1994) *Going for Gold: Men, Mines and Migration.* Berkeley and Los Angeles: University of California Press.

Murray J and C van Walbeek (2007) Impact of the sectoral determination for farm workers on the South African sugar industry: Case Study of the Kwazulu-Natal North and South Coasts'. CSSR Working Paper No. 181, University of Cape Town.

Nkosi M (2013) The changing working conditions in commercial agriculture in South Africa: A case study of horticulture in Gauteng. Paper presented at the conference 'Political Economy, Activism and Alternative Economic Strategies'. International Institute for Social Studies, The Hague, July 9-11.

OECD (2011) *African Economic Outlook.* Paris: OECD.

Oya C (2009) Ambiguities and biases in the definition and identification of the 'poor': Who is missing? What is missing. *Afriche Orienti,* Special Issue on Poverty II: 34-51.

Oya C (2013) Rural wage employment in Africa: methodological issues and emerging evidence. *Review of African Political Economy* 40:136, 251-273.

Pollin R, G Epstein, J Heintz and L Ndikumana (2006) *An Employment-Targeted Economic Programme for South Africa* Northampton: Edward Elgar Publishers.

Pons-Vignon N (forthcoming) Caught in the grip of the market: Agricultural and forestry workers in post-apartheid South Africa. In Oya C and N Pontara (eds) Rural Wage Employment in Developing Countries: Theory, Evidence and Policy. London: Routledge.

Pons-Vignon N and W Anseeuw (2009) Great expectations: Working conditions in South Africa since the end of apartheid. *Journal of Southern African Studies* 35 (4): 883-899.

Posel D, D Casale and C Vermaak (2013) The unemployed in South Africa: Why are so many not counted? Econ 3x3, February.

Segatti A and N Pons-Vignon (2013) Stuck in stabilisation? South Africa's post-apartheid macroeconomic policy between ideological conversion and technocratic capture. *Review of African Political Economy* 40(138).

Sender J and N Pontara (2010) The informal labour market: Conceptual issues and implication for research. Paper presented at the World Bank Headline Seminar on 'Promoting Inclusive Growth and Employment in Fragile Situations', April 12 and 13, Cape Town.

Stanwix B (2013) Minimum wages and compliance in South African agriculture, Econ 3x3, 22 January, available at http://www.econ3x3.org/article/minimum-wages-and-compliance-south-african-agriculture.

StatsSA (2013) Quarterly labour force survey. Quarter 3, 2013, 29 October. Available from www.statssa.gov.za.

StatsSA (Statistics South Africa) (2008) Labour force survey. Historical revision March series, 2001 to 2007, 28 August. Available from www.statssa.gov.za.

Strauss I (2013) Wages and productivity in post-apartheid South Africa. CSID Working Paper No.1/2013, University of the Witwatersrand.

Todd C (2004) Collective Bargaining Law. Cape Town: SiberInk.

Tshandu Z and S Kariuki (2010) Public administration and service delivery reforms: a post-1994 South African case. *South African Journal of International Affairs* 17(2): 189-208.

Unctad (2012) *Trade and Development Report, 2012. Policies for Inclusive and Balanced Growth.* New York and Geneva: United Nations.

Von Holdt K (2003) *Transition from Below: Forging Trade Unionism and Workplace Change in South Africa.* Scottsville: UKZN Press.

Von Holdt K (2010) Nationalism, bureaucracy and the developmental state: The South African case. *South African Review of Sociology* 41(1): 4-27.

Webster E (2013) The promise and the possibility: South Africa's contested industrial relations path. *Transformation* 81-82: 208-235.

Webster E and K von Holdt (eds) (2005) *Beyond the Apartheid Workplace. Studies in Transition.* Scottsville: UKZN Press.

Webster E et al. (2008) Making visible the invisible. Confronting South Africa's decent work deficit. Report prepared for the Department of Labour by the Sociology of Work Unit, University of the Witwatersrand.

NOTES

1   Thanks to John Sender and Claire Benit-Gbaffou for comments on earlier drafts.

2   This is the same argument which Amsden (2010) makes in her critique of strategies inspired by Say's law, according to which supply (in this case of skilled workers) creates its own demand, which argue for education or micro-credit as silver bullet solutions to unemployment and poverty.

3   The tendency to over-estimate self-employment (and under-estimate wage employment, especially of a casual nature) has been documented by Oya (2013) in relation to most African and aid donor statistics.

4   Privatised services often curtail access for the poor (Dugard 2013), while service delivery by 'New Public Management'-restructured state agencies or hospitals has overall been ineffective (Von Holdt 2010; Tshandu and Kariuki 2010).

5   This is very significant in a context of high dependency ratios, which is a direct consequence of high unemployment and a social grant system which barely covers able-bodied adults.

6   The EEC is not directly involved in research but typically outsources it, sometimes resulting in serious misrepresentation of issues, as in the case of forestry (Pons-Vignon, forthcoming). Radically different proposals were made in the MERG report (1993) for the establishment of sectoral wage boards, staffed with qualified researchers, and tasked with the establishment of minimum wages and monitoring of employment in different sectors.

7   Von Holdt (2003) shows how 'disobedient' black workers could be punished either for ignoring an order from a white colleague, or for obeying it when this order diverted them from their task.

8   Sectoral determinations can be found online at: www.labour.gov.za/legislation/sectoral-determinations/sectoral-determination.

9   One can wonder whether, beyond some isolated initiatives, there was ever any serious intent in Cosatu to recruit and organise poor workers in sectors such as agriculture or domestic work.

CHAPTER 2

The state of organised labour:
Still living like there's no tomorrow

Ian Macun

INTRODUCTION

One of the features of the past few years has been the extent to which the role of trade unionism and collective bargaining in South Africa have been called into question. Some commentators have gone as far as referring to an 'opportunity to smash the unions and enhance the economy's long-term job-creation potential' (Sharp 2012). Others acknowledge the importance of organised labour in South Africa's industrial landscape, 'but not in its current form' (*Business Day* 5 July 2012). By the end of 2012, and with some normality having returned in the wake of the tragedy at Marikana on 16 August when thirty-four mineworkers were killed by members of the South African Police Services, and an uneasy truce having returned in the farming sector of the Western Cape after violent protest actions, it was clear that something of a turning point had been reached.

The general assumption is that there has been a significant weakening of trade unionism, most clearly pronounced in relation to the shifting allegiance in the platinum mining sector from the National Union of Mineworkers (NUM) to the Association of Mineworkers and Construction Union (Amcu). Parallel to the weakening thesis sits a thesis of political power exercised by the Congress of South African Trade Unions (Cosatu) over the African National Congress (ANC) and government in how to regulate labour and the labour market. This has been most commonly argued in relation to Cosatu's opposition to labour brokers and the youth wage subsidy – both complex policy issues whose implementation was stalled for some time due to political difficulties. A similar argument has emerged in relation to the extension of the collective agreement between employers and trade unions in the clothing sector and its impact on jobs in the Newcastle area of KwaZulu-Natal.

What then is the reality of trade unionism in South Africa in the wake of Marikana? A divided and weakened union movement, or one that continues to command substantial power and is able to exercise significant political influence? And what are some of the challenges for trade unionism and for policy in the wake of the events of 2012?

Concerned with these issues, this chapter will start by looking back to the vision contained in the 1995 Labour Relations Act (LRA) for trade unionism to identify the major supports introduced in law to ensure state support for organised labour. It will provide an overview of the size and shape of the trade union movement post-1994 and will analyse what were arguably the most significant instances of industrial conflict during 2012 in order to identify some key challenges facing labour and the state.

THE VISION OF THE LABOUR RELATIONS ACT

The drafting of a new Labour Relations Bill began in the latter part of 1994 and a draft negotiating document in the form of a Labour Relations Bill was ready for public discussion and negotiation in February 1995 (Du Toit et al. 1996: 26). Key factors driving the urgency for a new labour relations dispensation were the interim constitution that had been adopted and that included fundamental rights (including in the area of labour relations) and a commitment by government to uphold international labour standards.

An International Labour Organisation (ILO) Fact Finding and Conciliation Commission on Freedom of Association had earlier found certain provisions of the previous LRA to be incompatible with principles of freedom of association. The new government had also undertaken to submit to Parliament for ratification the ILO Conventions dealing with freedom of association and the right to organise and collective bargaining. Both ILO conventions were ratified shortly after South Africa's readmission to the ILO in 1994, thus setting the stage for amendments to the LRA to bring it in line with the conventions and to significantly alter the legal framework for trade union organisation and engagement in collective bargaining.

The key areas of change affecting trade unions were:
i.   Curtailing the power of the state to interfere in the internal affairs of trade unions;
ii. Extending organisational rights to trade unions;
iii. Simplifying the registration procedure for trade unions; and
iv. Making provision for closed shop and agency shop agreements.

Organisational rights under the pre-1994 LRA were limited and were generally obtained through the negotiation of recognition agreements. The amendments that were incorporated in the new Labour Relations Act (No 66 of 1995) marked a significant shift in bringing the legislation in line with the ILO conventions, but also in making the operation of trade unions easier and extending legal support for trade union organisation.

Provided that trade unions achieve sufficient representation in a workplace, they can acquire organisation rights such as access to a workplace and deduction of union subscriptions without an employer having to agree. The LRA also makes provision for unions acting jointly to acquire rights that they may not be able to gain on their own. In other words, smaller unions could join together to become sufficiently representative and acquire organisational rights or apply to become parties to bargaining councils.

The provision for unions to act jointly could be seen as a way of encouraging greater cooperation between trade unions and possibly greater unity through mergers and amalgamations. More importantly, as Du Toit notes: 'The ease of registration may mean that new and predominantly small unions and employers' organisations could mushroom. It could also lead to increased union density, especially in sectors traditionally avoided by unions such as agriculture and small enterprises' (Du Toit et al. 1996: 63).

In parallel to the support for trade union organisation through the law, the use of representivity as a requirement for gaining organisational rights, applying for the establishment of statutory councils, entering into agency and closed shop agreements and applying for the establishment of workplace forums, led many to view the LRA as favouring larger unions and containing a majoritarian tendency. This view was clearly articulated by Baskin and Satgar who wrote: 'The LRA is profoundly majoritarian. Unions with majority support get distinct advantages. Small, minority and craft-based unions are disadvantaged. The message for unions is clear … grow or stagnate!' (Baskin and Satgar 1995:12).

In extending organisational rights to trade unions and in supporting centralised collective bargaining, the 1995 LRA was sending a clear message that stable labour relations depended on capable parties that could bargain effectively. The exercise of power should be reserved for the pursuit of matters of interest in an orderly fashion and as a last resort. The vision of the law was expressed clearly in the report of the Comprehensive Labour Market Commission which placed a strong emphasis on 'voice regulation' in the labour market:

> It is the need to balance flexibility with security that justifies the Commission's emphasis on *voice regulation* of the labour market, namely, the constructive role that bargaining between workers (and their unions) and employers (and their associations) can play in the productivity-enhancing redesign of the work process, in training and skills development, in employment equity planning and in many other aspects of the employment relationship. The ILO argues, and the Commission agrees, that excessively bureaucratic regulation is inimical to flexibility while an over-reliance on market forces is incompatible with labour market security and may result in increased inequality. Voice regulation provides the best means of charting a course that avoids both of these undesirable outcomes' (Report of the Commission to Develop a Comprehensive Labour Market Policy 1996: 3).

Relying on voice regulation requires bargained arrangements between strong, stable and well-informed employer and employee representatives. This policy approach articulated well with the legal framework in the LRA in relation to trade union rights and collective bargaining.

TRADE UNION GROWTH AND STRUCTURE

In the period 1994 to 2012, union membership increased by 557 919, or 18.4 per cent. Membership peaked between 2000 and 2004 and this coincided with a mushrooming in the number of registered trade unions (see Table 1 below). The sharp increase in the number of trade unions (but with a relatively modest increase in membership) was caused first by an unintended consequence of the new, open approach to freedom of association and trade union registration. This open approach led to the exploitation of union status for financial gain by individuals; a number of trade unions were established by labour consultants to gain rights of appearance available to unions and employer organisations in processes at the Commission for Conciliation Mediation and Arbitration (CCMA).

Minor amendments to the Labour Relations Act in 2002 and a concerted drive by the registrar of labour relations to de-register non-genuine trade unions led to a sharp decrease in the number of registered trade unions. The exploitation of union status for financial gain did, however, signal the arrival of an entrepreneurial orientation to trade unionism. This darker side of trade unionism has continued in different guises.

A second, expected, consequence of the new labour dispensation, was the spread of unionisation to the public sector and the public service in particular. Prior to 1993, unions had not been formally recognised in the public service. A number of unions had been active in parastatals such as Eskom and Transnet since the late 1980s and a few unions had begun to recruit members in the health services, in education and the police service. In the civil service itself, only staff associations had been recognised and it was only in the early 1990s that the state began informal discussion with the newly emerging unions and with staff associations that began to transform themselves into trade unions. Between the early 1980s and 1996 the number of organisations within the public service increased from one to over twenty, representing roughly 760 000 employees. In December 2011, there were 1 168 774 union members in the public service (excluding parastatals) – roughly 36 per cent of total union membership in the country.

Developments in other sectors were not as spectacular. Mining has increased in union density to a high of 77 per cent. In 1980, union density in mining was at 6.8 per cent, rocketing to 55.2 per cent in 1990. Manufacturing increased from 41 per cent in 1980 to 70 per cent in 1990, before declining to 31 per cent in 2012. The change in union density is, of course, explained not only by changing union membership but also by changes in employment. Declining employment in mining has contributed to the increased density, although the declining union density in manufacturing is certainly affected by changing employment patterns combined with a drop in union membership.

Table 1: Trade unions, union membership and density, 1994 to 2012

Year	Registered Trade Unions	TU Membership	TU Density (per cent)
1994	213	2470481	47.2
1995	248	2690727	51.5
1996	334	3016933	57.5
1997	417	3412645	
1998	463	3801388	
1999	499	3359497	
2000	464	3552113	
2001	485	3939075	30.7
2002	365	3277685	29.5
2003	504	4069000	30.4
2004	369	3134865	29
2005	341	3134865	30.2
2006	335	3049860	28.9
2007	261	3220245	30.3
2008	216	3298559	
2009	205	3238519	
2010	196	3057772	29.7
2011	195	3192530	29
2012	191	3028400	29.1

Note that density figures for 1994 to 1996 are based on non-agricultural employment, hence the higher density. The figures for 2001 to 2007 are from the former Labour Force Survey (all sectors) and the 2010 to 2012 figures are from the Quarterly Labour Force Survey. Figures for trade unions and their membership are from the records of the Department of Labour.

The change in employment patterns is also likely to have affected union density in sectors such as construction and wholesale and retail which have been characterised by a growth in contracting and sub-contracting arrangements that have made it difficult for unions to retain members. Although the post-1994 legal dispensation has supported unionisation and collective bargaining, it has not regulated non-standard employment. This has very likely been a factor in impeding union growth in a number of sectors.

Table 2: Trade union density by main industry sector 1980 to 2012 (per cent)

Main Industry	1980*	1990*	LFS 2002	LFS 2007	QLFS 2012
Agriculture			6.1	10.1	7.6
Mining	6.8	55.16	75.2	73.8	77.4
Manufacturing	41.72	70.16	35.1	35.8	31.2
Electricity, gas and water	12.83	42.39	49.6	43.4	59.2
Construction	11.79	31.53	13.3	9.4	11.3
Wholesale & retail trade	4.56	18.40	19.3	22.0	16.6
Transport	30.61	70.95	33.0	31.2	32.6
Finance	37.52	34.55	21.9	27.3	20.5
Community & Social Services	9.65	28.86	57.8	56.4	54.9
Private households			1.0	2.1	0.4
Total	**20.7**	**46.0**	**29.5**	**30.3**	**29.1**

Figures for 1980 and 1990 (from Hinks et al. 2007) exclude employment in agriculture and domestic work from the denominator, in part accounting for the high density in some sectors.

An important feature of union growth is that unionisation has not grown in sectors that have historically been characterised by low union density, sectors such as agriculture, construction and domestic work (private households). The particular difficulties posed by these sectors, such as diffuse employment, low numbers of employees per workplace, and difficulty of access to workplaces, have continued to elude union organisation both before 1994 and afterwards.

The trajectory of union growth post-1994 has thus been one of stable union membership overall and a reasonably stable union density, with some significant variation in different sectors. Compared to the pre-1994 period, the most significant growth has been in the public, mining and electricity sectors with other sectors such as manufacturing and finance showing a decline in unionisation. In the pre-1994 period, trade unionism showed a spectacular growth, particularly during the 1980s, which constituted the take-off phase in union growth in South Africa. This growth was a product not only of effective organisation at factory level by the emerging, independent unions, but also a product of the increased bargaining position of African workers (Hinks et al. 2007; Macun 2002).

The post-1994 period is perhaps best characterised as a phase in which trade unionism has held its own. This stabilising of unionisation should be viewed in the context of gradually declining employment, changing patterns of employment and low economic growth. The market power of trade unions associated with numerical strength has helped to sustain unionisation, as evidenced by the higher earnings of union members compared to non-members.

South Africa's unionisation rates are not unusually high, as some would think, but are comparable to the OECD countries and other large middle-income countries (Budlender 2012: 30). Where South Africa differs is that unionisation has not been declining as it has in a number of the advanced economies. South Africa also differs from many industrialised countries in having a large number of trade unions, most of which are small and unaffiliated to the major trade union federations.

UNION STRATEGY AND STRUCTURE

An analysis of union growth would not be complete without an examination of how union membership is distributed between the country's major federations and what trends there have been in the strategic choices of unions. In 1994, there were five major union federations which represented 89 per cent of all union members in seventy-seven affiliated unions. By far the largest federation was Cosatu with a 45 per cent share of union membership. The National Council of Trade Unions (Nactu) was the second largest – roughly a quarter of Cosatu's size. Table 3 shows the details of the major trade union federations, comparing their membership size in 1994 and in 2011.

Table 3: Trade union federations, affiliates and membership, 1994 and 2011

Federation	Affiliates	Member-ship	Per cent share	Affiliates	Member-ship	Per cent share
		1994			2011	
Cosatu	15	1 317 496	45	20	1 813 933	72
Nactu	18	334 733	15.2	22	145 008	5.79
Fedusa				19	367 106	14.6
Consawu				20	177 538	7
Fedsal	16	257 258	11.69			
Fitu	24	236 000	10.7			
Sacol	4	54 290	2.4			
Total	**77**	**2 199 777**		**81**	**2 503 585**	

By 2011 the configuration of the major federations had changed significantly. Cosatu has increased its number of affiliates, taking on a few smaller trade unions, such as the South African State and Allied Workers Union (Sasawu), the South African Football Players Union (Safpu) and a few others. More importantly, Cosatu's share of the union membership has jumped to 72 per cent of all workers represented by the major federations or 56.8 per cent of total union membership in the country. Its largest affiliate remains the NUM with just over 300 000 members followed by Numsa and the National Education Health and Allied Workers' Union (Nehawu), the largest unions in the manufacturing and public service respectively. While Cosatu was committed to a policy of 'one industry, one union' at the time of its formation in 1987, this has not been systematically pursued by the federation in the post-1994 period. Mergers have taken place between the old Construction and Allied Workers Union (Cawu) and the NUM and between unions in the chemical and paper and forestry sectors to form the Chemical Energy Paper Printing Wood and Allied Workers Union (Ceppwawu), but the original affiliates of Cosatu in the public service remain intact as separate unions focussing on different parts of the public service. More significant has been the blurring of organisational boundaries between the NUM and Numsa, in particular in mining and in the energy sector, with Numsa taking on members in both these sectors.

In contrast to Cosatu's growth, Nactu's membership has dropped by more than half. Recent developments, such as the growth of Amcu in the mining sector and the affiliation of the National Transport Movement may affect this decline, but Nactu remains a federation of relatively small unions spread throughout most sectors of the economy and representing predominantly less skilled and semi-skilled workers. What Nactu retains as a common characteristic with Cosatu is a distinct political unionism, both federations being aligned to party political traditions. The declining significance and support for the Pan Africanist Congress (PAC) post-1994 may well have a bearing on the decline in the membership of Nactu. The relationship of Cosatu to the African National Congress (ANC) and the South African Communist Party (SACP) has arguably had the opposite effect, although this political relationship is a far more complex one – and will be touched on in the final section.

The formation of the Federation of Unions of South Africa (Fedusa) through the merger of the old Federation of South African Labour Unions and Force in 1997 established the second largest federation with a membership of predominantly semi-skilled and skilled workers. A substantial proportion of Fedusa's membership was concentrated in the public service – which was the exclusive domain of the unions affiliated to Force. One of Fedusa's largest affiliates, the Public Service Association (PSA), disaffiliated, leaving it with a substantially reduced representation in the public service. In the last few years, Fedusa has increased its membership, also among less skilled workers, and now represents workers in most sectors. The largest affiliate of Fedusa is now the United Association of South Africa (Uasa), a general union in mining, manufacturing and the services sectors with over 70 000 members. This feature may well foreshadow the future trajectory of Fedusa as a federation characterised by political neutrality and focussed more on particular strata of the labour force across all sectors of the economy.

The Confederation of South African Workers Unions (Consawu) carried the mantle of the more conservative element in the union movement, taking over from the former South African Confederation of Labour (Sacol). Its major affiliate, Solidarity, grew out of the old Mineworkers Union (MWU) and recently disaffiliated from Consawu to pursue its representation of primarily white workers independently of any federation. This leaves Consawu as a small federation of unions concentrated mainly in the public sector, with a number of small unions in mining, construction, fishing and retail sectors.

The major fissures in the union movement that existed prior to 1994 have thus carried through into the post-1994 period with a trade union landscape characterised by a few federations of unions representing the overwhelming majority of all union members. In 1994, 89 per cent of all union members were concentrated in five federations whereas by 2011 this declined by roughly ten per cent to 78 per cent of union members in four major federations. The most significant shifts have been the increased dominance of Cosatu within the union movement and the growth of Fedusa as an independent voice.

The small grouping of trade unions that remain nonaligned to any of the main federations continues to characterise the union movement although their number has declined slightly from 136 in 1994 to 103 in 2011. Although slightly more union members are concentrated in the nonaligned trade unions, this is most likely explained by a few large unions, such as the PSA and Solidarity, choosing to disaffiliate from union federations.

While the total number of trade unions has declined, the number of applications to register new unions has averaged eighty-eight applications per year over the past ten years. At the same time, the Department of Labour cancelled the registration of approximately twenty-eight trade unions per year over the same period, mainly because of noncompliance with legal obligations under the Labour Relations Act.

The turnover in trade union organisations can be viewed in the context of the post-1994 era of freedom of association and easier access to registration. The main motive for union formation remains a genuine attempt at representing and protecting worker interests, but within the new dispensation trade union organisation has become fair game for those seeking access to resources and opportunities – ranging from labour consultants seeking to represent employees in dispute resolution processes to a few who have made union officialdom a livelihood. The formation of breakaway unions is not a new feature, and includes breakaways from Cosatu affiliates. Amcu was registered in 2001; there has been a break-away from Food and Allied Workers Union (Fawu) in the fishing sector, and 2012 saw a break-away from South African Transport and Allied Workers Union (Satawu) with the formation of the National Transport Movement. While the formation of breakaway unions fragments and weakens union organisation they cannot be read solely as a reflection of internal weaknesses. Internal splits in unions often relate to particular circumstances even though they are most commonly associated with divisions among union leaders and officials.

The above has suggested a relatively stable pattern of union growth and structure since 1994. What remains is an assessment of the character of trade unionism and, especially, of the significance of the industrial conflict of 2012 for trade unionism and for the legal framework.

CHANGES IN UNION ORGANISATION AND LABOUR LAW

A key factor in sustaining trade unions, particularly during apartheid, has been their organisational tradition of shop-floor democracy and worker control. The emphasis on worker control over their leadership and their organisations was critical to the survival and growth of these unions, and continues to be important in explaining how unions sustain themselves. The 1996 LRA does not interfere in the internal operations of unions and, in fact, promotes accountability within trade unions in the legal requirements with which unions have to comply and the way in which these requirements are enforced.

Recently, however, this organisational tradition has shown signs of stress in which 'the arrival of political democracy in 1994 has been associated with a decline in the intensity and vitality of local union democracy' (Hirschohn 2011: 2). Reporting on the fourth iteration of a survey of members of Cosatu affiliates, Hirschsohn and the researchers associated with the Taking Democracy Seriously project present findings that suggest a weakening of the key role played by shop stewards in the workplace and in relation to the members they represent. Two findings, in particular, are striking. The first is the sharp decline between the first survey in 1994 and the fourth survey in 2008 in the number of respondents who agreed that shop stewards can only act on a mandate from members. This fell from 72 per cent in 1994 to 46 per cent in 2008. Despite a problem of comparability between the first and the following three surveys due to methodological changes, the fact that less than half of the respondents in 2008 felt that shop stewards may act without a mandate points to a decline in accountability between shop-floor leaders and union members. A similar finding emerged from the Cosatu Workers Survey where less than 40 per cent of the respondents felt they were able to exercise a lot of influence over their shop-steward representatives (Naledi 2012: 23).

A second striking finding is the decline in policy knowledge levels among shop stewards. When shop stewards were asked, for example, whether they had ever been in a meeting where there was a report-back on Nedlac, the number dropped from 59 per cent in 1998 to 21 per cent in 2008. As Hirschsohn (op. cit.: 20) concludes: 'Although individual members are far removed from policy negotiations at Nedlac, the limited participation of their representatives in meetings where policy issues are discussed raises substantive questions about the extent to which effective mandating processes are in place.' Not surprisingly, Hirschsohn concludes that although the formal structure of democracy remains in place in the country's largest trade unions, the model of shop-floor democracy and worker control on which the unions were built has been substantially weakened.

This understanding of unions' internal organisational problems has been echoed by a number of commentators over the past few years (see, *inter alia*, Buhlungu 2010). It was, however, the dramatic industrial conflict during 2012, particularly the conflict in the mining sector, that pushed these issues into the open and no doubt influenced the self-critical agenda of Cosatu's 11th Congress in late 2012 and its collective bargaining conference in March 2013.

In his address to the collective bargaining conference, Zwelinzima Vavi (2013:7), the general secretary of Cosatu, outlined key organisational problems:

> On the issue of the social distance of leaders, we have to acknowledge that even at the level of full time shop stewards, and even more so at the level of elected leadership, we have allowed a situation where a physical and material distance often exists. How often do we hear of full time shop stewards having absolutely no connection to their original constituency? Sometimes these are elected office bearers, who have not been re-elected by their constituency, and yet get protected by a fudging of their union constitution. Then there is often a material distance. Sometimes in an effort to find a solution to the challenge of a full time shop steward being taken out of the normal pay and progression structure of a company, we have agreed to conditions which provide undue privilege. This privilege becomes the source of envy as well as derision (disdain and scorn). Where it becomes the source of envy it produces leadership battles based not on principle but on material competition. Whether the response of workers is envy or derision, the ultimate product is the same – the creation of conditions ripe for splits and splinter unions.

The fact that the NUM became the victim of widespread member dissatisfaction in the platinum mining sector is perhaps instructive of the range of challenges that have been facing many Cosatu affiliates. In the case of unions such as the NUM, its sheer size and scale has presented it with the challenge of maintaining a balance between worker control and shop-floor democracy on the one hand, and maintaining an effective union administration and level of service to its members on the other. In the face of a high outflow of experienced unionists to the public service, political office and other pursuits, maintaining an effective organisational machinery would clearly be difficult – as it has been in many other institutional and organisational settings in the country.

The first significant change in union organisation highlighted by the 2012 conflicts has therefore been a gradual but systematic weakening of the organisational power vested in the tradition of shop-floor democracy and worker control. This is not to suggest that organisational weakness spans the entire union movement – but the fact that some of the largest and most influential trade unions have suffered setbacks highlights the significance of the problem and the potential for greater instability in union developments in the future.

A second key feature of 2012 that relates to problems of union organisation was the upsurge in independent and often uncoordinated worker action in the mining and agricultural sectors. In the mining sector, the relationship between the action by workers and trade unions was complex. On the one hand, workers engaged in industrial action after communication between the NUM, management and workers broke down (Alexander et al. 2012: 119). On the other hand, worker committees were established on some mines, and although they seemed to be independent it is possible that rival unions such as

Amcu played a role in the formation and operation of certain committees. On the mines, independent worker action could therefore be viewed in the context of disillusionment with management, dissatisfaction with the established majority union, and a response to the emergence of a militant, rival union trying to gain a foothold among workers. Dissatisfaction with levels of pay, particularly among rock drill operators, was also a driving factor in the mining unrest from its inception at Anglo American Platinum in January 2012.

The upsurge of worker action in the Western Cape agricultural sector in September 2012, starting in De Doorns and spreading to Ceres, Robertson, Prince Alfred and Somerset West, saw worker action, independently of any union formation in the area, demanding a minimum wage of R150 per day. Within a short space of time, a number of trade unions established a presence among workers in areas such as De Doorns and engaged with government and employers in the talks that followed and that were aimed at reviewing the minimum wage contained in the sectoral determination. As was the case in the platinum mines, the underlying cause of worker action was dissatisfaction with existing levels of pay. Poor working and living conditions were frequently cited as aggravating factors fuelling the strikes and protest action among these workers. As Hartford (2012: 7-8) states: 'There is no doubt that the gross poverty and inequality in South Africa (amongst the worst in the world in respect of Gini coefficient measures) provides the social and economic context to heightened expectations of wage increases.'

The industrial action of 2012 in agriculture, in particular, was perhaps the first widespread expression of how socioeconomic pressures on workers, on income levels and on general living conditions have led directly to instability in industrial relations.

A third feature of 2012 was the persistence of violent action during industrial disputes. The tragic shooting of mineworkers on 16 August 2012 at Marikana served as a grim reminder of the repressive capability of the state, irrespective of political regime. The violence of Marikana was accompanied by violence during the farmworker protest and the strike during August 2012 in the road freight sector. In both, violence was accompanied by the burning of vineyards and trucks. In many ways, the violence that characterised industrial conflict during 2012 served also as a reminder of the persistence of violence in South Africa's industrial relations system. Strikes, and violence during strikes, has been a recurring theme from the early part of the twentieth century to the present.

The implications of recurring strike violence by unionised and non-unionised workers are twofold. On the one hand, violent action serves as a reminder of the limits to institutionalisation of industrial relations; irrespective of the legitimacy of industrial relations, the exercise of class power remains a possibility. On the other hand, the use of violence reminds one of the ways in which workers will exercise power – with violence an extreme form, but one frequently resorted to in South Africa. As Von Holdt (2008: 17) argues:

> It is clear from this that industrial conflict is only partially institutionalised in post-apartheid South Africa. On the one hand, trade unions and employers make regular, indeed daily, use of the institutions and procedures for resolving conflict between

individual employees and employers, as well as for collective dispute resolution and collective-bargaining. On the other hand, procedures may be disputed or regarded as unfair, and collective action not infrequently involves violence and intimidation, including violence by the police. Explaining the partial quality of institutionalisation needs to take account both of the industrial relations factors as well as the factors located in the broader society.

What are the likely implications of these features of the 2012 industrial conflict for the future of trade unionism? The weakening of internal union organisation and the ability of trade unions to rely on organisational power is likely to have three consequences. First, the chances of fragmentation through the formation of new, breakaway unions is increased. Fragmentation may lead to a short- term decline in overall union membership as some workers give up their union affiliation. Over time, workers may well join other unions or re-join the union to which they originally belonged, and the overall effect on aggregate union membership may be minimal. A second consequence of the weakening of union organisation is that it lays a basis for greater instability in workplace labour relations and may lead to a weakening of collective bargaining. The risk of instability is clearly heightened where unions compete for recognition and organisational rights, or where new unions adopt a militant stance in pursuit of organisational rights, which has been seen in the platinum mining and transport sectors. A third consequence is that trade unions turn to the state to support them in retaining their workplace influence – either through legislative change or through intervention with management. Such a strategy is not only contrary to the rationale underlying the current legal dispensation but is also likely to be the most damaging to the long-term prospects of strong, democratic trade union organisation.

The use of industrial protest action to deal with socioeconomic pressures experienced by workers can have many consequences. The obvious effects are instability in workplaces, with associated risks of deterioration in existing relations between management and workers and in such collective bargaining arrangements as may exist. It may be tempting to view spontaneous industrial action as an opportunity for trade union organisation, but such opportunities are complicated by a lack of familiarity with trade unionism on the part of workers, who are often in vulnerable positions, as are farmworkers, and for whom trade union subscriptions are not always affordable. The fact that workers who engage in industrial protest may be seasonal or contract workers, as was the case in the farmworker protests, also makes union membership an unlikely prospect. As has been pointed out in relation to obstacles to effective collective bargaining for non-standard workers, 'a fragmented workforce implies that there are different segments of workers in the same workplace with diverse interests and different contractual status, which can trigger and intensify conflicts among workers themselves instead of labour-management conflict, thereby hindering solidarity among workers' (Ebisui 2012: 5).

Finally, the consequence (apart from legal consequences) of violence during strikes and industrial action is likely to be a growing problem of trade union legitimacy. Declining legitimacy and growing distrust in unionism can only lead to declining affiliation and membership of trade unions.

In light of these developments in industrial relations and trade unionism, some have argued for a review of labour legislation to craft a different dispensation that is better able to deal with the challenges that have arisen over the past few years.

What then are the strategic and policy implications of the industrial conflict of 2012? The first implication is that the problems in labour relations cannot be resolved simply by further amendments to labour legislation. Some would argue that the legislative framework is not suited to current dynamics, especially when it comes to assisting low-paid, vulnerable workers and nor does it assist in regulating competition for resources between the employed and unemployed, as labour legislation supports collective bargaining structures that create barriers to entry into the labour market and excludes minority unions and outsiders. Such arguments tend to over-emphasise the role of law in resolving conflicts relating to socioeconomic conditions. As outlined above, the LRA clearly supports collective bargaining arrangements, in particular between strong bargaining partners. But the LRA does not compel parties to enter into specific arrangements, including arrangements relating to majority unions and the rights that they may enjoy. The LRA also does not prescribe what agency shop agreements employers and unions should enter, and nor does it set down hard and fast criteria for thresholds of representivity and access to organisational rights and collective bargaining arrangements. A distinction should be drawn between the statutory framework and the labour relations frameworks and practices that are adopted by employers and trade unions in workplaces and in bargaining structures, including bargaining and statutory councils. As Van Niekerk argues (2012: 5): 'It is not necessary in these circumstances to rewrite the LRA, nor is it necessary to reconvene another Wiehahn-like commission to consider alternative legislative models. What is required is for both unions and employers to revisit their agreements to determine whether they are grounded in historical circumstances that are no longer part of workplace reality, and to make the necessary changes.'

Placing the responsibility for change on business and organised labour, and not the state, does however run the risk of stalemate, as the parties resort to a power play that will inevitably inhibit innovation and change. If unions are to continue to grow in the face of the labour market and socioeconomic challenges that face workers it will be necessary to re-build democracy within trade union structures and also to restore legitimacy in trade unionism, particularly in the eyes of those who remain as prospective union members. Revisiting employer and trade union agreements in workplaces will also be necessary to craft a more inclusive trade union regime in the workplace so as to avoid conflict and encourage more inter-union cooperation.

As key elements of the LRA's vision for trade unionism and collective bargaining have not been realised over the past twenty years, the prospects for change in the future are not encouraging. In the light of increased labour market fragmentation, a weakening of organisational power of some of the largest trade unions and an increased politicisation of trade unionism, union growth in the future is likely to be limited, uneven across sectors and occupational groups, and constrained by the responsiveness of union organisation to changing labour market conditions.

CONCLUSION

The two competing theses about trade union growth and influence alluded to at the beginning of this chapter can be approached by recognising the many dimensions of power that may be exercised by trade unions. Trade unions exercise power through numbers – not only absolute membership, but also membership as a proportion of potential membership, that is, the degree of union density. At roughly 30 per cent, South African trade unions have retained a relatively high density across sectors and have demonstrated very substantial membership in sectors such as mining, energy and the public service. The stable growth of trade unions has continued despite adverse economic conditions over the past five years and a decline in real wages of workers, although negotiated increases have continued to outpace inflation.

To assume that trade unions are in crisis on the basis of a loss of membership by one union is misleading and underestimates the resilience of trade unions as organisations that further the interests of workers. The NUM may be facing particular challenges, but that does not mean that the whole of Cosatu or the union movement is weakening. This review of trade union growth after apartheid suggests that the numerical strength of the South African union movement has been relatively stable and that Cosatu has become even more dominant within the union movement as a whole.

Trade unions also exercise institutional power – that is, the ability to shape decision making in order to serve their members' interests. Cosatu's role in the Alliance and its relationship to the ANC clearly places it in a position of considerable power to influence national politics. This power has arguably grown during the past few years, although not without considerable risk to the cohesiveness of the federation and in individual affiliates, as witnessed by the investigation into the role of the general secretary, Zwelinzima Vavi, during 2013. The union movement's influence on government – and that of Cosatu in particular – has also ensured the continuation of a supportive legal and policy environment.

A critical dimension to trade union power is clearly its organisational strength, not only in a numerical sense, but in relation to the degree of unity and cohesion within union structures and their ability to represent the interests of members democratically and coherently, including their administrative capacity. In his analysis of the 2012 mining strike wave, Hartford (op. cit.: 6) summed up the dilemma facing the NUM and other large unions as follows:

> The union like any social organisation, is not a static, monolithic entity. It's a complex entity whose most constant feature is change – change in both its internal processes and a change in its external processes as a social actor and change agent itself. But the

change that happens at the very bottom of the union, at the interface of the union shop steward with the member, is the key driver which determines much of the strategic change processes in any union. To understand what is happening in any union, one must investigate this relationship between the member and the shop floor leader in particular. Because if a union loses its capacity to democratically account and promote the views of members, it loses the capacity to hold the loyalty of those members.

This same challenge of ensuring democratic worker control will face new unions such as Amcu who will, over time, have to find ways of responding to these pressures if they are to sustain themselves organisationally. Similarly, trade unions whose internal operations have not been characterised by democratic practices and worker control may well find themselves having to adapt and to ensure greater accountability to members where members demand this as a condition for loyalty and trust.

While trade unions operate along different dimensions of power, it is perhaps this dimension, the organisational power of trade unions, that has been exposed as the Achilles heel of a number of trade unions. After almost two decades of survival and growth in post-apartheid South Africa, continued growth will be significantly affected by the ability of unions to strengthen their day-to-day operations and their representation of their members' interests.

REFERENCES

Alexander P, T Lekgowa, B Mmope, L Sinwell and B Xezwi (2012) *Marikana A View From the Mountain and a Case to Answer.* Auckland Park: Jacana.
Baskin J and V Satgar (1995) South Africa's new Labour Relations Act: A critical assessment and challenges for labour. National Labour Economic and Development Institute (Naledi), Johannesburg.
Budlender D (2012) Key issues in the South African Labour Market. Unpublished paper prepared for the Department of Labour and the Economic Development Department.
Buhlungu S (2010) *A Paradox of Victory – COSATU and the Democratic Transformation in South Africa.* Scottsville: University of KwaZulu-Natal Press.
Du Toit D, D Woolfrey, J Murphy, S Godfrey, D Bosch and S Christie (1996) *The Labour Relations Act of 1995.* Durban: Butterworth.
Ebisui M (2012) Non-standard workers: Good practices of social dialogue and collective bargaining. ILO Working Paper No.36 ILO, Geneva.
Hartford G (2012) The Mining strike wave: What are the causes and what are the solutions? Unpublished paper.
Hinks T, I Macun and G Wood (2007) Comprehending union growth in South Africa, 1970-1990. *Historical Studies in Industrial Relations* 23/24:125-54.
Hirschsohn P (2011) The 'hollowing-out' of trade union democracy in Cosatu members, shop stewards and the South African Communist Party. *Law, Democracy & Development* 15: 279-310.
Macun I (2002) The Dynamics of Trade Union Growth in South Africa: 1970-1996. Sociology of Work Unit, Labour Studies Report Series 10, University of the Witwatersrand.
National Labour and Economic Development Institute (Naledi) (2013) Findings of the Cosatu Workers' Survey, 2012. Unpublished paper.

Report of the Commission to Investigate the Development of a Comprehensive Labour Market Policy (1996) *Restructuring the South Africa Labour Market*. Cape Town.: CTP Book Printers.

Sharp L (2012) 'SA's trade unions the biggest obstacle to job creation'. *Business Day* 25 May.

Van Niekerk A (2012) Marikana: The perspective of the Labour Court. Keynote address SASLAW Conference October.

Vavi Z (2013) An Overview of the Collective Bargaining, Organising and Campaigns Challenges that we face. www.Cosatu.org.za/events.php?cat=conferences. [Accessed March-April 2013]

Von Holdt K (2008) Institutionalisation, strike violence and local moral orders. Paper presented to the International Sociological Association (ISA) Conference, Barcelona, Spain, September.

CHAPTER 3

Citizen Wal-Mart?
South African food retailing and selling development[1]

Bridget Kenny

———•———

INTRODUCTION

In public debate throughout 2011 and much of 2012, Wal-Mart's entry into South Africa's economy sparked fierce debate. The Competition Tribunal and Competition Appeal Court processes became a match between the formidable US multinational – the world's largest private employer with some 2.1 million employees in fifteen countries[2] – and what appeared to many as activist ministries within the state, fighting to uphold 'public interest' in its merger with Johannesburg Stock Exchange (JSE) listed Massmart Holdings, Inc., trading as subsidiaries Game, Dion, Makro, Builder's Warehouse and Cambridge Foods, among others. South African unions, most notably the South African Commercial, Catering and Allied Workers Union (Saccawu), with support from global union federation UNI Global and the US union the United Food and Commerical Workers (UFCW), put up a resolute defence against an uncomplicated and quick merger approval (Kenny 2012b).

Wal-Mart/Massmart claimed to offer cheap goods to a growing middle and working class consumer base, and as such their 'everyday low prices (EDLP)' would bring the majority of South African consumers, previously excluded from consumption, into participation in this market. The chief executive officer (CEO) of Wal-Mart International,

Doug McMillon, wrote in an op-ed in *Business Day* on 26 January 2011 that the company's 'core mission – to save people money so they can live better' would be its contribution to South Africa. He concluded, 'Walmart looks forward to earning our credentials as a responsible and productive citizen of SA.'

But the protracted merger approval process was to belie any easy acceptance of Wal-Mart. In its report in February 2011, the Competition Commission recommended, in what can only be acknowledged as a political misstep, that the deal be approved with no conditions. When the Competition Tribunal in March and May of 2011 rolled around, the hearings had become the terrain of battle. The state's representatives, led by the minister of economic development, Ebrahim Patel, became increasingly frustrated with the merging parties' unwillingness to provide information or come to informal agreement over conditions for the merger. The Departments of Economic Development (EDD), Trade and Industry (DTI) and Agriculture, Forestry and Fisheries (DAFF) were concerned about the effects of Wal-Mart's entry on South African manufacturing and agricultural jobs in the context of the power of this global buyer to import through its supply chain the most competitive commodities from around the world. They sought stricter conditions on the merger, primarily through expanded commitments to sourcing locally and to opening access to Wal-Mart global networks for local companies. The departments made a joint submission, based on their request to intervene on matters of public interest, particularly around local sourcing. The unions Saccawu, Southern African Clothing and Textile Workers Union (Sactwu) and Fawu and the Small, Medium and Micro Enterprise Forum also raised public interest concerns over Wal-Mart's substitution effect, poor labour conditions, history of anti-union relations, and sourcing practices.

South African competition law demands that any large merger must go through an evaluation of the anti-competitive effects of the transaction on the economy. Meant to address the highly concentrated, deeply intertwined, and generally white capital dominating the South African economy under apartheid, the reformed Competition Act sought to open up the market and also to diversify it for black ownership and participation (Roberts 2004). South Africa's new law included a public interest clause which is relatively wide in scope. It requires a consideration of any concerns over the effect on employment, small business operations and social welfare. The stated purposes of the Act are threefold: 'To promote efficiency, adaptability and development of the economy; to provide consumers with competitive prices and product choice; and to promote employment and advance the social and economic welfare of South Africans' (Competition Act, 1998, section 2). Large mergers, specifically, must be assessed for their impact on a sector, on employment, on the competitiveness of small businesses, and on the ability of national industries to compete in international markets (Competition Act, 1998, section 12A; and see Hodge et al. 2013).

Without rehearsing the drama of those events (see Kenny 2012a), the Tribunal hearings largely revolved around whether a public interest case could be made around Wal-Mart's poor record on labour rights and on potential job losses/business closure upstream in local suppliers, manufacturers and producers as a result of Wal-Mart's global sourcing. Acknowledging uncomfortably that there was some issue to provoke concerns of public interest, in May 2011 the Tribunal recommended the deal with four conditions: 1) that there be no retrenchments in Massmart stores for two years; 2) that the company give hiring preference to 503 retrenched (in June 2010) workers; 3) that the company honour existing labour agreements and continue to recognise Saccawu as majority union for three years; and, 4) that the company resource a fund of R100 million to help develop local suppliers and train local suppliers in how to do business with Wal-Mart (Competition Tribunal 2011).

Saccawu appealed and the three ministers requested that the Tribunal decision be set aside by the Competition Appeal Court.[3] Patel explained: 'As government we are guided by the Constitution and the policies placed before the electorate … Employment and decent work are at the centre of our policies. They [the merging parties] will need to secure better protection for jobs in the Massmart supply chain than what we currently have in place.'[4] They sought stricter conditions on the merger.

The Appeal Court heard the case in late October. In March 2012, Judges Davis and Zondi rejected both the Department's request for review and the union's appeal of the merger. However, they strengthened the ruling's conditions, and ruled that the 503 retrenched workers should be reinstated (rather than receiving preferential hiring) and that a committee of experts, one nominated from each of the merging parties, the union, and the government should convene to research and report on the financial costs and process requirements to facilitate access of small business to the company's supply chain, rather than accept as evident the merging parties' proposal of R100m. This expert committee included Joseph Stiglitz for the state, James Hodge for the unions, and Mike Morris for the merging parties. In June 2012, two reports were produced, with different recommendations (Stiglitz and Hodge authoring one and Morris the second). In October 2012, the Appeal Court judgment ultimately followed Morris's narrower recommendations and determined that Massmart should contribute a maximum amount of R200m to a fund that would be used for the development of small and medium enterprises only. The judgment cautioned against 'competition law being employed as a surrogate for coherent industrial policy' and found no basis for the larger and longer-term fund proposed by Stiglitz and Hodge 'which we consider falls outside of the parameters of the Act' (Planting 2012). Debate over the use of public interest provisions in competition law to posit limits on capital returned to the position that these constricted competitive behaviour. The Wal-Mart merger case, then, opened up the possibility of using competition law towards broader developmental aims and, by its conclusion, shut it down again, in a firm confirmation of supply-side economics.

The state moved to reassure capital that it was committed to facilitating foreign direct investment (FDI). The minister of agriculture, Tina Joemat-Pettersson, journeyed to Wal-Mart-supported strawberry fields in Costa Rica, posing with her Wal-Mart cap, to see the effects of small producers' access to Wal-Mart supply chains (Mashala 2012), and Rob Davies, the minister of trade and industry, said he had changed his position, and now argued that Wal-Mart's work with small producers was a model of developing South African capacity (Crotty 2013).

The debates about the Wal-Mart/Massmart merger raised concerns over procurement because of the reputation of Wal-Mart, but missed the longer trend of state deregulation of the agro-food system in South Africa, in which South African retailers have very much followed the techniques pioneered by Wal-Mart and others, and have benefited from them –to the point of making Massmart an appealing acquisition in the first place. The merger of Wal-Mart with Massmart offers us an opportunity to engage with other questions about how development is being formulated in South Africa: what have been the relationships between retail capital, smallholder access, service employment and food security? Authors examining the internationalisation of retailing, as does Reardon (2005), have argued precisely that retailing can facilitate development in emerging economies through supply chain programmes. Retail appears as merely having capacity to support 'development', without promoting its own interests. In the same way, the state's impulse to bind the deal to sourcing locally seems a willing myopia, disengaged from what retail's role already suggests about our economic choices. Finally, using the merger to examine 'development' points to a similar shortsightedness of the labour movement, rallying mainly around conditions within shops and to protect jobs.

FOOD RETAIL INTERNATIONALISATION AND THE ENTRY OF WAL-MART

The South African retail sector had predicted the entry of a major transnational retail firm for some time. It was the inevitable progression seen in other parts of the world, and it made sense given the relative sophistication of its sector. Thus, Wal-Mart's approach was not a surprise. The global circulation of retail capital has been a trend since the 1990s, particularly led by food and general merchandisers (Wrigley 2000; Reardon and Berdegue 2002; Weatherspoon and Reardon 2003; Humphrey 2007). By the 2000s, this investment turned toward the global South with a 'deluge of retail FDI into the emerging markets' (Coe and Wrigley 2007:342), and Wal-Mart was a prime mover. The share of Wal-Mart's international sales increased steadily from 4 per cent in 1995 to greater than 20 per cent by 2005 (Durand and Wrigley 2009: 3). Wal-Mart is the world's leading international retailer at the moment.

The same expansionary impulse, of course, has been followed by South African retailers into Africa and other parts of the world, most robustly by Shoprite, with all major corporate firms increasing the percentage of their turnover from business outside South Africa over the past ten to fifteen years (Macquarie 2013; Weatherspoon and Reardon 2003; Miller 2008).

Yet the discussions on international retail expansion have moved beyond noting this rapid and visible phenomenon to become more nuanced, suggesting that there are many reasons why transnational retailers do better in some markets than in others. In general, a number of writers have made the important point that transnational retailers require the firm to embed within specific regulatory, cultural and market relations, which changes both local contexts and the retailer itself (Coe and Wrigley 2007; Tilly 2007; Wrigley et al.

2005; Christopherson 2007; Bianchi and Arnold 2004). Writing about Wal-Mart's entry into Mexico, Tilly (2006) argues that the conditions of entry helped set the terms of its advantage over local firms. Wal-Mart used the North American Free Trade Agreement (NAFTA) to enable it to import products and avoid building local distribution centres; it aggressively reduced prices to challenge local suppliers; and it managed product specifications in detail, putting remaining suppliers under pressure. Yet Tilly also found that local competitors benefited from imitating Wal-Mart's strategies, and reduced the advantage to the company over time (Tilly 2006:198). In contrast, Christopherson (2006) explains that Wal-Mart's unsuccessful entry into Germany (with its decision to disinvest) related to the very different character of market governance there than in the US – the power of German manufacturing, the system of occupational skills and training, the local regulatory context favouring existing firms—and ultimately to the disjuncture of Wal-Mart's firm culture. Thus, analysis of the existing conditions of the retailing, food manufacturing and distributive systems is critical to understanding the effect that Wal-Mart will have on an economy.

Durand and Wrigley (2009) usefully consolidate much of this literature into three key issues which explain the success of the firm within host economies: the timing and mode of entry into the host economy, the ability to exercise and benefit from upstream market power, and the responsiveness to labour regimes.

As we know, Wal-Mart entered South Africa through the majority share acquisition of Massmart, which looked fairly similar in operation to Wal-Mart. Massmart has focused on low-income consumers and has operated through 'big box retailing'.

Wal-Mart entered an already highly formalised retail context. South Africa's mass grocery retail sector (another name for the formal sector of food retailing) is Africa's largest in terms of value, worth about US$29 billion (BMI 2013). In 2003, the share of the food retailing market for formal stores (in comparison to informal routes) was already 55 per cent (Weatherspoon and Reardon 2003:1). In 2012, formal channels had increased to account for 62.3 per cent of the food market (meaning that 37.7 per cent was in the informal sector – for instance, hawkers and spaza shops), which is higher than many other developing countries, including Brazil, Russia and India (BMI 2013; see also Weatherspoon and Reardon 2003). Another estimate puts formal food retailing as high as 68 per cent (Planting 2010:34). Regardless of the exact figures, analysts agree that the food retail market is increasingly becoming formalised, with distribution happening through supermarkets.[5] Furthermore, it is a growing market in terms of sales: in 2012 mass grocery retail sales were up by 10.4 per cent, with this kind of growth rate forecast to continue through to 2016 (BMI 2013).

South Africa's formal food retail sector has been highly concentrated into four large corporations – Shoprite, Pick n Pay, Spar and Woolworths – that have accounted for over 94 per cent of supermarket sales (Weatherspoon and Reardon 2003). Another way to put this corporate dominance is that just four firms have held about 50 per cent of the total food market (not just supermarkets) (Ingham 2009)! In 2012, Christo Wiese, chairman of the Shoprite Holdings board, wrote that '67 per cent of the country's adult population buy groceries from our stores. That is more than 23 million people.'[6] Indeed, the South African food retail sector has been characterised as 'an extremely tight oligopoly' (Botha and Van Schalkwyk, cited in Louw et al., 2007:19). Domestic retailers have also consolidated through mergers and acquisitions to expand to smaller towns and rural areas.

In 2009 on the eve of Wal-Mart's approach, Massmart represented only 2 per cent of the formal food retailing market but 22.4 per cent of food wholesaling (RBB Economics 2011). Currently, Massmart's total food sales places it third highest in food retail and wholesale in South Africa. If the wholesale division is excluded, Massmart ranks as the fifth largest of the firms (Macquarie 2013:46).

Thus it is into this retailing context of already existing firm dominance that Wal-Mart entered. Format trends did not result from transnational corporation (TNC) investment, but predated it, with domestic retailers as drivers. Yet Wal-Mart is expected to vastly increase short-term competition in the food market, until it consolidates. Massmart is expected to spend significantly on expanding its food retailing operations in the immediate future (BMI 2013; Kew 2011). For instance, Massmart acquired Cambridge Food retail stores, which it has grown in central business districts and townships, particularly focusing on taxi ranks and other public transit routes. They now have twenty-five stores: 'Focussing [sic] on consumers within the living standards measure (LSM) 2-7 range, our customers are characterised by high levels of unemployment, reliance on social grants as a primary source of income, and heavy dependence on taxis, trains and busses to travel between work and home.'[7] Massmart has posted strong growth of sales across its divisions (BMI 2013). Analysts have noted that Massmart's late entry into food retailing carries some disadvantages, such as its difficulty in obtaining available sites for expansion; but all see future dominance.[8] They remark that Shoprite, with its deeper presence in Africa, and Woolworths, with is specific market differentiation into high LSMs, have the best chance of surviving Wal-Mart's effect, while Pick n Pay and Spar are most likely to be hit by immediate competition (Macquarie 2013:46).[9] Weatherspoon and Reardon (2003:2) noted a 'rapid transformation of the African food retail sector' since the mid-1990s towards increasing formalisation, corporate consolidation, the introduction of supply chain management technology, and logistics. Thus, efficient procurement systems, 'modern' supermarket formats, and corporate dominance of South African retail were already well underway (and expanding into Africa). While it is early to discern the impact that Wal-Mart's majority share in Massmart will have on South Africa's food retail sector, it is clear that it certainly does not diminish the concentrated market power of corporate chains. If anything, it will probably be a mover to push the intensification of formalisation in food retailing.

And, as this analyst report comments: 'With Walmart likely to be bearing down on prices it is in the supply chain that we think the winners and losers will be separated' (BMI 2013).

PROCUREMENT AND POWER: SUPPLY CHAINS, LOCAL PRODUCTION AND SMALLHOLDERS

Formal food retailing through supermarkets implies a distribution system which demands larger volumes and, typically, better standards of quality for food. The system also demands coordination between suppliers and retailers. As Durand and Wrigley (2009) note, the ability of retailers to make use of upstream relations with suppliers within host economies, as well as within their global networks, is a critical factor explaining the success of transnational retail capital in different contexts. Indeed, the concentration and expansion of corporate food retailing in South Africa has relied on efficient logistics systems, which have benefited from trade liberalisation and the deregulation of South Africa's agro-food economy.

Wal-Mart's legendary centralised distribution and information technology systems, which record 'real time' data from branches, allows the store to cut costs through responding quickly to consumer demand and to reduce stock shortages or over-estimations. Stock is controlled through category managers who are responsible for an entire group of merchandise and who work closely with suppliers, not only to specify products but also to promote the efficiency of distribution (Lichtenstein 2009; Fishman 2006). Logistics technology and inventory management have reduced costs to retailers and outsourced risk to suppliers. This 'retail revolution' is what Wal-Mart is known for (Lichtenstein 2009; see also Lichtenstein 2006). It has proved to be an important strategy of operation and comparative advantage to Wal-Mart in its overseas operations (Durand and Wrigley 2009:18). Maintaining contracts or relations becomes competitive business for suppliers, where increasing pressure is brought to bear on them to reduce their costs to the point where some supply for below cost to maintain their market with this retailer (Fishman 2006; Hong 2011). Centralisation gives retailers flexibility, then, through economies of scale and the ability to hedge market fluctuations, in part through global sourcing. Additional costs of transportation and storage are channelled back to suppliers with just-in-time sourcing.

In South Africa, a shift from wholesale distribution to the greater use of centralised warehousing and the use of information technology (IT) systems to coordinate supply has been underway since the 1990s (Weatherspoon and Reardon 2003). The corporate chains tend to use distribution centres and direct contracts with producers for fresh produce, while smaller chains rely on wholesale markets and fresh produce markets (Weatherspoon and Reardon 2003:10).

With Wal-Mart's entry, South African firms are working to compete with anticipated improvements in Massmart's supply chain systems. Massmart has recently upgraded its distribution network and benefits from Wal-Mart's technical knowledge and 'large purse' available to assist with logistics (BMI 2013). Thus, between 2011 and 2013 Shoprite upgraded its distribution centres and is building new ones in Cape Town, Durban and Port Elizabeth, all with the 'latest technological developments'.[10] Industry experts acknowledge that Shoprite has the best developed centralised distribution system of South African food retailers, 'a first-class centralised distribution network' (BMI 2013).[11]

The first preferred supplier programmes by retailers appear to have been focused mainly on larger farmers, many of whom were also exporters to European supermarkets, and already meeting food safety standards, volume and consistency expectations and quality measures (Weatherspoon and Reardon 2003:11). Most producers supplying to Freshmark, Shoprite's wholly-owned distributor, had to ensure that washing, packing, labelling and bar-coding were done before the produce reached the distribution centre (Weatherspoon and Reardon 2003:11). The producers were required to make deliveries daily in refrigerated trucks, which they provided. A preferred suppliers list ensured that producers who remained on the list had to meet all requirements. Pick n Pay ran a similar preferred supplier arrangement with larger and better-capitalised farmers, who could meet the requirements and standards (Weatherspoon and Reardon 2003:12). Retailers squeezed suppliers through regularly negotiated discounts and rebates, charging suppliers extra for promotions, returning unsold products, delaying payment and using own-label branding to undercut processors (Mather 2005; Mather and Kenny 2005). Yet suppliers continued to try to absorb these costs. Being on the list meant supplying these market channels, increasingly dominating access to consumers, as we have just seen.

Weatherspoon and Reardon (2003) suggest that standards for domestic food retailing were driven by retailer procurement from exporting farmers: retailers linked in to existing networks developed through deregulation of agricultural production, which encouraged export to global markets to benefit from private standards. They note that this exacted 'hefty entry requirements and even barriers to many farmers' (Weatherspoon and Reardon 2003:13) at the time, including investments in coordination, farming practices, packing-shed facilities, and fleet and cold chain infrastructure. They suggested that retailers would expand to lower market consumer segments and increase price pressure on suppliers to remain competitive while meeting standards (Weatherspoon and Reardon 2003:13). They concluded their seminal article by noting three trends: the use of large, well-resourced farmers; where these were not available, the use of importing; and an 'eagerness' to develop programmes to 'upgrade' the small farmers to meet the needs of supermarkets' (Weatherspoon and Reardon 2003:14). They suggested that this would produce a bifurcation of producers when smaller farmers, unable to cope, faced 'rapid exclusion' (Weatherspoon and Reardon 2003:14).

At the crux of the debate about Wal-Mart's entry was its ability to source from its global suppliers, understood as far more competitive than South African manufacturers and producers in their ability to meet cost and quality standards (for instance, see Chan 2011). The ultimate resolution was the creation of the Supplier Development Fund to assist small-scale producers to enter Massmart's supply chain. This model emerged out of Massmart's own voluntary fund, set up during the Tribunal process, with R100 million over three years to assist small-scale black farmers to meet the requirements to source to them. The focus of the fund, which targeted 1 500 small farmers, was on loans and providing equipment (Visser 2011). Massmart saw its significance in cutting out intermediaries, much as Wal-Mart does, to source directly from the producers, who then must pack their produce on the farms, ready for distribution through Massmart's controlled cold chain.

The R200 million fund that ultimately was mandated by the Appeal judgment was thus limited to developing the capacities of small-scale producers. As Morris puts it in his contribution to the expert committee report, the task is 'how to institutionally build the *competitive capabilities* of small and medium size enterprises within these supply chains' (Morris 2012:9, italics in original). As he notes, retailers '*do not do so as acts of beneficence to suppliers, but because it is in direct corporate interest*' (Morris 2012:14, italics in original).

There is a longer history of supplier programmes that focus on bringing small-scale producers into the market. The current fixation is on integrating smallholders in the production and distribution of fresh fruit and vegetables into supermarket supply chains. Thus, the extended discussion into Massmart/Wal-Mart's supplier fund becomes a condensation of the logics of the development agenda, in which retailers are well aware of the political imperatives of smallholder 'inclusion'.

In 2009, the ANC positioned agricultural production at the centre of its focus on rural development which, in turn, highlighted smallholder production as an arena of intervention.[12] Because of the concentration within the agro-food system in South Africa, any development of smallholders is seen to rest on access to local supermarket shelves rather than through production for export (Greenberg 2013; Aliber 2013).[13] Furthermore, job creation in agriculture is understood by DAFF as being best facilitated through small-holder schemes and agro-processing through inclusion into value chains (Aliber 2013).[14]

This policy shift toward smallholder development corresponds to a growing consensus within the state that food security rests primarily on access by consumers to cheaper food (rather than, for instance, through subsistence farming), with a new-found enthusiasm for the expansion of supermarkets to rural areas and townships (for example, the Comprehensive Rural Development Programme, DRDLR 2009, as cited in Greenberg and Paradza 2013: 55). In general, the state's approach to food security has been through providing social grants to underpin food purchases.

In short, the state sees supermarkets as an efficient means of coordination and distribution which can bring cheaper food to rural areas and townships and can provide small-scale producers with market channels. Within the long history of dominance by large-scale, capital-intensive agricultural production in South Africa reinforcing high barriers to entry, the state now looks to retailers to provide markets to small-scale farmers rather than transforming the embedded power of capitalist agriculture in South Africa.

Yet if we examine the food value chain, corporate concentration increases (along with deregulation) in the 1970s around the world (McMichael 1994) as well as in South Africa. Private coordination relies on power in the chain. As Greenberg (2010:3) writes: 'It does not merely replace the state, but alters the terms of governance and regulation to serve specific interests.' In South Africa, the deregulation and privatisation of single-channel marketing and pricing systems, starting in the 1970s and clinched with the 1996 Marketing of Agricultural Products Act, shifted power to corporate retailers over producers, who had previously had a guaranteed price for their product.[15] The corporatisation of former commodity cooperatives occurred at the same time that trade liberalisation in South Africa increased imports of foodstuffs – also accentuating the power of retailers, as they could now source food products globally (Greenberg 2010; Kenny 2012a). We enter the terrain of buyer-driven commodity chains, where retailers exact increasing control over product development and specification by controlling marketing channels (Gereffi 1994). While the state may set regulatory limits on, for instance, quality and health standards for food, it is private standards that have worked to enforce compliance and also to help shift power towards retailers who list preferred suppliers by their ability to meet volume, consistency, presentation and quality measures, increasingly defined and agreed at a global corporate level (Greenberg 2010).[16] The corporate retail control of food chains has introduced ever stricter entrance barriers to producers.

Smallholders are encouraged to participate in programmes which can facilitate their access to retailers' chains yet many of these programmes have low rates of success of sustainability (Nkomo 2013). TechnoServe SA, an international nonprofit organisation that 'empowers entrepreneurs' (Mashala 2013:48) manages the contract for Massmart's Direct Farm programme within its Supplier Development Fund. It has also run similar projects to bring small, medium and micro-sized enterprises (SMMEs) into other retailers' chains. Working with projects in Limpopo, Mpumalanga and KwaZulu-Natal, it provides training and assistance in finding markets and finance. TechnoServe reports that forty smallholder farmers currently supply Massmart with fresh produce (Mashala 2013:48). Given the skewed resource and skills sets that mean that large scale agriculture dominates South Africa, their interventions assist smallholders to build sustainability within this highly concentrated environment. A key way in which they ensure that a farmer may reach this goal is 'stringent' selection (Mashala 2013:49) – TechnoServe works with farmers who are better resourced, with their own access to land, equipment, labour, and those who have an 'already demonstrable access' to markets (Nkomo 2013:40). TechnoServe also argues that it focuses on value chains where commercial farmers are not already dominant because the competition would be too high. Beyond choosing feasible commodities, the farmer has to show some ability 'to access correct seed variables'; to know the crop requirements; to access and use fertilisers; to 'meet minimum quality requirements and understand these requirements from a market perspective'; and to have access to infrastructure, including irrigation and tillage equipment, storage facilities and packhouses, and logistics in the form of cold-chain friendly trucks to deliver produce (Nkomo 2013:40).We have little research that details the relationship and nature of contract of suppliers to retailers – highly sensitive information frequently governed by nondisclosure clauses (but see Mather 2005; Mather and Kenny 2005). Recent research by the Institute for Poverty, Land and Agrarian Studies (PLAAS) begins to detail the requirements of smallholders who participate in these programmes. Survey results from smallholder tomato farmers in Limpopo show that net incomes are higher for farmers supplying traditional market channels than through supermarkets or agro-processors (Chikazunga 2013), participation in which, as has consistently been found, requires 'production infrastructure such as greenhouses and irrigation technology' and enough land. 'Given poor yields, inferior quality and production risks, traditional channels are more relevant to the majority of the smallholder farmers' in the area (Chikazunga 2013:22).

Another study of a development programme aimed at getting smallholder farmers in the Vhembe district into the avocado value chain to supermarkets found that growers felt they benefited from the secured market of retailers, but nevertheless found that most farmers had turnovers below production costs because their farming units were too small to produce volumes high enough to spread costs. In this project, high costs included pesticide spraying to counter a fungus that damaged the aesthetic appeal of the fruit (necessary if the fruit is to be sold to a supermarket). Lower market prices, caused by unusually high volumes entering the market, were difficult for farmers to absorb. Farmers were poorly skilled in reading financial statements. The project also suggested that higher entry barriers, including viable minimum land size and tree numbers, existed for these farmers (Khumalo 2013:32).

In their dissenting report Stiglitz and Hodge noted concern that the Massmart Supplier Development Fund would have little influence on local sourcing precisely because it is limited to SMMEs and to local producers of fresh produce, a commodity category already more likely to be sourced locally. We can see that the debate over local sourcing in both state policy and retailer programmes has focused on the small-scale production of fresh produce. Where smallholders are able successfully to maintain the relationship, they have been selected for having already demonstrated capacities of infrastructure, land access, business skills, and safety standard measures that presume a prior capital base. Most of the already well-capitalised farmers will benefit from Wal-Mart's entry. Thus, smallholder procurement programmes are a high profile political intervention, but whether they can effect substantial changes to the structure of the economy or the food system is unlikely. The state has basically bought into a development path which has effectively accepted a large-scale, corporate agro-food system as the means of producing and distributing food. Retail capital is a core driver of this process.

LABOUR CONDITIONS WITHIN STORES

In their comparison of Wal-Mart and Carrefour international entries, Durand and Wrigley suggest that Wal-Mart subsidiaries have lasted longer and grown in host countries where there is weaker labour organisation and trade union independence, where labour regulatory enforcement is weaker, where wage bargaining tends to be more individualised and where job security is weaker (Durand and Wrigley 2009:16). We know that Wal-Mart agrees to recognise unions outside the US (see Tilly 2007; Bank Munoz forthcoming) but this may not be a sign of willingness to relate to strong and independent unions in meaningful collective bargaining. Maintaining parity conditions of employment and union recognition was a key demand in the Tribunal process of Saccawu, the majority union and Cosatu affiliate in the sector.

In general, South African retail employment is precarious, with low wages, low skills, part-time hours and few benefits describing many workers' conditions (Kenny 2001; 2005). In 2005 in the retail trade as a whole, 75 per cent of the workforce was permanent.

In large enterprises this figure dropped to 67.8 per cent, with 32.2 per cent being casual (Statistics South Africa 2007: xii). In the category 'non-specialised stores with food, beverages and tobacco predominating', permanent employment fell to 55.3 per cent, and casual and temporary was 44.6 per cent (Statistics South Africa 2007:14). In the same category but of only large enterprises, the figures for permanent employment dropped again, to 51.9 per cent; casual and temporary employment was 48 per cent (Statistics South Africa 2007:15). It must be remembered that the sectoral determination promulgated in 2003 made a much wider category of 'casual' workers technically 'permanent' but part-time. These statistics are therefore likely to hide the extent of part-time employment within the category 'permanent' (Kenny 2009).

In preliminary results of a non-representative, qualitative survey that colleagues and I have conducted in Cambridge stores, Massmart's newly-expanding food retail subsidiary, unionisation is almost nonexistent, and conditions are basic. In the sample of 109 workers interviewed from six branches in Johannesburg,[17] most workers were not even employees of the retailer: over 74 per cent were employees of labour brokers, with only 14.7 per cent being employees of Cambridge (the remaining 12 per cent were direct employees of suppliers); 42 per cent earned R2 000 per month or less,[18] and 78 per cent earned R3 000 or less. Although nearly 92 per cent said that they had a written contract with their employer, 81 per cent said that they did not personally have a copy of it. In focus group interviews, workers told us in fact that managers and contractors would not allow them to take a copy of the contract home to read, and some said that they were instructed to leave the date blank when signing the contract; it was explained that a date would be filled in when a worker was 'dismissed' enabling ease of firing even for employees meant to be on fixed term contracts. Only 31 per cent of workers reported that they received a pension or provident fund and 4.7 per cent of workers reported that they had medical aid. Nearly 60 per cent of workers said that they did not have opportunities for promotion.

Only 28.4 per cent of workers reported being members of a union, although the survey would have self-selected for union members through access and sampling through Saccawu networks. Of the thirty-one people reporting to be union members, only eight were members of Saccawu, seven were members of Fawu (typical for merchandisers employed by a major food supplier company), and fourteen were members of another retail union, the Federal Council of Retail and Allied Workers (Fedcraw). The mean length of time for which union members reported being members was over five years and 96 per cent of workers had not engaged in any form of collective action in these stores.

When asked what were the most important problems they faced on the job, 29 per cent of workers cited relations with management or supervisors; 29 per cent cited low wages or pay issues; over 30 per cent cited poor working conditions, job security or their contracts; and 9.7 per cent cited store operations. Thus, some 68 per cent of workers complained about the level of conditions, work organisation, surveillance and pay, followed by nearly 30 per cent about relations with management. In short, preliminary results at store level with retail workers in Cambridge Foods suggest a pattern of low-skill low-wage jobs with little worker attachment and less possibility of advancement. Notably, a large percentage of this workforce was contracted-in through labour brokers. Such corporate retailers grow employment in South Africa but continue to do so through precarious jobs.

CONCLUSION

Retail is not just a passive or benevolent conduit between food production and the consumer. In order to provide 'cheap food', retailers rely on low-wage labour in shops and the efficiencies met through a capital-intensive agro-food system. If we take seriously the embedded relations through which retailers operate in local economies, then there is a much wider scope around which to engage both state policy and labour movement politics.

The focus on smallholder integration into markets via corporate supply chains carries with it the assumption that production for profit is the only logic available. There is room here to push a direct examination of the power of retail firms, imbricated as they are with state deregulation of the agro-food economy, trade liberalisation, financialisation of capital, precarious service employment, and promotion of processed foodstuff generally of lower nutritional value.

Saccawu has focused attention on its All-Africa Wal-Mart Alliance, which seeks to network around conditions of employment across Massmart subsidiaries in Africa. Although this is an important effort, it has the effect of limiting its focus on the employer (see Kenny 2012b). This chapter sought to examine how Wal-Mart's entry into South Africa raises questions about the embedded context of corporate retail capital and its power in the agro-food system in South Africa. It highlights the mutual interests of the state and retail capital in promoting supermarkets as providers of cheap food and as leverage points for smallholder development. Yet it also suggests that Wal-Mart's 'citizenship' status, based on bringing consumer choice at a cheap price, has other costs bound into a system that relies on precarious employment and large-scale corporate control of the food system. Access to supermarkets may seem to be an easy way of ensuring food security for South Africans but we bind ourselves into a 'reverse Fordism' where cheap food is necessary because wages are so low (Collins 2009). Numsa and Fawu have recently launched a campaign to transform the agro-food system in South Africa, emphasising food security by focusing on ownership and inequality throughout the food sector. Low-wage food retail workers could contribute to this campaign. These efforts provoke hard questions about how the labour movement is organised by sector and employer in South Africa.

Corporate food retailers have been portrayed as the guardians of quality, the champions of reducing inefficiencies in the chain, the advocates for smallholder development, and our compatriots who bring us cheaper food; but if Wal-Mart's entry tells us anything it is that the public debate over the Tribunal process has had no effect on the relations of inequality structuring South Africa's food system based on a low-wage, racist labour regime. In accepting Wal-Mart as our fellow 'citizen', we may find choice in supermarket aisles, but we ultimately continue to reinforce a development agenda which reproduces poor quality jobs, excludes vast numbers of people from active economic participation, and offers little by way of food security.

REFERENCES

Aliber M (2013) Conceptualising approaches to smallholders and markets. In Greenberg S (ed.) *Smallholders and Agro-food Value Chains in South Africa: Emerging Practices, Emerging Challenges.* Cape Town: Institute for Poverty, Land and Agrarian Studies (PLAAS).

BFAP (2012) Farm sectoral determination: An analysis of agricultural wages in South Africa. Stellenbosch: Bureau for Food and Agricultural Policy (BFAP).

Bianchi C and S Arnold (2004) An institutional perspective on retail internationalisation success. *International Review of Retail, Distribution and Consumer Research*, 14: 149-169.

BMI (2013) *Food and Drink Report: South Africa Food and Drink Report.* London: Business Monitor International (BMI).

Chan A (ed.) (2011) *Walmart in China.* Ithaca and London: ILR Press.

Chikazunga D (2013) Determinants of smallholder farmers' participation in modern food markets: the case of tomato supply chains in Limpopo. In Greenberg S (ed.) *Smallholders and Agro-food Value Chains in South Africa: Emerging Practices, Emerging Challenges.* Cape Town: Institute for Poverty, Land and Agrarian Studies (PLAAS).

Christopherson S (2007) Barriers to 'US style' lean retailing: the case of Wal-Mart's failure in Germany. *Journal of Economic Geography*, 7: 451-469.

Christopherson S (2006) Challenges facing Wal-Mart in the German market. In Brunn SD (ed.) *Wal-Mart World: The World's Biggest Corporation in the Global Economy.* New York and London: Routledge.

Coe N and N Wrigley (2007) Host economy impacts of transnational retail: the research agenda. *Journal of Economic Geography* 7: 341-371.

Collins JL (2009) America in the age of Wal-Mart. In Bestemann C and H Gusterson (eds) *The Insecure American: How We Got Here and What We Should Do About It.* Berkeley: University of California Press.

Competition Tribunal (2011) Tribunal statement on the conditional approval of the merger between Wal-mart Stores Inc. and Massmart Holdings Limited – 31 May 2011. http://www.comptrib.co.za/publications/press-releases/wal-mart-and-massmart-31-may-2011/

Crotty A (2013) State changes tune on Wal-Mart. *Business Report*, 12 April http://www.iol.co.za/business/business-news/state-changes-tune-on-walmart-1.1499140#.UdHFzBYmxFI [Accessed 12 April 2013].

Durand C and N Wrigley (2009) Institutional and economic determinants of transnational retailer expansion and performance: a comparative analysis of Wal-Mart and Carrefour. *Environment and Planning A*, 41(7): 1534-1555.

Fishman C (2006) *The Wal-Mart Effect: How the World's Most Powerful Company really Works – And How it's Transformed the American Economy.* New York: Penguin.

Gereffi G (1994) The organisation of buyer-driven commodity chains: How the US retailers shape overseas production networks. In Gereffri G and M Korzeniewicz (eds) *Commodity Chains and Global Capitalism.* New York: Praeger.

Greenberg S (2013) Introduction: Smallholders and value chain integration in South Africa. In Greenberg S (ed.) *Smallholders and Agro-food Value Chains in South Africa: Emerging Practices, Emerging Challenges* Cape Town: Institute for Poverty, Land and Agrarian Studies (PLAAS).

Greenberg S (2010) Contesting the food system in South Africa: Issues and opportunities, Research Report 42. Cape Town: Institute for Poverty, Land and Agrarian Studies (PLAAS).

Greenberg S and G Paradza (2013) Smallholders and the 'Walmart effect' in South Africa. In Greenberg S (ed.) *Smallholders and Agro-food Value Chains in South Africa: Emerging Practices, Emerging Challenges*. Cape Town: Institute for Poverty, Land and Agrarian Studies (PLAAS).

Hodge J, S Goga and T Moahloli (2013). Public-interest provisions in the South African Competition Act: A critical review. In Moodaliyar K and S Roberts (eds) *The Development of Competition Law and Economics in South Africa*. Cape Town: HSRC Press.

Hong X (2011) Outsourcing in China: Walmart and Chinese manufacturers. In Chan A (ed.) *Walmart in China*. Ithaca and London: ILR Press.

Humphrey J (2007) The supermarket revolution in developing countries: tidal wave or tough competitive struggle. *Journal of Economic Geography*, 7: 433-450.

Ingham M (2009) South African FMCG retailing, Sasfin Securities newsletter, 16 July. http://www.sasfin.com/Portals/0/Mark/Perspectivesper cent20onper cent20theper cent20SAper cent20groceryper cent20marketper cent2016per cent20Julper cent2009.pdf [Accessed 6 September 2011].

Kenny B (2012a) The politics of global merger: Wal-Mart and the South African retail industry. Paper presented at Big Food in Africa conference, HSRC, 23-24 January, Cape Town.

Kenny B (2012b) Wal-Mart and transnational union solidarity in the South African Competition Tribunal process. Paper presented at the Second ISA Forum of Sociology, International Sociological Association, Buenos Aires, Argentina, 1-4 August.

Kenny B (2009) Mothers, extra-ordinary labour, and *amacasual*: Law and politics of nonstandard employment in the South African retail sector. *Law & Policy*, 31(3): 282-306.

Kenny B (2005) Militant divisions, collective possibilities: Lessons for labour mobilisation from South African retail sector workers. *Labour, Capital and Society*, 38(1&2): 156-183.

Kenny B (2001) 'We are nursing these jobs': The impact of labour market flexibility on South African retail sector workers. In Newman N, J Pape, and H Jansen (eds). *Is There an Alternative? South African Workers Confronting Globalisation*. Cape Town: ILRIG.

Kew J (2011) Wal-Mart's Massmart expands in Africa as regional competition increases. Bloomberg, 25 August http://www.bloomberg.com/news/2011-08-25/wal-mart-s-massmart-expands-in-africa-as-regional-competition-increases.html [Accessed 8 September 2011].

Khumalo L (2013) Big business for small farmers: The case of Venda avocado growers. In Greenberg S (ed.) *Smallholders and Agro-food Value Chains in South Africa: Emerging Practices, Emerging Challenges*. Cape Town: Institute for Poverty, Land and Agrarian Studies (PLAAS).

Lichtenstein N (2009) *The Retail Revolution: How Wal-Mart Created a Brave New World of Business*. New York: Metropolitan Books.

Lichtenstein N (2006) Wal-Mart: A template for twenty-first century capitalism. In Lichtenstein N (ed.) *Wal-Mart: The Face of Twenty-First Century Capitalism*. New York and London: The New Press.

Louw A, D Chikazunga, D Jordaan and E Biénabé (2007) Restructuring food markets in the southern Africa region: Dynamics within the context of the tomato subsector. In *Regoverning Markets Agrifood Sector Studies*. London: IIED.

Macquarie First South (2013) South African Food Retailers. Report published by Macquarie First South Securities, Johannesburg.

McMichael P (ed.) (1994) *The Global Restructuring of Agro-Food Systems*. Ithaca and London: Cornell University Press.

Miller D (2008) Retail renaissance or company rhetoric? The failed partnership of a South African corporation and local suppliers in Zambia. *Labour, Capital and Society*, 41(1): 35-55.

Marsden TK, M Harrison and A Flynn (1998) Creating competitive space: Exploring the social and political maintenance of retail power. *Environment and Planning A*, 30: 481-498.

Mashala P (2013) Supporting new farming entrepreneurs. *Farmer's Weekly* 31 May: 48-49.

Mashala P (2012) Walmart's 'direct farming' revolution. *Farmer's Weekly*, 27 July: 58-60.

Mather C (2005) The growth challenges of small and medium enterprises (SMEs) in South Africa's food processing complex. *Development Southern Africa,* 22 (5): 607-22.

Mather C and B Kenny (2005) The difficulties of 'emerging markets': Cross-continental investment in the South African dairy sector. In Fold N and B Pritchard (eds) *Cross-Continental Food Chains.* London and New York: Routledge.

National Planning Commission (2011) *National Development Plan: Vision for 2030.* Pretoria: Office of the President.

Nkomo M (2013) Experiences and insights on smallholder farmer value chain integration. In Greenberg S (ed.) *Smallholders and Agro-food Value Chains in South Africa: Emerging Practices, Emerging Challenges.* Cape Town: Institute for Poverty, Land and Agrarian Studies (PLAAS).

Planting S (2012) Massmart ordered to pay R200m fund, 9 October. http://www.moneyweb.co.za/moneyweb-economic-trends/massmart-ordered-to-pay-r200m-to-fund [Accessed 9 October 2012].

Planting S (2010) 'Into the trolley' *Financial Mail,* 23 July: 32–35.

RBB Economics (2011) The merger of Walmart and Massmart: Economic issues. Redacted statement to the Competition Commission, 3 May.

Reardon T (2005) Retail companies as integrators of value-chains in developing countries. Report prepared for Deutsche Gesselschaft fure Technische Zusammenarbeit (GTZ): Eschborn.

Reardon T and J Berdegue (2002) The rapid rise of supermarkets in Latin America: Challenges and opportunities for development. *Development Policy Review,* 20:317-334.

Roberts S (2004) The role for competition policy in economic development: The South African experience. TIPS Working Paper Series (WP8-2004). Johannesburg: Trade and Industrial Policy Strategies (TIPS).

Statistics South Africa (2013) Labour Force Survey. Pretoria: Statistics South Africa.

Statistics South Africa (2007) Retail trade, Statistical report 62-01-02. Pretoria: Statistics South Africa.

Tilly C (2007) Wal-Mart and its workers: NOT the same all over the world. *Connecticut Law Review,* Vol. 39: 1805- 1823.

Tilly C (2006) Wal-Mart in Mexico: the limits of growth. In Lichtenstein N (ed.) *Wal-Mart: Template for 21st Century Capitalism?* New York and London: The New Press.

Weatherspoon D and T Reardon (2003) The rise of supermarkets in Africa: Implications for agrifood systems and the rural poor. *Development Policy Review,* 21 (3): 1-17.

Wrigley N (2000) The globalisation of retail capital: Themes for economic geography. In Clark GL, MP Feldman and MS Gertler (eds) *The Oxford Handbook of Economic Geography.* Oxford: Oxford University Press.

Wrigley N, N Coe and A Currah (2005) Globalising retail: Conceptualising the distribution-based transational corporation (TNC). *Progress in Human Geography,* 29: 437-457.

NOTES

1   This chapter benefitted from discussions with Michael Aliber, Stephen Greenberg and Neva Makgetla. Interpretation and any errors, of course, remain mine.

2   See http://www.economist.com/blogs/dailychart/2011/09/employment, accessed 26/09/2011.

3   The state requested the judgment be set aside through an argument around discovery (information requested but not provided) in the Tribunal process that prevented full evidence being heard that would have supported its case.

4   Times Live 2/8/2011, http://www.timeslive.co.za/politics/2011/08/02/walmart-massmart-merger-poses-risk-to-sa-ministers, accessed 2/8/2011.

5   Compare South Africa's high degree of formalisation to Mexico, where only 7 per cent of the market was through formal channels when Wal-Mart entered (Tilly 2006).

6   See http://www.shopriteholdings.co.za/files/1019812640/Investor_Centre_Files/Annual_Reports/
      Annual-Report-2012/7_4521_Chairmans_Report.pdf, accessed 29 June 2013.

7   See http://www.cambridgefood.co.za/about.asp, accessed 1 June 2013.

8   Also, all expect Massmart to grow through expanding its African operations, understood as being
      a major growth area (BMI 2013; Macquarie 2013). Massmart already operates in 13 countries in
      sub-Saharan Africa through four divisions comprising 235 stores, and one buying association serv-
      ing 480 independent retailers and wholesalers (http://www.fastmoving.co.za/retailers/retailer-pro-
      files-132/massmart-198). Massmart has already announced plans to expand its operations espe-
      cially in Africa in 2013 ('Massmart to focus on store growth in Africa' FMCG SUPPLIER NEWS
      Ventures Africa - May 30th, http://www.fastmoving.co.za/news/supplier-news-17/massmart-to-
      focus-on-store-growth-in-africa-3802; accessed 11 June 2013).

9   Indeed, Pick n Pay has made efforts to upgrade its centralised distribution systems in line with
      competitive pressures from Wal-Mart's entry (BMI 2013). Rumours also abound about Tesco's
      move to acquire Pick n Pay.

10   See http://www.shopriteholdings.co.za/files/1019812640/Investor_Centre_Files/Annual_Reports/
      Annual-Report-2012/8_4521_Chief_Executives_Report.pdf, accessed 29 June 2013.

11   Shoprite operates a wholly owned subsidiary Freshmark, which runs its distribution centres in
      South Africa. It procures both South African fresh fruit and vegetables and imports. Its website
      says, 'It operates its own network of distribution centres and refridgerated trucks; negotiates pro-
      duction contracts with some 459 large- and small-scale farmers in South Africa and as well as
      354 suppliers in the 11 African countries we operate in; sources specialty fruit and vegetables on
      international markets, and plays a key role in equipping emerging farmers with the knowledge and
      skills to produce and meet international GLOBALG.A.P. standards (http://www.shopriteholdings.
      co.za/pages/1019812640/retailing-services/Freshmark.asp, accessed 29 June 2013).

12   Although, the ANC signalled this shift in policy priorities in 2007 at Polokwane (Greenberg
      2010:14). See PLAAS research on the varied definition (and class position) of 'smallholder' pro-
      ducers as sited in Greenberg 2013. A wide range of descriptions may be used to categorise small-
      holder producers, which are obscured by the term, particularly the amalgamation of subsistence
      producers with commercial producers. Nevertheless, the term broadly refers to small-scale produc-
      ers (either by income, land holdings, or type of production). Greenberg suggests 60-80 hectares as
      the maximum land holding (Greenberg 2013:3).

13   The National Development Plan outlines what it sees to be the importance of smallholder farmers
      to rural development through job creation and food security in terms of integration into supply
      chains (see Chapter 6, National Planning Commission 2011).

14   See Strategic Plan for Smallholder Producers, DAFF.

15   The regulated control of marketing and pricing of food products characterised the apartheid
      period. 'More than 75 per cent of agricultural products in South Africa were sold under controlled
      marketing schemes in 1990' (Greenberg 2010:4).

16   Most South African retailers require EurepGAP standards at farm level and HACCP (Hazard
      Analysis and Critical Control Point) at pack-house/processing level from fresh produce suppliers.
      Through the Global Food Safety Initiative (GFSI), seven major South African retailers have agreed
      to the four GFSI benchmarked food safety schemes: the British Retail Consortium Global Food
      Standard; the International Food Standard; the Safe Quality Food Scheme (2000); and the Dutch
      HACCP Scheme (Option B). The International Committee of Food Retail Chains co-ordinates the
      GFSI (Greenberg 2010:8-9).

17   A non-representative, qualitative questionnaire was administered to 109 workers and focus group
      interviews conducted in 6 branches of Cambridge through access provided by Saccawu. The proj-
      ect was funded by UNI Global. Project researchers included Bongani Xezwi, Ntsiki Mackay, Lesego
      Ndala, Matlhako Mahapa, Zakhele Dlamini, Tlaleng Letsheleha and Zivai Sunungukai.

18   Compare these retail workers' wages to the latest farm workers' minimum wages of R105/day (raised to this –itself a 35 per cent increase – in the latest Sectoral Determination following militant and violent strikes on farms where workers contested their poverty conditions). This works out to about R2 200 per month, a figure that mainstream economists from Stellenbosch and Pretoria have reported as unable to provide enough to meet the nutritional needs of their households (BFAP 2012). Farmworkers had demanded R150/day in the strikes. The report summarises, 'The real problem is that even at what seems to be an unaffordable minimum wage of R150 per day, most households cannot provide the nutrition that is needed to make them food secure' (BFAP 2012:vi).

CHAPTER 4

Transcending South Africa's oil dependency

Jeremy Wakeford

———•———

INTRODUCTION

Oil is the master resource that fuels the world economy, providing 33 per cent of global primary energy supply, supplying 95 per cent of the energy powering global transport systems, and providing feedstock for the diverse petrochemicals industry (IEA 2013). Since the Second World War, growth in the world economy has been strongly correlated with growth in oil consumption. Similarly, demand for oil products in South Africa has grown in step with the economy, and our passenger and freight transport systems depend overwhelmingly on petroleum fuels. In the apartheid era, the nationalist government's approach to liquid fuel security in the face of international sanctions was to build expensive, capital intensive coal-to-liquid and gas-to-liquid synthetic fuel plants to compensate for South Africa's lack of indigenous oil reserves. Since 1994, by contrast, the democratically elected government has pursued reintegration with the world economy, and South Africa's growing liquid fuel demand has been met almost entirely by rising imports of crude oil and – in recent years – refined fuels as well. The country currently relies on imports to meet at least 70 per cent of its liquid fuel needs, and is therefore vulnerable to global oil price hikes. There are both short-term and long-term threats to global oil supplies and prices which, if not mitigated, could have very serious effects on our economy and society.

This chapter provides a brief overview of a complex set of issues related to the risks inherent in South Africa's dependency on imported oil. Section 2 deals with the global oil outlook, highlighting projections of demand for oil, conventional oil supply, unconventional oil resources, world oil exports, energy return on investment for oil, and the implications of these trends for international crude oil prices. Section 3 focuses on South Africa's liquid fuel-related vulnerabilities and the likely implications of pursuing a business-as-usual path. Section 4 considers the main alternatives to imported petroleum, including options for domestic liquid fuel production and a shift to electrified transport systems. The concluding section interprets the oil dilemma from the perspective of a societal transition toward greater sustainability.

THE END OF CHEAP OIL

Over the past decade, a strident debate has raged among academics, industry analysts and representatives of government agencies about the prognosis for future oil supplies (see Wakeford 2012 for a critical review). For the layperson, it is very difficult to distinguish between research-based evidence and industry or media hype, and to judge between the sometimes wildly conflicting forecasts of future world oil production. However, there are some key facts, represented plainly in publicly available data, which show that the world has recently entered a new era of increasing oil scarcity, which is being reflected in persistently high oil prices. There is space here only to highlight the most important trends.

The International Energy Agency has forecast that global demand for oil could grow by 14 per cent by 2035, with all of the net additional demand projected to come from emerging economies (IEA 2012). This rise in demand is expected to be driven almost entirely by increasing use of motorised transport for both passengers and freight as incomes rise in developing countries. The forecast is, however, premised on the assumption that the world economy will grow by an average annual rate of 3.5 per cent over the period, and that oil prices will reach only US$125 (in 2011 dollars) by 2035. But there are many reasons to doubt these assumptions.

A growing body of literature by academics and oil industry experts is warning that the historical trend of increasing supplies of oil cannot continue indefinitely (see Sorrell et al. 2010a, 2010b) because oil (like other fossil fuels), having been formed in the geological past, is a finite resource subject to depletion. Finiteness necessarily implies that at some point in time the annual production of oil at a global scale must reach an all-time maximum and begin an irreversible decline (Hubbert 1956). This 'peak oil' phenomenon, as it is commonly termed, has already been observed to occur in the majority of individual oil producing countries and in large regions such as North America and Europe. Evidence suggests that the world is nearing the global oil production peak. Global new oil discoveries reached a maximum in the 1960s and have been declining ever since, despite remarkable improvements in exploration, drilling and extraction technologies – and record high prices in recent years. The International Energy Agency stated in its *World*

Energy Outlook 2012 that conventional crude oil production – oil obtained through typical drilling and refining techniques – peaked in 2008.

Much of the new oil that has come onstream in recent years has come from unconventional sources of oil such as Venezuela's 'heavy oil', Canada's oil sands, and shale or 'tight' oil from the American states of North Dakota and Texas, all of which require special – and costly – extraction and refining techniques. Although the resource estimates for unconventional oil are generally large, the annual flow rate of production is constrained by a number of economic, physical and environmental factors. First, the hugely capital-intensive nature of these production processes means that marginal production costs for unconventional oil are much higher than those of conventional oil; and that there are physical limits to the amount of capital equipment that can be deployed in the industry in the medium term. Second, the environmental effects of unconventional oil production are significantly worse than those of conventional oil: the fresh water demands are much greater; the CO_2 emissions can be up to twice as high per barrel of oil; and hydraulic fracturing and oil sand production may pollute fresh water sources (Hughes 2011).

While unconventional oil production has allowed total world oil production to continue to expand slowly in recent years while conventional oil output has stagnated, unconventional sources have come with substantially higher economic and environmental costs and several independent analysts warn that they may not offset the depletion of conventional oil production for long. For example, a report by the Canadian geologist David Hughes, which involves detailed analysis of shale oil production in the US, suggests that the shale oil 'revolution' might turn out to be a ten-year bubble (Hughes 2013). Eventually – and possibly within a decade – global production of all liquid fuels will begin to fall. The post-peak rate of decline could be between two and five per cent per annum, depending on a complex combination of geological, economic and political factors (Hirsch 2008).

For net oil importing nations such as South Africa, and for international crude oil prices, the quantity of oil traded on international markets is of more immediate significance than total world oil production. Data from the United States Energy Information Administration (EIA 2013a) show that world oil exports reached a peak of 43.4 million barrels per day (mbpd) in 2005, and have been slowly decreasing since then, largely explaining the steep rise in oil prices in recent years (see Figure 1). It is highly likely that world oil exports have passed their all-time peak because domestic consumption of oil is rising in most oil-exporting countries, driven by growing populations and rising incomes.

Not only is the quantity of oil available on world markets set to diminish, but the quality (ease of access and refining) of available oil is also deteriorating. This is principally because the easier to access oil deposits, typically discovered decades ago, are being rapidly depleted and the frontier for new oil has moved into more remote areas such as deep off-shore wells, polar regions and unconventional oil sources that are more costly and technically more difficult to access and process (Gagnon, Hall and Brinker 2009). The energy return on (energy) investment (EROI) for oil, which measures the ratio of

Figure 1: World oil exports and crude oil price, 1986-2010

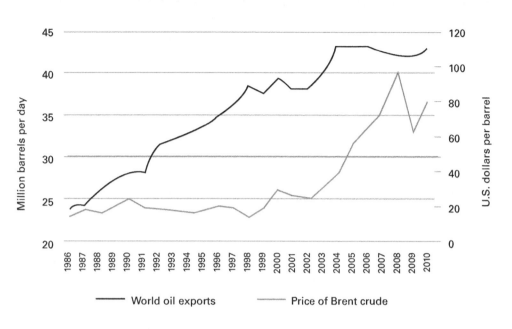

Source: Data from EIA (2013a) and BP (2013)

energy delivered by the process of oil exploration and extraction to the energy input, is diminishing in the world as a whole and in most individual countries. The EROI for unconventional oil resources such as oil sands and shale oil is estimated to be less than 5:1, compared to a global average of over 15:1 for conventional oil (Murphy and Hall 2010). Thus the net energy surplus (the energy output minus the energy input) yielded by oil is set to decline at a faster rate than the gross quantity of oil produced; and this will put further upward pressure on oil prices.

The International Energy Agency has confirmed that the era of cheap oil is over, but its relatively benign price forecasts are contradicted by recent modelling by International Monetary Fund (IMF) researchers. A paper that examined the interactions of rising demand and geological supply constraints warned that the price of oil could double to US$200 per barrel (measured in 2012 dollars) by 2020 (Benes et al. 2012). A second IMF working paper modelled various scenarios for oil prices and their impact on global growth (Kumhof and Muir 2012). In their relatively optimistic 'baseline scenario', which assumes that oil supply growth is constrained to one percentage point below its 1.8 per cent average attained between 1981-2005, and that there is a high degree of substitut-ability of other energy sources for oil, the price of oil nevertheless rises 100 per cent by 2020 and 200 per cent after twenty years. If it turns out to be more difficult than expected to find adequate substitutes for oil, or if world oil production begins to decline soon, the oil price could rise to devastating levels. Indeed, the historical record shows that international oil price spikes and temporary supply shortages have had serious negative economic effects in oil importing nations, resulting *inter alia* in higher rates of price inflation, slower economic growth, deepening poverty and food insecurity, debt crises, and in some cases civil unrest. In the light of these risks, we turn now to examine South Africa's oil vulnerabilities.

SOUTH AFRICA'S OIL DEPENDENCIES AND THE PERILS OF BUSINESS-AS-USUAL

This section details the ways in which the South African economy and society depend on oil, and highlights the risks of continuing this addiction.

Petroleum consumption

Oil comprised 11 per cent of South Africa's total primary energy supply (TPES) in 2010, while refined petroleum fuels constituted the largest share (30 per cent) of total final energy consumption (IEA 2013). Some three-quarters of petroleum products are burned by the transport sector, which depends on liquid fuels for 98 per cent of its energy requirements (the balance being supplied by electricity). Agriculture relies on petroleum fuels to satisfy two-thirds of its energy needs. Many poor households use paraffin for illumination and, in some cases, cooking. Total annual sales of petroleum products grew largely in line with the economy (real gross domestic product or GDP) in the period 1994 to 2012 (see Figure 2). Petrol and diesel together make up more than 80 per cent of petroleum product sales. Liquefied petroleum gas (LPG) sales in the figures below relate mainly to household use for cooking and heating. The average growth rate for sales of all petroleum products was 2.8 per cent for the period 1995 to 2007. However, these growth rates fell steeply from 2008 as a result of sharply rising fuel prices (crude oil traded at nearly US$100 per barrel on average for the year) as well as rising costs of living and higher interest rates. The recession in 2009 led to a marked fall in demand for diesel, but consumption has since resumed its upward trend.

Liquid fuel imports

Imported crude oil and refined products contribute approximately 70 per cent of South Africa's annual consumption of petroleum products. The remainder is derived from Sasol's coal-to-liquids (CTL) synthetic fuels (about 26 per cent) and state oil company PetroSA (about 4 per cent), which produces gas-to-liquid (GTL) synthetic fuels and a very small amount of domestic crude oil. South Africa's crude oil reserves stood at a meagre fifteen million barrels as of January 2013 (EIA 2013b), and are likely to be depleted within a few years in the absence of significant new oil field discoveries. Encouraged by significant offshore oil discoveries in Namibia in recent years, local and foreign oil firms are

Figure 2: Annual petroleum product sales and real GDP, 1994-2012

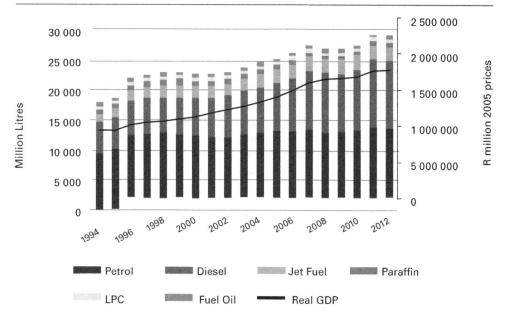

Source: Data from SAPIA (2013) and SARB (2013)

actively exploring for oil off the west coast of South Africa – but as of this writing no discoveries had been announced. In 2011, South Africa relied mostly on members of the Organisation of Petroleum Exporting Countries (OPEC) for its oil imports, notably Iran (27 per cent), Saudi Arabia (27 per cent), Nigeria (20 per cent) and Angola (11 per cent) (EIA 2013b). Reliance on Iranian crude oil imports was curtailed in 2012 and 2013 under pressure from the sanctions placed on the Iranian oil industry by the United States and the European Union. Imports were increased from Saudi Arabia and other suppliers to compensate, but the risk of disruptions to imports of Iranian oil remains a key vulnerability to South Africa's liquid fuel supply security, since some of our refineries are specifically configured to process Iranian crude.

PetroSA's Project Mthombo refinery: a great white elephant
The government's approach to security of liquid fuel supply, summarised in the *Energy Security Master Plan – Liquid Fuels* (DME 2007), is predicated on the assumption that South Africa's liquid fuel demand will continue to grow indefinitely. The plan contained two main infrastructure proposals: first for Transnet Pipelines to build a new multi-product fuel pipeline between the port city of Durban and the fuel-thirsty industrial heartland in Gauteng, which was duly commissioned in 2012; and second a proposal for

PetroSA to construct a large new oil refinery at the port of Coega in the Eastern Cape. The rationale given by the national oil company for this 'Project Mthombo' is threefold: to boost economic development and job creation in the impoverished Eastern Cape; to produce cleaner fuels in line with the latest European standards, leading to cleaner air and better health; and to ensure the national security of fuel supply by meeting the growing demand for refined fuels in the southern African region. All three justifications are problematic. While a few local jobs would be created – at massive capital expense – the Coega location makes no logistical or economic sense since most of the fuel would have to be transported to the main markets in Gauteng and other metros, which would require the construction of costly new pipelines or shipping the refined fuels to Transnet's new pipeline at Durban. Then, another 360 000 barrels per day of refining capacity in SA would render a substantial portion of existing capacity redundant. It would be far cheaper to upgrade existing refineries, even if the government had to provide the oil majors with sufficient financial incentives, to be recovered in higher fuel levies. Environmental and health concerns would be much better served by replacing petroleum fuels with more efficient and cleaner electric powered transport (as discussed below). The third and main reason to scrap the Mthombo idea is that it will do nothing in itself to ensure liquid fuel security of supply because it would rely on imported crude oil feedstock. By entrenching dependence on ever scarcer and costly crude oil imports, Mthombo would *increase* our long-term vulnerability to fuel supply shocks, not alleviate it. With an estimated price tag of over R100 billion, it would become the country's greatest white elephant. Even if offshore drilling yields substantial oil finds, it would still be more economical to process this crude in the existing refineries and invest the extra funds in more efficient transport systems and low-carbon energy.

Impact of oil price spikes on fuel demand and the economy

South Africa is a price taker on the international oil market. Domestically, the downstream liquid fuels industry is subject to extensive government regulation. Prices of petroleum fuels (petrol, diesel, paraffin and LPG) are administered by the Department of Energy, which imposes various levies and taxes and determines retail and wholesale margins, over and above a 'basic fuel price' (BFP). The BFP is benchmarked on the international spot price of refined oil, and is also influenced by the rand/dollar exchange rate. Sasol and PetroSA's synthetic liquid fuels are accorded the same status in the domestic market as fuels that are refined from imported crude oil, so domestic fuel production provides no buffer against the impacts of oil price spikes or currency depreciation. The same would apply if commercial offshore oil fields were discovered: the balance of payments would benefit, but consumers would still feel the pinch of world oil prices. If the price of crude oil spiked to US$300 per barrel and the rand traded at R10 per dollar, the local price of petrol would rise to about R24 per litre.

There are two major transmission channels whereby international oil price hikes have an impact on South Africa. One is an indirect channel via the slowing down of global economic growth and consequent dampening of foreign demand for South Africa's exports. This in turn tends to reduce the domestic rate of economic growth and slacken demand for liquid fuels in South Africa. The second transmission channel is the direct effect of higher fuel prices on the economy. Econometric modelling shows that the demand for petrol in South Africa is quite unresponsive to prices in the short run (less than a year), but that over the course of a few years a doubling in the price of petrol could reduce demand for this fuel by 50 per cent (Wakeford 2012). Demand for diesel is tied more closely to GDP than to price, and tends to contract in a recession – as it did in 2009. Overall, oil price shocks such as that experienced in 2007-2008 tend to result in higher transport costs, rising price inflation, and slowing GDP growth. This pattern can be expected to hold for future oil price shocks as long as the economy proceeds along a business-as-usual path of petroleum dependence. If the quantity of available world oil exports continues its trend decline in coming years, the world oil price will continue to rise – with heightened volatility. This will in all likelihood slow both global and local rates of economic growth. Slowing growth and rising fuel prices mean that at some point the demand for liquid fuels in South Africa can be expected to stagnate and eventually decline – in contrast with the Department of Energy's projections of robust growth for decades to come.

ALTERNATIVES TO IMPORTED OIL

There are two fundamental strategies for weaning South Africa off imported oil. One is to develop domestic sources of liquid fuels to substitute for imported crude oil. The other is more radical: to transform our transport systems to run on electricity derived increasingly from renewable energy sources.

Developing domestic liquid fuels

In 2012, South Africa's state-owned oil company PetroSA produced about 1 800 barrels per day of crude oil from its Oribi and Oryx oil fields off the southern tip of the country. Although oil exploration is continuing off the western and southern coasts, no new oil discoveries have been announced to date (December 2013) and therefore there is no expectation of a notable increase in domestic crude production in the foreseeable future. The realistic prospects for domestic liquid fuel production rest on coal-to-liquids, gas-to-liquids and biofuels.

Coal-to-liquids

Sasol currently supplies about 26 per cent of South Africa's annual liquid fuel demand from its CTL plant at Secunda. The major advantage of CTL is that it is a reliable technology with a proven track record producing synthetic petroleum fuels (synfuels), including petrol, diesel and jet fuel, that are usable in existing transport infrastructure. Expanding domestic CTL production would therefore reduce South Africa's dependency on oil imports and save foreign exchange. In March 2010, Sasol's board approved the first phase of a project to expand the synfuels and electricity generation capacity of the Secunda plant by approximately 3.2 per cent, using natural gas imported from Mozambique as feedstock. The Secunda expansion is due to come onstream in 2014.

Sasol has also investigated a proposed new CTL plant to be located at the Waterberg coal field in Limpopo. Named Project Mafutha, the proposed plant was to have a capacity of 80 000 barrels of liquid fuels per day, about half of Sasol's 2010 synfuel production volume. From the start, Sasol indicated that it would not be the sole investor in such a large-scale project – estimated to cost in the region of R160 billion – and the company sought financial support from government. According to Sasol, Project Mafutha would probably take up to 10 years to complete. If both Project Mafutha and the Secunda extension materialised, Sasol's synfuels would meet about 40 per cent of the country's 2012 liquid fuel demand.

Construction of a new CTL plant faces several risks and would entail costs other than purely financial. Such a project would be viable only if sufficient coal feedstock could be secured for the lifetime of the project and whereas the Waterberg coal field is relatively underutilised, South Africa's remaining coal reserves are the subject of much contention. The official figure for reserves is 30 billion tonnes (or gigatonnes, Gt) (BP 2013), but independent research casts doubt on this. David Rutledge (2011) of Caltech University estimates that remaining recoverable coal reserves in southern Africa (the vast majority of which are in South Africa) may be as low as 10 billion tonnes. Local geologist Chris Hartnady (2010) forecasts a peak in domestic coal production at about 284 million tonnes (mt) per annum in 2020. On the other hand, Eskom's demand for coal for electricity generation is set to rise by approximately 30 mt a year (to feed its new Medupi and Kusile power plants) to a peak of around 155 mt in 2021, thereafter declining as old power plants are decommissioned (Eberhard 2011). Meanwhile, the coal industry has plans to increase exports from about 65 mt in 2010 to over 90 mt by 2020. The proposed Mafutha CTL plant would require approximately 25 million tonnes of additional coal per annum. If the conservative coal production forecasts above turn out to be accurate, then coal production in the country as a whole will not be able to rise sufficiently to meet projected growth in demand by Eskom, other domestic users, exports and a new CTL plant. Trade-offs among these competing uses of coal would have to be made at some point, and domestic coal prices would probably rise considerably. Under these circumstances, it might make more sense for the Waterberg coal to be used to maintain electricity production from existing power plants rather than to feed a costly new CTL plant. Some of this electricity could be used to power transportation (for example, electric trains and road vehicles).

The second major area of risk to building a new CTL plant concerns potentially high environmental and health costs resulting from water and air pollution, including additional greenhouse gas (GHG) emissions. In view of South Africa's climate mitigation commitments under the Copenhagen Accord of 2009, Sasol may be required to install carbon capture and storage (CCS) technology at a new CTL plant, which would raise its costs considerably. Costs of CTL fuels will also rise considerably as the National Treasury's carbon tax is ramped up over the coming years. Furthermore, CTL facilities require prodigious quantities of water, which is an increasingly scarce resource in southern Africa in general, and in the Waterberg area in particular. Finally, the pollution resulting from coal mining and combustion can also have negative effects, such as respiratory diseases, on human health.

In view of these risks, Sasol put Project Mafutha on the shelf. Given the substantial lead times required for new investments of this scale, it is probably safe to assume that no new CTL plant will be built in South Africa for the remainder of this decade at least.

Gas-to-liquids

PetroSA produces liquid fuels using natural gas feedstock at its GTL refinery at Mossel Bay. Maximum production capacity is 45 000 barrels per day (bpd) of synfuels, although in recent years actual production has been curtailed to about half of this because of maintenance issues and gas feedstock supply constraints. The existing gas fields in the Bredasdorp basin, including the newly authorised F-O field (dubbed Project Ikhwezi), are expected to last until at least 2018, according to PetroSA. The company states on its website that 'further development of other gas prospects near the F-O field could potentially help to sustain the life of the Mossel Bay refinery until 2025'. PetroSA is also conducting exploration activities off the west coast, but has not yet announced any discoveries.

There are at least three other potential sources of natural gas that could supply feedstock to the Mossel Bay GTL refinery or possibly even a new GTL plant (which could in principle be built by either Sasol or PetroSA): imported gas; shale gas; and underground coal gasification (UCG). In recent years there have been very substantial discoveries of conventional natural gas offshore of Namibia and Mozambique, which led the Department of Energy and PetroSA to explore the feasibility of importing liquefied natural gas (LNG). However, LNG has to be transported in special tanker ships and then re-gasified before it can be used onshore, which requires costly new infrastructure. In 2010, PetroSA's management decided against the LNG option and chose Project Ikhwezi instead. Although LNG prices have in the past been quite closely correlated to oil prices, the development of shale gas in North America over the past few years has lowered gas prices in that region and also softened world LNG prices. If South Africa pursues the LNG option, it will have to compete on the global LNG market with the likes of China, India and South Korea.

Another potential, albeit highly contentious, source of feedstock for GTL plants is shale gas. In April 2011, the South African Cabinet placed a moratorium on shale gas exploration and appointed an interdepartmental task team to investigate the economic, social and environmental implications of shale gas development. The Working Group on Hydraulic Fracturing delivered its report in July 2012 (DMR 2012), and the report was subsequently endorsed by the Cabinet. A study commissioned for the US Energy Information Administration (EIA 2011) indicated that South Africa may have potential for shale gas deposits in the Karoo Basin amounting to 485 trillion cubic feet (Tcf) of technically recoverable resources. The Working Group stated however that 'owing to the limited amount of available data in the area, it is impossible to quantify the resource accurately, other than to say that it is potentially very large.' Experience from the United States and other countries suggests that the commercially viable portion of shale gas resources is likely to be much smaller than the technically recoverable resource (Hughes 2011) and serious concerns have been raised about potential negative social and environmental side-effects related to the contamination of water and air pollution (Hughes 2011; Howarth et al. 2011). Of particular concern is the limited availability of and possible contamination of fresh water, which is a very scarce resource in the Karoo.

In September 2012 the Cabinet, on the recommendations of the task team, endorsed the lifting of the eighteen-month moratorium on shale gas exploration – however, only 'normal' exploration methods, and not hydraulic fracturing, would be allowed for an initial six to twelve month period while the regulatory framework was augmented. The companies that have been awarded exploration licences still have to complete environmental impact assessments before any exploratory drilling can take place. According to the Working Group report (DMR 2012: 29), 'It may take ten or more years for a successful project to progress from the issuing of an exploration right, through the drilling of a discovery well, the drilling of a number of appraisal wells, the development of an economic feasibility plan, the application for and issuing of a production right, the drilling of production wells and the installation of the pipeline infrastructure before gas is delivered to the end user.' The potential of shale gas to contribute to the energy supply in South Africa therefore remains speculative, and it seems unlikely to play a meaningful role in this decade but could have a major impact on domestic energy markets after 2020. If a commercially recoverable resource of, say, 30 Tcf were established, this could potentially sustain PetroSA's current operations and provide feedstock for new GTL production – but possibly at a very high cost to the environment, as pointed out by David Fig in the previous edition of the *New South African Review*. At this point, the government seems determined to pursue shale gas and if early exploration activities indicate a likelihood of commercially viable gas reserves, environmentalists will have an uphill battle to stop the fracking juggernaut from rolling across the Karoo landscape.

A third source of feedstock for GTL could come from a process called underground coal gasification (UCG), whereby coal is ignited *in situ* underground, fed through a borehole with air or oxygen to yield a synthetic gas (syngas). The syngas can be used for electricity generation, for the production of synthetic liquid fuels or for industrial purposes. In addition to this flexibility, several other advantages are claimed for UCG, including utilisation of otherwise uneconomical resources; lower capital investment costs compared to conventional coal plants; no costs incurred for transporting coal; avoidance of the health and safety risks associated with traditional mining; and potentially lower environmental effects (Shafirovich and Varma 2009; Eskom 2010). The potential disadvantages and risks attached to UCG include GHG emissions and possible underground water contamination and land subsidence. Eskom has a small pilot UCG plant in operation at its Majuba power station in Mpumalanga, and the utility seems optimistic that the costs will compare favourably with those of conventional coal mining and power generation. Nevertheless, UCG has yet to be proven commercially, and is a highly uncertain potential contributor to domestic gas supplies. In any event, since the coal fields are located in the northern areas of the country while PetroSA's GTL refinery is in the southern Cape, costly pipeline infrastructure or a new GTL plant would be required to convert coal gas into liquid fuels.

It is reasonably assured that PetroSA will continue to produce GTL from its Mossel Bay refinery until at least 2018, using gas from the southern Cape offshore fields. Beyond that, there are various possibilities for expanding GTL production from domestically produced gas (if new conventional fields are found or if shale gas is found and developed), or from imported gas. However, each of these options would require costly infrastructure investments and could have seriously detrimental environmental side-effects.

Biofuels

In December 2007 the South African government approved the Department of Minerals and Energy's Biofuels Industrial Strategy which excluded maize as a feedstock for ethanol (citing food security concerns), advocating instead grain sorghum, sugar cane and sugar beet. The strategy also proposed that biodiesel be produced from soya beans, canola and sunflower oil. The target for biofuel penetration was set as 2 per cent of liquid road fuels by 2013, in an initial five-year pilot phase. In August 2012 the Department of Energy gazetted regulations pertaining to the Mandatory Blending of Biofuel with Petrol and Diesel in South Africa, although the implementation date is still to be determined by the minister. The regulations stipulate that bioethanol must comprise between 2 per cent and 10 per cent of petrol on a volumetric basis, while diesel should have a minimum concentration of 5 per cent of diesel volumes.

Obstacles to the development of biofuels in South Africa thus far have included low levels of awareness about the opportunities inherent in biofuels; technical challenges; food insecurity concerns; difficulties accessing financing; human capacity constraints; and an uncertain policy and regulatory environment (Amigun et al. 2008). Although large-scale production of biofuels may now become viable under the new regulations, the constraints imposed by water and land scarcity suggest that it is unlikely that biofuels will make a significant contribution to national liquid fuel supplies beyond what is envisaged in the blending regulations – that is approximately 5 per cent of current liquid fuel demand.

In the longer term there may be scope for so-called 'second-generation' biofuels, such as cellulosic ethanol, which utilises non-food crops, agricultural waste and wood chips as feedstock, and perhaps biodiesel produced from algae. The problem with cellulosic ethanol is that there is no ecological 'free lunch': for arable land to remain fertile, a significant proportion of the nutrients contained in the 'waste' must be returned to the soil – the more so when synthetic fertilisers become relatively scarcer and more expensive. These second generation technologies are still in the research and development stage and high costs have thus far prohibited their commercialisation, which may take a decade or longer.

Reducing demand for liquid fuels

A much cheaper and quicker alternative to investing tens of billions of rands in new infrastructure to produce (mostly fossil) substitutes for imported oil is to introduce policies and measures that reduce demand for fuel by encouraging greater energy conservation and efficiency. And for long term sustainability, our liquid fuel-based transport system needs to be replaced by one that is powered by renewable electricity.

Fuel conservation and efficiency

Since transport consumes the lion's share of petroleum fuels, this sector must be prioritised for demand reduction. Fortunately, there is a wide array of measures than can reduce fuel consumption substantially in the short- to medium-term and which do not require substantial financial outlays for infrastructure. The simplest way to save fuel is through eco-driving techniques such as use of correct gears, avoiding unnecessary acceleration and braking, appropriate inflation of tyres, and adequate maintenance of vehicles. These measures can be encouraged by information campaigns, although individual behaviour is not easy to change unless supported by economic incentives. Rising fuel prices will help. One of the most cost-effective measures for significant fuel savings is car-pooling, which can be fostered by the allocation of dedicated car pool lanes on highways and/or congestion charges in city centres. Traffic management measures – such as reducing road speed limits and imposing selective driving bans in cities – are generally a quick, relatively cheap and effective means of reducing fuel use. Local governments can partner with companies to encourage telecommuting and compressed work weeks, while the provision of safe cycle lanes can encourage commuters to leave their cars at home. Similarly, the most cost-effective measures for reducing oil consumption in freight transport are those requiring little new infrastructure and which can be implemented relatively easily in the short to medium term: improved vehicle maintenance, optimised routing and scheduling, and intelligent traffic management solutions.

Another way of reducing fuel consumption over the medium to longer term is to incentivise consumers to buy more efficient motor vehicles. This could work through the introduction of a 'feebate' system, whereby extra taxes are imposed on larger, gas guzzling vehicles while rebates are given on purchases of more fuel-efficient models. The carbon tax will also help to shift buying patterns toward greater efficiency. Even greater reductions in liquid fuel use can be achieved through the replacement of internal combustion engine vehicles (ICEVs) with battery electric vehicles, hybrids and plug-in hybrid vehicles. However, replacement of the vehicle fleet will take decades and require a large capital expenditure on the part of households and firms – money that could be spent more effectively if transport is revolutionised more dramatically.

Electrified mass transport

The quantitatively largest opportunities for reducing oil dependence are presented by modal shifts – from private motor vehicles to non-motorised transport and public transit such as buses, trains and trams for passengers, and from road to rail in the case of freight.

The bus rapid transit systems that are being developed in several metros and cities are a step in the right direction, but need to be accelerated and, ideally, electrified. The R123 billion budgeted over the coming eighteen years for the upgrade of passenger rail rolling stock is also welcome but, again, needs to be accelerated. This may sound like a large amount of money, but it is trivial compared to the R80 billion spent by households on personal motor vehicles in 2012 alone (SARB 2013). Taxes on vehicle sales and subsidies for public transport can address this gross imbalance and inefficiency in expenditure patterns although attracting passengers from cars to public transport will also require improvements in the provision of public transport services in terms of speed, reliability, regularity, safety and security, convenience, comfort and cost. What South Africa does not need is more investment in airports and planes, for triple digit oil prices are already exacting a heavy toll on airline companies, several of which have gone bankrupt in recent years, and with sky-high fuel prices the national carrier SAA keeps on asking for multi-billion rand bailouts from taxpayer money. In the case of freight, there is great scope for shifting bulk loads from trucks travelling on the main corridors (Gauteng-Cape Town and Gauteng-Durban) to electrified railways. Transnet's R300 billion capital expenditure programme is welcome, but much of this is geared towards expanding mineral export lines rather than general freight. Again, a reallocation of expenditure away from widening highways towards upgrading rail infrastructure will boost long-term energy security and mobility.

The gradual electrification of both passenger and freight transport will certainly place increasing demand on Eskom and independent power producers, which are already struggling to meet the country's power demands, but electric drive trains are much more energy efficient than internal combustion engines so there will be net energy savings over the long term, as well as greater transport energy security. Critically, future revisions of the Integrated Resource Plan for electricity generation must take account of growing demand from the transport sector. Much of the additional power generation must come from renewable sources like solar and wind, which suffer from the drawback of intermittency. And yet there are potential synergies to exploit: perhaps the most promising scenario is a marriage of renewable electricity production with integrated smart grids and plug-in hybrid vehicles that act as a storage mechanism for intermittent energy sources (see Rifkin 2011). What seems clear is that transport is set to undergo a fundamental revolution in the coming decades, with grid-connected electric vehicles gradually replacing stand-alone ICEVs (Gilbert and Perl 2008).

CONCLUSION

Over the past century we have structured our human settlements and our economic systems on the basis of an ever-increasing availability of affordable petroleum fuels. Twenty years into the democratic era, South Africa is largely pursuing a business-as-usual approach of building roads and airports, and meeting the rising thirst for fuel by increasing imports. But the evidence is now clear that the world has left behind the era of cheap and abundant oil and faces a future of increasing oil scarcity reflected in rising oil prices, for which this country is ill prepared. The bulk of our highly interconnected critical systems – transport, power generation, food production and distribution, the financial system and economic value chains – are vulnerable to the effects of global oil supply disruptions and price shocks. We urgently need to chart a new course.

Global oil depletion is just one of a whole suite of resource depletion and environmental degradation challenges that face our society. These should be tackled in an integrated way by the National Planning Commission, government departments, businesses and civil society. The coming decade is a critical time for South Africa, as the government and its parastatal companies embark on a massive infrastructure rollout. It is critical that this infrastructure is planned in a way that reduces South Africa's dependency on imported oil, rather than entrenching our addiction to the black liquid. What we don't need is our limited tax revenues being wasted on white elephants like new oil refineries, enlarged highways (with or without e-tolling), and never-ending airline bailouts.

Climate change and other pollution concerns, together with uncertainty over the quantity and quality of remaining coal reserves, demand that the nation forsake the route taken by the apartheid government and eschew additional coal-to-liquid production. Shale gas, and its potential to feed gas-to-liquid refineries, will remain a bitterly contested issue, but will probably do nothing to shield the country from oil shocks within the next decade. South Africa may be able to tap into its neighbours' gas deposits, but will face stiff international competition and world market prices for these resources. Biofuels are unlikely to contribute more than a token fraction of liquid fuel demand owing to constraints on arable land and water supplies, which will be increasingly necessary to meet the population's food security needs. The future of transport, therefore, lies in much greater energy efficiency. This can be achieved in a myriad ways, the most important being a shift of bulk freight from roads to railways and a massive expansion of public transport in cities. Although important strides have been taken towards the rehabilitation of passenger railways and the construction of bus rapid transit systems, they are receiving insufficient funding and urgency. Over the long term, our transport systems should be progressively electrified, bearing in mind that this will require prodigious investments in new renewable power generation and upgrading and extending the national grid. To achieve this transition, the body politic must somehow escape the crushing grip of the minerals-energy complex and the fossil fuel lobby.

South Africa surprised the world in 1994 when it achieved a largely peaceful democratic transition after centuries of colonialist exploitation and race-based minority rule. The country also became the first nation in the world to unilaterally disarm all its nuclear weapons in the early 1990s. Can our nation rise to the challenge of global oil depletion and lead the world in a transition towards a more sustainable future? The resources and technologies are available; what are needed above all are sufficient awareness, political will, enlightened leadership and individual resolve. The choice is ours, and time is of the essence.

REFERENCES

Amigun B, R Sigamoney and H von Blottnitz (2008) Commercialisation of biofuel industry in Africa: A review. *Renewable & Sustainable Energy Reviews* 12(3): 690-711.

Benes J, M Chauvet, O Kamenik, M Kumhof, D Laxton, S Mursula and J Selody (2012) The future of oil: Geology versus technology. IMF Working Paper WP12/109, Washington, DC: IMF.

BP (2012) Statistical Review of World Energy. London: BP plc.

DME (2007) Energy Security Master Plan – Liquid Fuels. Pretoria: Department of Minerals and Energy.

DMR (2012) Report on Investigation of Hydraulic Fracturing in the Karoo Basin of South Africa. Pretoria: Department of Mineral Resources.

Eberhard A (2011) The future of South African coal: market, investment and policy challenges. Stanford Program on Energy and Sustainable Development, Working Paper #100. San Francisco: Stanford University.

EIA (2013b) South Africa Country Analysis Brief. http://www.eia.gov/countries/cab.cfm?fips=SF [Accessed 1 June 2013].

EIA (2013a) International Energy Statistics. US Energy Information Administration. http://www.eia. doe.gov/emeu/international/contents.html [Accessed 1 June 2013].

EIA (2011) World Shale Gas Resources: An Initial Assessment of 14 Regions outside the United States. Washington, DC: US Energy Information Administration.

Eskom (2010) Underground Coal Gasification. http://www.eskom.co.za/live/content.php?Item_ID= 14077 [Accessed 18 February 2011].

Gagnon N, CAS Hall and L Brinker (2009) A preliminary investigation of energy return on energy investment for global oil and gas production. *Energies* 2: 490-503.

Gilbert R and A Perl (2008) *Transport Revolutions: Moving People and Freight without Oil.* London: Earthscan.

Hartnady C (2010) South Africa's diminishing coal reserves. *South African Journal of Science* 106(9/10): 1-5.

Hirsch RL (2008) Mitigation of maximum world oil production: Shortage scenarios. *Energy Policy* 36(2): 881-889.

Howarth RW, R Santoro and A Ingraffea (2011) Methane and the greenhouse-gas footprint of natural gas from shale formations. *Climatic Change* 106(4): 679-690.

Hubbert MK (1956) Nuclear Energy and the Fossil Fuels. Proceedings of Spring Meeting, American Petroleum Institute Drilling & Production Practice. San Antonio, Texas.

Hughes JD (2013) Drill baby drill: Can unconventional fuels usher in a new era of energy abundance? Santa Rosa, CA: Post Carbon Institute.

Hughes JD (2011) Will natural gas fuel America in the 21st century? Santa Rosa, CA: Post Carbon Institute.

IEA (2013) Statistics and Balances. International Energy Agency. http://www.iea.org/stats/index.asp [Accessed 5 September 2013].

IEA (2012) World Energy Outlook 2012. Paris: International Energy Agency.

Kumhof M and D Muir (2012) Oil and the world economy: Some possible futures. IMF Working Paper WP/12/256. Washington, DC: International Monetary Fund.

Murphy D and CAS Hall (2010) Year in review – EROI or energy return on (energy) invested. *Annals of the New York Academy of Sciences* 1185: 102-118.

Rifkin J (2011) *The Third Industrial Revolution.* New York: Palgrave Macmillan.

Rutledge D (2011) Estimating long-term world coal production with logit and probit transforms. *International Journal of Coal Geology* 85: 23-33.

SAPIA (2013) Annual Report 2012. South African Petroleum Industry Association. www.sapia.co.za [Accessed 5 June 2013].

SARB (2013) Quarterly Bulletin. June. Pretoria: South African Reserve Bank.

Shafirovich E and A Varma (2009) Underground coal gasification: A brief review of current status. *Industrial & Engineering Chemistry Research* 48(17): 7865-7875.

Sorrell S, R Miller, R Bentley and J Speirs (2010a) Oil futures: A comparison of global supply forecasts. *Energy Policy* 38(9): 4990-5003.

Sorrell S, J Speirs, R Bentley, A Brandt and R Miller (2010b). Global oil depletion: A review of the evidence. *Energy Policy* 38(9): 5290-5295.

Wakeford JJ (2012) Implications of global oil depletion for South Africa: vulnerabilities, impacts and transition to sustainability. PhD Dissertation, Stellenbosch University, South Africa.

CHAPTER 5

The politics of electricity generation in South Africa

Keith Gottschalk

INTRODUCTION

Other research (for example, McDonald 2009) has problematised the politics of social justice in electricity distribution and reticulation. This chapter will primarily explore the question of why a democratic government – under four successive presidents, and under seven successive ministers responsible for energy – has persisted in privileging the atomic industry lobby, regardless of the consequences for opportunity cost, cost-effectiveness, complexity, the potential for catastrophe, and constant change on the supply-side of the market and in technology.

HISTORICAL BACKGROUND

In 1923 the government founded the Electricity Supply Commission, Escom (later changed to the Afrikaans acronym Eskom) to nationalise some of the existing power stations, to build extra ones, and to start work on connecting what incrementally became a national power grid by 1975. For non-electricity sources of energy, the apartheid regime established Sasol, the world's largest coal-to-oil plant, which started production in 1955 and greatly ramped up production in 1981-82 when it feared that oil sanctions might become far more efficient than they were, and would be backed up by a naval blockade. It founded UKOR, the uranium enrichment corporation, primarily for a future atomic weapons programme, but which could have dual use to provide fuel for potential nuclear power stations. UKOR started operations in 1976, enriching the fissile isotope of uranium, ^{235}U, from 0.7 per cent to 5 per cent strength, later increased to 45 per cent.

Today, 93 per cent of South Africa's electricity is generated by coal-fired power stations. The Medupi and Kusile power stations under construction will each rank as the fourth-largest coal-fired power stations in the world, and the largest to use dry-cooling and desulphurisation.

DEVELOPMENTS IN NEW SOURCES OF ENERGY FOR THE GRID

In recent decades, new sources for energy became both technologically and financially feasible. While South Africa, largely a semi-arid country, has only small hydropower stations such as the !Gariep Dam, imported hydropower can be orders of magnitude larger, with energy security assured by tapping different sources and using different routes for transmission cables. Starting in 1976, Mozambique's Cahora Bassa hydro-power plant (a project initiated by then presidents Hendrik Verwoerd of South Africa and Antonio Salazar of Portugal) exported around 1 100 MW to South Africa. Incredibly, the apartheid-era South African Defence Force (SADF) flew tons of munitions quarterly to the Mozambican counter-revolutionary Renamo to sabotage the pylons for some fifteen years. This was a world record in cutting off your nose to spite your face: the militarists' motivation was to prevent Mozambique receiving any royalties, as it could not export electricity. After the liberation of South Africa ended these arms lifts to Renamo, the pylons were repaired and from the late 1990s Cahora Bassa resumed export of electricity to South Africa.

In Zaire, (today the Democratic Republic of Congo (DRC)), the Inga 1 hydropower plant (351 MW) was commissioned in 1972. In 1976, Henry Olivier, a civil engineer in private practice, proposed that: 'A pan-African power transmission grid ... will make it possible to send Inga power to any part of southern Africa' (Olivier 1976: 26, 60). By 1994, the end of apartheid and economic sanctions made it politically feasible to export hydropower from the DRC to South Africa. This started from Inga 1 and 2 through the Southern African Power Pool by the late 1990s, with typically a capacity averaging 110 MW through an 'eastern corridor' of transmission cables running across the DRC, Zambia, Zimbabwe and Botswana to South Africa.

The killing of the formerly SADF-supplied Jonas Savimbi led to the prompt surrender of his Unita and the end of the Angolan civil war in 2002; and so made it politically feasible to propose a 'western corridor' of power cables running from Inga through Angola, Namibia, and Botswana to South Africa. This enabled proposals for an Inga 3 hydropower plant for up to 4 800 MW.

Eskom led a consortium of national power parastatals (Botswana Power Corporation (BPC), Angola's Empresa Nacional de Electricidade (ENE), Nampower, and the DRC's Société nationale d'électricité (SNEL)) to incorporate Westcor (the Western Power Corridor Company) in Botswana in 2003 – who all signed an intergovernmental memorandum of understanding in 2004. The pre-feasibility study was completed in 2005. But neither Eskom nor the South African government ever put up the capital required, unlike the eight billion rands they simultaneously poured into the pebble-bed modular reactor (PBMR) project. The opportunity cost was that the DRC government lost patience, considered that Westcor offered them an unfairly small proportion of the anticipated royalties, and pulled the plug on Westcor participation in 2009 to seek alternative partners.

All told, this lost six more years before Presidents Kabila and Zuma signed a new treaty in October 2013. Fund-raising resumed for Inga 3 with an anchor contract to sell Eskom 2 500 MW, with the other half of the power servicing the DRC. When this is followed by the proposed Grand Inga cascades, Eskom will also buy at least 30 per cent of the up to 40 000 MW extra that will become available (Engineering News: 2013).

As far back as 1913, Egypt had used concentrated solar power (CSP) to drive a steam engine pumping irrigation water. CSP stations have, for two decades, generated a total of 350MW in California, at US$0.08 kWh. The physicist Bernard Scheffler's 'Solar Energy in Southern Africa' paper to the 1995 South African Institute of Physics conference noted that the world's most commercially viable location to produce CSP, with an insolation of 6.5 kWh per square metre per day, is in South Africa's Northern Cape, North-West and northern Free State provinces; and the southern parts of Botswana and Namibia. Had Eskom acted promptly on Scheffler's research, it could have avoided the widespread 2008 power failures and instead become, by that year, the world leader in solar power for the grid.

But in fact Morocco (20 MW in 2010, with a further 1 160 MW under construction), Algeria (25 MW in 2011), and Egypt (20 MW in 2011) all overtook Eskom in adopting CSP to feed electricity into their grid – even though Scheffler had noted that Saharan dust storms reduced their insolation per square metre to lower levels than those found in southern Africa. While the Department of Energy proposed a 5 000 MW solar park at Upington, it again failed to put up capital on the scale fruitlessly and wastefully spent on the pebble-bed modular reactor, nor – for a whole decade – would it offer tenders. Eskom will only start to buy 150 MW of CSP by 2014 at the earliest. The total of all renewable energy (CSP, photo-voltaic, wind) that will be under construction by 2016 will amount to only 3 725 MW (www.bdelive.co.za). Technology development saw thin-film photo-voltaic (PV) undercutting the price of CSP, the competitive advantage of which now lies in storing heat through molten salt for the peak power consumption between 17h00 and 21h00 in South Africa.

The third new source of energy is imported gas. The 865 km Mozambique-South African gas pipeline started operating in 2004, bringing gas to both Sasol and the Gauteng industrial conurbation. Subsequent vast gas field discoveries in Tanzania and in Mozambique have the potential to make major shifts in the cost-optimal blend of power sources for South Africa. The energy academic Anton Eberhard has also pointed out the low price of liquid natural gas (LNG) on the international market, which has a mature infrastructure for transportation by ship (Eberhard 2013).

Other sources are less important, and mentioned here merely to be noted. The wind atlas and Darling wind farm confirm that the South African west coast is one peak locality to generate wind power. Stellenbosch University, cognisant of overseas research into wave power, located the energetic south-west coast as the optimal littoral zone to generate electricity from this source, and has started a research project.

These supply-side drivers, which undercut the total costs of atomic power, enable us to test whether economic or political factors are primary in the government's choice of electricity generation options.

FOREIGN CORPORATE ENERGY LOBBIES

Foreign energy sector corporations seeking business in South Africa fall into two categories. First are those, such as ABB, Alstom, and Siemens, selling electrical technology that is needed regardless of which options are chosen for power generation. The same applies to large civil engineering companies which seek contracts to construct power stations, regardless of the generation option chosen.

The second category consists of corporations primarily active in one generation technology. Because the wealthy countries have colder climates than Africa's, the corporations with the most lobbying spend are those marketing atomic power – and wind turbines, solar and hydropower are not major business options for them back home. Danish companies have been active in promoting wind turbines, whose load factor (percentage of each twenty-four hours) producing electricity is at best less than half the load factor of solar power. The mega-corporations are Areva and others seeking atomic power station construction orders in the Third World to replace their declining markets in the Convention on the Organisation for Economic Cooperation and Development (OECD) countries.

DOMESTIC ENERGY LOBBIES

Coal-fired power stations are the comfort zone of most of the Eskom establishment of engineers and management. Their inclination for innovation focuses on higher efficiencies for furnaces and boilers, dry cooling, desulphurisation, and turning waste fly ash into concrete bricks.

The golden age of the atomic industry in South Africa was late apartheid. Hidden under military censorship, the apartheid regime built up an end-to-end atomic industry including uranium enrichment, fabrication of zirconium fuel cans for reactors, and the manufacture of six and a half atom bombs. The two nuclear reactors at the Koeberg power station served as camouflage for the destination of enriched uranium and as public relations for the atomic industry. By the time they were synchronised with the grid in 1984-85, the Koeberg power station had cost more than triple the original price told to the South African public, and its electricity cost the grid triple the price per kilowatt-hour of Eskom's coal-fired power stations. (Auf der Heyde et al. 1987: 481) The De Klerk interregnum saw the atom bombs dismantled and the enrichment plants taken apart and sold to China.

THE ATOMIC LOBBY FIGHT-BACK AFTER 1990

In February 1994, 240 delegates participated in a conference to debate nuclear policy for a democratic South Africa. It was co-hosted by the Western Cape sections of the Environmental Monitoring Group, and the African National Congress (ANC) Science and Technology Policy Group. In brief, its main recommendations were that South Africa should:

- oppose nuclear weapons and strengthen the Non-Proliferation Treaty;
- after historic over-investment, give no further subsidies to the atomic industry, but let those parts of it which make a profit continue; and
- research electricity generation through solar, hydro, wind, and other renewables.

The second and third of these recommendations were never even rejected by the ANC – they simply vanished without a trace. What happened?

Hindsight suggests four reasons. The first is formalistic. The recommendations from a conference had no standing within the ANC unless they were subsequently adopted by its National Executive Committee or other structure. Still less would they have any standing in the government unless they were accepted by a director general or cabinet minister.

The second reason is that before 27 April 1994 the ANC regarded the bureaucracy as hostile Afrikaner Nationalists. What civil society did not realise was that, from May 1994, ANC ministers, deputy ministers and other political appointees such as directors general, would grant daily access to existing civil servants to advise them and draft policy. By contrast, intellectuals and activists in ANC support groups and the nongovernmental organisations (NGOs) were from now on marginalised. They were now the outsiders, who had to request an appointment to make presentations to any political appointee, which requests were increasingly refused or ignored more frequently than they were granted. Even when the new decision makers granted activists occasional space and time to make presentations, these had decreasing influence as incoming ministers slowly meshed with the bureaucracy, who used their insider status to counter activist proposals.

The third reason is that within a month the *Financial Mail* published a half-page 'nuclear feature' which concluded: 'The ANC is doing its best to be polite to all past allies. But the case for sending the nuclear nutters packing after the April general elections is unanswerable' (*Financial Mail* 11 March 1994: 43).

By 'nuclear nutters' the *Financial Mail* meant not the nuclear industry but those opposed to it, who advocated renewable electricity generation. In short, the atomic industrial lobby had already won over most of the mainstream media, including editors, columnists and journalists. Newspapers repeatedly, after 1994, uncritically published Eskom's pro-atomic articles verbatim, but their editorial and other pages are often rationed to those advocating renewable sources of grid electricity. And media were not the only institution the atomic establishment lobbied.

The fourth reason is that a public relations firm hired by Eskom in 1994 recommended setting up a Koeberg task team; that Eskom's Nuclear Division should engage with ANC officials outside the conference; and that it should lobby members of the ANC National Executive Council. All this they diligently did, with success..

The atom bomb team, now incarnated as the PBMR team, fought hard for two decades to claw back from this reverse in their fortunes.

You are dealing with some of the most intelligent men in South Africa (there were no women) when you listen to heads of atomic establishments argue the case why their public funding should continue at its historic highest level. Their sophisticated arguments included that otherwise the capabilities and expertise built up over twenty years would be destroyed. If you retrenched nuclear engineers they might be recruited by Pakistan, Libya, Iran or other governments to proliferate A-bombs. Analysis of this special pleading indicates its flaw – that the young democracy should acquiesce and allow its priorities for capital spending and human resource allocation to be set in concrete by the choices of the apartheid military-industrial complex, and suffer the opportunity costs. In the two decades of democracy, there are no known cases of Afrikaner engineers from the A-bomb team emigrating to North Korea or Iran and battling to adjust to strange languages, creeds and climates.

They persuaded the government to continue to employ them to take up research and the development of a failed German technology for a type of 'generation four' high temperature reactor: a PBMR. This technology was abandoned by its companies owing to the pebbles' structural integrity failing from radiation embrittlement, inability for real-time detection of hot spots in its core, and other design flaws. The PBMR team were from the start able to tap into the Armscor old boy network to lobby for government support.

A series of *Noseweek* reports unearthed how the PBMR, allied companies, and its construction and component vendors, had generated business, or shareholdings, which successfully set up a revolving door that recruited – directly or indirectly – key insider public sector personnel ranging from a chairman of Eskom to a director general of the Department of Science and Technology. The PBMR team worked smartly to recruit black economic empowerment (BEE) partners, whose roles would include lobbying on behalf of the PBMR with top ANC decision makers inside and outside government.

The team first argued that they could produce a 'naval' PBMR. This was bizarre, as South Africa lacks a shipbuilding industry beyond luxury yachts accommodating from four to eight persons, with no capability to construct an atomic-propelled submarine or ship. Then, the team pledged that for two billion rands they would design and build a

PBMR to produce electricity for the grid. This argument was equally flawed, because a PBMR produces less electricity (under 100 MW) than any other type of nuclear reactor – for example, it would take over forty PBMRs to generate the same electricity as the Medupi power station. Third, when this argument was debunked, the team argued that their PBMR could produce 'process heat' for desalination, production of hydrogen through disassociation of water, or other industry or hot air for other industries. This claim was equally fallacious, for a PBMR has a far lower energy density than any other type of nuclear reactor – 2 MW per cubic metre, versus 100 MW per cubic metre in the average atomic reactor. Also, if a PBMR generated electricity at higher prices than any other source, the power could at least be blended in the national grid and the price averaged out with other generation. But process heat could only be used by factories adjacent to the PBMR. The idea that a company would pay thirty billion rands to access process heat was literally a lot of hot air.

In 2003, the atomic division within Eskom launched a major propaganda offensive in the media, with full-page advertisements. The peak was its advertisements of 9 December. The ads flighted equally-sized photos which projected an impartial and objective image to readers. In *Business Day*, the photo of Koeberg power station measured 11 x 17 cms; the photo of the wind farm 7 x 8 cms; the concentrated solar power photo 17 x 12 cms. The text on the page, however, allocated only two sentences to all non-nuclear sources of power generation combined versus forty-four column centimetres – *the entire page* – to atomic power.

The text was crudely one-sided propaganda for the PBMR, pushing assertions with no substantiation. For example, the text alleged that the PBMR 'will have short construction times' when in fact atomic power stations have longer construction times than any other type of power station (the text evaded giving those times in years). It alleged that 'nuclear energy also produces very small volumes of waste' but censored the fact that PBMRs generate ten times the volume of waste produced by any other reactor.

Above all, the text alleged that the PBMR 'will be economically competitive', but gave no comparison of the price per kW between that reactor and other generation options. It also alleged that the PBMR 'is environmentally friendly' without facts explaining how it compared to CSP or hydro generation.

In the *Cape Argus* version of this advertisement, the equal-sized images were run as wind farm (9 x 10 cms); solar dish Stirling technology (13 x 10 cms); Koeberg (12 x 14 cms). Again, this misled readers into thinking that they were about to peruse an impartial discussion of the generation options but the text mentioned 'imported hydro power from Southern Africa' and 'an abundance of sunshine suitable for solar power' in only two sentences, with the rest of the page devoted to atomic propaganda.

A further way in which the ad's text deceived its readers was through the misleading claim: 'Eskom is investigating various electricity supply options, including renewable energy (wind, solar and wave power), gas-fire power, coal-fired power using clean coal technologies, imported hydro power from Southern Africa, hydro power pumped storage schemes and nuclear power.'

This sentence would lead readers to assume that Eskom allocated roughly equal research and development funds to each of these options (nuclear, solar, wind and wave power). Questions in Parliament from Lance Greyling (then of the Independent Democrats (ID), now Democratic Alliance (DA) spokesperson on Energy) squeezed out of the government the admission that Eskom and government departments had allocated eight billion rands to the PBMR versus twenty million rands to *all* renewable sources of electricity combined. That is, *all renewable sources of grid electricity combined* have been allocated, not equal funds, but 0.25 per cent of the research and development funds allocated to atomic generation of electricity: a research and development ratio of 400:1.

This bias was capped by a headline: 'A verdict for nuclear power'. One week later, the atomic lobby media offensive continued in *ThisDay*, with a full-page ad headlined 'Koeberg showcases South Africa's excellent history of nuclear power operations'. The ad mentioned nuclear fuel reprocessing plants in France, the UK and Russia, with zero mention of the well-publicised leaks from Windscale alias Sellafield in the UK, and similar leaks elsewhere.

Eskom ran no similar ads on the work of its renewable energy division. Further rounds of Eskom ads appeared in the *Sunday Argus* in July 2004 with a headline repeating the mantra of 'A verdict for nuclear energy'. This ran four images of an atomic power station – but now dropped the images of solar and wind power generators, as a facade no longer necessary. The sixty column-centimetres of text rationed mention of renewable generation of electricity to four words in the first column, plus the put-down: 'Renewable energy sources such as the wind, solar and tidal are feasible but expensive.'

Again, the text avoided pricing the PRMR or Areva tender versus renewables per kW generated.

Eskom paid for a half-page ad in the *Cape Argus* of March 2005 headlined 'Nuclear energy – don't say no until you know' with text yet again a one-sided propaganda for atomic power. This repeated, without proof or comparative figures, the misleading claim that the 'PBMR will be economically competitive, environmentally friendly, and will have short construction times.'

With this ad campaign, the atomic industry lobby in South Africa achieved two world records. This was the first time in the history of advertising, and the first time in corporate history, that a company had paid for full-page ads in all the main newspapers, so that one division of that company could publically marginalise and denigrate the research and development work of another division of that company. There could be no clearer measurement of the power of the atomic division within Eskom, and the powerlessness and defencelessness of its renewables division.

One may reasonably assume that this media campaign was merely the public dimension, and that at the same time the atomic industry lobby put equal energy into lobbying cabinet ministers, deputy ministers, ANC members of parliament and National Executive Council members. One such example was the 'highly confidential' South Africa Power Project Strategic Implementation Proposal recommendation of 2007 was spending on nuclear power stations should be ten times higher than on all renewables combined (TSAPRO: 2007: slide 8).

This is also the place to flag another tactic consistently used by the PBMR lobby. When it came to demanding more money, the PBMR projected itself as a public entity, with entitlement to escalating grants from the taxpayers. But when they faced demands to prove their assertions that they had attracted foreign investors, or to cost their electricity per kW compared to renewable sources of grid power, they invoked 'commercial confidentiality' and asserted the right to behave as a private company. The PBMR team claimed they could build one for two billion rands, then four billion rands. By the time the project had spent over eight billion rands there was no PBMR; the money seemed to have gone mostly on the team's paying themselves corporate-level remuneration while they worked in the public sector. David Fig (2005:103) cites *Business Report* as calculating that the fruitless and wasteful expenditure on the PBMR had reached fourteen billion rands.

After seventeen years, from 1993 to 2010, the PBMR team then admitted that they would need a further thirty billion rands. The then minister for public enterprises, Barbara Hogan, stopped pouring good money after bad and terminated the project. Her reasoning was that the PBMR team consistently missed deadlines, failed to find any customers for their reactor, failed to get an opportunity to participate in the USA Nextgen nuclear plant round of research and development funding, and failed to secure private sector financing (bar miniscule shareholdings of Westinghouse at 4.9 per cent; and Exelon at 1.1 per cent before it withdrew). Within months, the minister was dismissed from the cabinet, and her political career was over.

Since 1994 South Africa has had seven ministers responsible for energy.[1] After Pik Botha, these were ANC politicians with no previous record of any interest in or statement about the atomic industry. Yet each minister, within a week or so of appointment, issued a statement reaffirming the government's commitment to atomic power stations. This implies, first, that this strategy is considered more important than any other policy under their domain; and, second, that someone invisible to the public has the power to pressure each new minister to issue such statements. Such a bureaucrat is unlikely to be lower than the rank of a deputy director general.

The roll-back offensive against the 1994 ANC Science & Technology Policy conference steadily mounted. The government's 1998 White Paper on Energy Policy pledged that it would investigate atomic power. In 2007 the Department of Energy published a draft Nuclear Energy Policy for comment, and the Cabinet promulgated the final version in 2008.

Principle One was that nuclear energy 'shall' be used (DME 2008: 7). The government was again committed to 'the development of a fuel fabrication capacity' (op. cit., p.27); would 'investigate the re-establishment of a uranium enrichment capacity' (p.26); and would start the 'construction of nuclear power plants' between 2011 and 2015 (p.29).

The Department of Energy seemingly considered that the Eskom advertising campaign discussed above had failed to convince, for it noted: 'The use of nuclear energy is generally misunderstood by the public due in part to lack of appropriate information … it is important to inform the public about the risks, benefits and safety of nuclear energy' and so resolved to 'roll out the public information programme' between 2008 and 2010 (pp.29, 31). One key strategy was for the atomic lobby to set up a National Nuclear Energy Executive Coordinating Committee (NNEECC) headed by the deputy president, to drive it at the highest level, and packed to ensure a majority of atomic power station supporters from the Department of Energy, the Department of Trade and Industry and others who could outvote the minister of finance. The political strength of the NNEECC soon became tangible. Renewable energy managers in the Department of Energy publically announced at a 2010 solar energy conference that they would found a 5 000 MW solar park in Upington, which later morphed into a 5 000 MW 'solar corridor'. But when the Integrated Resource Plan 2010-2030, endorsed by Cabinet, was published in 2011, solar power was slashed back to a derisory 200 MW. Instead, the Integrated Resource Plan proposed 9 600 MW of atomic power, even though it admitted that 'some' governments choosing atomic power 'are facing delays and cost overruns'.

A Department of Energy advertisement of February 2013 announced: 'Thuyspunt has been earmarked as the next nuclear plant site after Koeberg ... Preparations to launch the procurement of nuclear power plants are currently underway in South Africa. This is being led by the National Nuclear Energy Executive Coordination Committee' (*City Press* 2013).

The National Development Commission (NDC) had recommended that a thorough comparative financial analysis of different power generation options should be made before taking decisions. Instead, the NNEECC invoked 'strategic' interests to overrule the NDC. One political scientist, Anthony Butler, claimed that:

> In energy policy, an amalgam of foreign policy gurus, parastatal barons, securo-crats, and industrial policy enthusiasts are keen to buy six nuclear power plants from a Franco-Chinese consortium at a cost of up to R1 trillion. The long-range, cross-sectoral and irreversible aspects of this proposal should have made it a matter for National Development Commission deliberation.
>
> Instead, commissioners have been excluded from this 'strategic' decision and a way forward is being charted by an ad hoc committee comprised of [sic] vested interests and officials who are already committed.
> (*Business Day* 25 January 2013)

COSTS AND CORRUPTION

Press reports were that Eskom had shortlisted Areva to build over a dozen atomic power stations. Areva is reported to have paid large sums of money to two government officials in the Central African Republic. The journalist who reported this was arrested (*City Press* 13 January 2008). During his visit to South Africa, the French president Nicolas Sarkozy said: 'African civil society and public opinion wants us to be directly involved by for example denouncing corruption' (*Cape Times* 29 February 2008). Subsequently, an Areva vice-president in South Africa stood as an ANC ward candidate in municipal elections.

The Areva president and chief executive officer oversaw their corporate sponsorship of the 2012 and 2013 'French seasons' which paid for extensive cultural events throughout South Africa (www.france-southafrica.com). Their business rival, Westinghouse, appointed a former Azanian People's Organisation (Azapo) president and former director general of the then Department of Arts, Culture, Science and Technology, Itumeleng Mosala, as its regional president for South Africa (Westinghouse 2010).

Incredibly, Eskom also outsourced evaluation of rival tenders to Lahmeyer. This is the firm convicted in 2003 of bribery in the Lesotho Highlands Water Project, paying the largest bribe in the history of the kingdom. The World Bank banned Lahmeyer for seven years from any business with any project with which it was associated (*Business Report* 2008). The government and Eskom should uphold the OECD, African Union (AU), New Partnership for Africa's Development (NEPAD) and Southern African Development Community (SADC) conventions against corruption; demand the termination of any contracts with Lahmeyer and Areva; and also demand that they be barred from doing business with any South African entity.

Time and again, the atomic industry's choices are neither cost-effective nor the simplest, but the most expensive and most complex. The most cost-effective production of medical radioisotopes is by using a cyclotron, as the 200 MeV cyclotron at the iThemba laboratory at Faure has done for decades. The same choice predominates overseas. The 2013 decision to build another reactor at Pelindaba for increased production of medical radioisotopes, instead of a second cyclotron, is not cost-optimal, but can only be explained as part of a stratagem to rebuild a large atomic establishment. Similarly, global practice is to use lead containers for shipping industrial radioisotopes. The Valindaba choice of depleted uranium for radioisotope containers can only be explained by the intention to build capacity for producing both depleted and enriched uranium.

Analysing claims of the cost of generating electricity per kwH through different options flags four issues for attention. First, Eskom applies full market discipline only to renewable energy independent producers, and not to nuclear power. Renewable energy producers have to agree to sell their electricity to Eskom for a contractually-enforceable price. Any cost overrun is a risk for their shareholders. By contrast, atomic power stations have their cost overruns worked into the power bills of their consumers. The cost per kwH claimed in advance to win political approval and state buy-in is not justiciable: it is at best public relations spin, at worst science fiction.

Second, and related to the above, is that atomic power station vendors have become notorious for larger cost overruns than any other type of power station (a power station in Finland is the latest example). A revealing pattern is that corporate capital has for a decade avoided risk-taking such as buying shares in the PBMR. It only wants to be a vendor and to tender for public funds, with guaranteed, risk-free profits.

Third, the prices quoted to the public for the cost of atomic power stations is the 'overnight cost' (as if the cost was paid entirely from Eskom's internal funds) paid in one lump sum, and the vendor was on a fixed-cost contract. Such prices omit financing charges for credit, charges which typically raise the real costs by 40 per cent (Gurzynski 2010: 4).

Also, inflation ensures that construction costs rise over the typical decade it takes to build a nuclear power plant.

Fourth, the prices claimed in public for building atomic power stations externalise many costs, which then fall upon the power consumers and taxpayers. Vendors, for example, deem the cost of the land, administrative buildings, and constructing breakwaters for the power station water inlets as 'owners' costs'. These and other excluded costs add from 10 to 20 per cent to the nuclear industry's claimed costs.

Decommissioning costs are for guarding the site for three decades after closure until declining radioactivity makes demolition safe. The UK considers 130 years necessary before dismantling a used reactor core. All told, decommissioning costs are most probably 25 per cent of construction costs (op. cit.: 13).

The cost of building and maintaining high-level radioactive waste depositaries are not usually included, but fall on taxpayers. The commercial costs of this are R2.4m per cubic metre over the radioactive waste's lifetime ('commercial' here means the rates charged by other countries to receive radioactive waste (op. cit.: 11)).

Eskom's insurance liability for compensating homeowners in the event of major catastrophe and evacuation is R66 million. The real costs of a major catastrophe including evacuation of suburbs and rehousing will be at least three orders of magnitude higher. This is another burden that will be shared between taxpayers and only partly-compensated householders.

Comparisons of the cost of electricity between atomic power stations and power from grid PV, CSP, imported hydro, and imported gas need to be rigorously checked for the these four red flag issues.

SAFETY AND SECRECY

Under the apartheid-vintage National Key Points Act, it is a crime punishable by imprisonment to publish any incident inside an atomic power station (such as a massive leak of radioactivity) without the permission of Eskom. That this power has not been used by prosecutors after 1994 does not mean it cannot be used in future, should a bureaucrat or politician feel defensive, or vengeful towards whistle-blowers.

Nuclear safety in South Africa is intrinsically flawed. It is entrusted to the National Nuclear Regulator (NNR), which is answerable to the Department of Energy – not the Departments of Health or Environmental Affairs. This is a clear conflict of interests. The conflict was aggravated when the minister appointed a former senior employee of the PBMR as the chief executive of the NNR. Similarly, the National Nuclear Regulator makes provision for one NNR representative to represent civil society. At the start of democracy in South Africa, the civil society representative was in fact an ex-Eskom employee who had worked at Koeberg (Fig 2005:60). When all civil society organisations active in nuclear-related issues nominated a delegate, the Cabinet rejected this and instead appointed their own choice in 2012 from the ANC-allied SA National Civic Organisation (Sanco).

The minister of energy deems radioactivity from mine dumps to fall outside the remit of the NNR. Half of the Gauteng and North-West mine dumps are radioactive, with runoff that has ten times the maximum limit of radioactivity permitted by health regulations decanting into rivers. In the dry season, radioactive dust blows off them and is inhaled by the surrounding residents. Water pumped out of mines can have up to twelve times the maximum radioactivity limit that health permits for potable water (Madzvire 2013)

When secrecy legislation is applied to nuclear safety, public concern is more than merited. The NNR refused to release its emergency plans when asked for them by NGOs. It even rejected two Promotion of Access to Information Act (PAIA) applications for their release. When the plans finally came to light after an appeal in 2011, the reasons for the NNR defensiveness became apparent – the emergency plans were both inadequate and out of date. Subsequently, the NNR has adopted the procedure of refusing *all* information as a matter of principle, so compelling the public to submit laborious, time-wasting and sometimes expensive PAIA applications for any data on anything (Becker 2013). The NNR suppressed the 2006 Coetzee report because this Water Research Commission team proved that the level of radioactive contamination throughout the Wonderfonteinspruit catchment posed a significant threat to the health of all who lived there or consumed its produce: there are 2 200 tons of uranium in its sediments. It took two years of 'relentless pressure' from environmentalist Mariette Liefferink to get this report published. All told, the highveld mine dumps contain 600 tons of uranium dust blowing in the air when dry, and leaching into streams and groundwater when wet (*Noseweek* 162: 11-12).

The NNR has a severely inadequate budget and human resources for its current tasks, such as tracking all radioisotopes used industrially, and remediation of radioactive mine dumps. Its then head, advocate Boyce Mkhize, described it as 'mickey mouse' and then resigned. Since the NNR is so under-resourced for even current needs, it lacks the capacity and capability to ensure safety for the proposed three extra atomic power stations containing six nuclear reactors, plus the concomitant re-building of an end-to-end atomic industry.

Another procedural flaw is that in each case of an environmental impact assessment (EIA) for a proposed atomic power station, the 'independent' environmental consultant is hand-picked by the developer, not taken in taxi-cab rank order from a list of qualified professionals. The inevitable result is that any EIA recommending that a project should not be built ensures that the consultant will never again get corporate business. Every EIA concerning an atomic site unfailingly recommends that the installation should be built.

CONCLUSIONS

'Politics and power' has been defined as the allocation of scarce resources. As this book goes to print, Eskom and the government allocate the South African Nuclear Energy Corporation over R500 million rands per year for research versus forty million rands for research and development to the South African National Energy Development Institute for *all* renewable sources of electricity combined. That is, *all* renewable sources of grid electricity combined were allocated less than one-tenth of the research and development funds allocated to the atomic generation of electricity (Greyling 2013). This statistic is an irrefutable measure of the power of the atomic industrial lobby versus the powerlessness of the renewables lobby. Russian media reported in November 2013 that the South African government had signed an agreement to buy eight VVER atomic reactors for power stations.

Noseweek's strength is its *modus operandi*: follow the money. But this cannot explain the tenacious commitment to the PBMR, immune to tenfold ballooning costs, and subsequently, other nuclear reactors of successive presidents, deputy presidents, ministers and deputy ministers of minerals and energy, and of trade and industry. There was no known financial enticement to any of these top decision makers. Moreover, if a politician is able to extort bribes for contracts to build atomic power stations he can clearly extort the same bribes to build power stations which use any other option for generating electricity. So clientelism and corruption cannot explain the determination to demand nuclear power, as opposed to other generation options.

A more credible explanation is that the atomic industry lobby has successfully sold atomic power as projecting the ultimate political symbolism and aura of state power. Politicians are confident that they can assert unchallenged that atomic power is 'strategic', while none claim the same for 5 000 MW of solar or imported hydropower. This conclusion is substantiated by the fact that the government's commitment to the PBMR was not weakened when it cost double, then triple, then four times what was promised. Similarly, the total, all-included costs of the six proposed atomic reactors, including their breakwaters, decommissioning, and high-level radioactive waste storage are indisputably higher than imported hydro or gas power for grid electricity. The striking degree to which the government's determination to again become a nuclear power (this time in the civilian sense) is price-inelastic confirms that politics, not economics, is the driver. The only persuasion that might succeed against this tenacious belief is a public campaign, funded on the scale of the Eskom public relations analysed above, to explain that atomic power is a heritage technology of the Second World War, a legacy technology from the last century's Cold War.

An optimal, cost-effective programme for energy requires major revision of the 2010 Integrated Resource Plan to factor in demand-side management, the new availability of gas in the East African and global markets, and imported hydropower. Solar technologies have far better prospects of developing a South African export industry to the mostly tropical Third World, as they need less capital and high-level human resources, do not have risk of major catastrophes, and are not hindered by nuclear proliferation fears.

REFERENCES

Auf der Heyde T, D Fig, A Stoddart, J Venn and P Wilkinson (1987) The power of the state and the state of power: Recent developments in South Africa's nuclear industry. In Moss G and I Obery (eds) *South African Review 4*. Braamfontein: Ravan.

Butler A (2013a) 'Development plan may not be more than Zuma "fig leaf"'. *Business Day* 25 January.

Butler A (2013b) 'Brics bank may bankroll SA's nuclear ambition'. *Business Day* 22 February.

Department of Energy (2011) Integrated Resource Plan for Electricity 2010-2030 Revision 2 Final Report.

_____ (2013) Infrastructure for South Africa's nuclear programme. Insert 'BUILDING SA' *Sunday Times* 17 March 2013.

_____ Integrated Nuclear Infrastructure Review. *City Press* 3 February.

Department of Energy (2008) Nuclear Energy Policy for the Republic of South Africa. Official paper. http://www.energy.gov.za/files/policies/policy_nuclear_energy_2008.pdf [Accessed 14 October 2013].

Donnelly L (2013) 'No Clear Path to Ambitious Nuclear Goal'. *Mail & Guardian* Business News 1-7 March.

Du Plooy P (2012) 'Nuclear power. A splitting headache'. *Business Day Earth.* Johannesburg: *Business Day.*

Eberhard A (2013) 'Nuclear power is neither necessary nor cost effective' *Business Day* 19 March.

Environmental Monitoring Group Western Cape. and ANC Western Cape Science & Technology Policy Group. The Nuclear Debate. Proceedings of the Conference on Nuclear Policy for a Democratic South Africa. 11-13 February 1994.

Eskom Advertorial (2003): 'A Verdict for Nuclear Energy' *Cape Argus* 9 December.

Eskom Advertorial (2003) 'Koeberg Showcases South Africa's Excellent History of Nuclear Power Operations' *ThisDay* 15 December.

Eskom (2008) The South Africa Power Project (Tsapro) Strategic Implementation Proposal. Unpublished PowerPoint slide show.

Eskom Advertorial (2005) 'Nuclear Energy – Don't Say No Until You Know'. *Cape Argus* 17 March.

Eskom Advertorial (2004) 'A Verdict for Nuclear Energy'. *Sunday Argus* 18 July.

Fig D (2005) *Uranium Road: Questioning South Africa's Nuclear Direction.* Johannesburg: Jacana and Heinrich Böll-Stiftung.

Gurzynski R (2010) The Cost of Nuclear Power in South Africa. A Critique of the EPRI Methodology for Comparing Different Energy Options. Unpublished paper.

Madzivire G (2013) Chemistry and speciation of potentially toxic and radioactive contaminants during mine water treatment. Unpublished PhD thesis, University of the Western Cape.

Mail & Guardian (2013) 'Zuma slips into nuclear driver's seat. Takes over chair of NNEECC'. 26 July-1 August.

McDonald D (2009) *Electric Capitalism: Recolonising Africa on the Power Grid.* Cape Town: HSRC Press.

Naidoo P (nd) Westcor. Key Success Factors, Challenges. Powerpoint slide show.

Noseweek (2013) issue 162, April:10-16.

Noseweek (2013) issue 161, March: 24-27.

Noseweek (2008) issue 105, July: 6.

Noseweek (2006) issue 98, October: 12.

Noseweek (2005) issue 66, April: 14-16.

Noseweek (2003) 'All in the bed together'. issue 50, October.

Olivier H (1976) *Great Dams in Southern Africa.* Cape Town: Purnell.

Scheffler TB (1995) Solar Energy in Southern Africa. South African Institute of Physics conference paper.

Sibuyi P (2013) Irradiation effects on non-structured silicon carbide. Unpublished PhD Thesis, University of the Western Cape.

Van Wyk J-A (2013) South Africa's Nuclear Future. Johannesburg: SA Institute of International Affairs. Occasional Paper 150.

Venables H (2013) 'Can we trust our nuclear watchdog?' *Noseweek* issue 161, March.

Westinghouse (2010) News releases. Westinghouse appoints Professor Itumeleng Mosala as regional vice president, South Africa.

Wild F (2013) 'Inga deal to catalyse electricity expansion. Bloomberg'. *Business Report* in *Cape Times* 12 March.

World Bank (2007) Press Release No:129/2007/INT.

www. bdelive.co.za 20 February 2012 wind, solar power plans being built.

http://www.energy.gov.za/files/policies/policy_nuclear_energy_2008.pdf [Viewed 9 January 2013]
http://www.engineeringnews.co.za/article/sa-drc-to-sign-new-grand-inga-agreement-2011-11-10
    (viewed 20 November 2013)
http://www.engineeringnews.co.za/article/sa-drc-plan-regional-bilaterals-in-wake-of-inga-
    treaty-2013-11-08 (viewed 20 November 2013).
http://En.wikipedia.org/wiki/Barbara_Hogan [Viewed 9 January 2013].
http://en.wikipedia.org/wiki/Concentrated_solar_power [Viewed 12 March 2013].
http://www.france-southafrica.com [Viewed 12 March 2013].
http://www. World-nuclear.org/info/inf88.html [Viewed 21 December 2012].

NOTES

1   Pik Botha, Penuel Maduna, Phumzile Mlambo-Ngcuka, Lindiwe Hendricks, Buyelwa Sonjica, Dipuo Peters, Ben Martins.

POWER, POLITICS AND PARTICIPATION

2

Power, politics and participation

Prishani Naidoo

———

The character of the struggle against apartheid was such that it produced (and was sustained by) a sense that every person could be a part of and could contribute to its shaping and success, and an imagination among ordinary people that their participation was not merely possible but even necessary in the making of a politics that placed power in their hands.

While the memory of leaders such as Biko, Mandela, Sobukwe and Tambo served to produce shared histories of (and inspiration for) struggle, it was in the everyday that the majority of South Africans felt apartheid and chose to fight against it. It was here that an imagination of the political developed (both at the level of the individual and the collective), an imagination that saw the active participation of ordinary people in decisions affecting their lives, both in the struggle against apartheid and for the time after its defeat.

In the first twenty years of electoral democracy in South Africa there have been several instances where elected leaders have pushed ahead with policies with which people have voiced their discontent. These past twenty years have also seen the greater institutionalisation of struggle, with party political formations, movements and organisations coming to dominate the political sphere, and policy formulation processes and negotiating forums determining the frame for participation. Nevertheless, when people have felt aggrieved (or felt the effects of policy changes) they have often come together in protest in the streets, re-asserting their power and refusing to have their voices excluded from political processes.

Although the recent death of Nelson Mandela has ignited a largely uncritical celebration of the idea and practice of reconciliation and the virtues of electoral democracy, the chapters in this section suggest that there is much in South Africa's history that reconciliation did not allow us properly to confront, much that continues to trouble those whose imagination of power, of politics and of their own participation in it was shaped in the years of the struggle against apartheid – years when Mandela and other leaders were distant figures whose remembered lives inspired extraordinary courage and resilience from ordinary people in their everyday lives.

This section presents a set of diverse experiences and thoughts that speak to some of the ways in which power, politics and participation are being reconceptualised and reconfigured in struggles of people that continue today in spite of the institutions and processes of representative democracy and in relation to some of the problems and challenges created by apartheid but left untouched by the project of reconciliation. Each chapter offers a different experience as well as different ways in which to begin rethinking power, politics and participation today.

Aninka Claassens and Boitumelo Matlala turn our attention to the important issues of land ownership and redistribution, customary law and the power of traditional leaders in a chapter on the experiences of the Bakgatla ba Kgafela, a group in the platinum belt of the North West province, where flare-ups of local anger are not uncommon from communities excluded from lucrative mining deals conducted on land they occupy and work. They explore the ways in which recently-enacted laws have been interpreted by the North West High Court in 'thwarting the repeated and desperate attempts of community leaders to try to preserve their mineral assets and land base, and to hold traditional leaders to account', arguing that these new laws undermine 'inherently participatory features of customary systems' while entrenching the position and status of chiefs from the apartheid era as well as the contested tribal boundaries set by apartheid legislation. The chapter argues that it is the interests of a rich elite that are served by this new framework, and it homes in on the forms of protest and resistance that have emerged in response.

John Clarke looks at the experiences of the coastal residents of the amaDiba clan of the Mpondo in resisting the attempts of authorities to award mineral rights to an Australian-based venture capital mining company to mine in their ancestral lands. Drawing on his own experiences as a social worker involved in his professional capacity with the amaDiba community and the Mpondo royal family between 2005 and 2012, Clarke puts forward the idea that 'civil courage' is required in politics today. He uses the struggles of the amaDiba to develop a definition of civil courage as a practice that goes beyond that of civil disobedience by mobilising aspects of the Constitution and strengthening social bonds within the community.

In a chapter entitled 'Secrecy and Power', Dale McKinley examines the ways in which state security and the perceived need for secrecy around certain state and party processes, practices and people have become avenues through which to protect the interests of particular political and economic elites and, in so doing, to undermine democracy. Going back in history, McKinley unearths and explores several similarities and continuities between the apartheid regime, the corporate sector and parts of the liberation movement – and the current ANC Alliance and government with regard to their 'need' for secrecy, hence their undermining of democratic practices. McKinley looks at past and present legislation (for example, the regulation of protest, the surveillance of ordinary people and organisations by the state, and limits to access to information). He looks at the authoritarian culture of the organisations making up the ANC Alliance; the militarisation of the police; and, most importantly, resistance to the various attempts by the state to prevent people from having access to information about themselves and processes and decisions affecting them.

Xolela Mangcu returns us to questions of racial oppression in a chapter that considers the relevance of black consciousness today. He argues that the ascension of black people into government and the enactment of laws against racism means that black consciousness holds the potential for significance today very differently from the ways in which it was important in the 1970s when black people were excluded from the official political system and treated as inferior beings. Mangcu brings together aspects of Steve Biko's writing with more contemporary scholars such as Kwame Anthony Appiah, offering ways of addressing persistent problems related to race today, problems that stem from the old but that persist in the new frameworks said to be consciously working towards redress.

Finally, Zethu Matebeni confronts problems of race, gender, sexuality and representation through the story of the black lesbian in South Africa, identified increasingly and overwhelmingly, she argues, with death. Matebeni argues that whereas many black lesbian activists enter into the realm of identity politics strategically, appropriating the identity of black lesbian as a means through which to politicise their experience (individual and collective), in the South African case the discourse of death has come to permeate the representational experience of black lesbians, foreclosing their identity and their ability to be political in ways chosen by themselves. In spite of this, Matebeni is hopeful, offering the recent experience of Johannesburg People's Pride as a sign that life (as opposed to death) is capable once again of becoming part of the representational matrix of identity politics in South Africa.

CHAPTER 6

Platinum, poverty and princes in post-apartheid South Africa:
New laws, old repertoires

Aninka Claassens and Boitumelo Matlala[1]

INTRODUCTION

The Natives Land Act of 1913 delineated separate territories for black and white owner-ship and occupation of land, setting aside 7 per cent of the land for the black majority – subsequently increased to 13 per cent by the 1936 Natives Trust and Land Act. After the National Party came to power in 1948 it used the rural reserves established by the Land Acts as the basis for establishing ten ethnically defined 'homelands' for speakers of different African languages. Some of the 'homelands', such as Bophuthatswana, discussed here, became 'independent states'. A feature of the anti-apartheid struggle of the 1980s was anti-Bantustan uprisings in 'homelands' such as Bophuthatswana, KwaNdebele, Lebowa and Ciskei. The Bantustans were re-incorporated into a unitary South Africa with the transition to democracy in 1994, and a system of elected local government was put in place throughout the country, replacing the system of chiefly rule over separate 'tribes' that had formed the bedrock of the Bantustan system. There has been concerted opposition, by lobbies representing traditional leaders, to their loss of power with the end of apartheid, and various laws bolstering the powers of traditional leaders have been enacted since 2003. Deposits of valuable minerals such as platinum, chrome, vana-dium, titanium and coal have been discovered in former Bantustan areas, leading to a mining boom in recent years. South Africa's platinum belt spans the former Bantustans of Bophuthatswana and Lebowa and accounts for almost eighty per cent of the world's platinum production. Some of the most platinum-rich land in the western part of the bushveld was bought by groups of African purchasers either before the 1913 and 1936 Land Acts or through exemptions from them. These groups were subsumed within state-delineated 'tribes' during apartheid.

There are regular explosions of anger and frustration by local people in the platinum belt who are excluded from, and unable to get information about, the lucrative mining deals taking place on their mineral-rich land. These conditions gained national attention in 2012 with the massacre of thirty-four striking mineworkers at Marikana. Rural people living in former Bantustan areas continue to live in grinding poverty despite the valuable minerals in the land they have owned and occupied for generations. Instead, they read in the newspapers about mining companies and politically connected elites – in particular traditional leaders – flaunting vast amounts of money in opaque deals involving their land and mineral resources.[2]

This chapter focuses on the role and use of recently-enacted laws as they have been interpreted by the North West High Court in thwarting the repeated and desperate attempts of community leaders to try to preserve their mineral assets and land base, and to hold traditional leaders and government to account. It discusses the scale of the resources at stake, and unfolding events in one such group in the platinum belt, the Bakgatla ba Kgafela. The Bakgatla are by no means unique in relation to the scale of the billions of rands involved, or in relation to the web of laws and judgments that are repeatedly used to interdict community members from meeting or deny them information about the mineral deals concluded over land. Many other communities in the North West face similar problems (Manson 2013).

Key to the current conflicts is an interpretation of customary law that holds that only officially recognised traditional leaders have authority and *locus standi* in issues pertaining to land and mineral rights. Traditional leaders argue, and courts uphold, that only they, and officially constituted and recognised 'traditional councils', have the right to call meetings, to access information and to represent people living within the tribal jurisdictions delineated during apartheid. On this basis interdicts are routinely granted to stop community meetings that seek to get to the bottom of, and discuss remedies for, abuse of power. Concerned citizens seeking to crack open the opaque web of laws, regulations and multibillion mining deals are shut out and shut down, in some instances with punitive costs orders awarded against them for their troubles.

The irony is that this authoritarian and hierarchical approach to customary law is fundamentally at odds with a rich anthropological literature on the participatory and democratic (albeit only for men) aspects of Tswana law and process (Schapera 1994; Comaroff and Roberts 1981; Molema 1920). That literature stresses the multilayered levels of authority and decision making within Tswana society, extending upwards from the household, through the extended family, the clan and the village to the wider polity (Okoth-Ogendo 2008; Schapera 1938). Power is mediated by the existence of competing locuses of authority that exist in a state of constant tension (Delius 2008). The coexistence of these multiple and interlocking layers of consultation and decision making ensures a level of accountability that is fundamentally distorted and undermined when power is vested exclusively in a chief at the apex of the 'tribe',[3] especially where superimposed apartheid-created tribal boundaries remain deeply contested.

We argue that inherently participatory features of customary systems are undercut and undermined by new laws such as the Traditional Leadership and Governance Framework Act 41 of 2003 (Framework Act) and its provincial counterpart the North West Traditional Leadership and Governance Act 2 of 2005 (North West Act). These laws entrench the contested tribal boundaries inherited from the Bantu Authorities Act of 1951, and set in stone the official status of apartheid-era chiefs. Other legislation such as the Communal Land Rights Act of 2004 (CLRA)[4] and the Traditional Courts Bill of 2012 (TCB) then centralises power to 'senior traditional leaders' within these ascribed tribal boundaries.

A series of judgments involving the Bakgatla and the Bapo ba Mogale in the North West High Court suggest that the formal similarity between the new traditional leadership laws and their Bantustan predecessors is only part of the story. Of equal significance has been the jurisprudence of the North West High Court in relation to the interpretation of customary law. The legal conundrums confronting rural communities living on mining land are not restricted to problematic interpretations of customary law. Another fundamental problem is the lack of articulation between the opaque legal basis on which chiefs are made partners in mineral deals, and oversight mechanisms that would enable communities to hold them to account. Two bodies of law interact in creating this disjuncture. The first are the new traditional leadership laws, the second is the Mineral and Petroleum Resources Development Act 28 of 2002 (MPRDA), which was brought into operation in 2004, and the procedures used to issue 'new order' mining rights and identify black economic empowerment (BEE) partners.

Pre-existing problems of accountability are exacerbated by the changed nature of mining rights and complex financial deals introduced in terms of the MPRDA. Whereas previously the mineral rights vested in the owner of the land and mining companies paid royalties to the president of Bophuthatswana 'on behalf of' communities who held mineral rights, the MPRDA vests mineral rights in the state, and on that basis issues mining rights to companies provided they have BEE partners – and BEE shares seem to have replaced royalties as the mechanism for compensating communities with vested rights in the land.

This chapter begins by setting out the background of the new traditional leadership laws and how the MPRDA works in tandem with them to undermine accountability and the indigenous entitlements of ordinary people, and then moves to a discussion of the major disputes over mining revenue and traditional leadership among the Bakgatla and examines a series of judgments and interdicts that rely on and reinforce the 'official status' of *kgosi* Nyalala Pilane while insulating him from financial oversight. We discuss the differences and similarities between the application of the law in the Bakgatla and Bapo contexts and the jurisprudence of the North West high court in relation to the arbitrary powers of definition and appointment attributed to a 'paramount chief' of the Bakgatla in Botswana. Finally, we argue that the new traditional leadership legislation exacerbates pre-existing conflicts by creating a winner-takes-all situation which pre-empts the potential inherent in customary repertoires that accommodate layered and coexisting rights.

Our focus is on the laws and institutional arrangements that have elicited and condoned the levels of corruption and exclusion we describe, and on the use of distorted constructs of custom to impose contested identities on rural people, thereby undermining their capacity to protect their land and associated mineral rights.

BACKGROUND — NEW LAWS ENTRENCHING PAST DISTORTIONS

Various rural groupings and community-based organisations in the North West have rejected the new traditional leadership laws as re-entrenching the Bantustan legacy of distorted and autocratic custom which, they argue, was 'defeated' with the transition to democracy and the re-unification of South Africa in 1994. This is set out in numerous submissions to Parliament opposing the Framework Act, the CLRA, the TCB, and in relation to the repeal of the Bantu Authorities Act in 2010.[5] Indeed, one of the four applicant communities in the *Tongoane* case of 2010 that challenged the constitutionality of the CLRA in the Constitutional Court was from Makgobistad in North West.

The degree of popular opposition to the new laws came to a head in May 2012 during provincial public hearings about the TCB. The overwhelming majority of those who attended the four hearings held in North West vehemently opposed the TCB and related laws such as the Framework Act and the North West Act. In Potchefstroom the provincial legislature tried to close the hearing because of vociferous opposition to the Bill, but those attending prevailed on the officials present to hear them out. They argued that vesting more powers in traditional leaders would exacerbate a range of serious pre-existing boundary disputes and bolster abuse of power in many instances. Communities in the North West platinum belt raised a host of problems concerning the unilateral actions of traditional leaders in relation to mining deals on 'communal' land that had been purchased by black syndicates, as well as in respect of other land to which subgroups and families have specific customary entitlements. Ultimately, the North West legislature voted against the TCB. Their provincial mandate to the National Council of Provinces stated:

> The communities maintained that ... power is centralised to a senior traditional leader; hence living customary law is distorted. The bill is therefore arguably unconstitutional and unacceptable (North West Provincial Legislature 2013).

Opposition to the new laws does not, however, imply that people reject custom per se. On the contrary, claims to underlying historical and customary entitlements, including substantive rights to the land and procedural decision-making powers, are at the root of objections to the high-handed and unilateral approach of traditional leaders such as Nyalala Pilane. People assert that customarily they are entitled to a share of the mining proceeds, and that their consent is required before changes can be made to the land they occupy and use. The Constitutional Court has asserted the validity of customary entitlements to land and minerals rights in the *Alexkor* case of 2003, which dealt with the ownership status of both land and mineral rights in the Richtersveld. The Court rejected the 'official customary law' found in statutes emanating from our discriminatory past in favour of an inclusive construct of 'living customary law' that embodies actual practice and develops as communities 'change their patterns of life' (*Alexkor v Richtersveld* 2003, para 52; *Bhe v Magistrate* 2004; *Shilubana v Nwamitwa* 2008; *Pilane v Pilane* 2013).

In the North West platinum belt there is an additional and fundamental complication. Much of the land on which the platinum mines exist is not 'ordinary' communal land; it was purchased by groups of black people who constituted themselves in various ways but who were not allowed to hold the title directly because of racially discriminatory laws. The background is that very little of the seven per cent of the land that the Natives Land Act of 1913 set aside for black occupation and use was in the Transvaal (Delius and Beinart 2013) and thus many exemptions from the Act were granted in that province to African people seeking to buy land (Feinberg 1997; Claassens and Gilfillan 2008). In some cases, groups of African purchasers clubbed together as syndicates; in others clan members would each contribute an agreed number of cattle to raise the purchase price for a particular farm that was then exclusively occupied or used by that particular clan.

Historians (Feinberg 1997; Harries 1989) describe how government officials generally required groups of buyers of more than six people, regardless of their ethnic origins, to constitute themselves as 'tribes' in order to get approval to buy land. The 'six-native rule' was enforced for many years before its ultimate enactment in 1936, when section 11(2) of the Native Trust and Land Act provided that: 'No association, syndicate, partnership, aggregation or number of persons which includes more than six natives other than a recognised tribe, shall acquire land or hold land … save with the permission of the governor general.'

The rule forced groups of land buyers to associate themselves with 'recognised' tribes in order to buy land. Thus in the case of the Bafokeng some of the descendants of the original purchasers argue that they bought specific platinum-rich farms independently, and that this was recorded by missionaries who helped negotiate the transactions, and also understood by the 'officially recognised tribes' with whom they were forced to affiliate in order to be able to purchase land (Capps 2010; Manson 2013).

The already serious impact of the imposition of tribal ownership over sub-groupings with other identities was severely exacerbated by the implementation of the Bantu Authorities Act of 1951. The Act empowered the governor general to establish Bantu Authorities and to delineate the jurisdictional boundaries of the 'tribes' they would govern. Those who opposed the Act and the Bantustan agenda it embodied were relegated to small areas, and those who acquiesced were rewarded with large areas and elevated over their recalcitrant fellow chiefs (Delius 2008; Claassens 2001; Mbeki 1984). In the process, clans of roughly equal status were rearranged in new hierarchies that made some subservient to newly-elevated chiefs who now reigned over consolidated 'tribes' (Claassens and Hathorn 2008). This is the history described by Mmuthi Pilane, who argues that the clans who purchased much of the land now controlled by the Bakgatla 'tribe' were of equal status until one clan was elevated over the others from the 1950s (Pilane 2013).

The platinum belt is therefore beset by particularly intractable boundary disputes that pertain not only to the superimposition of apartheid-derived tribal boundaries, but also to the underlying ownership of much of the land. This powder keg of unresolved disputes has been ignited by the discovery of valuable platinum on the land in question. Instead of addressing this underlying complexity, the Framework Act and its provincial counterpart have exacerbated it. They entrench historically distorted tribal boundaries and hierarchies of authority – thereby eliciting and exacerbating winner-takes-all conflicts in relation to both land ownership and chieftainship disputes.

Nuanced approaches that seek to 'unpack' the superimposed constructs of 'tribe' and 'ownership' that obscure the history of vested rights in the land and the identities of current claimants are thus pre-empted by the new traditional leadership laws. The North West Act, for example, shares much of the same wording as the Bophuthatswana Traditional Authorities Act 23 of 1978 that it replaced. This preserves key features of the deeply centralised and discriminatory mining regime that subsidised the Bophuthatswana Bantustan at the expense of rural rights' holders.

The manifest institutional continuities between the Bophuthatswana regime and current-day control of mining revenue have not been offset by the promised 'transformational' component of the new traditional leadership laws – that 40 per cent of the members of traditional councils must be elected, and 30 per cent must be women. In addition, a commission on traditional leadership disputes and claims was set up in terms of the Framework Act to investigate and resolve chieftainship claims and boundary disputes arising from colonial and apartheid distortions. Ten years later both initiatives have failed. The Commission's findings have been challenged in courts throughout South Africa, and in the first such case to reach the Constitutional Court, the Court recently found it had adopted a flawed procedure in the *Sigcau* case. The proposed elections for traditional councils have not yet taken place in some provinces and where they have, they have been found to be fundamentally flawed (O'Donovan and Redpath, unpublished). The consequence, as elaborated in various judgments, is that none of the traditional councils in North West is validly constituted. The fact that traditional councils have no legal status has not, however, deterred judges in North West from interdicting meetings and rejecting requests for information, on the basis that 'others' should not purport to have legal authority.

A key feature of the Bophuthatswana regime was that mining revenue was deposited into 'D accounts'[6] under the control of President Mangope, rather than distributed to the people whose land was mined. The North West Act preserves these state-controlled D accounts for mining revenue under the supervision of the premier and they have been the subject of sustained interrogation and agitation by communities living on mining land for many years. There has been a renewed focus on them since the Marikana massacre in

August 2012 and in the light of complaints by the Bapo ba Mogale on whose land Lonmin is mining (Swart 2012; Manson 2013). It has emerged that mining revenue continues to be deposited into D accounts and that these D accounts have not been audited since the 1994 transition despite the vast amounts of money they hold 'on behalf of' traditional communities.[7] 'The approximate amount paid in royalties to the Bapo up to 2011 totalled R500 million, and [Lonmin] currently pays the Bapo R40 million per annum held in trust for them by the North West provincial government' (Manson 2013: 419). An investigation by the public protector began in the first quarter of 2013, paralleled by public hearings convened by the Standing Committee on Provincial Public Accounts during September and October and investigations by the North West premier's office. In late 2013 the various investigations were still underway.

In addition, the changed mineral rights regime introduced by the MPRDA raises a series of questions concerning the basis on which mining companies are transacting with traditional leaders – whether as 'custodians' of communal land or as BEE partners. Many suspect that community assets have been traded for BEE shares that vest in individuals and are not subject to community oversight (Hill 2006). In that situation there is little if any legal mechanism for the community to hold traditional leaders to account in relation to profits derived from the land.

It is common knowledge that mining houses transact with traditional leaders precisely because the reality of long-term communal ownership of much platinum land is plain to see, and the vested interests of the long term occupiers and users of the land cannot be denied. Yet the terms of post-1994 law do not provide the occupants of the land with tenure security or the ability to hold either the mines, or traditional leaders, to account. This is partly the fault of the centralised and unaccountable powers contained in the new traditional leadership laws, as has been described. But the MPRDA also carries a large share of the blame because its provision that holders of pre-existing 'old order' mineral rights must be allowed the opportunity to convert them into 'new order' mining rights did not apply equally to black owners whose rights had been undermined by discriminatory laws.[8] The conversion window was in recognition that pre-existing vested property rights were being removed. If it had not created a conversion mechanism, the Act would arguably have been invalid as an impermissible deprivation of property rights protected by section 25 of the Constitution. The timing of the conversion process meant, however, that the people who benefited from this protection were overwhelmingly white, and black owners were once again discriminated against because the majority of black owners had been prohibited by law from holding registered title to land or mineral rights, and so did not qualify to take advantage of the conversion window. When black owners obtain restitution of land that had the mineral rights intact when they were forcibly removed, it will be restored to them without the mineral rights, because in the interim the MPRDA has vested control over their mineral rights in the state.

Similarly, in tenure upgrades to give effect to underlying historical ownership, title will be awarded without the mineral rights that people enjoyed historically. The MPRDA, in failing to address and remedy the inherently unequal status of black and white mineral rights, cements past racial inequality. At the same time, however, it has been implemented in a way that cuts traditional leaders and the well-connected black elite into lucrative BEE deals, so pre-empting opposition from those quarters.

The complex entitlements to land in the North West embedded in the history of African land ownership in the area and Tswana customary law highlight the limiting nature of recent legislation on traditional leadership, land and mineral rights.

WEALTH AND POVERTY IN MORULENG

At one level the unfolding events among Bakgatla tell a familiar story of corruption and abuse of power exposed when the major players fall out with one another – but that story is on a grand scale because of the mining assets and billions of rands involved, in the context of extreme poverty and ongoing dispossession.

At another level the underlying story demonstrates how post-apartheid laws and institutional arrangements have built on Bantustan precedents to elicit, bolster and protect this scale of unilateral and unaccountable power in relation to land and minerals in the former Bantustans. Those who benefit at the expense of rural people include traditional leaders, government, the politically connected elite granted 'new order' mining rights and, in particular, the mining houses that play along.

Chiefly disputes: *kgosi* Pilane and *kgosikgolo* Kgafela

The details and scale of the problem have been blown into the open by a dramatic falling-out between two previously staunch allies, *kgosi* Nyalala Pilane, the officially appointed[9] chief of the Bakgatla ba Kgafela 'tribe' in South Africa, and 'paramount chief' or *kgosikgolo* Kgafela Kgafela, the deposed chief of Bakgatla ba Kgafela in Mochudi Botswana. Until very recently, Nyalala Pilane provided extensive financial support to Kgafela on the basis that the latter was paramount over all Bakgatla ba Kgafela, including those in South Africa. Bank statements of Bakgatla in Mochudi show that millions of rands were deposited into the Mochudi trust account at least quarterly after a resolution by the Bakgatla ba Kgafela Tribal Authority in Moruleng to contribute R5 million quarterly to the tribal office in Mochudi (Ntibinyane 2013).

The South African Bakgatla ba Kgafela number an estimated 350 000 people with their headquarters in Moruleng, also known as Saulspoort. In addition to vast platinum reserves they have a lucrative share in the Pilanesberg game reserve. The tribe is estimated to be worth R15 billion (Khanyile 2012). In June 2008, Nyalala Pilane was found guilty of fraud and corruption at Mogwase Regional Court, but this sentence was overturned on appeal in September 2010 in the Mafikeng High Court. However, complaints about Nyalala Pilane's unilateral and opaque financial dealings have only escalated since then (Molopyane 2012). A community member described this frustration, saying: 'We get to hear in the media about all the multimillion rand deals while our children remain unemployed and communities live in poverty' (Tau 2012).

People have demanded explanations of the announcement of a R3,2 billion Industrial Development Corporation (IDC) investment in Platmin, a mining company of which Nyalala Pilane is a director. It is reported that this is the biggest single IDC investment in five years (Cramer 2012). There are recurrent demands for access to the tribal books of account (Maleke 2012), previous and current premiers have been petitioned to depose Nyalala as chief (Dibakwane 2008), and the royal family has applied for court orders that the tribal accounts be audited – but all this to no avail. Instead, Nyalala has successfully obtained several court interdicts to stop community members from being allowed to meet, including six interdicts against meetings of the 'royal family'. In June 2012, community frustration exploded into violent conflict during which vehicles were burned and schools closed. This took place after the tribal administration failed to respond to a memorandum handed to them during a march in May; the memorandum called for a change in leadership, the election of a representative tribal council and for the state to intervene because of fears of large-scale corruption taking place in the tribal administration (Molopyane 2012). The community reiterated these claims during the June protest action (Tau 2012).

Kgosikgolo Kgafela Kgafela had also been having a torrid time in Botswana. He was charged with organising age regiments to 're-instill' traditional discipline by indiscriminately flogging villagers, and a warrant for his arrest was issued in Botswana (Ntibinyane 2013). In October 2011 he had been stripped of his official chieftainship status for undermining government development efforts and inciting *dikgosana* (headmen) to undermine government ministers (Selebi 2011). He characterised the prosecution as 'constitutional tyranny' and applied to court to have the Botswana Constitution set aside. His application failed. After the warrant for his arrest was issued in Botswana, Kgafela relocated to Moruleng in South Africa during 2012. He convinced Nyalala Pilane to abdicate as chief in August 2012 and turn over the chieftainship (and with it the platinum wealth) to a representative appointed by him (Selebi 2012). However, Nyalala subsequently withdrew his abdication, heightening conflict between the two formerly staunch allies. In retaliation, Kgafela released an internal audit report that details the scale of unauthorised, reckless and extravagant spending under Nyalala's watch. The report revealed a lack of accounting systems resulting in multimillion rand contracts with nonexistent service providers, and payments for services not rendered. Some employees were routinely paid double salaries. Substantial amounts of money were spent on extravagant overseas trips for the *kgosi* and his close associates.

The audit also found that only between one and five percent of the Bakgatla ba Kgafela Traditional Authority's (BBKTA) expenditure was spent on 'community upliftment' projects. Instead, large amounts of money appear to have been spent on dysfunctional investment companies. Farms belonging to the community, worth no less than R20 million, were placed under the care of Nyalala Pilane's co-accused in the fraud case, and basically ransacked. Fixtures in the farmhouses were either removed or damaged beyond repair. The audit investigators were told that, at night, cattle were captured, slaughtered and sold to a local butchery and that hunters with permits to hunt one eland would shoot four and pay the manager of the farms a bribe in lieu of the difference. Moreover, income from the farming business of the Bakgatla was not declared to the South African Revenue Services.

The audit was unable to ascertain the number and extent of several investments belonging to the tribe. In particular, mining revenue was unaccounted for. The audit annexes a letter by the auditor general revealing that the tribe's books had not been audited since 2005.

Kgafela points out that key assets belonging to the tribe are registered as Nyalala's personal property. Embarrassingly for Kgafela, the audit report also details the many millions that were channelled to his office in Botswana, and that the Bakgatla in South Africa financed his legal battles there. The Botswana papers also reveal commissioned architectural plans to construct a R28 million palace for Kgafela in Botswana (Ntibinyane 2013). Nyalala's financial support for Kgafela in Botswana has been a source of deep unhappiness among South Africans living on the platinum-rich farms (Letswamotse 2012). Kgafela made an affidavit to the Hawks detailing allegations of corruption against Nyalala in October 2012, also launching legal proceedings against the premier of the North West in December 2012 and demanding that she depose Nyalala Pilane in compliance with the Framework Act and the North West Act.

However, the North West Department of Cooperative Governance and Traditional Affairs reiterated on August 2012 that Nyalala remains the officially recognised traditional leader of the Bakgatla ba Kgafela in South Africa (Molopyane 2012). Spokespeople for the Department of Traditional Affairs have also said the accusations of financial mismanagement against Nyalala Pilane are not the concern of the provincial government, as the funds in question are not under their control. The premier's office has also distanced itself from the current turmoil, stating that it is not the role of the Department to intervene in issues of *bogosi* [chieftainship] (Molopyane 2012).

Resistance to the opaque financial dealings and high-handed actions of Nyalala Pilane has come from a range of different groupings within Bakgatla ba Kgafela society and include community activists such as Victor Modimokwane who is mentioned repeatedly in press reports; members of the Pilane royal family; and groups of concerned citizens in the thirty-two villages that make up the Bakgatla 'traditional community'. The names of a wide range of people appear in the various court applications that have been brought over the years to try and obtain financial information and hold Nyalala Pilane to account.

RESISTANCE TO CHIEFLY ABUSE OF POWER: MOTLHABE VILLAGE

Motlhabe is by no means unique among the other villages. Its significance lies mainly in the fact that it was the subject of a Constitutional Court judgment in February 2013. The background facts are that after numerous failed attempts to protect their local assets and to hold Nyalala Pilane to account, the leaders of the Bakgatla ba Kautlwale clan decided they had no option but to secede from the Bakgatla ba Kgafela tribe. They argued that historically the various clans that make up the Bakgatla ba Kgafela had enjoyed equal status, and were only consolidated into 'one tribe' in 1950 as the outcome of cooperation between *kgosi* Tidimane Pilane and officials of the Department of Bantu Affairs. The Kautlwale clan has exclusive use of three farms, two of which they bought historically and one of which they have occupied since time immemorial. The valuable Pilanesberg Platinum Mine falls on their land.

In 2010, Nyalala Pilane interdicted the leaders of the clan from going ahead with a meeting with neighbouring groups to discuss their secession plans. Justice Landman upheld the interdicts in a judgment of the North West High Court, awarding costs against the two applicants, Mmuthi Pilane and Ramoshibidu Dintwe.

The majority of the Constitutional Court disagreed. They upheld an appeal against the interdicts and set them aside in February 2013. The Court held that the interdicts infringed basic rights to freedom of expression, assembly and association, as well as the constitutional principle of accountability. The majority judgment by Justice Skweyiya also took notice that 'numerous matters of a similar nature involving the respondents [*kgosi* Nyalala Pilane and the traditional council] have appeared before the courts'. In that context the Court said that deciding the appeal would 'provide clarity on the rights of people living in the traditional community, and in traditional communities more generally'.

The Constitutional Court held that 'statutory authority accorded to traditional leadership does not necessarily preclude or restrict the operation of customary leadership that has not been recognised by legislation'. It reiterated that 'the true nature of customary law is a living body of law, active and dynamic, with an inherent capacity to evolve in keeping with the changing lives of the people it governs'. Ultimately, the judgment stated that 'there is an inherent value in allowing dissenting voices to be heard and, in doing so, permitting robust discussion which strengthens our democracy and its institutions.'

Two judges dissented from the majority judgment: Chief Justice Mogoeng Mogoeng and Judge Bess Nkabinde, both of them hailing from North West. Of the three interdicts upheld by Judge Landman they argued that only two should have been overturned. Their minority judgments starts with the sentence: 'This application has a long and toxic history.' It goes on to say that: 'Traditional leadership is a unique and fragile institution. If it is to be preserved it should be approached with the necessary understanding and sensitivity.' The two judges conclude that setting aside the first interdict will 'provide an avenue for undermining legitimate traditional structures, leadership and governance and the erosion of the rule of law'.

NORTH WEST JUDGMENTS, TRADITIONAL AUTHORITY AND MINING REVENUE

The interpretation of customary law developed by the North West High Court appears to have followed a distinctive and specific trajectory, indicating jurisprudential continuities between the Bophuthatswana era, current interpretations of customary law and the new traditional leadership laws. In that light, certain recent judgments of the North West

High Court have bearing on disputed custom and mining rights. These judgments have been pivotal in buttressing Nyalala Pilane's contested authority in the face of numerous challenges from the Bakgatla royal family and community members. The audit report reveals that 'the tribe' paid one attorney R49 million over a three-year (2009-2011) period, providing some evidence of the scale of the litigation. It is a bitter pill for community activists to swallow that the money used in litigation to shut them down is the very money generated by their mineral resources.

We begin by examining recent judgments interpreting the content of customary law, in particular the pre-eminent and arbitrary powers attributed to the Botswana paramount Kgafela Kgafela over Bakgatla in South Africa, and the implications this has had in relation to the royal family's attempts to hold Nyalala Pilane to account. This is a topical issue, as Kgafela relies on that version of custom in his ongoing dispute with Nyalala.

A theme running through this chapter is the importance attributed to the 'official status' of traditional leaders and traditional councils. The same law that provides for official recognition includes financial controls and checks and balances on the exercise of power. This was previously the Bophuthatswana Traditional Authorities Act 23 of 1978, and is currently the North West Traditional leadership and Governance Act of 2005. While the judgments reiterate the importance of the official status of Nyalala Pilane, the checks and balances contained in the law do not receive equal attention. Time and again the complaints of community members, and their attempts to enforce the protective provisions of the law, are dismissed on the basis of flawed *locus standi*.

Given the focus on statutorily inscribed official status, it is ironic that various judgments[10] of the North West High Court also point out fundamental flaws arising at the intersection between the 'transitional' mechanisms contained in the national Framework Act and the provincial North West Act. These range from the fact that proper elections have not been held and the women's quota has not been met, to issues pertaining to inconsistent provincial and national competencies. The outcome is that 'prior' tribal authorities have not been properly converted to validly constituted 'traditional councils'. The implications of this lack of official status have, however, been uneven. In the Bakgatla case the *locus standi* of the tribal authority has been upheld, with the result that it has been enabled (for example) to prevent members of the community from holding meetings; while in the Bapo case the tribal authority has been found to have no *locus standi*, with the perverse result that it was thereby prevented from disciplining a provincially appointed administrator accused of mismanaging the community's mining revenue.

The interpretation of customary law and the Botswana paramountcy

The pre-eminence of the Botswana paramountcy has been asserted time and again by Nyalala Pilane, starting with the litigation that upheld his disputed appointment as chief in 1994. In that case, the son of the previous chief at Moruleng, Tidimane Pilane, challenged Nyalala Pilane's appointment as chief. Nyalala relied heavily on the fact that *kgosi* Linchwe II of Botswana, Kgafela Kgafela's father and the previous 'paramount', supported his appointment. He argued that this support was pivotal because the Bakgatla tribe spans national boundaries, with the South African section subservient to the Botswana paramount. Nyalala Pilane's argument is now being used against him, as it forms the basis of Kgafela Kgafela's application to have him deposed and replaced. Be that as it may, it stood him in good stead in previous litigation, and for the many years that the Moruleng Bakgatla were on good terms with, and subsidised, the Bakgatla in Mochudi, Botswana.

The effect of the pre-eminence accorded to the Botswana paramount is illustrated by the 2011 judgment in a case between Nyalala Pilane and members of the Bakgatla royal family. The case was about the confirmation of an interim interdict granted on 2 April stopping a proposed meeting of the royal family. Mpule David Pheto and others had advertised the meeting in the *Sowetan* newspaper. The proposed agenda included matters such as the duties, functions and constitution of the traditional authority, and the implications for decision-making processes. The judgment also dealt with a counter application by Pheto, Segale Pilane, Oupa Pilane and Tiny Motshegwa that Nyalala Pilane and the Traditional Council be ordered to submit their financial books and statements to the North West Province and auditor general. They also requested the premier to appoint a commission of enquiry to ascertain whether Nyalala Pilane and the Traditional Council were guilty of fraud, gross irregularity or maladministration of the affairs of the tribe.

In his judgment on 30 September 2011, Judge Hendricks confirmed the interdict, dismissed the counter application, and awarded a punitive costs order against Pheto and his co-respondents. In justifying this outcome he found that Pheto and his co-respondents had no *locus standi* to call a meeting of the royal family, as they 'are not members of the inner circle or core of the royal family of the Bakgatla and also not royalty'. Judge Hendricks upheld the interpretation put forward by Nyalala Pilane that membership of the royal family and inner circle depends on the *kgosikgolo's* (paramount's) preferences, which may change over time. 'In other words, participation in the inner circle or core is at the discretion of the *Kgosikgolo* over and above an "entitlement" arising out of proximity to the royal family.'

Judge Hendricks found that Nyalala Pilane, being 'the nominated representative of the *kgosikgolo* in South Africa, has the necessary standing and clear right as a member of the royal family, as defined in terms of Bakgatla custom and law, to bring this application.' This is a disconcerting and novel interpretation of customary law – that membership of a royal family, and chiefly status depends on the discretion of a 'paramount' based in another country. During arguments in the Constitutional Court hearing of the recent Sigcau case, the justices reiterated that membership of a royal family is a self-evident customary law 'fact' – known and widely understood within customary communities.

Judge Hendricks's interpretation has far-reaching consequences for the concept and exercise of chiefly accountability. In effect it means that a traditional leader such as Nyalala Pilane cannot be held accountable by anyone in the customary community, including his royal family, apart from a more senior traditional leader. This flies in the face of a wide-ranging historical and anthropological literature about the role of councils and interlocking customary structures at various levels in mediating and shaping the exercise of chiefly power (Delius 2008; Schapera 1938)

It also introduces a new and entirely arbitrary element into the interpretation of age-old lineages and well-known family histories. The implications of that arbitrariness have been neatly illustrated by subsequent events. Having previously sworn in two affidavits that Pheto was merely the illegitimate son of an outsider and certainly not a member of the royal family, Kgafela Kgafela changed his mind in December 2012. In his pending application against the premier to depose Nyalala Pilane, he now proposes that the person to replace him as senior traditional leader of the Bakgatla in South Africa should be none other than the same Mpule David Pheto. His affidavit says that the royal family (being Kgafela and his uncles) designated Pheto to replace Nyalala Pilane on the basis of his being 'the rightful incumbent and/or successor to *bogosi* of the Bakgatla'.

Interpretations of the financial oversight provisions in traditional leadership laws

We turn now from the consideration of judgments dealing with the content of customary law per se, to look at judgments dealing with the interpretation of national and provincial legislation such as the Framework Act and the North West Act. The continuities between the North West Act and its predecessor, the Bophuthatswana Act, have already been remarked upon. Section 11 of the Bophuthatswana Act is almost identical to Section 30 of the North West Act, dealing with the accounts of tribal authorities and traditional councils respectively.

Section 11 of the Bophuthatswana Act was pivotal to Nyalala Pilane's conviction for theft and fraud in 2008 and also to that conviction being set aside on appeal in September 2010 by Judges Hendricks and Kgoele. In overturning the conviction, Judge Hendricks states: 'The state premised the prosecution of all counts on the monies involved being dealt with strictly in accordance with the dictates of section 11 of the Bophuthatswana Act, 1978,[11] as a matter of legal obligation.'

Section 11 of the Bophuthatswana Act, entitled 'Tribal Authority Account' reads as follows:

> 11. (1) The president shall cause to be opened in the office of every magistrate, in respect of each tribal authority an account into which shall be paid such amounts as are hereinafter specified and from which all expenditure incurred in connection with any matter within the power of the tribal authority concerned shall be met: Provided that the president may on such conditions as he may deem fit and subject to any regulations, transfer any such account or any portion thereof to the tribal authority concerned.
>
> (2) There shall be paid into the account of the tribal authority --
>
> (a) all fees and charges which according to the laws and custom of the tribe are payable to the tribal authority;
>
> (b) all amounts from any property of the tribal authority;
>
> (c) any donation made by any person for the benefit of the tribal authority;
>
> (d)[12] *all other amounts derived from any source whatsoever* [our emphasis] for the benefit of the tribal authority including any amounts payable to the tribal authority which the National Assembly may grant for the purpose.

Section 12 then deals with the auditing of tribal accounts by the auditor general. The judgment states: 'In my view, it is not necessary that a trust of a company conduct business in accordance with section 11 when the monies in question are not provided by the state but involve a commercial concern.' The judgment does not include an explanation of the reasoning that motivated the judge's interpretation of section 11(2)(d). That section, on the face of it, is all-encompassing. It applies to 'all other amounts derived from any source whatsoever' and includes money from the state only as a sub-category. Under the circumstances, the conclusion that the section applies only to monies provided by the state is mystifying.

This judicial interpretation of section 11 has had very far-reaching repercussions. It was pivotal to the setting aside of the fraud and theft convictions of Nyalala Pilane and Koos Motshegoe, and has been relied on by the Department of Cooperative Governance and Traditional Affairs (COGTA) in the North West, in justifying its hands-off approach in relation to subsequent and repeated complaints of financial mismanagement against Nyalala Pilane. The BDO Spencer audit report is testimony to the serious financial consequences for the community, including unaudited books of account since at least 2008.

Most striking is the consequence that Nyalala Pilane and the Bakgatla ba Kgafela Traditional Council are effectively insulated from the financial oversight provisions of the very laws that provide them with statutory authority and official status. The essence of Nyalala's position has been his assertion that his 'official status' provides him with the exclusive right to represent and administer the affairs of the Bakgatla, and that anyone who seeks to challenge or interfere with his actions attempts to usurp and undermine his officially conferred authority. This approach underlies the string of interdicts against community meetings and the recurrent focus on *locus standi* as opposed to the material facts and actions in dispute.

Official status and the North West Act

Given the far-reaching powers exercised by traditional leaders and traditional councils in respect of mining deals, and the recurrent focus on official status and *locus standi* in litigation, it is no wonder that local applicants have repeatedly pointed out that existing traditional councils have not been properly constituted in terms of the North West Act.

Judge Hendricks has twice found that the provisions of the North West Act have not been complied with in respect of the Bakgatla Ba Kgafela. The first time was in a case between Bito Victor Modimokwana and the Bakgatla ba Kgafela Traditional Council, decided in April 2011. Judge Hendricks accepted that the term of office of the Traditional Council had expired, but nevertheless dismissed Modimokwana's application 'on the basis that there can never be a lacuna in that no traditional council exists to run the affairs of the traditional community'.

The second time was in response to the counter application by Pheto and others. Again, he found that the Traditional Council was not properly constituted. He attributed the problem to the province's failure to take the necessary steps to reconstitute all traditional councils. On the basis that 'law abhors a vacuum', Judge Hendricks ruled that the Traditional Council did indeed have *locus standi* to obtain an interdict against Pheto, notwithstanding the expiry of its term of office. His judgment was handed down on 30 September 2011.

Judge Landman, of the previously discussed interdicts against Mmuthi Pilane and Ramoshibidu Dintwe, had similarly found that traditional councils in North West are not properly constituted in a prior case involving the Bapo. Given this prior finding, it is strange that the basis of the subsequent 2011 *Pilane v Pilane* judgment is about protecting officially recognised structures from those who only purport to have official status.

On 11 April 2011, the Department of Local Government and Traditional Affairs in North West issued a circular to all traditional councils stating that the term of office of traditional councils had expired. It warned of the danger that contracts/deals contracted by traditional councils after 24 September 2010 may be invalid, '… the basis therefore being that such traditional councils lacked legal standing at the time such contracts/deals were concluded'.[13] On 5 July, the same department announced the postponement of the scheduled 2013 traditional council elections. This followed an agreement between the department and the Independent Electoral Commission to postpone the elections indefinitely in light of several challenges with lack of participation and support for the electoral process (South African Government Information 2013).

The Bapo Traditional Authority: Official status and *locus standi*

The context of the *Mogale v Maakane* case was that the traditional council or tribal authority was seeking to discipline a provincially imposed administrator whom they accused of maladministration. The mining revenue belonging to the 75 000 strong Bapo group is, unlike that of Bakgatla ba Kgafela, deposited into their provincially held D account. The lack of information about, and access to, the D account has been the source of much strife and complaint, with repeated allegations made that the province is misappropriating the mineral resources of the community (Swart 2012; Manson 2013) which are currently estimated to have a value of R10 billion (Manson 2013).

The premier has appointed a series of external administrators to manage the affairs of Bapo since 2008, after recurrent complaints concerning the actions of *kgosi* Bob Mogale. The first of these was Makepe Kenoshi, who managed to extend his one-year term of office by concluding an agreement with the Bapo Traditional Authority (BTA) that they would employ him as their chief executive officer. Manson (2013) writes that far from being a neutral administrator, Kenoshi became a 'rogue element' who aligned himself closely with *kgosi* Bob Mogale in ignoring the instructions of the BTA, going as far as to sign a R234 million contract on their behalf, despite their explicit instructions against the deal. The BTA instituted disciplinary proceedings against Kenoshi and attempted to bar him from their offices, but the province intervened to demand that the disciplinary hearing be suspended.

Kgosi Bob Mogale then applied for and obtained an interim interdict to stop members of the Bapo Traditional Authority from 'interfering' in the affairs of the Bapo Ba Mogale traditional community, in particular from attending meetings at the tribal office, contacting any member of staff, or coming within a 200 metre radius of the

Bapo traditional authority office. This effectively barred the Traditional Authority from proceeding with disciplinary action against Kenoshi.

In examining the status and *locus standi* of the traditional authority, Judge Landman found that the timeframe in the Framework Act for converting traditional authorities into traditional councils had expired. While the North West Act purported to extend the period, he found this to be beyond the competency of provincial legislation. He thus found that a notice issued by the premier in 2008, which purported to reconstitute all traditional authorities as traditional councils, was defective on multiple grounds.

Judge Landman's judgment, which was handed down in October 2010, confirmed the interim interdict on the basis that members of the BTA had no *locus standi* to institute any proceedings related to the administration or mal-administration of the tribe, as the BTA was no longer a validly constituted authority. This would have let Kenoshi off the hook, had the members of the BTA not simultaneously applied, in another court, for an interdict restraining him from dealing with their assets and forcing him to submit to the disciplinary enquiry.

The latter case was heard in the North Gauteng High Court, where Judge Legodi took a different approach. He found that the scale of the resources entailed justified urgent action by the community to protect their assets and said that the status of the traditional authority and the issue of *locus standi* was 'nothing else than a smokescreen', and that members of the community had a direct and material interest, which was sufficient to provide them with *locus standi*. The traditional authority also had *locus standi* as the body that had employed Kenoshi, regardless of its official status. He referred to the province's attempt to stop the disciplinary action against Kenoshi, and said that the proceedings in the North West High Court appear to have been aimed at silencing Tshepo Maakane, a member of the community and the respondent in the North West case.

Judge Legodi pointed out that Kenoshi had relied on the *locus standi* issue instead of addressing the merits of the case and answering the serious allegations against him. He confirmed the interdicts preventing Kenoshi from interacting with the tribal authority and dealing with the assets of the Bapo. He also said that the premier and North West provincial government should fulfill their functions, roles and obligations in terms of sections 9 and 10 of the North West Act to support the BTA.

On this basis the BTA succeeded in firing Kenoshi. However, the North West province has continued to insist that they are not properly constituted as a traditional council, and has appointed two administrators since Kenoshi to handle the financial and other affairs of the Bapo community. Their assets continue to be locked in the provincially managed D account. Their lawyer, Hugh Eiser, said in 2012:

> The premier [of the North West province], the MEC and North West officials have done as they pleased with the community's money, while the community which owns the money is kept in the dark (Manson 2013; *City Press* 2012).

This is a very different outcome from that in Moruleng, where the money controlled by Nyalala Pilane is exempted from the strictures of the D account, and the judge who in 2010 insisted that traditional councils have no legal status in North West in 2011 confirmed an interdict protecting Nyalala Pilane and the Bakgatla ba Kgafela traditional council. On the basis that: "Any action by a parallel but unsanctioned structure that is neither recognised by the law or custom, seeking to perform and assume functions which are clearly the exclusive preserve of such recognised authorities, ought to incur the wrath of the law."

Suspicion and resistance

At the local level, the explanation for the different fates experienced by different players is attributed to 'political connections'. A community activist, Victor Modimokwane, told the *New Age* that the Bakgatla ba Kgafela community had realised that Chief Nyalala Pilane is protected because he has the African National Congress 'under his wing' (Molopyane 2012).

The levels of fury and suspicion concerning the premier's perceived support for specific factions in traditional leadership disputes involving mining assets run high in North West. Manson (2013) describes the example of the Bakwena ba Mogopa of Bethanie, who have significant deposits of vanadium and platinum on their land. In 2005 a regent was appointed who was accused of being a pawn of Edna Molewa, the then premier, and in cahoots with one Elias Tshepe who allegedly purported to represent Bakwena while he was a consultant to Amplats.

According to Manson (2013), when Molewa refused to reconsider her appointment of the regent, things turned violent. 'The royal homestead was set alight and police had to disperse the angry crowd with tear gas. Mathibedi [the regent] fled for her life' (Manson 2013).

Although a new and more acceptable traditional leader was subsequently appointed, problems persist in relation to financial accountability and transparency. A task team composed of royal family members discovered that two advisors to the *kgosi* were attempting to have the tribe's royalties of R97 million transferred into their personal account. The same task team complained in 2012 that millions are missing from the tribe's D account that is held by the premier's office. They infer that the *kgosi* is involved because he has signing powers. This may or may not be the case. It is difficult to ascertain this partly because these D accounts and the regulations governing them are shrouded in secrecy. In that context, and given the high stakes and convoluted background to these disputes, suspicion, alarm and division are inevitable (Manson 2013).

CONCLUSION

An examination of the two bodies of law that interact to govern relations on communal land in the platinum belt – the new traditional leadership laws and the MPRDA – suggests that the law reform agenda has been hijacked by elite interests that stand to profit from the value of the resources at issue. The MPRDA undercuts customary entitlements to mineral rights that vest in the people who have occupied the land for generations. The new traditional leadership laws centralise chiefly power in a way that is fundamentally at odds with indigenous accountability mechanisms.

In the process, democratic alternatives built on honouring substantive and procedural customary entitlements are pre-empted in favour of a version of custom that cements elite alliances and locks out rural people. Also discounted are approaches that acknowledge the complex and specific history of land occupation and African land purchases in the North West that would seek to 'unpack' the legacy of past racial discrimination and forced overlapping of rights on an inclusive basis premised on the acceptance of historical vested rights.

Instead, Parliament, in making these laws, has opted to cement Bantustan distortions that dovetail with the financial interests and autocratic leanings of the ruling elite, an approach that gives loyal allies a share of the spoils, but only on terms that exclude the majority of those with customary entitlements and the migrant workers who make up the bulk of the workforce. We see traditional leaders being cut a slice of mining profits on the one hand – and National Union of Mine Workers (NUM) shop stewards paid directly by mine management and increasingly insulated from the rest of the workforce on the other hand. The assumption appears to be that, in return, traditional leaders will deliver the rural vote, and that NUM will remain a loyal and powerful political ally within the Tripartite Alliance.

The levels of exclusion reinforced by the new laws are, however, simply too dysfunctional and distorted to be stable. They put at risk the survival of the very institutions they seek to support. The NUM on the platinum belt took a beating from the more responsive Association of Mineworker and Construction Union (AMCU) during 2013, and it remains to be seen whether traditional leaders in North West will garner or lose votes for the ruling party in the 2014 elections. The scale of violent protest on and around the platinum mines has provoked fears that the financial stability of the country is at stake, and calls for an 'emergency response' at the level of the deputy president (Paton 2013). Alongside this, the edifice created by the Framework Act is rapidly crumbling throughout South Africa. Ten years after the Framework Act was enacted there has still been no attempt to elect the required 40 per cent of members in Limpopo, and elections have been postponed indefinitely in the North West. In other provinces traditional council elections have been so deeply flawed as to call into question whether the election stipulation has been met at all (O'Donovan and Redpath, 2012). On this basis it is doubtful that any of the traditional councils currently supported and paid by government are properly and lawfully constituted.

This chapter suggests that post-apartheid laws have brought out and reinforced the scale of corruption and abuse of power exposed by the audit report and in press reports about other mining disputes in the platinum belt. The problem goes beyond the terms of the law, however, to include how the law is interpreted and applied in practice. In the North West, the combination of the two has resulted in fundamental continuities with Bantustan constructs and embedded institutional arrangements and understandings, with the result that ordinary rural people are excluded from processes and systems through which decisions are made and resources are allocated. With all avenues for redress effectively blocked, and those blockages sanctioned by law and court judgments, is it any wonder that people are turning to increasingly violent protest as the only means to draw attention to their plight?

The first step in addressing the situation in respect of mining ventures on customary land is to do away with superimposed tribal boundaries and to enable people to define their own identities and opt into customary systems and arrangements only where these have resonance for them. Next is to clarify the historical and customary entitlements held by different groups. This would require more nuanced mining agreements, taking into account and requiring the consent of those with specific interests in particular areas of land. It would also break down the autocratic control of officially recognised traditional leaders by requiring negotiation with structures representing the people directly affected, whether at the clan, family or syndicate level. Instead of profits and benefits being centrally controlled, they would be distributed through the different levels of authority operating at the local level. In the context of landownership by families, syndicates and clans rather than by overarching 'tribes' customary and historical entitlements to the land remain crucially important, the difference being that these entitlements would be disaggregated in accordance with history and the layered and inclusive nature of customary identities.

Laws and judgments emanating from the North West province have cemented the Bophuthatswana legacy of excluding the majority from access to resources and from processes of collective definition. The effects of this exclusion are made visible in the intensifying inequality and violent protest examined in this chapter. The risks entailed in using law in this manner go beyond entrenching dispossession, serious as that is; they include undermining the legitimacy of law, the law-making process and public confidence in the impartiality of the courts.

REFERENCES

Bennett T (2008) 'Official' vs. 'living' customary law: dilemmas of description and recognition. In Claassens A and B Cousins (2008) *Land, Power and Custom: Controversies Generated by South Africa's Communal Land Rights Act*. Cape Town: UCT Press.

Capps G (2010) Tribal-Landed Property: The Political Economy of the BaFokeng Chieftaincy, South Africa, 1837-1994. PhD Thesis, London School of Economics and Political Science.

City Press 'Madonsela to probe tribes' lost millions'. 11 February 2012.

Cousins B (2008) Characterising 'communal' tenure: nested systems and flexible boundaries. In Claassens A and B Cousins (2008) *Land, Power and Custom: Controversies Generated by South Africa's Communal Land Rights Act*. Cape Town: UCT Press.

Claassens A (2008) Power, accountability and apartheid borders: the impact of recent laws on struggles over land rights. In Claassens A and B Cousins (2008) *Land, Power and Custom: Controversies Generated by South Africa's Communal Land Rights Act*. Cape Town: UCT Press.

Claassens A (2008) Customary law and zones of chiefly sovereignty: the impact of government policy on whose voices prevail in the making and changing of customary law. In Claassens A and B Cousins (2008) *Land, Power and Custom: Controversies Generated by South Africa's Communal Land Rights Act*. Cape Town: UCT Press.

Claassens A and M Hathorn (2008) Stealing restitution and selling land allocations: Dixie, Mayaeyane and Mkuleke. In Claassens A and B Cousins (2008) *Land, Power and Custom: Controversies Generated by South Africa's Communal Land Rights Act*. Cape Town: UCT Press.

Claassens A and D Gilfillan (2008) The Kalkfontein land purchases: eighty years on and still struggling for ownership. In Claassens A and B Cousins (2008) *Land, Power and Custom: Controversies Generated by South Africa's Communal Land Rights Act*. Cape Town: UCT Press.

Comaroff JL and S Roberts (1981) *Rules and Processes: The Cultural Logic of Dispute in an African Context*. Chicago: University of Chicago Press.

Cramer M (2012) 'IDC invests big in Gilbertson/Frandsen new-look platinum integration', *Mining Weekly* 29 March.

Delius P (2008) Contested terrain: Land rights and chiefly power in historical perspective. In Claassens A and B Cousins (2008) *Land, Power and Custom: Controversies Generated by South Africa's Communal Land Rights Act*. Cape Town: UCT Press.

Delius P and W Beinart (2013) The historical context and legacy of the Natives Land Act of 1913. Paper presented at Land Divided Conference, University of Cape Town, Western Cape.

Department of Local Government and Traditional Affairs, March 2013. Circular/Minute 03/2011 – Ref 11/2/10/P.

Dibakwane W (2008) 'Bakgatla call for Molewa's removal'. *Sowetan*, 23 June.

Hill M (2006) 'Angloplat finalises royalty-for-equity empowerment deal'. *Mining Weekly* 14 December.

Khanyile G (2012) 'Bakgatla tribe men facing corruption probe'. *IOL News* 14 October.

Letswamotse P (2012) 'Fight over Kgafela's Hummer'. *Botswana Gazette* 15 August.

Luthuli A (1962) *Let My People Go: An Autobiography*. Johannesburg and London: Collins.

Maleke L (2012) 'Chaos at Moruleng meeting'. *MmegiOnline* 17 December.

Maleke L (2012) 'Kgafela: The troublemaker without borders'. *MmegiOnline* 21 December.

Manson A (2013) Mining and 'traditional communities' in South Africa's 'platinum belt': Contestations over land, leadership and assets in North-West Province c. 1996-2012. *Journal of Southern African studies* 39(2): 409-423.

Modise O (2011) 'Govt withdraws recognition of Kgafela as Bakgatla Kgosi'. *Sunday Standard* 31October.

Molema SM (1920) *The Bantu: Past and Present: An Ethnographical and Historical Study of the Native Races of South Africa*. Edinburgh: Green.

Molopyane O (2012) 'Special report – A chieftaincy 'ruled by greed''. *The New Age* 10 May.

Molopyane O (2012) 'Bakgatla tribe steps up its campaign to oust 'greedy' chief'. *The New Age* 30 May.

Molopyane O (2012) 'Feature: Bakgatla will probe audit report'. *The New Age* 21 June.

Molopyane O (2012) 'Bakgatla in probe call'. *The New Age* 9 August.

Molopyane O (2012) 'Bakgatla in royal dispute'. *The New Age* 21 August.

Morewagae S (2012) 'Pilane pleads for Kgafela's lonely co-accused'. *Mmegionline*, www.mmegi.bw.

North West Local Government and Traditional Affairs (2013) Postponement of traditional council elections 2013, *South African Government Information*. http://www.info.gov.za/speech/DynamicAction?pageid=461&sid=37794&tid=111994.

Ntibinyane N (2013) 'How Kgafela "ate" *madi a morafhe*'. *Botswana Guardian* February.

Ntibinyane N (2013) 'Inside Kgafela's lavish palace' .*Botswana Guardian* 11 January.

Ntibinyane N (2012) 'Kgafela vs Nyalala'. *The Midweek Sun* 14 November.

Okoth-Ogendo HWO (2008) The nature of land rights under indigenous law in Africa. In Claassens A and B Cousins (2008) *Land, Power and Custom: Controversies Generated by South Africa's Communal Land Rights Act*. Cape Town: UCT Press.

O'Donovan M and J Redpath J (2012) Traditional Council elections in South Africa: A critical review of performance since 2008. (2012) Unpublished. Centre for Law and Society, University of Cape Town.
Paton C (2013) 'Motlanthe seeks pledges to avert potential mining crisis'. *Business Day* 12 June.
Pilane M (2013) MPRDA and Traditional Communities, Submission to Parliament, Workshop: Redressing the legacy of the 1913 Land Act, 7-8 June 2013. Good Hope Chamber, Parliament of the Republic of South Africa, Western Cape.
Selebi M (2012) 'Bakgatla chief Pilane abdicates'. *Sowetan* 2 August.
Selebi M (2012) 'School disturbances will not be tolerated – chief'. *Sowetan* 12 June.
Schapera I (1938) *A Handbook of Tswana Law and Custom.* Oxford: Oxford University Press.
Swart H (2012) 'Bapo Ba Mogale community turns to public protector'. *Mail & Guardian* 14 September.
Tau P (2012) 'Locals demand their share'. *The Star* 12 June.

Case law

Alexkor Ltd and Another v Richtersveld Community and Others (CCT19/03) [2003] ZACC 18 (14 October 2003)
Bhe and Others v Khayelitsha Magistrate and Others (CCT 49/03) [2004] ZACC 17 (15 October 2004)
Chief Pilane v Chief Linchwe and Another [1995] (4) SA 686 (BG)
Kgafela III and Another v Premier of North West and Others 2012, Applicant Pleadings, North West High Court, Mafikeng
Modimokwana v Traditional Council of Bakgatla-Ba-Kgafela Traditional Community (706/2011) [2011] ZANWHC (26 April 2011)
Mogale v Maakane and Others (1106/2010) [2010] ZANWHC 18 (29 July 2010)
Pilane and Another v Pheto and Others (582/2011) [2011] ZANWHC 63 (30 September 2011)
Pilane and Another v Pilane and Another (263/2010) [2011] ZANWHC 80 (30 June 2011)
Pilane and Another v Pilane and Another (CCT 46/12) [2013] ZACC 3 (28 February 2013)
Pilane and Another v State (CA 59/2009) [2010] ZANWHC 20 (17 September 2010)
Sigcau v President of the Republic of South Africa and Others (CCT 93/12) [2013] ZACC 18 (13 June 2013)
Tongoane and Others v National Minister for Agriculture and Land Affairs and Others (CCT100/09) [2010] ZACC 10 (11 May 2010)
Traditional Authority of the Bapo Ba Mogale Community v Kenoshi and Another (31876/10) [2010] ZAGPPHC 72 (29 July 2010)

NOTES

1   We are grateful to our colleagues Thuto Thipe, Monica de Souza and Tara Weinberg for their input and assistance.

2   'Locals demand their share' (Tau 2012). 'Bakgatla bicker over royalties' (*Business Day* 2011),

3   We use inverted commas to indicate that this is a contentious construct, imposed in many instances by delineations in terms of the notorious Bantu Authorities Act of 1951. The continued imposition of overarching tribal boundaries undermines the varied ways in which groups of people (including historical syndicates of land buyers and previously autonomous customary clans) identify and constitute themselves.

4   Struck down by the Constitutional Court in 2010.

5   Charlotte Mokgosi, Makgobistad Community Committee. Submission on the Traditional Courts Bill. 2008.
Tsholofelo Zebulon Molwantwa, Baralokgadi Communal Property Association. Submission on the Traditional Courts Bill. 2012.
Constance Modingwana, Rhenosterskraal. Submission on the Traditional Courts Bill. 2012.
Bafokeng Land Buyers Association. Submission on Traditional Courts Bill. January 2012,

LAMOSA North West. Submission on the Traditional Courts Bill. 2012.

Constance Mogale, Land Access Movement of South Africa. Submission on the repeal of the Black Authorities Act. 2010.

Mary Mokgaetsi Pilane and Mmuti Pilane, Motlhabe Village. Submission on the repeal of the Black Authorities Act. 2010.

6   Also referred to as tribal trust accounts and in some cases trust accounts. The D in the name derives from section 11(2)(d) of the Bophuthatswana Traditional Authorities Act 23 of 1978, and section 30(d) of the North West Traditional Leadership and Governance Act of 2005 that replaced it. These are so similar that they enable the D accounts established during the Bophuthatswana era to remain in place.

7   Budget vote given by the MEC Paul Sebegoe in 2012 indicated that the North West Department of Local Government and Traditional Affairs would be allocated additional funds to the tune of R4 million for the investigation of tribal D accounts.

8   Old order mining rights are those that existed prior to the enactment of the MPRDA and new order mining rights are those issued by the Department of Minerals and Energy since it was brought into operation.

9   He was appointed in terms of the Bophuthatswana Traditional Authorities Act 23 of 1978.

10   In particular the *Mogale v Maakane* case decided by Justice Landman in 2010 and the *Modimokwana v Traditional Council* and *Pilane v Pheto* cases decided by Justice Hendricks in 2011.

11   The North West Act came into operation only in 2005, which means that most of the contentious transactions would have taken place under the ambit of the Bophuthatswana Act.

12   We assume this to be the origin of the 'D accounts' referred to in the introduction, and in the Bapo discussion that follows. Section 30(d) of the North West Act provides – 'Any other amounts derived from any sources whatsoever for the benefit of a traditional community.'

13   Department of Local Government and Traditional Affairs Circular/Minute 03/2011 – Ref 11/2/10/P.

CHAPTER 7

amaDiba moment:
How civil courage confronted state and corporate collusion

John Gl Clarke

Stories are the secret reservoir of values. Change the stories individuals and nations live by and tell themselves and you change the individuals and nations. If they tell themselves stories that are lies, they will suffer the future consequences of those lies. If they tell themselves stories that face their own truth they will free their histories for future flowerings.
(Ben Okri, poet and writer)

This chapter, written from the perspective of a social work practitioner rather than that of an academic, tells the story of a latter-day 'Mpondo revolt', of how the coastal residents of the amaDiba clan within the Mpondo traditional kingship stood their ground to force the minister and officials responsible for mineral resources to revoke the award of mineral rights to an Australian-based venture capital mining company for heavy mineral deposits buried in their ancestral lands.

Between 2006 and 2008 the mining protagonists used bullying and underhand tactics to subvert local community resistance to what the community perceived to be the desecration of sacred sites, the destruction of crop and grazing lands and the forced resettlement of homesteads. Human rights violations had been reported to the South African Human Rights Commission in 2007 and concerted citizen action ultimately forced the minister of mineral resources to revoke the mining rights in May 2011. However, the Mpondo found that proving the proposed mining development to be an unjust violation of human rights was ultimately a moral and ethical argument rather than simply a matter of proving a case by legal disputation through the courts. It required *civil courage*: a *praxis* that transcended the normal activist strategy of civil disobedience by taking the noble ideals espoused by the preamble of the South African Constitution and strengthening the social fabric of this historically marginalised community. Civil disobedience is hard to sustain in the long run. In contrast, civil courage draws from endogenous potential, which is metabolised by connecting people with shared interests, affirming life and managing creative ideas and innovations that arise. It is fundamentally about spirit and soul; about creating shared meaning and common purpose by telling and retelling stories of empowerment; about facing our own truths to 'free our history for future flowerings' (Okri 1998).

The vital importance of a spiritual/educational/moral undergirding of social activism to sustain civil courage came via the Scottish peace activist and author Alastair McIntosh (2001). His book *Soil and Soul: People vs Corporate Power* describes the success of two Hebridean island communities in community struggles in the 1990s against the fallen 'Powers that Be'. The crofter community of the Isle of Eigg raised the money to buy their ancestral island from the laird thus restoring communal land tenure and sparking widespread land reform in Scotland. The community of the Isle of Harris and Lewis, in turn, convinced a multinational corporate, Lefarge, to abandon plans to turn their island into 'the gravel pit of Europe': a scheme to blast the sacred Mount Roineabhal into the stone aggregate used in road construction.

The unlikely bond of spiritual solidarity between the Hebridean Islanders and the Mpondo amaDiba community stemmed from following the same threefold strategy of naming, unmasking and engaging the powers.

Having, in 2011, succeeded in stopping one large, unwanted, unsustainable and unjust imposition on them, the amaDiba, supported by their king and queen, were empowered by their learning to also expose the hidden agenda behind the intention of the South African National Roads Agency (Sanral) to shorten the N2 route between Port Shepstone and Umtata by constructing a new tolled highway over their ancestral lands in order to serve the dune mining interest. Mpondo resistance was met by extreme measures from the Powers that Be in the South African Government. Attempts were made to aggressively undermine local traditional leaders. The Mpondo king, *iKumkani* Justice Mpondombini Sigcau was deposed in favour of a compliant relative. Standing firm in civil courage, the Mpondo nevertheless prevailed to outwit, outplay and outlast the mining and N2 Toll Road protagonists, culminating in the Mpondo Royal Family succeeding with a court challenge when the Constitutional Court upheld King Justice Sigcau's application to regain the prerogative to decide royal succession according to the living customary law of the Mpondo instead of by presidential fiat (Constitutional Court 2013).

Over the eight-year period between 2005 and 2012, I worked in my professional capacity as a social worker with the amaDiba community and the Mpondo royal family to intervene in a situation that trembled on the edge of violence. I journeyed back and forth about six times a year between the rural Mpondoland communities and the urban megalopolis of Gauteng. The more involved I became in the *amaDiba*/Mpondo narrative, the clearer it became that their story was emblematic of the larger South African historical narrative of mining-induced social conflict and economic and environmental injustice.

However, the Mpondo ultimately showed that notwithstanding the nationalisation of mining rights (by the passing of the Mineral and Petroleum Resources Development Act of 2002) human rights do not belong to government but to people – and the solidarity and determination showed by rural Mpondo was to offer a salutary lesson in internalising the Bill of Rights and understanding civil courage.

HISTORICAL CONTEXT

When a youthful Henry Francis Fynn crossed the Mzamba River in 1824 in a prospecting expedition from Port Natal (now Durban), he was not prospecting for titanium. In his diary he reconstructed his experience of having traversed a stretch of 22 km of coastline between the Mzamba and Mntentu estuaries, where he met several droves of elephants.

Although he was encouraged to find elephants in 1824, Fynn did not find many people living along that stretch (on account of the *mfecane,* the 'crushing' under the despotic conquests of King Shaka). In 1996, some 172 years after Fynn's journey, a latter-day prospector named Mark Victor Caruso followed a similar path, and along the same 22 km stretch of coastal dunes that Fynn had traversed he also found what he was looking for: titanium and other heavy mineral deposits, (ilmenite, rutile, zircon, pig iron, leucoxene). By 1996, however, the area was well settled with people. One of twenty-four constituent clans of the amaMpondo nation, people known as the amaDiba, populated the area. The pioneering anthropologist Monica Hunter-Wilson had described them as the 'byword of conservatism' (Hunter-Wilson 1936).

It so happened that while Caruso was exploring the dunes in 1996, the drafters of the South African Constitution were putting the finishing touches to the document before it was unanimously adopted by Parliament. It was controversial for two innovations hitherto unseen in the constitutional democracies of the world. The first was the entrenchment of environmental rights in a Bill of Rights (Section 24 of Chapter 2); the other was the entrenchment of Traditional Leaders and Customary law (Chapter 12).

While human rights activists, environmentalists and traditional leaders were all celebrating the Constitution and its ambitious goal of merging different (some would say opposing) streams of consciousness, Caruso and his hosts (certain senior government officials) were busy optimistically planning a strategy to turn the heavy mineral deposits of what became known as the Xolobeni Mineral Sands into profit. At the time nobody realised that they were in fact opening up an opportunity for environmental rights to acquire meaning, in the way that Eleanor Roosevelt had advocated way back in 1948 when she said:

> Where, after all, do universal rights begin? In small places, close to home – close and so small that they cannot be seen on any maps of the world … Unless these rights have meaning there, they have little meaning anywhere. Without concerted citizen action to uphold them close to home, we shall look in vain for progress in the larger world.[1]

In 1996 the Xolobeni Mineral Sands on the Pondoland Wild Coast did not show up on the maps of the world. When, a few years later in 2003, Caruso reported to shareholders that it was the 'tenth largest deposit of heavy minerals in the world',[2] with the space-age mineral titanium the most plentiful, suddenly it did. Caruso re-floated a dormant Australian mining exploration company, MRC Ltd, on the Australian Securities Exchange to attract venture capital investment for a scheme to mine the deposits, assuring investors that he had met personally with the highest ranking Department of Minerals and Energy (DME) officers who supported the project – but he 'could not publicly say that'. He did not realise that he was in fact saying it publicly, for one of the 'investors' in his audience at the 2007 Shareholders' Annual General Meeting (AGM) was a proxy for a shareholder who had bought shares in the company precisely to obtain such information. The shares had been purchased on behalf of the amaDiba coastal residents, who suspected all along that the mining scheme was driven by the vested interests of corrupt officials.

Neither had the Wild Coast shown up on the national road map of South Africa, until Nazir Alli, the CEO of Sanral, announced that he had received an unsolicited bid from the private sector N2 Wild Coast Consortium to shorten the N2 between Durban and East London which currently runs inland from Port Shepstone, skirting around Pondoland, by constructing a new 'greenfields' shortcut along the Pondoland Wild Coast in return for a thirty-year tolling concession for the entire length of the N2 between Durban and East London. The N2 Wild Coast Toll Road scheme became one of Alli's greatest ambitions; he claimed that it would alleviate poverty and facilitate much-neglected development of one of the poorest regions of South Africa (Alli 2005: 24).

CONCERTED CITIZEN ACTION

The threshold moment which defined the amaDiba struggle as a classic human rights struggle occurred on 16 November 2003. The 'Mntentu moment' came about thanks to the insightful questioning of local amaDiba residents of the Mntentu Estuary for the South African Broadcasting Corporation (SABC) environmental programme '50/50' by the late Jonathan Rands on which he commented that the role of the media could not have been more obvious. The film was the first in-depth media investigation into the Xolobeni dune mining controversy. Wrapping up his report he put his finger on the issue.

> With an issue as controversial as this it really surprises me that no NGO or capacity building organisation has actually come into this area and said, 'what are the issues we are looking at? We are looking at mining, we are looking at a road, we are looking at eco-tourism', and said 'Lets look at the pros and cons of all of them. Let's give you the information that you as a community need, so you can make an informed decision. It seems that the debate is happening up here, and the people on the ground are actually being alienated and marginalised, and aren't really part of this decision-making process. That's a problem.[3]

A voluntary unfunded civil organisation called Save the Wild Coast (SWC) had just come into existence, led by the 'Green Bishop', Geoff Davies, who had for seventeen years served the Mpondo as Anglican bishop of the diocese of Umzimvubu. Over the ensuing years SWC shaped and reshaped itself to coordinate the 'concerted citizen action' that Eleanor Roosevelt had said was necessary to hold governments accountable.

First, in December 2004, they persuaded the minister of environmental affairs and tourism (at the time Marthinus van Schalkwyk) to set aside a decision by his director general (Crispian Olver) to grant environmental authorisation for the N2 Wild Coast Toll Road, for which a private sector construction consortium, the N2WCC, had submitted an unsolicited bid to construct a massively expensive shortcut for the N2 route between Durban and East London in return for a thirty-year private tolling concession. The fatal flaw was a conflict of interests that the late Rufus Maruma (the environmental consultant appointed by the construction consortium) had failed to declare. Besides owning Bohlweki Environmental, he was also a director of Stewart Scott International, a member of the consortium. Evidently embarrassed, the N2WCC vanished and it was Sanral which resubmitted the revised proposal for the N2 shortcut. The intervening years had given the local residents more opportunity to interrogate the scheme and it was local amaDiba residents who led the high court application to have it set aside. By that stage it was obvious that the 'Sanral preferred route' for the shortcut was to favour the mining of the coastal dunes. During 2006, Save the Wild Coast had reinvented itself as Sustaining the Wild Coast, to support local residents by doing what Jonathan Rands had called for in 2003. Local residents became ever more empowered as active protagonists of their own development process. The veteran human rights attorney Richard Spoor was approached and became actively involved as a legal advisor and strategist. When on 30 March 2007 the mining company lodged its mining rights application, the stage was set for an intense campaign to oppose it.

In June 2007, the local residents formed the amaDiba Crisis Committee (ACC) as a democratic participatory structure under the auspices of the Tribal Authority, to undertake a programme of action to ensure that all available measures were taken to stop the unwanted scheme. They were vehemently opposed to the mining of their ancestral lands and even more vehemently opposed to the Xolobeni Empowerment Company (Xolco) the BEE company which claimed to represent their interests for a 26 per cent stake in the project. They alleged that their constitutional rights – notably freedom of expression (Clause 16), and the right of access to information (Clause 32) – had been violated and that their environmental rights (Clause 24) would be violated in the future if the mining went ahead. Clause 24 of the Bill of Rights states that 'everyone has the right to an environment that is protected and conserved for the benefit of present and future generations'. Their assertion that this right would be violated was a key plank in their platform of alleged abuses.

Two individuals were specifically named as alleged perpetrators of the violations, Zamile 'Madiba' Qunya (who, together with Patrick Caruso of MRC and the attorney Maxwell Boqwana had founded Xolco in 2003) and Zoleka Capa, the executive mayor of the OR Tambo District Municipality and a member of the ANC National Executive Committee (NEC).

The Mpondo royal family, the South African Human Rights Commission and the South African Council of Churches were all engaged in support of the struggle. But a year later, in July 2008, it was finally announced that 'provisional mining rights' for one third of the tenement, the Kwanyana Block, had been awarded.

The announcement was first discovered in a statement on the Australian Securities Exchange website (www.asx.com.au), under the listing of the mining company MRC Ltd. The local landowners found it particularly offensive that they were the last to know, only after the investors had been informed. This served to intensify their determination and, thanks to extensive media coverage, the minister of minerals and energy, Buyelwa Sonjica paid a visit to the amaDiba in August to endeavour to convince them that the government had their interests at heart. A senior journalist with *The Sunday Tribune*, Fred Kockott (2008), described it as:

> … the strangest of meetings, and a blatant demonstration of the buying power of government, the mining industry and politicians [Zoleka Capa prominent among them] … The decision to award a mining licence even in the face of objections from the Department of Environmental Affairs has sparked one of South Africa's biggest environmental controversies, a growing campaign of protest from environmentalists and divisions within the community, particularly in areas earmarked for mining. Besides free food and a full day's entertainment, identity book registration and social welfare grants were also on offer for people throughout the amaDiba district, many of whom had been transported in from areas far from where the mining is planned. Marshalls kept a register, seemingly for mining lobbyists to record a huge groundswell of support for the project. But a snap survey by the Sunday Tribune revealed that many of those attending did not even know that a mining announcement was on the agenda of the day's proceedings.

At the conclusion of the meeting, the '50/50' producer Don Guy asked the minister, 'Isn't this about people's land rights?'

Somewhat taken aback, she replied, 'No, not according to my understanding. It is about competing interests. The one group feels that mining should happen. Another group feels that they want tourism.' (In the course of her speech, reported on the SABC on 26 August 2008, she had also decried how 'we lost St Lucia to tourism' when Richards Bay Minerals were denied rights to mine those coastal dunes of heavy mineral deposits in 1995.)

A NINTH DAY IN SEPTEMBER

The ACC successfully persuaded the minister to return a month later, on 12 September 2008. This time it was without all the political razzmatazz, without Zoleka Capa, and without Xolco's leader, Zamile Qunya, both of whom had accompanied her in August. This time the venue provided the appropriate opportunity for any discussion on land rights issues, the *Umgundlovu Komkulu* (the tribal courthouse, 'the great place of the elephants', ironically more or less where Fynn reported his sighting of droves of elephants in 1824). The hall was too small for the crowd so available benches were carried outside, but most sat on the grass. King Sigcau was represented by Princess Mazoe Sigcau. The senior traditional leader of the amaDiba, *Nkosi* Lunga Baleni, was present to emphatically state that he had never been consulted by any government official or mining company representative about the mining proposal.

To her credit, the minister endured the severe dressing-down she received. The ACC chairperson, Sikoshiphe 'Bazooka' Radebe, delivered well-aimed objections, and representatives from across the spectrum of age, gender and educational background backed him up with a well-prepared repertoire of speeches. She attentively listened to the fashionably attired young Mpondo woman Nonhle Mbuthuma's rhetorical questions: 'What is it about the Mpondo that makes us different from all other South Africans? Why is it only us who are expected to give up our land in order to get government service delivery?' Then she listened to the man whom Nonhle credits as having really educated her as to the realities of life, despite his having never been to school or university. A gifted orator, with skills honed by decades of struggle since his participation in the Mpondo Uprising of 1960, *uTata* Samson Gampe rose to his feet to confidently and politely inform Minister Sonjica that according to customary law no amount of top town consultation efforts would change the collective mind of the local residents. 'We do not want mining. Now or ever in the future,' he said to rapturous applause.

In response, Sonjica again tried to justify the mining as a means of alleviating 'chronic poverty'. Her words only served to provoke further outrage from the 450-strong gathering of local residents who resented the crude caricature of being a helpless, dependent community, at the mercy of government welfare programmes.

Afterwards, the journalist Don Guy again asked the question of the minister: is this not about people's land rights? 'Yes,' she replied this time, in a complete turnaround from the previous month. 'It is all about that, and again this is about sustainable development, it's about rights, it's about land and all of that. But I want to talk to the camera, and I hope you will record this one. It is not about human rights being violated. It is about a process of consultation which was not done properly.'[4]

From closely observing and filming the meeting, my impression was that Minister Sonjica had indeed been completely misled.[5] I suspect that the persons responsible for the misinformation included her director general, Advocate Sandile Nogxina, who had awarded the mining rights; Executive Mayor Zoleka Capa, who had shared the platform with her during the August 'political jamboree' (as one observer described it); and Zamile Qunya.

The Legal Resources Centre had by then joined Richard Spoor to put their weight behind the legal challenge to educate the state that a public consultation process that is not done properly is *ipso facto* a violation of human rights. The attorney Sarah Sephton prepared papers threatening high court action. Government capitulated to the threat and Minister Sonjica suspended the mining rights pending the outcome of an internal administrative review process.

Buyelwa Sonjica was one of the few survivors of the Mbeki cabinet to be retained by Jacob Zuma upon his election as president in April 2009. However, he redeployed her to a reconstituted ministry of water and environmental affairs. Within the anti-mining lobby there was much hope that the new president would bridge the enormous gulf between people and government that had widened under Mbeki's presidency, and that Sonjica would use her new position to recover lost moral authority by following through on her promise to ensure a proper consultation process. The amaDiba Crisis Committee tasked me to record interviews with Samson Gampe and other leaders on a DVD, to keep communication channels open. The DVD was hand-delivered to Minister Sonjica's office (and to her Cabinet colleagues Minister Susan Shabangu, who took over the mineral resources portfolio; Minister S'bu Ndebele of transport; and Minister Sicelo Shiceka of cooperative governance and traditional affairs). It took three months for Minister Sonjica to acknowledge the DVD, but indirectly there was evidence of her change of heart. An article appeared in the *iSimangaliso News*, an in-house publication written in her name and singing the praises of the success of the iSimangaliso World Heritage Site in alleviating poverty through nature-based tourism (Sonjica 2009:7). The picture she painted as minister of the environment could not have contrasted more starkly with her statements as minister of minerals one year earlier. A few months after the astonishing article appeared, President Zuma dropped her from his Cabinet altogether. No reasons were given.

While Sonjica had promised to consult with the king, her successor as minister, Susan Shabangu, did not respond to our efforts to brief her. Perhaps she knew what was coming, for in July 2010 President Zuma announced that King Justice Mpondombini Sigcau had been deposed by government in favour of a nephew, Zanuzuko Sigcau, who immediately showed himself eager to please.

Nevertheless, so overwhelming was the case against the award of mining rights that a year later, in May 2011, Shabangu finally yielded to the pressure brought by the amaDiba threatening High Court action, and revoked the mining rights completely. The fact that an executive decision was made to revoke a decision without the judiciary having to order it was unprecedented. The amaDiba had achieved something quite remarkable. It gave them the confidence to tackle claims by Nazir Alli's misleading claims that the purpose and intentions of the N2 Wild Coast toll road were developmental.

FAREWELL TO INNOCENCE

The revoke of the mining rights ought to have been the end of the matter, but it was not. A year later, in March 2012, the mining company announced their intention to start the process all over again from scratch, commencing with a mineral prospecting right application for the Kwanyana Block. With all that had transpired between 2003 and 2011, many were shocked that the Department of Mineral Resources could even entertain the possibility. I was not, because by then I had become immersed in supporting the Mpondo royal family in their court battle with government. By then, having drunk from the same wells of liberation and contextual theology that Frank Chikane, Albert Nolan, Allan Boesak, and Archbishop Desmond Tutu had drunk, I too had long bidden 'farewell to innocence' (Boesak: 1977).

The stories of how the campaign against the Xolobeni mining and the N2 toll road evolved are inspirational and edifying – but it is what transpired after the minister's reluctant decision to revoke the mining rights that called for further acts of civil courage.

The really hard part of my intervention only came after the mining rights were revoked in May 2011. Alastair McIntosh had warned that the really evil powers always used more presentable masks. After we had successfully unmasked the powers behind the BEE company Xolco to find the faces of Zamile Qunya, Maxwell Boqwana and Patrick Caruso, they hastily co-opted respected local leaders to give credible face to the company. Nkululeko Msabane, principal of the Baleni Senior Secondary School, had agreed to serve on the board, having been assured by Qunya that the coastal residents were all in favour of the mining. However Msabane proved to be a principal with principles and soon became disenchanted when Qunya and Boqwana declined to hand over the financial statements of Xolco. He and two others, Nomangezi Malunga (an ANC ward councillor from Umtata) and a Ms Luke, discovered that Qunya, Boqwana and Caruso were still pulling the strings. Mr Msabane spilled the beans in an in-depth interview with me on 10 February 2010. It was filmed and submitted to the minister of mineral resources as evidence of gross abuse and manipulation of BEE policy and practice, as well as to the Cape Law Society to substantiate a complaint against the attorney Maxwell Boqwana for unprofessional conduct. The three, Msabane, Malunga and Luke, subsequently resigned in protest against Xolco's behaviour.

After the mining rights were revoked, I continued to practice my social work obligation to 'engage the Powers' in Australia by speaking at length to the CEO of MRC, Mark Caruso, in the hope of making peace and to help him save some face. I learned that MRC was simply a mask of convenience and another power behind him needed to be named and unmasked. The power was much closer to home, deeply entrenched in the Department of Mineral Resources and kept in place by the perverse dynamics of black economic empowerment and the Mining Charter.

The situation begged for investigative journalists to probe the way that the mining rights were awarded and the dubious means whereby the BEE partners of Xolco had tried to obtain the manipulated consent of local residents, but the inaccessible amaDiba at the coast were too remote to secure the sustained interest of the media to highlight the injustices they were experiencing from the mining protagonists.

The writer David McKay of *Mining Mix* speculated in an opinion piece on 14 February 2011 that upon his impending retirement Advocate Nogxina, who had served as director general of mineral resources from 1996 until 2011: '… may return to his village on the KwaZulu-Natal south coast to bring his administrative experience to local matters rather than, as many suspect, take up a juicy non-executive post at a mining corporate' (McKay 2011). Such reports lacked the sort of hard content that journalists would get by actually travelling to Port Edward, the site of Nogxina's holiday home, where he had been spending a great deal of his time. Indeed, Nogxina was trying hard to persuade the leaders of the amaDiba community struggle to withdraw their opposition to the mining rights.

Nogxina was to be disappointed. Not only did the Amadiba community rebut his arguments, but in the run-up to the local government elections of 2011 the ANC local branch committees in the mining-affected area made sure that only those candidates with declared anti-mining sympathies were nominated as candidates. Nkululeko Msabane, as chairperson of the ANC regional branch committee again showed shrewd insight by ensuring that Qunya and his allies were completely thwarted in their anti-democratic subversion of the popular will. Five pro-mining candidates ran as independent candidates in a desperate strategy to regain the initiative. In the critical Mntentu/Baleni/Xolobeni ward no less than three pro-mining independent candidates were fielded to try and dilute the vote and leave the ANC candidate Nokwamkela Mteki without a majority mandate. She trounced them all, winning 65 per cent of the vote. The table below, compiled from data downloaded from the Independent Electoral Commission, shows how the cookie crumbled for the independents. Had they formed an electoral alliance by virtue of the proportional representation system, they could have secured one seat to represent their interests, but they were loath to be identified together in a common pro-mining platform.

Soon after the May 2011 local government election results showed that the pro-mining faction had been thoroughly defeated, Minister Shabangu, under threat of an investigation by the public protector for the long delay, revoked the mining rights. In June 2011, the *Business Report* journalist Ingi Salgado accompanied me to focus media attention on the revived efforts of the amaDiba in recovering the 400 eco-tourism jobs lost because of the mining conflict. With the defeat of the mining interest, the ACC decided the time was right to at last disclose, firstly, Advocate Sandile Nogxina's blatant failure to declare his conflict of interests and, secondly, his various attempts to influence the ACC to withdraw their objections to the award of mining rights.

After consultation with *Business Report* deputy editor Peter De Ionno, Salgado and I made sure the matter was simultaneously reported to the Public Protector for investigation. Before *Business Report* ran the story Advocate Nogxina was afforded the customary right to reply. He moved very quickly to stifle the story at source by threatening Independent Newspapers with legal action. Regrettably, the *Business Report* editors complied, despite the fact that a third allegation of intimidation was now made to the public protector. ACC members further alleged that Advocate Nogxina had threatened them with arrest if they did not retract their allegations, his threat backed up by the suspiciously convenient arrival of two police constables from the Port Edward police station. The ACC members duly signed the retraction, but Nogxina was not aware that I had filmed the relevant interviews as additional corroborating evidence.

To underscore the urgency another representative of the ACC joined me in a special meeting with a senior investigator at the Office of the Public Protector in Pretoria. We

Analysis of Amadiba Wards Affected by mining and toll road

	Kyanyayo, KwaNduna	Kwampisi	Lukolo, Gumzana	Mngungundlovu	Sigidi	Mtentu, Baleni, Xolobeni	Between Mphalana and Mnyameni and inland to Tyeni	
	Ward 15	Ward 16	Ward 22	Ward 23	Ward 24	Ward 25	Ward 28	Total
Total reg	4 007	3 636	3 998	3 781	3 146	4 139	3 785	26 492
Total voted	2 332	2 192	2 329	2 217	1 719	2 395	2 133	15 317
% Poll	58.20	60.29	58.25	58.64	54.64	57.86	56.35	57.82
ANC share	1 686	1 104	1 326	2 063	975	1 562	1 861	10 577
%	72.30	50.36	56.93	93.05	56.72	65.22	87.25	69.05
Independent share	333	1 016	882	0	646	717	124	3 718
%	14.28	46.35	37.87	0.00	37.58	29.94	5.81	24.27
Ward Councillor	Lusapho General Mcambalala	Simon Mfanafuthi Thukwana	Mazeneno Xesibe	Phillip Ndovela	Hlebo Ntlahla	Nokwamkela Mteki	Jackson Madayisa Dimane	
Independent Candidate(s)	1 Bonile Miya, 2. Nontyatyambo Nomlomo	Siboniso Sikali	Sibongile Mncanywa	None	Sobohle Jongikaya	1.Mandlenkosi Ndovela 2.Mtembeni Gxolonxa, 3. Ntethelo Madikizela	Nobuhle Gcaleka	
Previous Ward Councillor	Addison Bonile Miya (independent)	Ncayiyana Mthetheleli Clerkson	Simphiwe Mampofu	Gloria Phakati	Mpendulo Jama	Ncayiyana Mthetheleli Clerkson	Ntethelo Madikezela	
Number of non-voters	1 675	1 444	1 669	1 564	1 427	1 744	1 652	11 175
Total non supporters of Ward Councillor	2 321	2 532	2 672	1 718	2 171	2 577	1 924	15 915
%	57.92	69.64	66.83	45.44	69.01	62.26	50.83	60.07

explained what had happened. The investigator was most encouraged by a 'good news story' of civil courage. However because the allegations were of a criminal nature, Advocate Thuli Madonsela informed us that it exceeded her powers but undertook to officially refer the matter to the national director of public prosecutions, (at the time Advocate Menzi Simelane, who in September 2013 was forced to stand down after the Constitutional Court found that his appointment had been invalid). He in turn informed me, in a letter dated 2 September 2011, that the Directorate of Public Prosecutions did not have sufficient investigative capacity to explore the complaint but that I was 'at liberty to report the matter to the South African Police within [my] area of jurisdiction who will register a case docket and do the necessary investigations'. Notwithstanding a lack of confidence in the police, the ACC decided to go up the command, and reported the complaints to the commanding officer of the Lower South Coast region, Brigadier Moodley, providing a sworn affidavit and video evidence to substantiate their allegations. He passed the buck to his Eastern Cape counterpart, even though the alleged offences were committed at the Estuary Hotel, Port Edward, which falls within his jurisdiction. The editors of *Business Report* have yet to fulfil their undertaking to follow up the story.

REFLECTIONS

Where does this all this leave us?

It is the first duty of a social worker to challenge social injustice, with the Bill of Rights as our benchmark standard. As professionals, social workers leave it up to the media to keep the public informed (which they have failed spectacularly to do in the above instance) and to lawyers to go to court to seek legal remedies. However, before, during and especially after the adversarial battles have been fought in the courts of law, and debated in the court of public opinion, social workers must work to promote insight. In the multicultural context of South Africa this also means promoting cross-cultural sensitivity and understanding. While I was working with them to ensure the Bill of Rights became meaningful, the amaDiba community taught me what participatory democracy means in practice, and just how indispensable civil courage is if we are to effectively challenge social injustice.

King Mpondombini Sigcau paid an enormous price for taking the president and Commission for Traditional Leadership Disputes and Claims to court to challenge the decision to depose him in favour of a nephew. He kept going to the very end, the Constitutional Court hearing, but died before judgement was handed down.

After the news broke that King Mpondombini had been deposed, I wrote to Alastair McIntosh for some guidance, and to specifically ask him if he could help us get the scandalous abuse of power into the international media. He replied by letter:

> I can only wish you well in seeking to give strength to those who are connected to
> Truth and the soul rather than to power and money. This evening we had a group

of Peace Activist pilgrims visit the GalGael Trust with which I am involved here in Glasgow. One of them is a South African born activist. I had a little rant about our work here and about the way in which deepening of the soul, such as happens on pilgrimage, is where we must take the nuclear debate. She was very much in agreement with this, and came up afterwards to me and my colleague, Gehan, and said the following. I pass her words on to you and you might wish to convey them to the King and Queen of Pondoland. She said: 'Civil disobedience is difficult to sustain. Only civil courage can be sustained in the long run.'

I do not believe that things are now worse than the situation that prevailed under apartheid. The above narrative would never have been possible under apartheid: in 1960, when the amaDiba rose up in rebellion (at that time against their chiefs as much as against the apartheid government), they were ruthlessly crushed. There was every possibility that the amaDiba mining conflict would descend into violence, but for the moment at least violence has been averted because of the acts of civil courage by leaders at all tiers of the traditional leadership system, a system which has in this case acted in conformity with the wishes of the local people. Thus it is that the Constitutional Court judgement that handed King Mpondombini Sigcau his victory on Thursday 13 June 2013 is a cause for great hope. It pushed back the ominous tide of history that was threatening to repeat itself. The judgement was another stinging rebuke by the judiciary to curb executive power, provoking the *Mail & Guardian* to editorialise as follows in its issue of 14 to 30 June 2013:

> Lawfare over the constitution is among the most consequential features of our current political environment. There is a dimension to this contest, however, much less noticed than headline battles over President Jacob Zuma, the prosecutions service and the transformation of the judiciary, but equally important to millions of South Africans – in some ways more so.
> The Constitutional Court is now wrestling increasingly with the practical implications of developing customary law to ensure its continued function within a constitutional framework and its judgements are creating precedents, although at times revealing telling divisions on the Bench.

On Thursday, a unanimous court set aside a decision by President Zuma, acting on the advice of the Commission of Traditional Leadership Disputes and Claims, to appoint Zanuzuko Tyelovuyo Sigcau as king of amaMpondo ase Qaukeni. Had that decision stood, he would have taken over the title, and the considerable powers that come with it, from Mpondombini Sigcau who inherited the position in 1978.

Whatever 'customary settlement' the amaMpondo people arrive at in the ensuing months or years to fill the vacancy left by King Mpondombini's death, it is not only Chapter 12 of the Constitution (Traditional Leadership) which must give shape to it but another entrenched chapter, the Bill of Rights (Chapter 2).

As we look forward to the fourth democratic election perhaps the greatest lesson on offer from this narrative is that acting with civil courage to stand fast on matters of ethical and moral principle imbues the actors with authority, a quality that is quite different from the acquisition of power. Manfred Max-Neef (1988, 1991: 95) explains that power is a capacity of a person or group to use force in order to impose their will over others. Authority by contrast is 'understood as the capacity of influence exercised by the person (or group) to whom legitimacy is granted because of recognised capacities and qualities'. Max-Neef asks the question: 'Are things going wrong because it is the wrong group that is in power, or are things going wrong because there is something wrong with power?'

REFERENCES

Alli N (2005) Sanral Annual Report. www.nra.co.za.
Boesak AA (1977) *Farewell to Innocence: A Social Ethical Study Of Black Theology And Black Power*. Maryknoll, NY: Orbis Books.
Clarke JGI (2014) *The Promise of Justice: Book One, History*. Pietermaritzburg: Brevitas Books (forthcoming).
Clarke JGI (2013) *The Promise of Justice: Book Two, His Story*. E-book version.
Constitutional Court (2013) Justice Sigcau v President of the RSA and Others (CCT 84/12) 13 June 2013.
Hunter-Wilson M (1936) *Reaction to Conquest. Effects of Contact with Europeans on the Pondo of South Africa*. Re-issued 1961. Berlin: LIT Verlag.
Kockott F (2008) *The Sunday Tribune*, 17 August.
Max-Neef MA (1988, 1991) About the pruning of language. In *Human Scale Development: Conception, Applications and Further Reflections*. London: Apex Press.
McIntosh A (2001) *Soil and Soul: People Versus Corporate Power*. London: Aurum Press.
McKay D (2011) The House Nogxina Built, http://www.miningmx.com/opinion/columnists/The-house-Nogxina-built.htm
Okri B (1998) *A Way of Being Free*. London: Phoenix.
Sonjica B (2009) Independent View. *iSimangaliso News* November-December: 7.

NOTES

1   Quoted by Dr Mary Robinson in an address to the Business and Human Rights Conference, January 2007, Johannesburg.
2   Quotes from Caruso are taken from personal correspondence with the author.
3   See a re-edited version of the report on YouTube at this address http://www.youtube.com/watch?v=mLrJUshu8mQ&feature=share&list=UUg42uQEUdiuKmuAt6_-ij8g.
4   This was recorded in the SABC programme '50/50' on 23 September 2008.
5   The author was present at this meeting and his comments are made in respect of his own observations.

CHAPTER 8

Secrecy and power in South Africa

Dale T McKinley

—————

'The best weapon of a dictatorship is secrecy, but the best weapon of a democracy should be the weapon of openness.'
Niels Bohr (1885-1962: Danish physicist, Nobel Laureate)

Secrecy has always been one of the most dangerous enemies of democracy. Any meaningful democracy, by its very nature, demands openness, transparency and accountability – the currencies of democratic freedom. On the other hand secrecy, as human history has so often shown, is the currency of authoritarianism (whatever the ideological variety), of social, economic and political control by those for whom the securing and maintenance of power is the ultimate goal.

Yet, despite these foundational understandings and historical experiences,[1] all indications point to the reality that in our contemporary South Africa (and indeed our world) secrecy is back in fashion with a vengeance. While secrecy's 'new' look might appear different from those of the past – after all, power has regularly had to change its appearance precisely because of democratic struggles – the essence of what its mask is trying to hide has changed little.

As the WikiLeaks saga has so convincingly shown, there are few things that those in (or with) power, whether in the public or private sectors, fear more than for ordinary people to have access to the truth: the truth about how they spend (and earn) money; the truth about what they say and do behind closed doors and what they say and do in public; the truth about how decisions are made and who influences (and benefits from) those decisions; the truth about what we all simply don't know – but should.

Our early twenty-first century conundrum is that the rapid advances in information technology, networking and dissemination have catalysed an equally rapid growth of this fear-induced, suffocating secrecy industry. While there is now more information available than ever before (leaving aside the issue of the dominant character and content of that information as well as huge disparities in the ability to gain access to it), there are also more secrets than ever before and thus the intensified desire by those in or with power, to hide them.

To take a contemporary international example: according to a two-year long *Washington Post* investigation[2] the number of new (government-induced) secrets in the United States rose 75 per cent between 1996 and 2009, with the number of documents using those secrets exploding from 5,6 million to 54,6 million during the same period. Similar (even if quantitatively less) indicators of the burgeoning secrecy industry are visible across the globe. Ask the ordinary Zimbabwean, Chinese or British citizen. South Africa is no exception.

EMBEDDED IN HISTORY

Although the symbiotic relationship between secrecy and power was at the core of the entire edifice of colonialism and imperialism across the global South, the implementation of formal apartheid in South Africa took this relationship to a new level. After narrowly securing victory in South Africa's 1948 all-white elections, the prime minister, Dr Daniel Malan, and his Afrikaner-dominated National Party quickly set about instituting a range of laws and decrees that would not only deepen existing legalised racism but also lay the foundation for complete political and administrative control of the state. This ideologically saturated securitisation of the state was then used to control all social, economic and political relations across South African society and to suppress any resistance from the oppressed black majority.[3]

The passage of the Suppression of Communism Act of 1950 gave the apartheid state the legal basis to ban all organisations, protests and publications that were deemed 'communist', alongside banning, detaining or restricting those seeking any 'political, industrial, social or economic change' (Bunting 1969: 199). This was quickly followed by: the Criminal Laws Amendment Act of 1953 (outlawing all protests/gatherings not approved by the state); the Public Safety Act of 1953 (allowing states of emergency for up to twelve months as well as associated detentions without trial); and, the Riotous Assemblies Act of 1956 (criminalising 'intimidation' related to strikes/stayaways/pickets, the joining of a non-state approved union and incitement to public violence).

The 1960s saw three more pieces of related legislation being passed to complete the circle: the Internal Security Act of 1963 (allowing for various types of preventative detention and interrogation of political-social activists); the Civil Defence Act of 1966 (providing for the seizure of people and property during states of emergency or threats of emergency); and the Terrorism Act of 1967. This legislation allowed for indefinite detention without trial of 'suspected terrorists or persons in possession of information about terroristic activities' (op. cit.: 236). Later in 1982, the omnibus Internal Security Act was passed, effectively replacing all previous 'security' legislation and providing even harsher regimes for the criminalisation and banning of individuals, organisations, publications and gatherings as well as for detention without trial. The axle on which the use of such concentrated political and socioeconomic power turned was institutionalised secrecy, as evinced by the Protection of Information Bill of 1982.

Such state-centred secrecy was, not surprisingly, mirrored in the thinking and practice of the (white dominated) corporate sector, whose sociopolitical and economic interests dovetailed nicely with the main demands and needs of apartheid's racial capitalism. However, one crucial aspect of apartheid's heart of secrecy and power that most often goes unrecognised was its impact – individual and organisational – on the main forces of liberation. The closing down of any meaningful space for democratic involvement by the black majority, alongside the banning of liberation organisations, saw those forces embracing armed struggle and moving either into exile or an internal underground. On the armed struggle front, the tactical dominance of a sabotage campaign, by its very character, demanded highly secretive organisation and minimal involvement of the oppressed sectors of the population. As the former South African Communist Party (SACP) and present African National Congress (ANC) stalwart Ben Turok (1974: 360) noted perceptively:

> Sabotage had the effect of isolating the organised movement from the mass ... The sabotage campaign failed on the main count – it did not raise the level of action of the masses themselves ... they were left on the threshold, frustrated bystanders of a battle being waged on their behalf.

Over time, this was combined with an increasing centralisation of power centred on a small collection of exiled leadership[4] and framed, in the case of the ANC and its exiled ally the SACP, by general adherence to Soviet-style commandist politics and an overarching ideology and rhetoric that did not distinguish between the liberation movement and the people. As Raymond Suttner (2006 and 2008: 119) points out, the cumulative result was the adoption of a 'warrior culture, the militarist tradition' which 'entailed not only heroic acts but also many cases of abuse of power', leading to the emergence of a liberation movement as a prototype of a state within a state, in which it sees itself as the only legitimate source of power.[5]

The growth and variety of grassroots organisational forms that emerged during the internal resistance to apartheid-capitalism during the 1980s was accompanied by the ever-increasing influence of the decidedly bureaucratic, centralised and hierarchical organisational form of the exiled ANC and its allies (mainly grouped together in the United Democratic Front (UDF)). While those forces associated with the ANC (internally and externally) gained a dominant organisational and symbolic position by the late 1980s, the actual liberation struggle on the ground was replete with divergent, contradictory and often overtly hostile positions, locations, and organisational and ideological traditions. Indeed, by the late 1980s the ANC's 'calls for unity increasingly referred only to those who accepted the leadership of the UDF and its exiled ANC allies' (Marx 1992: 171). While there certainly was a broad-based unity around getting rid of apartheid, there was also a marked intolerance and fear of internal dissent and external opposition that developed within the ranks of the respective leaderships of the ANC and its alliance partners. The supreme historical irony was that as the twilight of apartheid approached the very forces of liberation poised to take political power had imbibed much of the toxic concoction of secrecy and power so beloved by their own oppressors.

SAME WINE, NEW BOTTLES?

The unbanning, return from exile and entrance into political negotiations of the ANC and other liberation organisations marked the opening up of a new terrain in the struggle for national liberation. But it was not the terrain that many had envisioned. The ANC leadership, as the dominant liberation movement 'players', quickly adopted the position that there was no need for militant grassroots organisations and struggles since the institutional space, through the negotiations, would now act as the fulcrum of 'democratic' engagement (McKinley 1997). What this logically required, then, was an enforced unity in the name of 'the people', wherein such organisations were no longer needed now that the ANC and its allies had effectively ended formal apartheid. In turn, this was framed by an approach to 'nation-building' that demanded (of 'the people') political obedience to the 'new' state – which was just around the corner – and the party that would soon control it.

The most immediate result of the political triumph over apartheid as evinced through the April 1994 elections was, as Salim Vally (2003: 67) has argued, a continuity of 'the dominant interests that determine the strategic thrust of the South African state … [including] ownership of the commanding heights of the economy [and] the repressive apparatus of the state … '. Crucially, then, the mindsets and practices that structured apartheid responses to dissent and conflict found a generally warm embrace amongst the ANC leadership and, as we shall see, especially within the new state's security and intelligence apparatus. Such continuities were, however, over-determined by the particular position that was adopted by the state and ruling ANC in relation to questions of economic policy as revealed by the adoption of the neoliberal Growth, Employment and Redistribution (GEAR) policy. Indeed, the (early) transitional genesis of the ANC state's approach to (democratic) power and space is to be found in its heavy-handed reactions to, and effective marginalisation of, widespread dissent over GEAR.

Besides the ANC leadership's declaration that GEAR was 'non-negotiable',[6] the central political tenet of that response was provided by senior ANC and state official, Joel Netshitenzhe (1996) who argued: '… when pressure from below is exerted it should aim at complimenting the work of those who are exerting pressure against the old order from above'. In the context of the historical 'entry-points' as analysed above, this was simply another way of saying that the ANC and the state it now controlled viewed any political or socioeconomic struggle and dissent against its own practices and policies (the exercise of power) as unacceptable and even illegitimate. The implicit assumption was, and remains, clear; that the post-1994 state and the people that put it in power are one and the same and that going outside the organisational and institutional boundaries of democratic engagement set by the ruling party and the state itself should be treated as an act of political heresy and, if necessary, a betrayal of the liberation struggle itself.

In practice, this is more or less what happened. As opposition from within and outside the ANC, its alliance partners and the state intensified, a climate of hostility took hold towards any radical critique of and active opposition to ANC policy. Labels such as 'ultra-left', 'unpatriotic' and 'counter-revolutionary' were increasingly used to label critics, and some were expelled from the ANC, Congress of South African Trade Unions (Cosatu) and the SACP.[7] The then president, Thabo Mbeki, declared that 'the people know that ... historically, those who opposed and worked to destroy the ANC, and tried to mobilise the workers to act against our movement, were the same people who sought to entrench and perpetuate their oppression' (Mbeki 2002).

Unsurprisingly, the practical effects of GEAR and the gradual foreclosure of any real dialogue between the state and poor communities in relation to issues of economic import catalysed a new wave of resistance. Engagements between the two began to take on an increasingly conflictual character, mediated by the criminal justice system in the context of post-1994 security and related legislation (McKinley and Veriava 2005: 45-53). Although the South African Parliament passed the Safety Matters Rationalisation Act of 1996 which repealed thirty four apartheid-era laws dealing with security legislation, several pieces of legislation from the apartheid days were maintained (and remain as law today). These include the 'Riotous Assemblies Act of 1956' which gives the president the power to take 'special precautions to maintain public order' and makes 'incitement to public violence' a crime; the National Key Points Act of 1980 (NKPA) which makes it a crime punishable by up to twenty years in prison for 'disrupting' the operations of secretly designated key points such as airports, military bases, government buildings, water storage and distribution facilities and oil refineries; the Protection of Information Act of 1982 (PIA) whose approach to the protection and dissemination of information is informed by the demands of an authoritarian and secretive apartheid state; and, the 'Regulation of Gatherings Act of 1993' (RGA) that determines how, where and when individuals and groups can gather and defines the shape, size and location of protests.

Besides these laws, the Cabinet unilaterally implemented the Minimum Information Security Standards of 1996 (MISS) which, in the name of ensuring 'that the national interests of the Republic are protected', set down information security standards for all government departments and institutions based on four categories of classification for handling 'sensitive information' (restricted, confidential, secret and top secret). Besides going a long way to prevent the free flow of government information, the MISS placed a thick veil of secrecy over whatever was left of apartheid-era state information. Even though the much-celebrated Promotion of Access to Information Act of 2000 (PAIA) was subsequently passed,[8] its immediate (and longer-term) effectiveness and influence was seriously compromised by a huge lack of public awareness, education and human resources within the state to implement it, the poor state of public records management, and an alarming absence of accountability in those entrusted with ensuring its implementation (McKinley 2003).

Further, the state introduced an 'Anti-Terrorism Bill' to Parliament in 2003, the name of which was later disingenuously changed to the 'Protection of Constitutional Democracy against Terrorist and Related Activities Act' when it was passed in 2004 after intense public debate and opposition. As in its apartheid predecessor (the 'Internal Security Act' of 1982, some of which remained in effect from 1994 until the passage of the new Act), terrorism includes any act designed to 'intimidate, or to induce or cause feelings of insecurity within, the public'. Critically for social movements and local community organisations whose protest activities have most often revolved around a lack of basic needs and services, the Act makes 'interference with or serious disruption of an essential service, facility or system, or the delivery of any such service, facility-system, whether public or private' a terrorist act (Republic of South Africa 2004).

Before the first decade of South Africa's democracy had drawn to a close the ANC and the state it was increasingly running with a velvet-lined clenched fist, had 'succeeded' in closing down many institutional avenues of democratic participation and redress; in actively utilising repressive apartheid-era legislation and the coercive forces of the state to intimidate and harass activists and their organisations, crack down on popular dissent as well as prevent open access to state information, both past and present; and in invoking an exclusionary and accusatory political discourse wrapped in one-sided understandings of power. Such 'successes' were much too close a match to those of the apartheid regime in that they revealed states of fear and loathing, reflecting both individual and organisational-institutional insecurities about power and place, about acceptance and legitimacy – the perfect incubator for secrecy.

OLD HABITS DIE HARD

When then president Mbeki (with Nelson Mandela and half of the government's Cabinet in tow) joyously celebrated the awarding of the Fédération Internationale de Football Association (FIFA) 2010 Soccer World Cup to South Africa in 2003, not a single 'ordinary' South African had any idea what their elected government had agreed to in order to get the prize. Not that this bothered the ANC politicians, given their hyper-secretive conduct in concluding a wholly unnecessary late 1990s multi-billion rand arms deal on 'behalf' of the South African citizenry. Indeed, despite overwhelming evidence of massive corruption involving senior ANC and government officials – a result of whistleblowing and some courageous investigative research and journalism[9] – to this day, there remains an ongoing battle in the legal/court system to try and force the government to reveal information about the arms deal.

So successful was the wall of secrecy thrown up around the Soccer World Cup deal between the government and FIFA (protected by an inbuilt confidentiality clause) that it took another seven years after the actual signing of the contractual agreement with FIFA for the South African public to find out what their 'democratic' representatives had agreed to, in their name. The 'guarantees' in the agreement (SA 2010 FIFA World Cup, 2010) included providing FIFA with 'the support of officers of relevant authorities, such as police and customs, to assist in the protection of the marketing and broadcast rights'; ensuring 'that there are no legal restrictions or prohibitions on the sale or distribution of commercial affiliates products'; indemnifying 'FIFA and defend[ing] and hold[ing] it harmless against all proceedings, claims and related costs which may be incurred or suffered by or threatened by others against FIFA'; providing 'at no cost to the users, all telecommunications infrastructure'; 'not [to] impose any kind of taxes, duties or other levies on FIFA, FIFA's subsidiaries, the FIFA delegation and the host broadcaster'; 'unrestricted import and export of all foreign currencies to and from the country as well as the exchange of these currencies into US dollars, euros or Swiss francs'; and, 'to enact laws to ensure that hotel prices for the FIFA delegation [and] representatives of FIFA's commercial affiliates … shall be frozen as of 1 January 2010 … and that hotel prices for the FIFA delegation are 20 per cent less than the frozen rate … with no minimum stay'.

Neither did anyone outside the World Cup 'inner-circle' elite, comprising top politicians, South Africa's soccer hierarchy and leading corporate capitalists, know that the original estimates in 2003 for the entire cost to the government (and thus all South Africans) for the 'privilege' to host the event, amounted to around R2,3 billion. What they eventually discovered was that the final cost was a shade under R40 billion, a 1700 per cent increase (*Business Report* 2 July 2010). One of the main reasons for this outrageous over-expenditure was the government's acceptance of confidential 'host city agreements' and 'stadium agreements' in which 'many of the terms in the contracts had been framed in an undetermined fashion' (Parliamentary Monitoring Group 2006). The ensuing levels of fraud and corruption surrounding everything from stadium construction to fan parks (not to mention the murders of whistleblowers and the intimidation of journalists) are only now beginning to come to the surface thanks to a web of secrecy having been thrown up by the various power elites involved, at local provincial and national levels (McKinley 2011; Media24 Investigations 2013; IOL News 2013).

Nowhere was the local version of this web more intense than in the province of Mpumalanga, not only in respect of the local Mbombela stadium but also with that most sensitive of post-apartheid issues – land. Starting in 2003, a motley crew of corrupt officials and politicians, local white farmers, politically connected businessmen and greedy trustees of the local Ndwandwa community trust, went about hijacking the Ndwandwa Trust. They did so as a means of milking available land reform funds with impunity, exploiting legitimate beneficiaries ruthlessly and launching a sustained campaign against the person and properties of local whistleblowers Fred Daniel and Robert Nkosi, who exposed and blew the lid off what remains the biggest land scam in South African history. Despite damning evidence from three independent and government-backed forensic investigations into the scam that confirmed a R50 million fraud, no one has been convicted of any crime (McKinley 2012a).

The flourishing affair between secrecy and power began to show its face all over the place. Soon after the passage of the Promotion of Access to Information Act (PAIA), a law explicitly designed, in the words of the then minister of justice and constitutional development, Penuell Maduna, 'to bring to an end the secrecy and silence that characterised decades of apartheid rule and administration' (South African Press Association 25 January 2000), the government granted the National Intelligence Agency a five-year exemption. Not long thereafter, then Reserve Bank governor Tito Mboweni, after refusing to release two damning reports on Saambou Bank, publicly stated that 'it would be in the best interests of the banking sector as a whole' for the Reserve Bank to have a PAIA exemption. In what can only be described as a classic case of perverse logic, Mboweni, arguing in defence of blocking access to information about banking operations, stated that, 'people do not understand the detail of what's going on' (Loxton 2003).

It was in the myriad back corridors of power within the ruling ANC where the affair was 'outed' on a much grander scale. As the early 2000s battles between the Mbeki and Zuma factions within the ANC (and its alliance partners) became ever more intense, so too did the involvement of the state's intelligence services. Charges between the two factions flew thick and fast, revolving largely around the involvement of senior ANC and government leaders in spying for the apartheid regime, corruptly benefiting from the arms deal, and abusing the state security and intelligence services to dig up dirt and to spy on each other (Hefer Commission of Inquiry 2004; *Mail & Guardian* 2009; *Mail & Guardian* 2013b). Even if there was a huge gap between the protagonists' stated embrace of the constitutional values and laws respecting the privacy, dignity and human rights of all South Africans, acknowledgement of the past abuse of security and intelligence services for political and oppressive ends and what was actually going on,[10] by 2006 things were bad enough for the then minister of intelligence, Ronnie Kasrils, to appoint a ministerial review commission on intelligence (the Matthews Commission).[11]

The Commission's mandate was to review the operations of all intelligence entities (excepting crime and defence intelligence) with the aim of strengthening 'mechanisms of control of the civilian intelligence structures in order to ensure full compliance and alignment with the Constitution, constitutional principles and the rule of law, and particularly to minimise the potential for illegal conduct and abuse of power.' Its main findings confirmed that the services had indeed been politicised and 'drawn into the realm of party politics [which] required it to monitor and investigate legal political activity and, … undermined political rights that are entrenched in the Constitution.'

It also found that accountability to the public was weak, a 'consequence of excessive secrecy, which is inconsistent with the constitutional tenet that all spheres of government must be transparent and accountable.' Importantly, it confirmed that the mandate of the intelligence services was far too broad, which 'can lead to … focusing in an inappropriate manner on lawful political and social activities.' The excessive mandate was largely attributable to an equally over-broad conception of national security wherein the services had come to see themselves as the main watchdog of society, almost separate and above the constitutional and democratic order. In this respect, the Commission noted that, 'national security should thus not be conceived as separate from, and potentially in conflict with, human security and human rights. It encompasses the security of the country, its people, the state and the constitutional order.'

Many other problems were identified by the Commission: a lack of adequate oversight and regulation in respect of counter-intelligence functions as well as the finances and budget of the services; that the inspector general of intelligence lacks independence and resources; that the National Communication Centre 'appears to be engaged in signals monitoring that is unlawful and unconstitutional' because it 'fails to comply with the requirements of the Regulation of Interception of Communications and Provision of Communication-Related Information Act of 2002 (RICA), which prohibits the interception of communication without judicial authorisation'; and that 'some senior officials believe that it is legitimate to break the rules when dealing with serious security threats'. The conclusion of the report, besides calling for a public review of the intelligence mandate and several specific measures to improve accountability, crucially argued that, 'the right of access to information lies at the heart of democratic accountability and an open and free society. Secrecy should therefore be regarded as an exception … the intelligence organisations have not shed sufficiently the apartheid-era security obsession with secrecy.'

But just when there seemed to be the real possibility of a serious push for the democratisation of the intelligence services, and also for a range of opportunities to reign in those who had increasingly become intoxicated with the power-secrecy potion, factional politics within the ANC took centre stage again. The triumphant Zuma faction,[12] with Zuma himself having been given a 'get-out-of-jail-free' card by the timely intervention of some individuals within the very security-intelligence and prosecutorial agencies at the heart of the burgeoning secrecy industry, quickly put the Matthews Commission report in the closet and set about mixing up its own even more powerful cocktail of secrecy and power.

RIDING ROUGHSHOD: ZUMA AND THE SECUROCRATS

'There is too much information in the hands of citizens.'
Nkenke Kekana, former ANC parliamentary Communications Portfolio Committee chair, 2011.

In many ways, South Africans should not be that surprised with what has happened, in respect of the secrecy and power equation, over the last few years under the 'reign' of a government and ANC of which Zuma is the president. First, Zuma had been very much central to the leadership of both since the beginning of the transition, and part of all major policy, organisational and overall political developments. Second, Zuma cut and sharpened his political and organisational teeth as head of ANC intelligence during the later part of the exile years. Old habits die hard.

One of the arenas of secrecy which Zuma and his lieutenants quickly made clear they would not only continue to uphold but would expand, was political party funding. With the embers of the Polokwane 'victory' fire still hot, the ANC's investment arm, Chancellor House, as 25 per cent owner of Hitachi Power Africa, signed a hugely lucrative contract worth an estimated R3 billion with Eskom as part of Eskom's power station infrastructure project (Brümmer and Sole 2008). Not surprisingly, the ANC has flatly refused to divulge the contents of the contract or to answer questions about how the party is using the money.

Similarly, Zuma's ANC has consistently refused to reveal the sources and amounts of private funding it receives or to act on unregulated private funding of all political parties. It is estimated that the amount of such private donations to political parties during the 2009 elections was in the region of R550 million (Right2Know Campaign 2013b). Unbeknownst to most South Africans, almost R1 billion has been paid out by provincial governments to political parties (the lion's share of which goes to the ANC) even though it appears that such payments are unconstitutional (Phoshoko, Timse and Brümmer 2013).

Much as it did in the Mandela and Mbeki years, the Zuma government has maintained (and in many cases expanded) the ANC's and the state's cosy relationship with the corporate sector. Predictably, this has seen an even greater wall of secrecy built by both the state and the corporate sector, and often in conjunction with public infrastructure tenders, environmental impact assessments, personal/business relationships, workplace conditions, energy tariff deals, mining licences, service contracts and road tolls. In one of the most outrageous examples, the activities of Aurora Empowerment Systems (in which President Zuma's nephew, Khulubuse Zuma and his lawyer Michael Hulley are key shareholders) in stripping the assets and destroying the lives of thousands of workers at the Grootvlei and Orkney gold mines has been actively covered up for years. A judicial inquiry where both testified about their roles was held behind closed doors (Smith 2011) and no one has yet been held responsible.

When civil society organisations and the media have attempted to access information related to the impact of industrial and mining activities on the environment, many government departments and private companies have flatly refused access and treated the hidden information as state secrets. During 2011-2012 the Mineral Resources Department refused 97 per cent of over a hundred PAIA requests for information on environmental health and protection made by the Centre for Environmental Rights. The refusal rate by private companies was almost as high, with CRE's director Melissa Fourie noting that they 'encountered reluctance, resistance and suspicion from both public and private bodies … we were frequently interrogated about our and our clients' motives, use and need for the information' (Carnie 2012).

Similarly, over the past two years there has been a consistent pattern of collusive blocking of information related to the proposed expansion of the Durban Port and new Dug-out Port that is crucial to the environmental and physical health of communities in the South Durban basin (South Durban Community Environmental Alliance 2012). The same kind of secrecy by default behaviour has also been applied to the state's proposed R1 trillion nuclear build programme (which makes the earlier arms deal seem like small change), with Greenpeace Africa's PAIA requests to the Department of Energy for its Integrated Nuclear Infrastructure Review (INIR) which contains information on process, environmental assessment and financing, being either refused or simply ignored (Greenpeace Africa 2012).

Even information related to government-initiated commissions of inquiry, the impetus for which have mostly come from public pressure and media exposure, has been kept in the secrecy closet by Zuma and his securocrats (Freedom of Expression Institute 2010, *Mail & Guardian* 2013b). To give a recent example of the extent of such generalised secrecy: the South African History Archive (SAHA) administered 159 PAIA requests for information held by various public and private bodies during 2012; of these, 102 (64 per cent) were refused or received no answer (Right2Know Campaign 2013b).

Two of the most publicly contentious issues where the ANC, state and private sector have jointly waged intense battles to prevent public access to information have been over energy pricing and e-tolling. In the case of energy (electricity) pricing, it took almost four years of PAIA requests, protests, and expensive court proceedings to finally (in March 2013) force Eskom, along with corporate behemoth BHP Billiton, to reveal a secretive contract that gives preferential prices far below those charged to ordinary South Africans (Business Report 2013). Linked to this is the Department of Energy's promulgation in 2012 of two draft bills, the National Energy Regulator Amendment Bill and the Electricity Regulation Second Amendment Bill. Combined, these will effectively transfer the regulatory power of the present statutory body, the National Energy Regulator of South Africa (Nersa) to the minister of energy, which in practice will mean that the one space where the public can access crucial energy information as well as actively participate in decision-making processes will be taken away (Earthlife Africa 2012).

On e-tolling, national and provincial government have repeatedly stonewalled widespread public calls to come clean on the decision-making process leading to, and content of, a bevy of contracts signed with the Electronic Toll Collection (ETC) consortium that will run the e-toll system in Gauteng and which will see road users paying steep tariffs for the privilege of travelling on roads built with public funds (*The Times* 2012). Despite public protests largely led by Cosatu, a lengthy legal battle engaged by the Opposition to Urban Tolling Alliance (Outa), and revelations that ANC-linked businesses have benefited and will continue to benefit handsomely (Rasool 2012), the toll system is on the verge of being implemented after President Zuma signed the 'Transport Laws and Related Matters Amendment Bill; (otherwise known as the E-Toll Bill) into law in late September 2013.

This conscious, politically and materially driven closing down of the constitutionally-enshrined right of access to information under the Zuma-led ANC/state (with the active encouragement and collusion of corporate capital) is one side of a three-pronged secrecy-power matrix. While that matrix has been in operation from the start of the South African transition, the ascension to power of the Zuma faction since 2007-2008 has taken it to another level. The second side is the militarisation and centralisation of power within, the coercive forces of the state alongside the massive and largely de-regulated growth of the private security industry. As Karl Marx so clearly understood, the sustenance of societal consent under capitalism demands enforcement through the combined coercive power of the state and the capitalist class.

In the case of the capitalist class, the dominant vehicle for such coercive power in contemporary South Africa has become the private security industry, which has doubled in size over the last five years and now has more than two-and-a-half times the number of personnel (many of whom are armed to the teeth) in the South African Police Services (De Waal 2012). The state has largely abandoned its oversight and regulation mandate, with the result that there is no available information on the number of firearms held or deaths and violent incidents involving the industry (Jaynes 2012). There is a massive unregulated private 'army' spread out all over the country, largely protecting private interests (although in many cases, public infrastructure and services through outsourced state contracts) and doing more or less what it pleases without any meaningful consequences.

As far as the coercive forces of the state are concerned, Zuma's *umshini wami*-inspired militarisation of the police force has catalysed an even harsher crackdown on surging worker and community protests – protests that themselves are largely a direct response to a lack of basic services and/or the closing down of democratic space. Outright, and illegal, bans on marches, a shoot first ask questions later approach (as at Marikana), and a huge upsurge in the number of people who have died either through police action or in police custody (with over eight hundred deaths in 2010-2011 alone) are now the order of the day (Duncan 2010; Independent Police Investigative Directorate 2010/2011). In the specific case of the Marikana massacre, there has been a particularly energetic effort by Zuma's securocrats to bottle up relevant police and intelligence information that might actually force them to take responsibility (Kasrils 2012). Such systematic use and abuse of the state's coercive forces is all the more damning when the minister of state security himself openly admits that there are 'no discernable threats to our constitutional order' (Cwele 2011).

The third side of the matrix is the law, past and pending. As previously noted the Regulation of Gatherings Act of 1993 has been kept on the books and, under the Zuma state, has been (mis)used more than ever before to frustrate and prevent people's legitimate right to protest, and thus to bring consistent popular pressure for transparency and accountability. But that has clearly not satisfied the seemingly insatiable need of Zuma and his securocrats to hide behind their self-constructed walls. What better way to buttress those walls of secrecy around the physical representations of state and private (capitalist) power than to dust off and actively employ the NKPA of 1980. This apartheid dinosaur gives the minister of police the power to declare any place a 'national key point' if it is considered vital to 'national security'. Once a site is declared, a range of strict anti-disclosure provisions which criminalise any person disclosing 'any information' in 'any manner whatsoever' about security measures of a national key point comes into effect as does the curtailment of the right of assembly in or near any key point (South African Police Service 2007). No surprise then that Zuma and his securocrats have increased the number of national key points by over 50 per cent in the last five years, famously adding Zuma's private rural residence in Nkandla to prevent disclosing details of the expenditure of large sums of public money, although they continue to refuse to publicly reveal the rapidly expanding list for 'national security' reasons (Right2Know Campaign, 2012b).

There's more though. Completely ignoring almost every warning and recommendation of the Matthews Commission report, the ANC reintroduced the Protection of Information Bill in 2010. Since renamed the Protection of State Information Bill, but popularly known as the 'Secrecy Bill', it is on the verge of being passed into law despite spirited and widely supported opposition[13] led by the Right2Know Campaign – a fight that has seen the Bill go through twenty-nine versions and in the process become the most debated piece of legislation in post-apartheid South Africa. Even though some of the most draconian aspects have been excised, the Bill remains hugely problematic for a number of reasons: the definition of 'national security' is open-ended and thus ripe for abuse in determining what information can be 'protected', particularly due to the inclusion of undefined 'state security matters' and 'economic, scientific and technological secrets'; it will give the minister of state security (and, to lesser degrees, other state bodies like the police) incredibly wide powers over classification procedures and overall management of state information; it will ensure that previously classified information (including some from the apartheid era) enjoys protection; it criminalises (with extremely harsh sentences) simple possession and/or disclosure of classified information; and there is no full public interest defence nor public domain defence, thus further exposing activists, whistle blowers and journalists to criminal prosecution (Right2Know Campaign 2012c).

The fight is not over, though. In mid-September 2013, several months after the Bill was passed by Parliament and sent to President Zuma, he referred the Bill back to Parliament. Even though Zuma citied two specific clauses in the Bill as being 'irrational and … unconstitutional' he did not explain the specific reasons why these two clauses, neither of which address any of the major problems as outlined above, are problematic. It remains to be seen whether any parliamentary time and space is opened up to address the various unconstitutional aspects of the Bill, and the likelihood is that the Bill will be passed into law within months. It will then immediately face a Constitutional Court challenge by an increasingly combative civil society which is also looking to new technology and creative avenues such as open data to prise open the doors of information in South Africa (McKinley 2012b).

Another piece of securocrat legislation that has only recently been signed into law by Zuma is the General Intelligence Laws Amendment Bill (otherwise known as the 'Spy Bill'). It faced extensive public opposition which was largely ignored. While the opposition engendered some positive changes to the initial Bill, it did not prevent Zuma and his securocrats from retaining the most worrying provisions, among them the centralisation of every intelligence structure, foreign and domestic (with the exception of the oversight body, the National Intelligence Coordinating Committee) into a 'super' State Security Agency (SSA) and an overly broad intelligence mandate that includes 'political intelligence', which could result in the monitoring of journalists, unionists and activists.

While a clause that would have made it legal for the new SSA to tap into the private communications of ordinary citizens without a warrant through the monitoring of 'foreign signals' which could include Skype, Gmail and Facebook (McKinley 2012c; Right2Know Campaign 2012a; Bhardwaj 2013) was scrapped, the matter is not closed since the SSA has indicated it will address this in a future policy review during 2014.

There is enough evidence exposed in the media which suggests this kind of monitoring continues to happen, even though it is illegal. When combined with the Secrecy Bill the clear picture that is emerging is one of a 'superpower' state security and intelligence establishment answering largely to itself and its political masters. That sounds eerily familiar.

QUO VADIS?

South Africa's apartheid and more recent transitional past have a dual but intertwined history: one of repression, injustice, inequality and secrecy; another of freedom, justice, equality and openness. The battle between these two did not end in 1994 – it simply changed faces and shifted gears. As democratic South Africa approaches the twenty year mark we are at a crossroads on many fronts, but no more so than when it comes to the collusive and corrosive mix of secrecy and power. The longer it goes on, the more dominant it will become and the harder it will be to resist and defeat.

Those who are determined to force the toxic mix down our throats cannot be the ones entrusted to be the overseers and implementers of openness and transparency in a democracy. If the powerful are fearful of what ordinary people think, know and do, then they are fearful of democracy itself. It is not, as they would have it, simply a matter of 'balancing' self-constructed notions of state/national security against the rights and freedoms of our democracy. Those rights and freedoms, which are not static but have been and remain continuously fought and struggled for, are the foundational basis for our collective intelligence and security in the present and the future.

REFERENCES

Bhardwaj V (2013) Briefing note: developments on GILAB thus far. E-mail correspondence to the Right2Know working groups list, 11 March.
Brümmer S and S Sole (2008) 'ANC's power grab'. *Mail & Guardian* 1 February http://www.mg.co.za/articlePage.aspx?articleid=331152&area=/insight/insight__national/ [Accessed 19 April 2008].
Bunting B (1969) *The Rise of the South African Reich*. Harmondsworth: Penguin.
Business Report (2010) 'World Cup 2010: the legacy'. 12 July.
Carnie T (2012) 'Secrecy over environment information'. *The Mercury*, 16 April.
Cawthra G and R Luckham (eds) (2003) *Governing Insecurity: Democratic Control of Military and Security Establishments in Transitional Societies.* London and New York: Zed Books.
Cwele S (2011), Address by the minister of state security, Dr Siyabonga Cwele, on the occasion of the State Security Budget Vote, 2 June. http://www.ssa.gov.za/Portals/0/SSA%20docs/Speeches/2011/Minister_Budget%20Vote%202011%20Revised.pd [Accessed 7 August 2011].
De Waal M (2012) 'Unregulated and taking root: SA's private security peril'. *Daily Maverick*, 19 November. http://www.dailymaverick.co.za/article/2012-11-19-unregulated-and-taking-root-sas-private-security-peril#.UVV2xRc7FrM [Accessed 6 December 2012].
Duncan J (2010) 'The Return of State Repression', 31 May. http://www.sacsis.org.za/site/article/489.1 [Accessed 12 June 2010].
Duncan J (2011) 'How Deep Is the Rot in South Africa's Intelligence Services?', 23 October http://www.sacsis.org.za/site/article/771.1 [Accessed 28 October 2011].

Earthlife Africa (2012) Department of Energy's strike against democracy. Press Release, 16 February.

Ellis S and T Sechaba (1992) *Comrades Against Apartheid: The ANC and the South African Communist Party in Exile*. London: James Currey.

Fenster M (2008) *Conspiracy Theories: Secrecy and Power in American Culture* (Revised Ed.). Minneapolis: University of Minnesota Press.

Freedom of Expression Institute (2010) FXI Challenges Justice Department's decision to deny access to the state's submissions to the Ginwala Inquiry'. Press Release, 8 December.

Gill P (1994) *Policing Politics: Security Intelligence and the Liberal Democratic State*. London: Frank Cass.

Greenpeace Africa (2012) Greenpeace lodges complaint with public protector and the SA Human Rights Commission'. Press Release, 19 November. http://www.greenpeace.org/africa/en/Press-Centre-Hub/Press-releases/Greenpeace-lodges-complaint-with-Public-Protector-and-the-SA-Human-Rights-Commission/ [Accessed 2 December 2012].

Hefer Commission of Inquiry (2004) Report to President Thabo Mbeki, 7 January. http://www.info.gov.za/view/DownloadFileAction?id=164664 [Accessed 8 November 2012].

Independent Police Investigative Directorate (2010/2011) Annual Reports. http://www.ipid.gov.za/documents/annual_reports.asp [Accessed 10 October 2012].

IOL News (2013) 'Bobby Motaung faces more charges', 3 March. http://www.iol.co.za/news/crime-courts/bobby-motaung-faces-more-charges-1.1479773#.UVLzsxc7FrM [Accessed 10 March 2013].

Jaynes N (2012) Flying below the radar? The armed private security sector in South Africa. Open Society Foundation Occasional Paper. http://osf.org.za/wp/wp-content/uploads/2012/10/CJI-Occasional-Paper-11.pdf [Accessed 24 January 2013].

Kasrils R (2012) 'It was like poking a hornet's nest'. *Sunday Times*, 26 August.

Legassick M (1974) South Africa: Capital accumulation and violence. *Economy and Society* 3(3): 253-291.

Leigh I and L Lustgarten (1994) *In From the Cold: National Security and Parliamentary Democracy*. Oxford: Clarendon Press.

Loxton L (2003) 'Mboweni wants to block access to banking information'. *Business Report*, 31 March.

Maharaj M (2009) 'Walking tall in the face of adversity is a collective effort'. *Sunday Times*, 12 April.

Mail & Guardian (2013a) 'Editorial, Khampepe report: Keeping you in the dark', 1 March. http://mg.co.za/article/2013-02-01-00-khampepe-report-keeping-you-in-the-dark.

Mail & Guardian (2013b) 'Lawyers: Zuma will fight release of Spy Tapes', 10 March. http://mg.co.za/article/2013-03-10-president-zuma-to-fight-release-of-spy-tapes [Accessed 13 March 2013].

Mail & Guardian (2009) 'Spooks Haunt our Democracy', 22 May. http://mg.co.za/article/2009-05-22-spooks-haunt-our-democracy [Accessed 18 February 2012].

Marx A (1992) *Lessons of Struggle: South African Internal Opposition, 1960-1990*. Cape Town: Oxford University Press.

Mbeki T (2002) Letter from the President: The Masses are Not Blind. *ANC Today*, 2(40): 4-10 October.

McKinley D T (2012a) Beauty and the beast: A historical timeline of corruption, greed and conflict in Badplaas, Mpumalanga (1998-2012). Unpublished research report undertaken on behalf of Fred Daniel.

McKinley D T (2012b) The Right to Know, The Right to Live, Open Data in South Africa. Research Report for the Open Democracy Advice Centre.

McKinley DT (2012c) Back to the Future? Securitising the South Africa State, 6 March. http://www.sacsis.org.za/site/article/1228 [Accessed 6 March 2012].

McKinley D T (2011) FIFA and the sports-accumulation Complex and, Mbombela: Corruption, murder, false promises and resistance. In Cottle E (ed) *South Africa's World Cup: A Legacy for Whom?* Scottsville: University of KwaZulu-Natal Press.

McKinley D T and A Veriava (2005) *Arresting Dissent: State Repression and Post-Apartheid Social Movements*. Johannesburg: Centre for the Study of Violence and Reconciliation.

McKinley D T (2003) The State of Access to Information in South Africa. Research Report for the Centre for the Study of Violence and Reconciliation.

McKinley D T (2001) Democracy, power and patronage: Debate and opposition within the ANC and Tripartite Alliance since 1994. In R Southall (ed.) *Opposition and Democracy in South Africa.* London: Frank Cass.

McKinley D T (2000) The end of 'innocence': the Alliance and the left. *South African Labour Bulletin* 24 (5): 55-60.

McKinley D T (1997) *The ANC and the Liberation Struggle: A Critical Political Biography.* London: Pluto.

Media 24 Investigations (2013) Hawks probe construction industry price-fixing, 4 February. http://www. m24i.co.za/2013/02/04/hawks-probe-construction-industry-price-fixing [Accessed 16 February 2013].

Ministerial Commission on Intelligence (2008) Intelligence in a Constitutional Democracy, 10 September. http://www.ssronline.org/edocs/review_commission_final_report20080910.doc [Accessed 15 October 2011].

Netshitenzhe J (1996) State and Social Transformation. African National Congress Discussion Document, http://www.anc.org.za/show.php?id=306 [Accessed 16 July 2001].

Parliamentary Monitoring Group (2006) 'Sport and Recreation and Provincial and Local Government Portfolio Committees - 2010 Agreements with Municipalities Briefing', 6 June. http://www.pmg. org.za/node.7874 [Accessed 13 July 2010].

Phoshoko F, T Timse and S Brümmer (2013) 'R1-billion in "illegal" party payouts'. *Mail and Guardian*, 8 March. http://mg.co.za/article/2013-03-08-00-r1-billion-in-illegal-party-payouts [Accessed 15 March 2013].

Priest D and W Arkin (2010) 'A hidden world growing beyond control' *Washington Post.* http://projects.washingtonpost.com/top-secret-america/articles/a-hidden-world-growing-beyond-control/ [Accessed 27 March 2011].

Rasool F (2012) 'E-tolling: It's all about the money'. ITWeb, 24 May.

Republic of South Africa (2004) Protection of Constitutional Democracy Against Terrorist and Related Activities Act, http://www.info.gov.za/view/DownloadFileAction?id=67972 [Accessed 12 June 2005].

Right2KnowCampaign(2013a)TheMatthewsCommission,GILABandwhywe'reworriedaboutSA'sspies. 11 February, http://www.r2k.org.za/2013/02/11/matthews-commission-gilab-south-africa-spies/ [Accessed 15 February 2013].

Right2Know Campaign (2013b) R2K's Secret State of the Nation Report, 17 February. http://www.r2k. org.za/2013/02/17/secret-state-of-the-nation-report/ [Accessed 18 February 2013].

Right2KnowCampaign(2012a)R2SubmissionontheGeneralIntelligenceLawsAmendmentBill,16March. http://www.r2k.org.za/2012/03/16/r2k-submission-on-the-general-intelligence-laws-amendment-bill/ [Accessed 24 March 2012].

Right2Know Campaign (2012b) How the National Key Points Act undermines the public's right to know, 4 October. http://www.r2k.org.za/2012/10/04/how-the-national-key-points-act-undermines-the-publics-right-to-know/ [Accessed 17 October 2012].

Right2Know Campaign (2012c). Why the Secrecy Bill still fails the Freedom Test, 28 November. http://www.r2k.org.za/2012/11/28/guide-why-secrecy-bill-fails/ [Accessed 29 November 2012].

SA 2010 FIFA World Cup (2010) Government's Guarantees. http://www.sa2010.gov.za /en/guarantees [Accessed 24 July 2010].

Sanders J (2006) *Apartheid's Friends: The Rise and Fall of South Africa's Secret Service.* London: John Murray.

Smith N (2011) 'Aurora's "plunder" of mines secret as liquidation hearing is held in camera'. *Business Day*, 3 August.

South African Police Service (2007). *National Key Points Act 102 of 1980* (updated to 31 August 2007). http://www.saps.gov.za/docs_publs/legislation/juta/a102of1980.pdf [Accessed 3 November 2012].

South Africa Press Association (2000) 'Bill Will End Secrecy: Maduna'. Press Release, 25 January.

South Africa Press Association (2013) 'BHP Billiton Loses Court Bid', 17 March. http://www.iol.co.za/business/companies/bhp-billiton-loses-court-bid-1.1487704#.UVR-WBc7FrM [Accessed 18 March 2013].

South Durban Community Environmental Alliance (2012) Trucking, the Port Expansion, the Dug-out Port, Back of Port Plan, and Link Road: How will these developments impact on communities, the environment, and contribute to climate change? http://www.sdcea.co.za/images/stories/pdfs/trucking_port_expansion_dugout_port_info.pdf [Accessed 2 March 2013].

Suttner R (2008) *The ANC Underground in South* Africa. Auckland Park: Jacana Media. *The Times* (2012) 'Why won't the government come clean on e-tolling?' 27 November, http://www.timeslive.co.za/opinion/editorials/2012/11/27/why-won-t-the-government-come-clean-on-e-tolling [Accessed 3 December 2012].

Suttner R (2006) Talking to the ancestors: national heritage, the Freedom Charter and nation-building in South Africa in 2005. *Development Southern Africa* 23 (1): 3-27.

Turok B (1974) South Africa: The search for a strategy. In Miliband R and J Saville (eds) *Socialist Register 1973*. New York: Monthly Review Press.

Vally S (2003) The Political Economy of State Repression in South Africa. In S Ndung'u (ed.) *The Right to Dissent*. Johannesburg: Freedom of Expression Institute.

NOTES

1   For more holistic and historical analyses of the varied relationships between secrecy and power (in relation to South Africa and internationally) and subsequent sociopolitical effects see Gill (1994), Leigh and Lustgarten (1994), Cawthra and Luckham (2003), Saunders (2006) and Fenster (2008).

2   The project was called *Top Secret America* and consisted of a series of online articles. For figures quoted see Priest and Arkin (2010).

3   Although the historical development of apartheid always had as much to do with class considerations as those of race, the racism of the National Party and racial history of South Africa provided a firm foundation on which to construct apartheid. In this light the historical development of South Africa has been labelled 'racial capitalism'. For extended discussions on this see Legassick (1974).

4   For a critical analysis of the ANC and SACP's exiled politics and organisation, see Ellis and Sechaba (1992).

5   Acknowledgements to Henning Melber (2010) 'Beyond settler colonialism is not yet emancipation: On the limits to liberation in Southern Africa', Research Paper for the Nordic Africa Institute.

6   This was first announced (publicly) by then finance minister Trevor Manuel and subsequently repeated (publicly) on more than one occasion by then president Nelson Mandela.

7   This included the expulsion of the author from the SACP in 2000. For a more extended (and polemical) discussion see McKinley (2000).

8   The then minister of justice and constitutional development, Penuell Maduna, foreshadowed the positive expectations that accompanied the legislation when he stated: 'We are turning on the light to bring to an end the secrecy and silence that characterised decades of apartheid rule and administration' [South Africa Press Association Press Release, 25 January 2000, Bill Will End Secrecy: Maduna].

9   Which included dozens of newspaper articles, numerous academic research reports and at least two books.

10 For example see, Address of the President of South Africa, Thabo Mbeki, at the Intelligence Services Day 10th Anniversary Awards Ceremony and Inauguration of the Wall and Garden of Remembrance: Musanda, Tshwane: 24 November 2005. http://www.dfa.gov.za/docs/speeches/2005/mbek1125.htm [Accessed 4 March 2013].

11 All subsequent quotes are taken from the Commission Report. Also see: Jane Duncan (2011) and Right2Know Campaign (2013a).

12 For a classic example of the Zuma faction's clearly self-interested public attempts to paint themselves as the saviours of South Africa's constitutional democracy, and Zuma as the victim of an elaborate conspiracy, see Maharaj (2009).

13 The Bill has been opposed by many other civil society organisations, sections of the media, opposition political parties as well as Cosatu. Not surprisingly, though, the SACP has once again chosen to line up behind their ANC masters.

CHAPTER 9

The contemporary relevance of Black Consciousness in South Africa

Xolela Mangcu

INTRODUCTION

The most obvious difference between Black Consciousness under apartheid and in the democratic era is the change in the political-legal position of black people. For the first time in four hundred years black people are in control of the country's governmental machinery and have enacted laws to prohibit racism. Section 9 of the Constitution extends equal protection under the law to everyone, and Subsection 9 (2) enjoins government to take affirmative measures to remedy the injury done to black people in the past. Steve Biko's (1972:52) definition of black people as 'those who are by law or tradition, politically, economically, socially discriminated against as a group in South African society and identify themselves as a unit in the struggle towards the realization of their aspirations', would therefore be anachronistic under these changed circumstances.

Although white people continue to dominate the country's economic, financial and institutional infrastructure, it would be politically implausible to speak of the 'unnerving totality of the white power structure' (Biko 1972:54). Social stratification within the black community also means that we cannot really sustain the idea of a solid black bloc that would confront such a 'totality'. Instead of being huddled together with the poor and working classes, the middle classes have fled the townships at the slightest chance. Young people started forming new social relationships across the colour line in a way that was unimaginable during the days of Black Consciousness. Many of these young people have had little or no experience of apartheid or of the anti-apartheid struggle.

Biko (1972:53) wrote that 'the interrelationship between consciousness of self and the emancipatory programme was of paramount importance' in understanding Black Consciousness. But what happens to the black self when the emancipatory programme has been taken to its political conclusion? In what follows I argue that the absence of the political predicate – 'all those who are by law and tradition oppressed' – allows us to explore other aspects of Black Consciousness. In what follows I argue that Black Consciousness remains relevant in contemporary South Africa to the extent that it can:

    i.   foster self-reliant development among black people
    ii. provide an archive for the preservation of a black cultural patrimony
    iii. contribute to our conceptualisation of race
    iv. provide a diagnostic tool in the ongoing battle against racism while promoting self-reliance (affirmative action is used as an example).

The chapter is accordingly divided into four thematic sections.

I. BLACK CONSCIOUSNESS AS A TOOL FOR SELF-RELIANT DEVELOPMENT

Twenty years into democracy, South Africa is still characterised by the spatial geography of apartheid – worsened by post-1994 policies that distributed black people to far flung places away from localities of work. Too many black people are still unable to work their way out of grinding poverty or find decent jobs. The black poor – what Frantz Fanon (1963) called the 'wretched of the earth'– constitute the majority of the poor. Houston Baker gives more of a sociological than a political definition to the concept of the 'black majority'. He describes this majority as those black people who 'inhabit the most wretched states, spaces and places of our national geography' (Baker 2008: 7). Albie Sachs (2006: 11) describes the salience of race for this segment of the population:

> Colour rather than need or ability is still the greatest factor in deciding who will wear shoes and who will go barefoot, who will get water by switching on a tap and who has to walk miles each day to fetch it, who will matriculate and who will be unable to write his or her name, who will die of measles or malnutrition and who will go on to sail around the world. Now that the battle for equal voting rights has been won we have to press on with the even more arduous task of guaranteeing equal access to the resources of the country.

The starkness of racial inequality was recently confirmed in a recent survey of the South African Institute of Race Relations which found that between 1994 and 2012 the rate of unemployment among white people increased from 3 per cent to 5.7 per cent whereas that for blacks increased from 16 per cent to 29 per cent. The number of the white poor declined from 2 per cent to 1 per cent between 1994 and 2012 while that for black people declined from 50 per cent to 45 per cent for the same period. For all intents and purposes South Africa's social challenges lie in solving the problems facing the 'black majority' without ignoring the minority of the white poor and unemployed.

But if the problems are of an economic nature, what is the need for a racial politics of Black Consciousness instead of a class-based approach? Black Consciousness is necessary precisely because economic statistics do not even begin to capture the cultural, social and institutional degradation that poverty brings about in communities. Karl Polanyi (1944: 157-158) described the multifaceted nature of poverty as follows:

> Not economic exploitation as often assumed, but the disintegration of the cultural environment of the victim is, then, the cause of the degradation. The economic process may naturally supply the vehicle of the destruction, and almost invariably economic inferiority will make the weaker yield, but the immediate cause of his undoing is not for that reason economic; it lies in the lethal injury to the institutions in which his existence is embodied. The result is a loss of self-respect, and standards, whether the unit is a people or a class…

Biko captured the cultural dimension of poverty by saying 'material poverty is bad enough, coupled with spiritual poverty it kills' (Biko 1972:30). This is the degradation that Black Consciousness would need to address in order to have relevance for the impoverished and powerless sections of the black community. Despite the obvious cultural and institutional dimensions of poverty, South Africa's development discourse is stuck on economic solutions such as service delivery and welfare grants instead of the self-reliant development that was the hallmark of the Black Consciousness Movement.

To be sure, the culture of self-reliant development did not originate with the Black Consciousness Movement. It has always been part of what Baker calls the 'resistive current' of black life. He remembers how his otherwise middle class mother explained why she was selling clothes to poorer members of the community in Little Africa, in Louisville, Kentucky: 'I had to charge them something or they wouldn't have taken them – they didn't want charity' (2008:6). Cornel West similarly speaks about the 'cultural structures of meaning and feeling that created and sustained communities…' (West 1993: 23).

The Black Consciousness Movement's success lay in the ability of its leaders to connect to these 'resistive currents' or 'cultural structures of meaning' of black communities. The Movement did this by working closely with community-based religious, educational and cultural institutions – including music and sports clubs. In *Biko: A Biography* (2012), I describe how Biko was shaped by the culture of civic duty that obtained in the Ginsberg Township of his youth, and how that social environment in turn provided him with a script for his political and development work. He described the thinking behind self-reliant development after helping the community to build a crèche in Ginsberg:

For instance where I stay in King William's Town we revived a community crèche which was serving a basic need for the community in that a number of mothers could not go to work because they had to look after their babies and toddlers. Or if they go to work it implies that kids who are supposed to be school-going must stay behind looking after the toddlers. So that it became clear to us that there was a need to provide a crèche to that community. And we revived a crèche which I attended actually when I was young … but it had gone defunct … we call it the Ginsberg Crèche (Arnold 1979: 94).

What was even more important for Biko was the psychological empowerment of the locals by these initiatives, empowerment that in turn heightened their political consciousness:

We believe that black people, as they rub shoulders with the particular project, as they benefit from that project, with their perception of it, they begin to ask them-selves questions and we surely believe that they are going to give themselves answers, and they understand, you know, that this kind of lesson has been a lesson for me, I must have hope. In most of the projects we tend to pass over the maintenance to the community (Biko 1992: 94).

This psycho-cultural approach to community empowerment was replicated on a nation-wide basis in different parts of the country. Among the better known examples was the building of the Zanempilo Health Clinic in Zinyoka just outside King William's Town. People travelled long distances to obtained free health services for themselves and their children. Another project was in the rural village of Njwaxa, outside Alice, home to the University of Fort Hare. Here Biko and his colleagues set up a workshop for the manu-facture of garments and other leather products.

The Movement also set up various research institutes such as the Institute for Black Research under the leadership of veteran activist and academic, Fatima Meer. The Institute promoted a culture of writing and research in the black community. The Movement published journals such as *Black Review*, *Black Perspectives* and *Black Viewpoints*. In an introduction to a collection of essays for *Black Viewpoint* – the essays were by Njabulo Ndebele, Mangosuthu Buthelezi and Curnick Ndamase – Biko expressed frustration at the absence of intellectual initiatives in the black community:

We have felt and observed in the past the existence of a great vacuum in our literary and newspaper world. So many things are said to us, for us and seldom by us. This has created a dependency mood among us which has led to the tendency to look at ourselves in terms of how we are interpreted by the white press.

This intellectual history is crucial given the culture of anti-intellectualism that has gripped the black world in the democratic era. Ironically, the assault on intellectuals started under Thabo Mbeki, a man who fancied himself as an intellectual president. But like many other African leaders before him, Mbeki could not fathom the idea that there could be intellectuals other than himself. According to Mkandawire (2005: 23-24), 'the default position of the African political class was a profound distrust of its country's intellectuals'. And because of their mistrust of intellectuals, African presidents took on the role of philosopher-king with Kwame Nkrumah, Jomo Kenyatta, Kenneth Kaunda and Julius Nyerere as the more prominent examples. The results were disastrous: 'Even characters adamantly committed to mediocrity and obscurantism promulgated ideologies that were supposed to inform their countries' transformation.'

In South Africa, this obscurantism took place through a Mbeki-inspired 'Native Club' consisting only of black intellectuals considered loyal enough to the government. More recently, Jacob Zuma's administration has announced plans to establish a school of government whose curriculum will be devised by government itself. It will be interesting to see who will be asked to teach in this institution. If history is anything to go by, the party will deploy its own cadres – but as there will not be enough deployees to work as university professors the party will resort to the very whites it so often decries.

Having no pretensions to intellectual leadership, Zuma simply dismisses intellectuals as the 'clever blacks'. They may shout from the rooftops but they don't really count in the greater scheme of things. The mediocrity that characterised Mbeki has turned into what I have described as a 'sediment of systemic ineptitude' (2013). One of the worst examples was the choice of the current chief justice, Mogoeng Mogoeng, over the much better qualified and experienced Dikgang Moseneke, who had been serving as deputy chief justice for years. Moseneke's 'crime' was that he came from the Pan Africanist Congress (PAC), and was reported to have said something unpalatable to the African National Congress (ANC) at his birthday party. As it turns out, what Moseneke said is exactly what he is enjoined to do by the Constitution, which is that his responsibility is not to the ANC but to the constitution of the country

It is important to keep in mind, though, that the culture of sycophancy is not a peculiarly African phenomenon. The veteran American presidential adviser David Gergen described a similar phenomenon around Richard Nixon during Watergate – a rather unfortunate example for Mbeki and Zuma:

> We held tight to our belief that, whatever the shenanigans of his team, Richard Nixon himself was innocent and so were the people in his inner circle. In politics there is a will to believe in your man, especially if he is elected to the presidency, and even more so if you are working for him in the White House. It's a natural human tendency, strongest among the young, to idealise your leader, persuaded that you are part of some larger crusade for good and ignoring evidence to the contrary. Your wagon is hitched to a star, you resent those on the outside who tarnish the adventure (2000: 67-68).

However, to put the intellectual decline on the shoulders of individual leaders would be to miss seeing the forest for the trees. Elaboration on the origins of this anti-intellectualism would require a separate paper, but suffice to say that in order to understand the decline we would have to go back to the transition from the Black Consciousness Movement's organisation building to the mass mobilisation of the 1980s – a transition that was marked by political intolerance and interminable violence within the black community. Having decimated their political opponents in the black community, the ANC clasped the hands of their erstwhile enemies in the National Party, and together they hashed out a political transition based on the twin concepts of elections and service delivery. The discourse of self-reliant development and intellectual reflection had long been replaced by the new terminology of delivery and practicality.

Es'kia Mphahlele (2013: 224-225) described this cultural change in black life as follows:

> Today we blacks are not accustomed to hard thinking. We do not even pick up and pursue the stimulating ideas from our thinkers ... We depend excessively on mass action and decisions we pitifully mistake for true democracy. We fail to realise that mass action is no substitute for analytical reflection, for the think tank, to which 'group mobilisation' is best suited.

As if recalling the era of Black Consciousness Mphahlele adds:

> Yet we have some brave men and women countrywide who launch and manage crèches, pre-schools, children's homes, centres for the physically and mentally disabled and support structures for students, but receive very little if any of our patronage. This way we frustrate self-reliance among our people at its very roots, forever leaning on white folks.

This is not to argue at all that the practical delivery of services to black people is not important – but an approach that had self-reliance at its core might have had less disastrous consequences for our public culture.

BLACK CONSCIOUSNESS AND RACIAL IDENTITY

The second dimension in which Black Consciousness remains relevant is in terms of how we think about our racial identities. As elsewhere in the world, but particularly in the United States, the debate on race has taken on the familiar division between advocates of colour blindness and of colour consciousness. The former are opposed to race on the grounds that it has no scientific basis or that class is a better indicator of deprivation. Despite the ANC's latter-day turn to racial politics, its approach to race has historically been contradictory. For example, whites were not allowed into the national executive of the organisation until 1985. By then the ANC –through its internal proxy, the United Democratic Front – was violently (literally and figuratively) opposed to any form of racial consciousness. The Congress movement (as it is also called) carried high the banner of nonracialism as the vision of the future.

Nelson Mandela and Desmond Tutu became the embodiments of the new nonracial society. Mandela stretched out his hand of reconciliation through several symbolic acts: he kept repeating the speech he gave at the Rivonia Trial in which he pledged to fight against white and black domination; he came out in support of an all-white Springbok rugby team, an event that is memorialised through books and movies. He even had tea with Hendrik Verwoerd's widow, and visited the prosecutor who sent him away for all those long years.

But there was also a counter-narrative to this nonracialism, and it was coming from within the ANC itself. Mandela's biographer, Anthony Sampson, described what happened as follows: 'In his first months as president, he [Mandela] enjoyed a brilliant honeymoon, particularly with white South Africans, to whom this tolerant old man came as a wondrous relief … at the end of the first hundred days in office the *Financial Times* could find no whites who had a bad word for him. It was a normality which carried its own dangers, as black militants saw the revolution betrayed, and younger ANC leaders including Thabo Mbeki knew they must make reforms which would offend the whites' (1999: 504).

And thus was inaugurated the politics of redress based on colour consciousness as the *sine qua non* for racial reconciliation. Heralding this change in mood was Mandela's successor, Thabo Mbeki. Mbeki and other advocates of colour consciousness did not think they needed to prove anything beyond pointing to the empirical reality of the abject living conditions of most black people. Initially the recognition of race as a consideration in public policy caused a great deal of excitement for former Black Consciousness activists, some of whom actually became members of Mbeki's inner circle or 'kitchen cabinet' (the most prominent member of that cabinet was Mojanku Gumbi, whom Richard Calland (1996) described as the most powerful woman in South Africa). Mbeki also invited the head of the main Black Consciousness organisation, the Azanian People's Organisation (Azapo), Mosibudi Mangena, to serve on his cabinet.

A debate soon ensued about whether Mbeki had become a latter-day convert to Black Consciousness or whether he was simply co-opting these movements to solidify his own powerful image as an advocate of black people's interests. This was at about the same time that Mbeki was facing increasing criticism – from within and outside the ANC – for his economic policies, the 'arms deal', his advocacy of 'silent diplomacy' on Zimbabwe and his refusal to provide anti-retroviral drugs to pregnant women living with HIV/AIDS. In return Mbeki attacked his critics, either as white racists or black sell-outs.

As I argued in *To the Brink*, the politics of colour consciousness had now morphed into a crude racial nativism that 'harkens to purist essentialist conceptions of what it means to be African …' (2008:6). It was suddenly seen as enough that one should have a black skin and plead loyalty to the 'chief'. This provided the new 'race men' with the licence to speak or to banish those with opposing views. Skin colour soon became the main consideration in public appointments – and sometimes this meant that well-qualified white individuals with far greater liberation struggle credentials were overlooked.

This racial nativism was a contrast to the syncretic political approach to blackness that had characterised the Black Consciousness Movement, particularly its emphasis on consciousness as the basis of political identity. Biko, after all, had declared that 'being black is not a matter of pigmentation – being black is a reflection of a mental attitude' (2004: 52).

In yet another ironic departure, the leader of the liberal opposition, Tony Leon, unashamedly mobilised the white community on racial grounds. Leon saw no contradiction between the politics of colour blindness for which his party stood and the pandering to the white vote that the elections demanded. He said it was the only way to realistically build a base for the Democratic Party (before it amalgamated with the National Party to form the Democratic Alliance). And thus he entered the 1999 election as a true warrior ready to 'fight back', as the party's slogan announced. If anything this showed up the hypocrisy of those who say they don't 'see race'. Leon's denialism was matched only by Mbeki's nativism.

But is there no way out of the Scylla of racial nativism deployed by advocates of colour consciousness and the Charybdis of racial denialism displayed by advocates of colour blindness?

Appiah's distinction between 'strict criterial' and 'vague criterial' definitions of racial identity could provide a useful way of thinking about race in South Africa. He agrees that race has no scientific basis, and that it has taken on different meanings – from its early application to plants and animals to its adaptation to human beings by natural scientists in the eighteenth century. The 'strict criterial' approach refers to the things that would *strictly* have to be shown to be in existence as the basis of racial identity. The 'vague criterial' approach is satisfied with the existence of *most but not* all of the criteria associated with race. What the 'vague criterial' approach suggests is that we may have a social *idea* (instead of scientific knowledge) of racial identity. In other words, even if race can be shown to have no scientific basis it is still important to know what people believe or think about it. As Appiah (1998:38) put it:

> People act on their beliefs, whether or not they are true. Even if there are no races we could use a grasp of the vague criteria for the concept of race in predicting what their thoughts and their talk about race will lead them to do; we could use it too to predict what thoughts about races various experiences would lead them to have.

I can only add that we can even use understanding of such thought to anticipate how people are likely to act.

Biko's definition of race cited at the beginning of this chapter is an example of a 'vague criterial' theory of race. As Black Consciousness student activists in the 1980s we spent endless hours arguing with ANC members who were opposed to any talk of race and to those PAC members who sometimes veered towards jingoistic interpretations of black-ness – and this was ironic given that the PAC were the original founders of the concept of nonracialism. If Black Consciousness had had a 'strict criterial' conception of race we would have gone along with the jingoists but we did not. We insisted on defending our watertight but admittedly complex definition of blackness. In our view one's racial iden-tity was not a given because of pigmentation but was conditional on one's consciousness.

In the next section of this chapter I use the same 'vague criterial' in setting out yet another task for Black Consciousness: the preservation of black cultural patrimony. By culture I do not mean 'culture writ small' (the rituals that people perform) but culture 'writ large': 'the great sea of practices, conventions, concepts, values' (Appiah, 2005: 130) – a definition vague enough to allow as many people as possible to participate in what I shall now refer to as 'consciousness of blackness'.

But I should first say a word about the concept of 'post-Blackness', which is one of the latest developments in discussions of race in the United States. Theorists of post-Blackness argue that the present generation of African Americans have 'a general sense of removal from the sacredness of history that inspires a feeling of independence and indi-viduality' (Touré 2011: 39). African American culture has now become popular culture, which is a great advance from the struggles for cultural recognition of the 1960s and 70s. In this conception Black culture has moved from the margins to become the *lingua franca* of the United States: 'Black culture is more like Starbucks, located on every corner in every major city and available to everyone who wants in … multiculturalism destroyed the idea that certain cultural legacies belong to certain cultural groups…' (Touré 2011: 41- 49).

At times, Touré seems ambivalent about whether post-Blackness means a complete disappearance of black racial identity. The very argument that African American culture has become part of universal American culture requires recognition of its cultural speci-ficity – another form of race consciousness. Thus, it seems, post-Blackness is incapable of speaking without blackness as a reference point. The contradiction can be seen in this definition of post-Blackness:

> The post-black era is filled with these sorts of cross-cultural mashups – from the Grey album where Jay-Z's lyrics are mixed up with Beatles music; to white singer-songwriter Nina Gordon's cover of NWA's Straight Outa Compton, slowly singing their vulgar autobiographical rhymes over sweet acoustic guitar, to Chapelle's 'Clayton Bigsby' sketch where a black man believes himself to be a Klansman, to the cultural schizo-phrenia of a world where Eminem is an elite MC and Tiger Woods and the Williams sisters dominate overwhelmingly white endeavours (Touré: 2013: 49).

While theorists of post-Blackness do not make a particularly convincing case for a world beyond race, they seem to be arguing for yet *another* way of thinking about racial identity. For them blackness is not a matter of political or even cultural identity but of cultural inte-rest, and this brings them closer to the idea of cultural patrimony that I will now outline.

II. BLACK CONSCIOUSNESS AS CULTURAL PATRIMONY

It is a fair generalisation to say that most black South Africans were affected negatively by the experience of colonial and apartheid rule. It is for this reason that I would argue that there is a shared cultural patrimony that cuts across social and political differences. Many people are nostalgic about Black Consciousness precisely because of its transcendent, cultural resonance with their search for identity, or as a matter of intellectual interest or personal motivation. Interestingly, this cultural approach is also how Steve Biko saw the role of the Black Consciousness Movement. He was opposed to the idea of a political formation. As he put it: 'I myself was opposed to the idea but finally voted with the resolution to form a political organisation' (Arnold 1979:75).

This transcendent cultural approach makes possible the understanding of the black self, not necessarily as part of a political project but of one's cultural history. This cultural consciousness can in turn become the basis of a new material culture that can find expression and manifestation through the educational system, research institutes, museums and so on. This patrimony can be given a lived reality through the arts: music, dance, painting and literature, not as government-controlled projects but as civic initiatives springing from the people themselves – as in the era of Black Consciousness. Black Consciousness would literally mean the consciousness of blackness by others interested in black history, cultures, languages, intellectual histories and all that has been effaced from the archive upon which black people constructed their lives. The archives are overfull with examples of how black people wrote, debated and sang about their experiences with the colonial encounter. The pioneer nineteenth century African intellectual, Tiyo Soga, described the crucial role of cultural patrimony in an article for the missionary newspaper, *Indaba*, in 1862:

> I see this newspaper as a secure container that will preserve our history, our stories, our wisdom. The deeds of the nation are worth more than our cattle herds, money and even food. Let the elderly pour their knowledge into this container. Let all our stories, folk and fairy tales, traditional views, and everything that was ever seen, heard, done, and all customs, let them be reported and kept in the national container. Did we not form nations in the past? Did we not have our traditional leaders? What has happened to the wisdom of these leaders? Did we not have poets? Where is their poetry? Was there no witchcraft in the past? Did we not fight wars? Who were the heroes? Where is the distinctive regalia of the royal regiment? Did we not hunt? Why was the meat of the chest of the rhino and the buffalo reserved for royalty? Where are the people to teach us our history, our knowledge, and our wisdom. Let even the spirit of the departed return to bless with the great gift of our heritage, which we must preserve (Williams 1998).

In 1927, SEK Mqhayi repeated Soga's call:

> How can anyone be grounded knowing nothing of his own people. Whatever his efforts in support of a national issue, he cannot be well grounded, he can expect to be struck down senseless by a puny little word so that he falls flat on his face, because he was hopping on one leg all along. A person who knows nothing of the historical events of his people lives his life with blunt teeth, he can't really get his teeth into anything that he does. That is why these educated people set up none but cowards for emulation, because their fathers did not narrate any history to them, and in those training schools they are taught a sequence of history, but in fact their education has entirely duped them, because in all our training schools the history of only one nation is studied, the English ... (Opland 2009:28).

Steve Biko followed in the steps of his ancestors in making a similarly historical argument as the basis of black consciousness:

> No doubt, therefore, part of the approach envisaged in bringing about 'black consciousness' has to be directed to the past, to seek to rewrite the history of the black man and to produce in it the heroes who form the core of the African background. To the extent that a vast literature about Gandhi in South Africa is accumulating it can be said that the Indian community already has started in this direction. But only scant reference is made to African heroes. A people without a history is like a vehicle without an engine. Their emotions cannot be easily controlled and channelled in a recognisable direction. They always live in the shadow of a more successful society (2004:32).

Thabo Mbeki (1996) asserted the vision of a multicultural patrimony in his goosebump-inducing speech, 'I am an African':

> I am the grandchild of the warrior men and women that Hintsa and Sekhukhune led, the patriots that Cetshwayo and Mpephu took to battle, the soldiers Moshoeshoe and Ngungunyane taught never to dishonor the cause of freedom. My mind and my knowledge of myself is formed by the victories that are the jewels in our African crown, the victories we earned from Isandlwana to Khartoum, as Ethiopians and as Ashanti of Ghana, as the Berbers of the desert. I am the grandchild who lays fresh flowers on the Boer graves at St Helena and the Bahamas, who sees in the mind's eye and suffers the suffering of a simple peasant folk, death, concentration camps, destroyed homesteads, a dream in ruins. I am the child of Nongqawuse, I am he who made it possible to trade in the world markets in diamonds, in gold, in the same food for which my stomach yearns. I come of those who were transported from India and China, whose being resided in the fact, solely, that they were able to provide physical labour, who taught me

that we could both be at home and be foreign, who taught me that human existence itself demanded that freedom was a necessary condition for human existence. Being part of all these people, and in the knowledge that none dare contest that assertion, I shall claim that – I am an African.

The decision by the leading Black Consciousness organisation, Azapo, to change its constitution to allow whites to join as members is one of the most remarkable departures from Black Consciousness of the 1970s to Black Consciousness in a free and democratic South Africa. I have long argued that an organisation such as Azapo would be much stronger if it were to de-register as a political party and take on the role of a broad-based community think tank, and perhaps take on this task of building a consciousness of blackness as part of South Africa's multicultural patrimony.

However, I am not so naive as to believe that this move towards a non-biological conception of blackness will satisfy hard-nosed opponents of racial discourse of any sort. Appiah (2005) refers to opponents of any talk of race as 'hard rationalists' who have little patience for anything that defies rational proof. And yet most of what goes on in the world of identities is based on non-rational grounds, particularly in religious and cultural belief systems. I should not be surprised if the 'hard rationalists' are also Christians who believe in a God they have never proved to exist – at least scientifically. The influence of religion in shaping their lives is no less real for that reason. Appiah is equally critical of those who yield too easily to fixed identities. He argues that while denial of racial identities constitutes a form of 'tyranny', a disregard of identities as they might become could easily lead to a form of 'defeatism' (2005:212). Black Consciousness as cultural patrimony could provide scripts for dialogues about identity among young people.

IV. BLACK CONSCIOUSNESS AS A DIAGNOSTIC TOOL: THE CASE OF AFFIRMATIVE ACTION

Over and above the continued relevance of Black Consciousness for black cultural patrimony, racial identity is important for diagnostic purposes. Without the use of 'race' the state is left without any way of monitoring the extent to which racist discrimination continues to be a social problem. In playing the diagnostic role, however, the state must also undertake the process of getting people to think beyond their racial identities. Randall Kennedy (2012: 17) describes this dual role as follows: 'Others desire an eventual move to colour blindness but believe that a wholesale disregarding of race in allocating opportunities can only be done justly after obstacles stemming from past and present wrongdoing have been removed.' Appiah (2005:164) similarly sees the role of the state as that of 'soul making'. He describes 'soul making' as the 'project of intervening in the process of interpretation through which each citizen develops an identity … with the aim of increasing the chances of living an ethically successful life'. In the case of race, soul-making thus entails 'reforming the social conception of the identity *black* with the aim of improving the success of the lives of black people through the reform of their identities'.

By calling out those who use derogatory and defamatory speech against members of other groups and by criminalising hate speech, states are already involved in 'soul making'. Combating racism is thus also a discursive, cultural process that seeks to change how people think about each other and to combat negative and dangerous stereotypes. There was a time when it was unimaginable that the United States would have an African American president. But through a process of discursive struggles by African Americans and other progressives that day came with the election of Barack Obama – even though his experience in office would suggest that the stereotypes remain. Soul making is a process of continual validation of certain values such as diversity and equality in the society.

An example of 'soul making' is what the US Supreme Court justice Sandra Day O'Connor said in her decision upholding affirmative action in *Grutter v Bollinger (2003)*. In that court case, a student, Barbara Grutter, had appealed against the University of Michigan for rejecting her in favour of lesser qualified African American students. The university, however, referred to a binding earlier Supreme Court ruling in *Regents of the University of California v Bakke*. In that ruling, Justice Lewis Powell wrote that race was a compelling interest in promoting diversity. In the Grutter, case O'Connor invoked Justice Lewis Powell's ruling: 'He [Powell] rejected the colour blind absolute because he was wary of the educational re-segregation that would have likely occurred in the absence of race conscious admissions programmes. And he rejected the benign race classification absolute, in turn, because he did not want to abandon the goal of transitioning , however deliberately, to a colour-blind society'.

Other scholars would still not be content with leaving the fight against racism or the responsibility of educating the public to the state. Guinier and Torres (2002) adopt a more collective, civil society approach, which offers the concept of political race as a diagnostic tool, to see whether people continue to face discrimination in access to health care, schooling and economic opportunities. While Appiah would focus on how racism hinders an individual's ability to lead a successful life, Guinier and Torres are concerned with the group effects of racist discrimination. Their focus is more on the role of civil society organisations in building cross-racial alliances.

There is indeed an affinity between their political approach to race and to that of the Black Consciousness of the 1970s. It is understandable why scholars concerned with minority groups would put emphasis on political race, a position also advocated by Tommie Shelby (1997), who argues that political solidarity is much more important for the fate of African Americans than are Afrocentric arguments for cultural sameness.

There is also an affinity between advocates of political race and Black Consciousness in the 1970s to the extent that they both advance what Kirstie MacClure describes as a horizontal politics of 'direct address' through which citizens interrogate each other's narratives. MacClure argues that the ultimate aim is to get to some sort of mutual intelligibility: 'identity on this account is not what one is but what one enacts ...' (1992:123). Consciousness of blackness is crucial to such an everyday politics of direct address and identity enactment for both black and white South Africans. Biko spoke about the need for such a radical engagement between black and white people if there was to be genuine reconciliation in South Africa. He believed strongly in the need for what he called a 'joint culture': 'Sure, it will have European experience because we have whites here who are descended from Europe. But for God's sake it must have African experience as well' (2004:148).

Affirmative action is indeed a classic example of how the state – or public institutions in general – can play the dual role of monitoring racist exclusion while also challenging people to think differently about race. As things now stand the debate on affirmative action is polarised between proponents who see race as a biological concept limited to skin colour, and opponents who argue that race should be replaced by economic disadvantage. And of course the discussion takes the conceptual divide between colour blindness – with all its liberal hypocrisy and colour consciousness – with all its radical pretensions. Absent is any serious discussion of race as a historical experience.

I can see why the biological and economic proxies for race would be useful to university bureaucrats – they are much easier to enumerate than the idea of race as expression of a particular social consciousness. And yet, whether our students are studying medicine or engineering or law or the social sciences, the capacity to think critically about racial identity should be both a requirement and a goal of higher education in a country that has been defined by racial identification. Thinking critically means being able to understand how race has historically shaped people's livelihoods for better (mostly for white people) and for worse (mostly for black people) and what would be required to have a consciousness of that history by everyone. Thus, Patricia Williams (1995:121) argues that affirmative action should be about the recognition of blacks as a 'social presence that is profoundly linked to the fate of blacks and whites and women and men either as subgroups or as one group. Justice is a continual balancing of competing visions, plural viewpoints, shifting histories, interests, allegiances. To acknowledge that level of complexity is to require, to seek, and to value a multiplicity of knowledge systems, in pursuit of a more complete sense of the world in which we all live.'

This social and historical complexity is difficult to capture through quantitative scores. In debates on affirmative action at the University of Cape Town I have suggested the use of biographical essays and letters of recommendation as part of the admissions process, instead of relying solely on quantitative scores, which as Bok and Bowen (1998) have demonstrated, tell us very little about the potential to do well at university. A Black Consciousness approach to affirmative action would seek out those students who have experiences and the potential to succeed and contribute to the project of combating racism while also inviting students to a greater 'consciousness of Blackness'.

What I have suggested in this essay is that democracy does not mean the disappearance of blackness as an identity. However, it does make possible the emergence of the multiple ways in which blackness can be invoked. As Steve Biko once put it: 'We don't want to be just political Africans ... we [want to be] social Africans' (2004:148).

REFERENCES

Appiah KA (1998) Race, culture and identity. In Gutman A and KA Appiah (eds), *Colour Conscious*. Princeton, NJ: Princeton University Press.

Appiah KA (1995) *The Ethics of Identity*. Princeton, NJ: Princeton University Press.

Arnold M (1979) *The Testimony of Steve Biko*. London: Maurice Templeton Publishers.

Baker H (2008) *Betrayal: How Black Intellectuals Have Abandoned the Ideals of the Civil Rights Era*. New York: Columbia University Press.

Biko S (1978) *I Write What I Like*. Johannesburg: Picador Africa, 2004.

Biko S (1972) Preface, *Black Perspectives*. Durban: SPRO-CAS.

Bowen WG and D Bok (1998) *The Shape of the River*. Princeton: Princeton University Press.

Bruge K in Rust K and S Rubenstein (1996) *Mandate to Build: Developing a Consensus Around a National Housing Policy in South Africa*. Johannesburg: Ravan.

Calland R (2006) *Anatomy of Power: Who Holds the Power*. Cape Town: Zebra Press.

Fanon F (1963) *The Wretched of the Earth*. New York: Grove Press.

Fatton R (1986) *Black Consciousness in South Africa: The Dialectics of Ideological Resistance to White Supremacy*. Albany: State University of New York Press.

Gergen D (2000) *Eyewitness to Power: The Essence of Leadership: Nixon to Clinton*. New York: Touchstone Books.

Guinier L and Torres (2002) *The Miners Canary: Enlisting Race, Resisting Power, Transforming Democracy*. Cambridge: Harvard University Press.

Kennedy R (2012) *The Persistence of the Color Line: Racial Politics and the Obama Presidency*. New York: Vintage.

Maclure K (1992) On the subject of rights: Pluralism, plurality and political identity. In Mouffe C (ed.) *Dimensions of Radical Democracy*. London: Verso.

Mangcu X (2012) *Biko: A Biography*. Cape Town: Tafelberg.

Mangcu X (2008) *To the Brink: The State of Democracy in South Africa*. Scottsville: University of KwaZulu-Natal Press.

Mkandawire T (2005) *African Intellectuals*. New York: Codesria and Zed Books.

Mphahlele E (2013) *A Lasting Tribute*. Johannesburg: Stainbank and Associates.

Opland J (2009) *Abantu Besizwe, Historical and Biographical Writings, 1902-1944, SEK Mqhayi*. Johannesburg: Wits University Press.

Polanyi K (1944) *The Great Transformation: The Political and Economic Origin of Our Time*. Boston: Beacon Press.

Sachs A (2007) The Constitutional Principles Underlining Black Economic Empowerment. In Mangcu X, G Marcus, K Shubane, and A Hadland (eds) *Visions of Black Economic Empowerment*. Cape Town: HSRC Press.

Sampson A (1999) *Mandela: The Authorised Biography*. Cape Town: Jonathan Ball.

Shelby T (2005) *We Who Are Dark: The Philosophical Foundations of Black Solidarity*. Cambridge: The Belknap of Harvard University.

Touré S (2011) *Who's Afraid of Post-Blackness: What it Means to Be Black Now*. New York: Free Press.

West C (1991) *Race Matter*. New York: Vintage Books.

Williams D (1978) *Umfundisi: A Biography of Tiyo Soga, 1829-1871*. Alice: Lovedale Press.

Williams P (1995) The obliging shell. In Danielson D and K Engle (eds) *After Identity*. New York: Routledge.

CHAPTER 10

Death and the modern black lesbian

Zethu Matebeni

'Those who are directly identified with same-sex desire most often end up dead;
if they manage to survive it is on such compromised terms that it makes death seem attractive.'
(Heather Love 2007:1)

'Another lesbian rape and murder,' read a beaded newspaper headline in the latest exhibition on black lesbian lives by photographer Zanele Muholi (2012). Its reference was to the Eastern Cape born Noxolo Nogwaza, a 24-year-old mother of two, who had been brutally murdered in KwaThema outside Johannesburg in April 2011. At her funeral, an old male family member cried out: 'We are disappearing because of crime and violence. We are disappearing because of jealousy. We will be non-existent because of battering.' Noxolo's name joined the list of many young black lesbian, gay and transgender people murdered because of their sexual or gender nonconformity.[1] Mourning such deaths had become ordinary as people's lives were cut short because of who they were.

In their recent publication, *What's in a Name? Language, Identity and the Politics of Resistance*, the One in Nine Campaign states: 'When people in other parts of the world hear about lesbians in South Africa through the media, almost the only thing they are likely to learn is that butch, black, soccer-playing lesbians in townships are raped, and sometimes killed, by black men who wish to "correct" them ...' (2013:1). A recent international media report read: 'Being a lesbian in South Africa can be a death sentence' (Turley 2012). This is the popular representation of black lesbians in South Africa today, in both public discourse and academic texts. In light of twenty years of democracy and the inclusion of sexual minorities in the Constitution, it is of concern that such representation still prevails.

Black lesbian life in South Africa (and on the African continent) has become synony-
mous with rape and even death. Death, as opposed to life, has received much attention
in relation to the black lesbian body. It is an unwanted site, a body constantly rejected,
excluded, marked as 'ungodly, unAfrican' or even not 'properly' woman, and it is no
surprise that black lesbians' relationship to death has been so close. Heather Love (2007:4)
argues that because of the rejection, social exclusion and historical 'impossibility' of
same-sex desire, people in same sex relationships often feel attracted to the idea of death.

IDENTITY IN THE TIME OF POLITICS

To understand the category 'black lesbian' in relation to South Africa requires an interrogation of the concept of identity on the one hand, and issues of gay and lesbian politics
on the other. Identity is a problematic concept that has undergone much critique and
scrutiny. Even defining the term is quite ambitious. When the concept is placed next to
gay and lesbian or sexual politics, a wilder figure emerges. The tendency, particularly in
scholarship on Africa, is to write lesbian as a same-sex (behaviour) issue, thus taking away
the focus on identity. Important though behaviour may be, it is not sufficient to explain
the injustices that people experience because of their personhood.

Although the notion of identity may be insufficient and can be ambiguous or have
contradictory meanings (Cooper and Broobaker 2005), making use of it in the context
of black lesbian life in South Africa is necessarily political. The 'problem' of identity is
a distinctively modern discourse. Evident in the social changes of modernity is the way
in which identity invokes the problem of 'reflexivity' – which in turn is brought by the
problems of self-recognition and recognition by others (Calhoun 1994). Another way
of thinking about identity would be to consider what Giddens (1991) suggests to be the
notion of how one has become that person and where they are going to have a sense of
who they are. For many lesbian, gay, bisexual and transgender people that narrative is
interrupted by various political and structural forces, including violence and death.

Although theoretically contested, identity remains useful in daily talk, activism and
other discourses in various ways. This is not to say that identity is stable or coherent; on
the contrary, even within different identity groups there are differing ideas of the useful-
ness of identity as a concept. Current struggles of identity politics include the pursuit of
recognition, legitimacy (and sometimes power), not merely (individual) expression or
autonomy. Pursuing these goals is political because it requires others (groups, organisations, the state) to pay attention and to respond to those who refuse to allow their identities to be reduced or displaced. For many people who take on lesbian, transgender, gay,
or bisexual identity labels, these struggles remain. At the same time, we should 'remain
seriously self-critical about our invocations of essence and identity' (Calhoun 1994).

In South Africa, gay politics is crucial in understanding ideas of lesbian and gay identity formation. Identity animates itself in a number of problematic ways, which further
narrow the way that black lesbians are seen. The black lesbian category (and identity)

did not arise out of a vacuum. A series of political struggles within the gay and lesbian movement in South Africa have given rise to what currently appears as a 'fixed' notion of identity – to illustrate this, a return to the beginnings of this movement is necessary to reveal the stark divisions and fractures that characterise current gay politics and identity politics today.

In its existence, the gay movement has changed its face over time but its core principles have remained the same. On the one hand, there are characteristics of the legacies of an apartheid regime that are unwavering. On the other, questions arise about the nature of the gay movement itself and the rights it has advanced over time. Within the movement, white gays remain the main beneficiaries of post-apartheid laws whereas black gays – and lesbians especially – continue to receive harsh penalties. That this has remained unchallenged in this democratic moment is startling.

FROM GAY POLITICS TO GAY RIGHTS

During apartheid, the first signs of a gay movement appeared under the Legal Reform Fund set up in 1966 to oppose anti-homosexual legislation in the form of the Immorality Amendment Bill. The fund was set up as direct action following a police raid at a party in Forest Town, one of Johannesburg's affluent suburbs; money raised by the fund would go towards legal representation established to investigate the proposed Bill. What was rather curious about the Forest Town party were the events after the arrest of many of Johannesburg's middle and upper class white gays which have come to symbolise the fractured state of gay, as well as lesbian, gay, bisexual and transgender (LGBT) politics in South Africa today. The Legal Reform Movement (LRM), set up through the fund, was careful not to align itself with black anti-apartheid movements of the time, as it feared antagonising the state (Gevisser and Cameron 1995). These were already the telling signs of where gay politics of the time would go.

By 1982 a national organisation, GASA (Gay Association of South Africa), was formed, differing from the LRM only in name. Its mission statement was: 'A nonmilitant, nonpolitical answer to gay needs' (Croucher 2002:318). It was clear from its name that the agenda of the organisation was specifically pro-gay (Epprecht 2012), unlike the unspecific Law Reform Movement. It soon linked up with an initiative in Cape Town, as well as other smaller groups in other parts of the country. GASA, which addressed the psychosocial needs of white gays and lesbians, had an explicit policy of being 'apolitical'. This was a very crucial time in South Africa as apartheid was at its most volatile and aggressive and anti-apartheid groups were working hard at overthrowing the government. It is odd to imagine that gay groups were choosing to remain outside politics.

Operating in a tense political climate, GASA's mainly white middle-class gay male members were forced to deal with their political conservatism when Simon Nkoli, a black gay man and anti-apartheid activist from the township, as well as other black gays and lesbians, joined in 1983. Because of its 'apolitical' stance and refusal not to 'antagonise' the state, GASA could not respond to Nkoli's needs and requests at the time he was imprisoned (while in prison, arrested for treason, Nkoli had asked GASA to assist him with his case). Some have suggested that GASA was patriarchal (Cock 2003) and 'apartheid-friendly' in the ways in which it imposed upon its members to change their behaviour, 'play it straight, keep a low profile, and ... not give offence' (Luirink 1998:21). This strategy was a political stance to benefit white gay interests (Gevisser 1995).

The early 1990s, characterised particularly by black gay and lesbian visibility, saw gay and racial liberation march hand in hand. This was exemplified by the first pride march in Johannesburg. At the core of that march, organised by GLOW (the Gay and Lesbian Organisation of the Witwatersrand), a predominantly black gay and lesbian organisation formed in the late 1980s, was the idea for pride to be a visual symbol for gay and racial liberation. And this was carried out in the speech made by Simon Nkoli at the pride march in 1990. Bev Ditsie (2006:19) recounts it as follows: 'I am black and I am gay. I cannot separate the two parts of me into secondary or primary struggles ... So when I fight for my freedom I must fight against both oppressions.'

GLOW's successes and ideologies were short-lived. By 1994, when the National Coalition for Gay and Lesbian Equality (NCGLE) campaigned for the inclusion of sexual orientation in the new constitution that was being drafted, gay politics had returned to GASA's ideology in pursuing white gay people's interests (Gevisser 1995:36). At the same time, although there had been a rise of black politics championed by GLOW prior to GASA, this soon receded. Oswin (2007) argues that the coalition, by virtue of being a coalition and thus an umbrella body of between twenty and seventy-five organisations, managed to create an idea that a community and a unified nonracial lesbian and gay movement existed. This, however, was not the case. As Gunkel (2010:71) argues, the NCGLE's strategy 'played down' class and racial differences and presented an idea that all gay people were similar and had similar interests. This was clear in the NCGLE's approach of focusing on a single issue that would supposedly change the lives of all gay people.

By 1996, sexual orientation was included in the equality clause in the Bill of Rights. Already at that time there was some dissent. Certain Christian leaders saw the clause as 'undemocratic' (Cock 2003). For gays and lesbians 'the Constitution created an impression of unity' (Craven 2011:32) but many recognised the existing fractures within the lesbian and gay movement, which would be played out by the infamous 'shopping list', a litigation strategy that started with decriminalisation of sodomy and ended with legal recognition of same-sex marriage in 2006 (Berger 2008:18). The NCGLE, which by then had changed to the Lesbian and Gay Equality Project (LGEP), championed many of the legal battles.

Although suggested as a poverty-alleviation strategy (Oswin 2007), the question of same-sex marriage was in reality directed at accessing benefits. It was to protect the economic interests of mainly white gay couples. Black gays and lesbians were made to believe that same-sex marriage promoted values of extended familial and community support. The LGEP's strategy on marriage and, similarly, same-sex marriage, begs to be problematised. It is very odd and worrying that in a country like South Africa, where the state is responsible for alleviating poverty and gross inequalities, gays and lesbians would seek marriage as a solution to these social ills.

Oswin (2007:650), following Spivak in Danius and Jonsson (1993), calls the LGEP's stance a 'politics of strategic essentialism'. She argues that the lobbying efforts deployed to advance constitutional gains have been a 'deliberately conservative approach that has been characterised as elitist, unrepresentative, and male dominated'. On the one hand this strategy created a constitution that would protect the rights of lesbians and gay people in South Africa. On the other, it created the category 'poor, black gay or lesbian', central to this chapter.

PRIDE AND POLITICS

Perhaps the most interesting period in gay and lesbian politics in South Africa is post-2000. It is at this point that the wild dramatisation of 'poor black lesbians and gays' becomes the spectacle that is 'gay' South Africa today. Since the early 2000s, two narratives have emerged to symbolise the experiences of gay and lesbian people in South Africa. One takes shape through the visual display of gay and lesbian pride marches throughout the major towns and cities of the country. The other (which is dealt with below) is the representation of the black lesbian as the perpetual victim of male sexual violence and murder. At times both are staged simultaneously, causing outbreaks of anger and racist claims within what is believed to be the gay and lesbian 'community'.

Epprecht (2012:223) argues that the 'spirit of gay liberation and pride (taking place on African soil) is as pioneered in the West'. While many may agree with Epprecht, particularly his reference to Western gay assimilation, the earlier gay and lesbian movement in South Africa suggests the contrary. There are significant moments that Epprecht misses in South African gay politics. The role that GLOW played in South Africa in the late 1980s and early 1990s (as discussed above) was precisely in answer to the question of being gay, black, and African within nationalist politics. This was unprecedented on African soil – no country on the continent had managed to put black African identity next to gay politics. GLOW linked gay politics to national liberation and the overthrow of racial domination. However, that was intercepted quite quickly within the South African gay and lesbian movement that subsequently formed, concealing identity and political differences. What happened to the project of black politics and nationalist politics within the gay 'movement' is the drama that remained unknown until it unfolded after 1994.

Many have accused Western cultural imperialism for its imposition of strong identitarian readings of the 'essentialist' terms 'gay' and 'lesbian' (Altman 1996; D'Emilio 1992; Massad 2007). These terms have been adopted and utilised outside European and American borders, sometimes problematically. In South Africa, the terms gay and lesbian have existed since, and as a result of, the gay movement. This is not to say that other forms of existence and expressions have not existed; studies have shown that same-sex social and sexual life in some parts of the country have existed without being labelled gay or lesbian (Morgan and Wieringa 2005; Murray and Roscoe 1998) or with identity labels being rejected completely. At the same time, for political reasons, labels have been called upon to access or fight for certain gains.

In a globalised world it is shallow to suggest that cultural artefacts, icons, ideas and languages do not circulate and are not attractive to the rest of the world. More interesting than the circulation of sexual identities globally, it is the manifestation and meaning of sexual identities in society and in social relations that begs attention. The best place to locate sexual identity and relations is in the staging and performance of gay pride. Although initially meant as a form of protest against the apartheid regime, gay pride marches (sometimes called 'parades' or 'mardi gras') have turned towards celebrating gay people's achievements in democratic South Africa.

Every year, these pride marches exhibit the stark inequalities existing within gay and lesbian groups as well as in the country as a whole. The history of gay and lesbian pride marches goes back to 1991, having started in the streets of downtown Johannesburg with only about 800 people. Just over twenty years later almost 20 000 people took part in the pride march in the affluent northern suburb of Rosebank. The Johannesburg gay and lesbian pride march has simultaneously reinvented itself while remaining a constant reflection of a splintered rainbow nation. This notion of a rainbow nation, while celebrated for displaying the diversity in South Africa today, is something of an illusion. Gqola (2001) argues that even though symbolic, the rainbow nation hides difference, political struggles and the sociocultural histories of the South African body politic. The rainbow flag, carried and flown religiously at every annual gay and lesbian pride march, works as a constant reminder of this illusion.

Ongoing challenges, including racial tensions within organising committees and numerous protests by groups of black lesbians demanding recognition and support for the injustices in their lives, have led to the closure of the nonprofit organisation that runs Johannesburg Pride. For many years, stark racial divisions and demarcations have symbolised Johannesburg Pride. It took place in the affluent suburb of Rosebank, and Pride participants were secured by a fence erected to control access. This was read by many black gays and lesbians as a way of enforcing that the fenced area belonged to those who could pay the cover charge (read as white gays) and thus support the commercial activities provided. Every year, many black participants would gather outside the fence in direct protest and defiance of the demarcations of space. In one year, a group of anarchists stood outside the Pride fence in Rosebank wearing t-shirts on which was printed 'equality for all – terms and conditions apply'.

These forms of protest illustrate the tensions that have always existed in lesbian and gay politics over the years. As one journalist pointed out: 'What transpired [at the Johannesburg Pride in 2012] also served to reveal the deep malady of racism in South Africa' (Schutte 2012). A number of Black Pride participants have criticised the way Pride marches have turned out in South Africa. Speaking about Cape Town Pride, Vanessa Ludwig, argues: 'Gay and lesbian people have not been part of eradicating racial domination. Many gay and lesbian people have been and continue to be part of the system that maintains the geographical apartheid that is in Cape Town today...' (Ludwig interview 21 February 2013). Similarly, Khwezilomso Mbandazayo, who was among the people staging a protest stated: 'Johannesburg Pride did not take seriously some of the issues affecting black lesbians in the townships. In particular, Pride has become a commercial venture benefitting only a few. The politics of resistance and change have taken a back seat, that Pride is now just a party, a parade' (Mbandazayo interview 21 February 2013).

Current gay politics can no longer continue avoiding structural inequalities and the forms of oppression and racism that exist in South African society. One of the challenges that local gay politics faces is the increasing demand for global ideals of gay or queer consumerism. The results of a commercialised and consumer-driven Pride have meant that other pressing local issues take a back seat. In Cape Town (as in Johannesburg), the Pride march is organised to fit Western consumerism and thus the needs of inter-national tourists, who are mainly white Euro-American gay men. The image portrayed of gay pride in South Africa is a version of what Joseph Massad (2007:160) calls the 'gay international' and Dennis Altman's (1996) notion of 'global gay', which internationalises homosexuality based on certain forms of cultural and social identity.

It has been argued that globalisation, consumerism and commercialisation tend to normalise gay and lesbian people for the global market (Gibson-Graham 2001). When this happens, local politics and resistance shift from a form of 'radicality' to a politics of 'palatability' (Oswin 2007) that serves the global gay image. Current gay politics in South Africa has resulted in a polarised image of the white gay/lesbian on the one hand and the black gay/lesbian on the other. Both have become, in different ways, commodified global figures. The former is a highly desirable image reproduced, coveted anywhere in the world by other 'queer consumers' (Altman 1996) and representing excess. Unlike the 'lipstick lesbian' portrayed and sought after, as Altman says, by mainstream and gay media, the butch/masculine black lesbian represents an undesirable, valueless commodity that disappears as quickly as it appears. Viewing black lesbians in this way leaves no room to interrogate issues of masculinities, femininities or varied genders in female bodies. Most problematically, it allows black lesbians to be seen only in relation to violence and death.

VICTORY TO VICTIM

Cameron (1995:93) argues that the 'traditional attitude of intolerance towards gay sexual conduct seems to be deeply ingrained in our legal history'. Prior to the 1996 South African Constitution, laws governing sexuality prohibited any form of sexual contact between people of the same sex. Such contact was regarded as 'unnatural', and outlawed. Society responded accordingly and stigmatised those involved in such acts, branding them as criminals and giving them pariah status. This has meant that legal struggles are closely related to social struggles and the two inevitably affect one another.

However, what current South African politics of sexual minorities show is the discon-nect between legal and social reform, with the latter lagging behind. It is difficult to make sense of such disparities twenty years after democracy. While there have been many laws advancing the rights and opportunities for gay, lesbian, transgender and intersex people, there have also been strong social attitudes viewing gays and lesbians, mainly, as shameful, and which continue to challenge some of the gains that democratic South Africa has advanced.

For a long time black lesbian life and existence have been portrayed not only as undesirable, but also through the narrative of victimhood and, to a lesser extent, criminality. In this narrative, the black lesbian remains the object that is made to disappear in various ways. One of the first stories to appear of a black lesbian-identified female figure, Gertrude 'Gertie' Williams, published in *Drum* magazine in 1956 and later reprinted in Gevisser and Cameron's *Defiant Desire* (1995) used this notion. Gertie was a coloured cross-dresser who passed as a man at different times in her life and had relationships with women. Outside the questions of her gender ambiguity, and thus her identity as a butch lesbian, Gertie appeared in these texts only as a gangster, a 'lesbian gangster' (Chetty 1995: 128), a criminal – a female figure who could not be seen as a woman.

Similar representations have not been uncommon in contemporary South Africa. The public violence that led to 19-year-old Zoliswa Nkonyane's death became a widely circulated and consumed media event. In the end, very little was known about Zoliswa, except that while she was walking home with a friend, a group of youngsters approached them. They claimed that Zoliswa and her friend wanted to be raped because they were tomboys and living as out lesbians. In the altercation Zoliswa was clubbed, kicked and beaten to death by a group of men in full view of people walking by (Thamm 2006). This kind of public violence works in ways that communicate to black lesbians and non-comforming women that their sexuality and gender can be done away with publicly, in the presence of witnesses. In addition, this is a way in which men not only control women's bodies, but also maintain patriarchal spaces.

The focus on lesbian murders and violations has given the impression that violence towards lesbians is not only 'special' but also that lesbians themselves are 'special victims'. The black lesbian becomes the victim of a form of violence easily deemed 'corrective'. The language used to describe the torments and violations she goes through is made to be palatable, precisely because she is an unwanted figure, a figure deemed to be 'cured' or corrected (Matebeni 2013). Without any form of interrogation, they have stripped her of any other existence but that of a victim of 'corrective rape' and, eventually, murder (Kelly 2009).

The language used to speak about violence towards lesbians has also contributed to the 'special' nature in which violence in portrayed. Lesbians are considered not only 'special' victims, but victims of 'corrective rape'. The concepts 'curative' or 'corrective' rape, now used widely by the media and the public, arise out of lesbian and feminist activist circles in South Africa (Muholi 2004; Mkhize, Bennett, Reddy and Moletsane 2010). Muthien (2007:323) defines 'curative' rape, as the 'rape of women perceived of as lesbian by men as an ostensible 'cure' for their (aberrant) sexualities'. Historically, the term had significance for a group of women who found themselves marginalised in various parts of society, and even within the women's movement, but I do not think the term is currently useful, for lesbians themselves as well as to describe the violence on their bodies. While recognising the difficult past which brought rise to such terminologies, we have to rework the words for current political uses (Love 2007) without alienating or branding the people spoken about.

Recent works have come out strongly criticising the use of this term (Hames 2011; Mtetwa 2011; One in Nine Campaign 2013). The language in which violence is constructed and communicated veils the violent essence of the actual experience. While the term continues to circulate, even within LGBT groups, it perhaps it does more damage than good to those it aims to speak about. In many ways, it takes away the humanity and visibility that many women struggle to attain. By using such language, we become complicit in silencing forms of resistance that black women have shown throughout history. We are, perhaps even consciously, disempowering black lesbians, and ensuring that they remain invisible. Their lives as black women and black lesbians remains only in the domain of experiences of the inhumane – the violated, tortured, humiliated and, finally, dead.

Gibson-Graham (2001:241) suggests different ways in which the victim narrative or victim role, which is 'prescribed by the rape script', can be challenged. The most obvious way would be a refusal to accept the victim role. A number of strategies can be put to use to do that, including 'using speech in unexpected ways, diminishing the power of the perpetrator, and rescripting the effects of the rape on the victim'. In particular, the strategies suggest a change in the representation of rape – to see rape as 'death, an event that is final and lasting in terms of the damage it does to self'.

'OUR LIVES ARE NOT FOR SALE'

Black lesbians themselves have started challenging the victim narrative and the way they have been represented. In November 2008 the Forum for the Empowerment of Women (FEW), a Johannesburg-based organisation for black lesbians, bisexual and transgender women, hosted a black lesbian conference entitled 'My life, my story, my terms'. This conference, which launched the Black Lesbian Memory Project, was a direct rejection of the victimhood narrative of black lesbians.

Already at that time, a huge industry had developed around capturing and writing about black bodies, black sexualities and black sexual orientation. The temptation to feed into the stereotypes was felt even among black lesbians. The imperative to change this stereotype lay with the group. The sub-theme of the conference, 'Our stories are not for sale', captured the struggles with the ways in which black lesbian stories and lives had become commodified and 'packaged' for public consumption in many problematic ways. Most important was the resistance to such commodification. One participant, K, shared her experiences of being traumatised and continuously objectified by organisations and the media, who chased after her story of surviving multiple violent rapes. She became the exemplary black lesbian, a stereotype whose identity and subjectivity was stripped from her. What remained behind, after the journalists and researchers had left with her story, was 'the personal cost of being made into a spectacle'.

Beverley Ditsie, who had been at the forefront of gay liberation in the late 1980s with Simon Nkoli argued that although violence and hate crimes have become the 'big issue' it is important that lesbians focus also on other ways of representing themselves. Lesbian narratives are not limited to poverty, shame, violence and death. There are many black lesbians who occupy different positions across class structures and who are not represented by narrow views which do not show the diversity of black lesbian existence in South Africa. In the absence of a narrative that specifically relates to and celebrates black lesbian lives, participants worked towards shaping their representation in different sectors of society, particularly in the media, photography and film. Specifically prioritised was the desire to challenge the victim status that black lesbians are made to occupy in society. The response was to engage with black lesbians about ways of developing and creating an archive of black lesbians that will represent the interests of this group.

In the search for the lesbian victim, what is left behind are the varied experiences of black lesbians in different social settings. When black lesbian life is captured only in relation to victimhood, their female sexuality is made to exist only in the realm of pain and violence. There is no space for love, play, fantasy or pleasure within this narrative, and without these the black lesbian is violated to the extent that she is only treated as dead.

Similar efforts have been carried out by black lesbians in fighting for justice for those who have been murdered. The success of the two cases of black lesbians that have made it to court have shown that lobbying and the advocacy strategies of lesbian groups are working towards challenging the lesbian victim role. Eudy Simelane and Zoliswa Nkonyane's cases became successes because of lesbian groups' determination to 'diminish the power of the perpetrator' (Gibson-Graham 2001:241). These struggles continue, and the biggest challenge is to move black lesbians from a place of death to where life is more attractive.

CONCLUSION

Democracy presents us with the power to choose and to create our own narrative about how we become who we are. While we cannot ignore or forget the past that is deeply influenced by the memory of violence and victimhood, particularly among black South Africans, there are possibilities of moving from this to a present that fashions varied narratives of being. For many black lesbian, gay, bisexual and transgender people who have been pursuing recognition, legitimacy, inclusion and acceptance in the face of rejection and violence, creating a new narrative may be an important project to undertake.

Although it seems easy to be enticed by the idea of death, we have to resist and not be complicit with this notion. With democracy comes the possibility of imagining identity through life. Death is not the only attractive option or possibility. The recent People's Pride march in Johannesburg in September 2013 attests to the desire for many LGBT people to carve new ways of existing. It was at this Pride march that black queers saw not only death, but also life as a possibility. A powerful visual display by a queer organisation, Iranti-org, took all marchers through a walk down 'hate crimes' lane. This was a different protest against hate crimes. Marchers were asked to walk slowly and silently. Volunteers from this organisation held thirty placards with the names and details of murdered LGBT persons. As each marcher walked past a name, they had to remember each victim's life. At the end of this lane, a white banner with the words 'They will never kill us all' flew above the marchers. This was a significant moment for many people who had imagined violent death as the only option for LGBT people.

For many marchers at People's Pride, the display of victims' names next to the possibility of life (or that we will not be all killed) culminated in an emotional realisation that death also has its limits. Perhaps the spirit of this recent march can be maintained for the generations that follow. Like the first march in 1991, which protested against many injustices, people marched in 2013 proudly and as defiant people who claim that 'choice of sexual orientation, choice of work, choice of identities can never, in our world, be a basis for discrimination' (People's Pride 2013). It was a powerful moment that signified that even with death, there is life.

REFERENCES

Altman D (1996) Rupture or continuity? The internationalisation of gay identities. *Social Text* 14(3): 77-94.

Berger J (2008) Getting to the Constitutional Court on time: litigation history of same-sex marriage. In Judge M, A Manion and S De Waal (eds) *To Have and to Hold: The Making of Same-Sex Marriage in South Africa.* Johannesburg: Fanele.

Calhoun C (1994) Social theory and the politics of identity. In Calhoun C (ed.) *Social Theory and the Politics of Identity.* USA: Wiley-Blackwell Publishers.

Cameron E (1995) Unapprehended felons: gays and lesbians and the law in South Arica. In Gevisser M and E Cameron (eds) *Defiant Desire: Gay and Lesbian Lives in South Africa.* Braamfontein and London: Ravan and Routledge.

Chetty D (1995) Lesbian gangster: Excerpted from *Golden City Post* and *Drum* magazine. In Gevisser M and E Cameron (eds) *Defiant Desire: Gay and Lesbian Lives in South Africa.* Braamfontein and London: Ravan and Routledge.

Cock J (2003) Engendering gay and lesbian rights: The equality clause in the South African constitution. *Women's Studies International Forum* 26(1): 35-45.

Cooper F and R Brubacker (2005) *Colonialism in Question: Theory, Knowledge, History.* Berkeley: University of California Press.

Craven E (2011) Racial identity and racism in the gay and lesbian community in post-apartheid South Africa. Unpublished MA thesis. Johannesburg: University of the Witwatersrand.

Croucher S (2002) South Africa's democratisation and the politics of gay liberation. *Journal of Southern African Studies* 28(2): 315-330.

Danius S and S Jonsson (1993) An interview with Gayatri Chakravorty Spivak. *Boundary* 2(20): 24-50.

D'Emilio J (1992) *Making Trouble: Essays On Gay History, Politics and the University.* New York: Routledge.

Ditsie B (2006) TODAY we are making history. In De Waal S and A Manion (eds) *PRIDE: Protest and Celebration.* Johannesburg: Jacana.

Epprecht M (2012) Sexual minorities, human rights and public sexual health strategies in Africa. *African Affairs* 111/443: 223-243.

Gevisser M (1995) A different fight for freedom: A history of South African lesbian and gay organisation from the 1950s to the 1990s. In Gevisser M and E Cameron (eds) *Defiant Desire: Gay and Lesbian Lives in South Africa*. Braamfontein and London: Ravan and Routledge.

Gibson-Graham JK (2001) Querying globalization. In Hawley JC (ed.) *Post-Colonial, Queer: Theoretical Intersections*. New York: State University of New York.

Giddens A (1991) *Modernity and Self-Identity: Self and Society in the Late Modern Age*. California: Stanford University Press.

Gqola PD (2001) Defining people: analysing power, language and representation in metaphors of the new South Africa. *Transformation* 47: 94-106.

Gunkel H (2010) *The Cultural Politics of Female Sexuality in South Africa*. New York: Routledge.

Hames M (2011) Violence against black lesbians: Minding our language. *Agenda: Empowering Women for Gender Equity*, 25(4): 87-91.

Kelly A (2009) Raped and Killed for Being a Lesbian: South Africa Ignores 'Corrective' Attacks. http://www.guardian.co.uk/world/2009/mar/12/eudy-simelane-corrective-rape-south-africa [Accessed 12 March 2009].

Love H (2007) *Feeling Backward: Loss and the Politics of Queer History*. Cambridge and London: Harvard University Press.

Luirink B (1998) *Moffies: Gay Life in South Africa*. Cape Town: Ink.

Massad J (2007) *Desiring Arabs*. Chicago: University of Chicago Press.

Matebeni Z (2013) Deconstructing violence towards black lesbians in South Africa. In Ekine S and H Abbas (eds) *Queer African Reader*. Oxford: Pambazuka Press.

Mkhize N, J Bennett, V Reddy and R Moletsane (2010) *The Country We Want To Live In: Hate Crimes and Homophobia in The Lives of Black Lesbian South Africans*. Cape Town: HSRC Press.

Morgan R and S Wieringa (2005) *Tommy Boys, Lesbian Men and Ancestral Wives*. Johannesburg: Jacana.

Mtetwa P (2011) 'Correct' the homophobes. *Amandla*, 20 July/August: 20-21.

Muholi Z ((2012) *MO(U)RNING*. Stevenson: Cape Town & Johannesburg. www.stevenson.info/exhibitions/muholi/index2012.html [Accessed 26 July 2012].

Muholi Z (2004) Thinking through lesbian rape. *Agenda*, Issue #61.

Muthien B (2007) Queerying borders: An Afrikan activist perspective. *Journal of Lesbian Studies* 11(3): 321-330.

Murray SO and W Roscoe (eds) (1998) *Boy-Wives and Female Husbands: Studies in African Homosexualities*. New York: St Martin's Press.

One in Nine Campaign (2013) *What's in a Name? Language, Identity and the Politics of Resistance*. Johannesburg: One in Nine Campaign.

Oswin N (2007) Producing homonormativity in neoliberal South Africa: recognition, redistribution, and the Equality Project. *Signs* 32(3): 649-669.

People's Pride (2013) Johannesburg People's Pride March for Freedom and Justice. http://peoplespride.blogspot.com [Accessed 5 October 2013].

Schutte G (2012) Johannesburg gay pride parade: not much to be proud of. *The South African Civil Society Information Service (SACSIS)* www.sacsis.org.za/site/article/1450 [Accessed 8 October 2012].

Thamm M (2006) Not just another murder. *Mail & Guardian Online* www.mg.co.za [Accessed 4 March 2006].

Turley M (2012) South Africa: The fight for acceptance in the rainbow nation. http://www.globalpost.com/dispatches/globalpost-blogs/rights/South-Africa-lesbians-violence-lgbt [Accessed 4 April 2013].

NOTES

1   Sizakele Sigasa and Salome Masoa, a black lesbian couple raped and murdered in 2007 in Meadowlands (Johannesburg); Thokozane Qwabe, a 23 year old black lesbian raped and murdered in 2007, Ezakheni (KwaZulu-Natal); Sibongile, a black lesbian raped and murdered in 2008 in Strand (Cape Town); Eudy Simelane, a black lesbian murdered and suffered attempted rape in 2008 in Kwa-Thema (Johannesburg); Khanyiswa, a black lesbian murdered in 2008 in New Brighton (Port Elizabeth); Ncumisa Mzamela, a 21 year old black lesbian burnt to death in Inanda (KwaZulu-Natal) in 2010, Nokuthula Radebe (20), Ntsiki Tyatyeka (21), Khanyiswa Hani (25), Tshuku Ncobo (26), Mpho Setshedi (27), Sanna Supa (28), Hendrietta Thapelo Morifi (29), Phumeza Nkolonzi (18) … and there are many others whose victimisation, rape and murder remains unreported and undocumented (source: www.iranti-org.co.za).

PUBLIC POLICY AND SOCIAL PRACTICE

3

Public policy and social practice

Roger Southall

The founding provisions of the South African Constitution lay down that all citizens are equally entitled to the rights, privileges and benefits of citizenship (RSA 1996, Ch.1, 3.2). The Bill of Rights elaborates further. Everyone is equal before the law and has the right to equal protection and benefit of the law; equality includes the full and equal enjoyment of rights and privileges and freedoms; and everyone has inherent dignity and the right to have their dignity respected and protected. Numerous rights follow, such as the freedoms of religion, belief and opinion, expression, movement and residence, and the right to have access to adequate housing, health care, sufficient food and water and social security. Ultimately these rights are protected by the Constitutional Court – whose duty is to defend citizens' rights against breach by government or any other body (such as large corporations) and, if convinced by appeals to its judgement, to order the government to implement policies to ensure that citizens' rights are realised.

Understandably, the role played by the Constitutional Court, and the African National Congress (ANC) government's relationship to it, have come under intense scrutiny, internationally as much as domestically. Generally, it is fair to say that the performance of the Constitutional Court has received highly favourable reviews. However, as was discussed in the Introduction, Theunis Roux has argued that the role of the Constitutional Court is as much political as it is legal – that is, in seeking to defend and secure implementation of the Constitution, the Court has to be advised not merely of what is politically possible but what is politically wise. Although it may well be the duty of a Constitutional Court to stand up against an oppressive government, when push comes to shove the latter is usually more powerful – and if such a government chooses to ride roughshod over a constitution, there may be little that a Constitutional Court can do about it (except shout from the sidelines).

Roux fears that after two decades of democracy the ANC may be more predisposed than it was to undermine the independent standing and the status of the Constitutional Court. The implication is that a Manichean struggle between the judiciary and the executive might be pending, the outcome of which could prove to be critical for South African democracy. Yet such a moment has not arrived yet, and more usually when we are looking at the failure of government to implement rights we need to be far more concerned with far more mundane problems of public policy than any suggestion of an unlicensed grab for power by the ruling party (even if the ANC's penchant for passing laws promoting official secrecy, as explored by McKinley above are worrying). At times, the government may act in bad faith, and it may regard the Constitution as an obstacle to its designs rather than as a fundamental testament to citizens' rights – but more often constitutional and public policy dilemmas arise out of inappropriate policy designs, contradictions between policies implemented by different departments, budgetary constraints, lack of human capacities, and unrealistic ambitions – not to mention sheer incompetence and even bureaucratic bloody-mindedness. In short, there are many reasons why the laudable aspirations of the Constitution have not been realised after twenty years of democracy – even if, as argued in the Introduction, there are fundamental tensions between South Africa's status as a constitutional state and a macroeconomic policy which, in line with neoliberal trends internationally, erodes the capacity and will of the state to attend to the needs and rights of ordinary citizens.

It is with these thoughts in mind that we now turn to issues of social policy, our four contributions dealing respectively with the public schooling system, higher education, the prisons, and the impact of poverty upon households.

EDUCATIONAL CHALLENGES

As ever, it is appropriate when we are addressing South African issues to keep international comparisons in mind. Martin Prew does this when he provides cautious suggestions as to why – despite Zimbabwe's disastrous economic experiences in recent years – its school system appears to perform better than that of post-apartheid South Africa. Similarly, Ahmed Bawa locates the state of our higher educational system within a global context.

> According to the Constitution (RSA 1996: 29.1):
> Everyone has the right –
> a) To a basic education, including adult basic education; and
> b) To further education, which the state must take reasonable measures to make progressively available and accessible.

As Prew points out, comparing school systems is 'a perilous venture' given different national cultures and experiences. Nonetheless, both Zimbabwe and South Africa were subject to white minority rule, and their black populations subject to systematic discrimination which reached far into their educational experiences. After Zimbabwean independence in 1980 and the attainment of democracy by South Africa in 1994, the respective governments launched programmes of racial redress designed to deliver quality education to all. In retrospect, despite the setbacks of the last decade and a half, the Zimbabwean school system continues to outperform the South African (or, at least, its public component) according to key measures. The post-independence government in Zimbabwe had problems enough, yet was nonetheless able to implement a coherent educational system subject to centralised national policy and guidance, backed by a vigorous school building programme in the 1980s, innovative teacher training and an important focus upon technical and science subjects. Until the economic crisis hit, teachers were highly valued by the government, pupils and communities. In contrast, the post-apartheid government faced the enormous problem, first of all, of consolidating some eighteen apartheid era education departments (for different race groups and the various bantustans) into one, often against the wishes of a still powerful 'old guard' in administrative positions and in the schools themselves. Mistakes were also made. Thousands of teachers were retrenched, in part because it was thought that there were too many of them, in part in pursuit of transforming the racial profile of the profession. Teacher training colleges were shut, and their functions taken over by 'reluctant' universities. Subsequently, a new curriculum was introduced, without many teachers being adequately prepared. Unsurprisingly, the morale of the teaching profession was severely affected, not least because during the 1980s the black schooling system had been severely disrupted by violence as the struggle against apartheid reached its zenith. This disruption was such that, arguably, the public school system for the majority of black pupils has yet to recover.

Both schooling systems continue to display gross inequality. In Zimbabwe, elite urban schools and mission schools received more funding than the majority of township and rural schools. In South Africa, similarly, former white schools – although now formally deracialised – continue to enjoy more resources and better teaching. In both countries, too, privilege is buttressed by the ability of better-off schools to charge fees. Where, nonetheless, the public educational system is seen by parents as failing, there is flight to a burgeoning private sector in education.[1]

The ANC government cannot be accused of deliberately failing the country's children, deliberately failing to ensure that they all receive their constitutional rights. Far from it; it is a well-known fact that it spends more on education (proportionately) than most governments throughout the world – but it is equally well known that it is not getting an adequate bang for its buck, because of its apparent inability to grapple with the legacy and other problems with which it has been confronted. So children's educational experiences vary greatly, although they are increasingly differentiated by class as much as by race.

Inequality likewise continues to divide the higher education system. Deep imbalances persist between the historically white institutions and those that were historically black. While the upward mobility of blacks has enabled student bodies in the former to (unevenly) 'transform', the trend of poor (overwhelmingly black) students going to poor (historically black) universities has been maintained, their disadvantage compounded by the poor governance which characterises such institutions. Furthermore, although the stronger and better resourced universities will be more able to navigate the changing higher educational terrain than their less advantaged counterparts, all South African higher education institutions face an uncertain future.

Higher education, argues Ahmed Bawa, is both intensely local (an elitest system wrestling with official demands for transformation) and intensely global (the pervasive triumph of managerialism accompanying the emergence of new forms of international organisation of knowledge production systems). Simultaneously, our universities are publicly funded yet fiercely autonomous, a tension that is intensified by budget cuts which are increasingly forcing them to corporatise. It is within this context that South African higher education institutions have failed the challenge to 'massify', a global phenomenon that is integrally related to the desire to build knowledge economies, and is driven by the passionate demand by youth for higher education. While there are local reasons for this (for instance, universities complain that the school system is not producing adequately prepared students), their failure compounds 'the legitimacy deficit': popular perceptions that they have remained elitest, exclusionary, untransformed and alienated from the developmental needs of society. Inevitably, this invites increased official intervention. Only by overcoming the legitimacy deficit will South African universities be able to prevent the further erosion of institutional autonomy and academic freedom.

PRISONS AND OVERCROWDING

If our tertiary sector is too restrictive, then the South African prison system is too inclusive – with Claire Ballard arguing that our prisons are overcrowded, with consequent infringements of inmates' constitutional rights.

Under apartheid, the human rights of those who were detained by the state were subject to massive abuse. It is therefore unsurprising that the longest and most elaborate paragraphs in the Bill of Rights refer to the rights of arrested, detained and accused persons (notably RSA 1996, 2.35). Among the key provisions are those which insist that persons subject to arrest be brought before a court as soon as reasonably possible; that they be released from detention if the interests of justice permit; and that all prisoners should be detained in conditions that are consistent with human dignity. Ballard argues that at present these demands of our Constitution are not being met.

Certainly the appropriate legislation is in place to ensure that prison inmates' rights are met, but the reality is that with 'remand detainees' (those awaiting trial or sentence) now constituting a third of the total prison population, the infrastructure of many (but not all) prisons is being severely stretched, and the conditions in which prisoners are kept is accordingly deteriorating. Although Ballard is careful to point out that, internationally, the South African prison system is not the worst offender in this regard (she cites some distressing examples from Africa), she nonetheless indicates that there are major concerns. Overcrowding (although uneven across prisons) not only compromises inmates' rights to adequate nutrition, medical treatment and exercise, but can cause major psychological strains for individuals and is associated with higher levels of assault, rape and sexual violence. As a result, any attempt to rehabilitate prisoners – one of the official objectives of the Department of Correctional Services in line with constitutional values – is severely compromised.

BASIC RIGHTS

The South African Constitution is aspirational:

> 27 (1) Everyone has the right to have access to
> a. Health care services, including reproductive health care;
> b. Sufficient food and water; and
> c. Social security, including, if they are unable to support themselves and their dependants, appropriate social assistance.
> (2) The state must take reasonable legislative and other measures, within its available sources, to achieve the progressive realisation of these rights.

It was indicated in the Introduction how the state's record, in terms of ensuring that these provisions of the Constitution are realised, has been mixed. Ambition and good intention has been embodied in the expansion in the number of social grant recipients and the delivery of water, electricity, sanitation and housing for the poor, and have brought improvements in living standards to many. At the same time, noble aims have been thwarted, in part by limited funds, limited governmental capacities, and (many would say) inappropriate cost-recovery models. Above all, however, the hopes of the Constitution have been undermined by the persistence of staggeringly high levels of unemployment. In the final chapter in this section, Sarah Mosoetsa considers the implications of poverty and unemployment for households at the bottom of South Africa's still highly unequal society.

Mosoetsa starts from the notion that the household is a site where economic resources are intertwined with social power relations which extend across gender and generation. Under apartheid, patriarchal household patterns were reshaped and reinforced by the migrant labour system. Through wage remittances, men's authority was reinforced, even during their long absences from home. In the democratic era, however, the household as an economic unit has been restructured in African communities by the pervasive levels of unemployment. Without jobs, men's patriarchal authority is undermined, as economic power shifts to recipients of social grants (notably old age pensions and child grants), with many female recipients also earning extra income from the informal economy. Fathers who cannot provide for their families lose status, dignity and power in the eyes of their parents, wives and children. Thus although the social grant system remains vital for the subsistence of the poor, an unintended consequence is that state pensions and grants become a source of conflict: old age pensions have to support entire households, and in many households men cling onto their power by resorting to domestic violence. The citizenship rights of the poor, concludes Mosoetsa, continue to be violated by the state's inability (and perhaps unwillingness) to address poverty in a comprehensive and all inclusive manner, and its hostility to those who resort to protests.

THE DANGERS OF FOILED HOPES

It has been argued previously in the *New South African Review* that the accountability of government under the Constitution is the foundation for South African democracy (Hoffman 2011: 83-99). Insofar as the hopes of the Constitution are realised, insofar as the rights it elaborates are claimed by the people, insofar as the government is rendered accountable, democracy will be maintained. However, where the reverse is true, and the rule of law undermined or frontally challenged by governmental arrogance or limitations, democracy will be endangered. The four contributions in this section all display a similar pattern – of good intentions foiled by a mix of the complexities of power, the state's limited administrative capacity and, not least, by the enduring inequalities of an economy which should be able (but does not) provide adequately for the basic needs of the poorer and most disadvantaged segments of its population. Suffice it to say in conclusion that the warning lights for our constitutional democracy are flashing.

REFERENCES

Hoffman P (2011) Democracy and accountability: Quo Vadis South Africa. In Daniel J, P Naidoo, D Pillay and R Southall (eds) *New South African Review 2: New Paths, Old Compromises*. Johannesburg: Wits University Press.

Republic of South Africa (RSA) Constitution of the Republic of South Africa as adopted by the Constitutional Assembly on 8 May 1996.

Roux T (2012) *The Politics of Principle: The First South African Constitutional Court, 1995-2005*. Cambridge: Cambridge University Press.

NOTE

1   Prew does not explore this aspect with regard to Zimbabwe in this chapter, but recent visits by this author to the country indicate that it is so: middle class Zimbabweans wanting to ensure a good education for their children increasingly feel compelled to send them to private schools.

CHAPTER 11

Why does Zimbabwe's school system out-perform South Africa's?

Martin Prew

INTRODUCTION

Since 1994 the South African school system is believed to have been performing relatively poorly in comparison to the Zimbabwean system, although the expenditure per learner is much higher and the Zimbabwean schooling system has been severely affected by the economic chaos of the last decade. Comparing school systems, however, is a dangerous academic exercise because every system is innately different, with its own history, structure and processes. With a warning, this chapter tries to do exactly that. The justification for this perilous venture is that as South Africans deal with the low performance and high cost of their school system some commentators have been comparing its failure to what is seen as the success of the Zimbabwean school system. This chapter explores to what extent that comparison is valid and, if if it is, what South Africa can learn from the Zimbabwean school system. It looks at the development of the school systems in both countries from before independence to the present and then engages in a limited comparison based on a few salient factors. It is not meant to be exhaustive and is more suggestive than conclusive.

The assertion that the South African school system is worse than the Zimbabwean school system is largely based on two indicators: the relative positions of the two countries' scores in the learner comparability tests and the claim that Zimbabweans living in

South Africa tend to speak better English and seem better educated and more employable than their South African counterparts. These are partial and subjective indicators.

COMPARATIVE DATA FROM BOTH SCHOOL SYSTEMS

The only international comparability testing process in which South Africa and Zimbabwe both participate is the Southern and Eastern African consortium for Monitoring Education Quality (SACMEQ). Zimbabwe is not a participant in either Trends in International Mathematics and Science Study (TIMSS) or Progress in International Reading Literacy Study (PIRLS). The basis for comparison based on test scores is therefore limited. However, it is worth exploring SACMEQ. In the Grade 6 tests in 2007 the scores were as follows:

Table 1: Comparison of South African and Zimbabwean SACMEQ III (2007) results

	Zimbabwe	South Africa	% points difference
Gr 6 literacy	507.7	494.9	12.8
Gr 6 mathematics	519.8	494.8	25.0

(Source: SACMEQ 2010)

There is a substantial difference between the two countries' scores, particularly for mathematics.

The other indicator that is used is the national literacy rate which is quoted by Unesco. Zimbabwe's, at 92.22 per cent, is considerably higher than South Africa's at 86.4 per cent, and is one of the highest in Africa. Even the Zimbabwe minister of education admits that he cannot support this figure, and questions how it was obtained (Coltart 2012). What is certain is that, with up to a quarter of the Zimbabwean population having emigrated since the late 1990s owing to the economic collapse, all statistics are likely to be skewed. Among those who left the country by 2009 were over 60 000 of the 160 000 teachers. Many children have also left and as a result there are schools all over the country which saw their rolls falling through the 2000s.

BACKGROUND TO THE SCHOOL SYSTEMS

Zimbabwe school system
Many commentators have written about the education success of the first decade of Zimbabwe African National Union (Patriotic Front) (Zanu PF) rule in Zimbabwe, from

1980 to 1990. Meldrum (2004) talks about the most obvious aspect of transformation immediately after independence, when he says:

> Zimbabwe had just experienced an education explosion, as Mugabe had opened up primary and secondary education to all. Enrolments doubled and tripled and the teachers were delighted to be working with students who were so eager to learn.

Table 2: Expansion of the school system after independence

	Learners in primary school	Number of primary schools	Learners in secondary school	Number of secondary schools
1979	819,000	2401	73,540	197 (1980)
1981	1,680,143	3418	145,363	694
1983	2,044,847	3960	316,438	790
1985	2,229,000	Approx 4000	497,766	+1200

(Source: Chung 1988 and Zvobgo 1987)

By 1995 Zimbabwe had 4 633 primary schools with 2 470 000 learners, and by 2007 it had 5 560 primary schools with no increase in learners (Makopa 2011).

Expansion was predicated by the fact that in 1979 only 42 per cent of primary school age black children were in school and only some 20 per cent of this minority of black children lucky enough to complete primary school were able to access secondary school places (Chung 1988). However, access to schooling before 1980 did not ensure access to quality teaching. The spending per black learner was 9.1 per cent of the spending on each white learner (Riddell 1980). This difference was reinforced by the inferior curriculum at black schools and the limited opportunities education created for black students, with only 8 000 tertiary education places available a year for them (Chung 1988), and with white access dominating places at university and in apprenticeships. As Zvobgo (1987: 319) explains: 'Racism was the cornerstone of colonial policy in education as it provided the ideological framework for economic and social policies.'

Education provision under colonial and settler rule

Colonial education was the basis for separate and differentiated development, with black schooling geared to reproduce a subservient, low-skill, cheap labour force which could not compete for 'white' jobs, but would be able to 'render more efficient service to European employers' (Katedza 1987: 51). This meant channelling bright black learners into junior technical secondary schools where they learned technical skills for positions as foremen and low level technicians in white-controlled industry (Riddell 1980). While the government tried to ensure that mission societies used schools to feed into the white supremacist master plan and ensure that at least half the lesson time was spent on 'industrial rather than academic education' (Zvobgo 1987: 320), many mission schools gained a reputation for having high academic standards and producing leaders who later caused political and labour troubles for the minority regime. Manipulation by the colonial government of the spending on black education, the curriculum delivered – and the provision and training of teachers – ensured that very few blacks had the chance to enter the professions and that education played a critical political and social role (Prew 1993). As Table 3 shows, every new phase in the schooling system was used to block access to the vast majority of black learners who had reached the end of the previous phase.

Table 3: Survival rate of the 1971 cohort of black learners across all schools

Year and Grade	Number of learners	% of 1971 cohort
1971 Grade 1	127 790	100 per cent
1978 Form 1	10 360	8.1 per cent
1981 Form 4	1 525	1.19 per cent
1982 Form 6	183	0.14 per cent

(Source: Zvobgo 1987: 331)

When the Rhodesian Front gained power in 1965 it increasingly transferred control of many existing African primary schools and all new primary schools from mission societies to African local councils. However, these newly created black councils lacked the funds, knowledge and policy space to run schools effectively. As in South Africa, resistance to the regime was sometimes expressed through school strikes and the burning of schools (Prew 1993), but this was on a small scale and left a legacy of rejecting technical education rather than schooling *per se* (Katedza 1987).

The fact that at independence in 1980 an estimated 45 per cent of black Zimbabweans were illiterate, and another 12.5 per cent semi-literate, was seen by Zanu PF as a potential 'brake' on development (Chung 1988: 118). The other concern, which was increasingly dominating political and economic discourse during the years after independence, was the lack of employment opportunities for Zimbabwean school leavers and university graduates (Prew 1993).

Expansion of schools

Education maintained its importance after 1980, but the politics, social and economic aims and particularly the symbolism had been transformed. The rhetoric was now Marxist and the aim was full access and the removal of all racist legacies. Zanu PF's 1980 election manifesto committed to deracialising education, while making it free and compulsory and fully accessible as a basic human right, and a driver for transforming society (Zanu Central Committee 1980). The party intended that the education revolution would 'enhance the socialist struggle to dismantle colonial imperialism' (Zvobgo 1987: 334). Zanu PF hit a popular chord in opening school access to all on an equal and free basis.

However, Zanu PF faced a dilemma: free primary and secondary schooling and the national adult literacy programme would leave the fiscus dry and so undermine the funding of other aspects of the transformation the party was driving. Cost sharing and user fees were put into effect by devolving considerable power over education to local councils, school committees (which included elected representatives of the community and educators) and through mobilising communities to build and maintain their schools. Other school owners, such as mission societies, were allowed to continue to finance and run their schools, but as part of the national system. At the same time, Zanu PF introduced a highly centralised governance system, allowing the state to train and deploy teachers, set the curriculum and provide low cost resources (including textbooks) where they were most needed. The lack of multiple bureaucratic layers between central office and schools meant that instructions reached schools reasonably efficiently and with minimal cost.

By the late 1980s it seemed that every settlement had a new brick primary school (Chung 1988). The design was simple, utilitarian and durable. Each school had classrooms, an administration block with staff room, principal's office and school office; and secondary schools had a library and laboratories. Thirty years later this physical infrastructure stands as testament to the quality of the buildings and design. The quality of teaching and learning was affected by the other, less visible reforms, which included a successful teacher training programme containing various models.

Innovative teacher training

With such a rapid expansion of education provision by 1988, only 4.2 per cent of teachers were university graduates and 17.1 per cent had 'O' levels and professional training (Chung 1988). Therefore the majority of teachers lacked basic minimum academic and/or professional qualifications (many primary school teachers had completed Form 2 (nine years of schooling) and had a primary school teaching qualification). To meet the need by 1990 all non-graduate trainee teachers spent half of their four-year training programme in schools on year-long attachments. This apprenticeship approach ensured that the teachers started their teaching careers with an understanding of the job, and afforded the system thousands of low-cost teachers. The other two years were spent in college. New high quality teacher training colleges were built, with Belvedere Technical Teachers' College the flagship, able to produce 500 combined subject (technical and academic) teachers per year (Chung 1988). As the traditional teacher training colleges were not able to meet the demand an alternative mass training model was introduced for primary teachers called ZINTEC (Zimbabwe Integrated National Teacher Education Course). This course pioneered an apprenticeship model of teacher training combined with a distance education component. It has been described as very successful (Chung 1988: 124), although the model perished during the economic and political crisis of the mid 2000s.

The Zimbabwean schooling system has a 7-4-2 structure, with seven years of primary schooling ending in a national Grade 7 exam, four years of secondary schooling leading to 'O' levels and then two further years where normally three subjects are taken for 'A' levels. Most learners leave the system after 'O' levels.

Funding of expanded school provision

The huge increase in access was led by the Zanu PF government making education a funded national development priority. From an annual education budget of about Z\$120m in 1979 it soared to Z\$224 in 1980 and Z\$517m in 1985 (Chung 1988; Zimbabwe Ministry of Education undated). The spending was structured to increase gradually so it was affordable while being enough to have dramatic effect (Chung 1988). However, the funding model after independence sustained an existing two-tier system. The elite urban and mission schools got more funds (through higher teacher salaries) than the majority of township and rural schools which were mainly district council and community owned and were staffed largely by untrained or undertrained teachers. Alongside state funding, schools were expected to charge fees. These deepened the division in quality, as most rural schools used funds to develop basic infrastructure, whereas urban schools used funds to reduce class sizes by hiring more teachers, buying extra equipment and generally enriching the schooling experience. This reality reinforced a dependent, dualistic economy and bred aspirations among poorer learners which were increasingly unrealisable (Prew 1993).

The expansion was also supported by the low-cost publishing of a limited number of texts provided free to schools as part of the capitation grant. These texts were chosen nationally by teachers, as the most appropriate for different syllabuses. The paper used in textbooks was cheap and of relatively poor quality, and so this policy was accompanied by strong textbook management and retrieval systems in all schools to ensure all textbooks were tracked and returned by the learners at the end of each term. Textbooks were supplemented by the national provision of science kits and technical equipment to support the focus on technical and scientific training. By 2007 the provision of resources, given the financial crisis, had become differentiated between rural and urban provinces, with the former having inadequate resources (Makopa 2011).

Racial integration in schools

Racial integration, particularly in the former elite urban schools, was speeded up by making these schools operate double sessions. This almost doubled the number of learners each school could enrol and dealt with any resistance related to class size and the school being declared 'full'. Formerly white schools (Group A) had 78.3 per cent black enrolment by 1985 (Chung 1988). The integration was also enforced in independent schools which, after 1985, had to have a minimum of 60 per cent black learners (Zvobgo 1987). Zvobgo argues, however, that Group B and C schools (township and rural schools) absorbed most of the increased post-independence enrolment, as Group A schools still had an average learner teacher ratio of 30:1 compared to 49:1 in Group B and C schools, and still represented colonial-style privilege.

Stability and gradual change

The curriculum, assessment system and teacher methodology were remarkably stable after independence. Although new syllabuses were introduced to primary and lower secondary schools the change was managed and was not radical, as the Ministry realised that it could not retrain huge numbers of teachers. The major innovations were in a greater focus on technical and science subjects and the introduction of 'education with production (EWP)' in which every school had to link education with gardening and other physical activities (Prew 2012b). However, in many schools EWP was used as punishment, as it had been before independence. EWP had been tried in the schools in liberation camps and the liberated areas of the country before independence. The aim, borrowed from Chinese communism, was to promote the nobility of labour and farming, and to assist schools to become self-sufficient. Other innovations in liberation schools were never mainstreamed (Prew 2013). The post-independence system was wedded to the overseas 'O' and 'A' level system even after the establishment of a local exam board in the 1990s.

The Zimbabwean schooling system, even with its undertrained teachers, was performing well until the economic and political crisis of the 2000s. According to a former minister of education (Coltart 2012), thousands of teachers left the service; textbook-per-learner ratios soared to 1:15; state funding of schooling almost dried up, leading to 8 000 schools closing; and a massive teachers' strike in 2009 over unpaid salaries and working conditions closed the rest for months. This situation was largely reversed between 2009 and 2013 and the schooling system stabilised, with teacher salaries seen as a priority in the national budget under the coalition government. The system is a shadow of its former self, but it still outperformed South Africa in SACMEQ 2007.

SOUTH AFRICAN SCHOOL SYSTEM

The system under white minority rule

As in Zimbabwe, access to schooling, and education more broadly, had been used by a minority white regime to restrict access to more complex and better paid jobs as a mechanism to ensure that white dominance could be maintained in the face of a majority black population. Famously, Hendrik Verwoerd, when minister of native affairs, declared that:

> Racial relations cannot improve if the wrong type of education is given to Natives, they cannot improve if the result of Native education is the creation of frustrated people, who, as a result of the education they received, have expectations in life which circumstances in South Africa do not allow to be fulfilled immediately (Fiske and Ladd 2004:1).

Later, Verwoerd made clear that an African would not be allowed to compete for jobs against whites and would be trained only to 'certain forms of labour' which would ensure 'he' could not be 'absorbed' into the 'European community' (Molteno 1984:92).

Limitation of access was enforced through various interlocking policies – the apartheid state taking over most mission schools, the differential spending on the schooling of the various racial groups depending on their 'whiteness', and the under-provisioning and under-training of teachers preparing to teach in schools in African areas. These policies were rooted in separate development which ensured that Africans lived in communities isolated from the main centres of industry and services, and away from whites.

The different provision was illustrated most effectively by the expenditure patterns under apartheid (Table 4). After the promulgation of the 1979 Education and Training Act and the publication of the subsequent De Lange Report 1981, the government set about creating a unitary system of education (but not including the Bantustans) where learners would in theory experience the same curriculum, exams, teacher pay levels and finance. However, as can be seen from Tables 4 and 5, the gap between provision for whites and blacks, even if it was closing, was still large up to the 1994 election.

Table 4: Expenditure on African and white learners and education 1953- 1988

	Total expenditure (millions of rands)		Expenditure per pupil (rands)		Ratio expenditure per pupil.
	African education	White education	African	White	White: African
1953	16.0		17.1	128.0	7.5:1
1955	15.8		15.7	n/a	-
1960	19.5	79.0	13.6	114.0	8.4:1
1965	24.9	252.3	12.7	357.0	28.1:1
1970	66.3	366.0	47.6	428.0	9.0:1
1975	160.2	738.7	50.0	605.0	12.1:1
1980	553.0	1360.9	87.3	1021.0	11.7:1
1985	1816.0	2973.7	293.9	2746.0	9.3:1
1988	4096.6	3727.5	582.9	3982.8	6.8:1

(Source: Prew (2003a); Unterhalter et al. (1991))

Differential treatment led to a race-based gap between the quality of provision and the outcomes of schooling. Of the cohort who entered school in South Africa in 1969,

70 per cent of the white cohort matriculated in 1978, while the figure for the black cohort was under 5 per cent. The reasons for high dropout rates in black schools included very large classes, poor teacher training, poor resources, parental poverty and political harassment. Increasingly, in the 1980s, violence which was becoming endemic in many townships and rural areas (with the complicity of the regime) engulfed many schools. Education analysts in KwaZulu-Natal illustrated the devastating effect this violence had on learners in local schools (Gultig and Hart 1990; Nzimande and Thusi 1991). By the early 1990s much of the African schooling system was tied up in what were conflict zones, with the associated trauma and learning difficulties (Nicolai 2009).

Somewhat differently from Zimbabwe, and because of the pressure created after the Soweto uprising of 1976, which was triggered by rejection of the schooling imposed on black communities, access to secondary education was fairly broad-based even for African students. This followed expansion of access to primary schooling for black children in the 1960s and 1970s. This first phase of expansion, however, had been achieved on shrinking allocations for African education (Hartshorne 1992), which in practice meant larger classes and double sessioning, with over seventy learners per teacher by 1970 (Hartshorne 1992), declining teacher qualifications, and the cost of school building relegated to communities. In the 1980s, secondary school expansion occurred, with the government committing to parity of spending per learner by 1996, but with no redress for past differentiation.

Table 5: School enrolment for whites and blacks in 1982

	Whites		Black Africans	
	Number	Percentage	Number	Percentage
Sub A	84 969	8.8	1 008 938	19.0
Standard 2	87 770	9.1	574 604	10.8
Lower Primary Total	*342 181*	*35.5*	*3 042 080*	*57.4*
Standard 3	89,517	9.3	526 363	9.9
Standard 5	83,442	8.7	381 441	7.2
Upper Primary Total	*261 165*	*27.1*	*1 349 009*	*25.4*
Standard 6	85 913	8.9	295 326	5.6
Standard 10	55 216	5.7	72 501	1.4
Secondary Total	*360 681*	*37.4*	*912 408*	*17.2*
Overall Total	**964 027**	**100**	**5 303 497**	**100**

(Source: Survey of Race Relations in South Africa, SAIRR, Johannesburg, 1983)

The contrast between the two systems could not be clearer – while white learners are spread fairly evenly across the various grades until the matric year (Standard 10), African learners are bunched in the early years, with 82.8 per cent in primary school. In 1982 there was clearly a filter at each stage blocking access up the system for all but a limited number of African learners.

The most radical change after 1980, in a mirror image of Zimbabwe, was the broadening of access to secondary schooling. Between 1975 and 1988 black enrolment in Standard 6 (Grade 8 – the start of secondary schooling) rose by six times, and Standard 10 (Grade 12) black enrolment rose by twenty-one times.

Table 6: Overall school enrolment 1970- 1985

	Primary school enrolment	*Secondary school enrolment*
1970	2 615 400[1]	122 489
1985	4 820 100	1 192 900

In 1989, 1.82 million African learners were in secondary school. This expansion may have been in part a reaction to secondary school expansion in Zimbabwe, but was explicitly in response to the requirements of industry and the need for more and better skills. However, as a result of the lack of access to equipment and resources (Harvey 1997); falling qualifications of teachers – with only 13.5 per cent having degrees (Hartshorne 1992); the arrival of many learners who needed more structured and remedial support; and political unrest in schools, matric pass rates for African learners plummeted. Between 1980 and 1989, 50.1 per cent of all black learners who did matric failed and only 12.9 per cent got an exemption allowing them to go on to higher education. In 1989, not one matriculant from the Department of Education and Training (DET) achieved an 'A' aggregate and Kahn (1994) estimated that one in a thousand black learners got a matric exemption in maths and science, compared to one in four whites.

White supremacist control of the schooling system was underpinned in South Africa with a pseudo-philosophy named Fundamental Pedagogics, which itself was underpinned by the Christian nationalism of the ruling National Party. Fundamental Pedagogics was prefaced by a highly damaging assumption that babies are born 'sinful' (Suransky 1995). It was the pervasive influence in most teacher training colleges for black teachers, in seeing the child as helpless, incompetent and sinful, and laid the basis for transmission modes of teaching supported by corporal punishment. This perverse form of teacher preparation had supplanted the more professional training before 1948 and created an under-trained teacher force which struggled to comprehend alternative methods of teaching and running a school. As Jansen (2003) puts it, they were skilled at 'structured compliance'.

ANC PLANS FOR EDUCATION IN THE NEW DISPENSATION

The African National Congress (ANC)-led government which came into power in 1994 inherited a low performing and skewed school system and it could be argued that the expansion of access in the 1980s created a dangerous legacy. The government inherited a schooling system which had become a key part of the struggle to resist the government and Bantustan fragmentation and to make townships and some rural areas ungovernable. Essentially protest had, in many communities and schools, turned to outright revolt against the apartheid state and its agents in the community, including, in some cases, teachers and principals (Naidoo 1990). From 1976 many African schools had been rent by divisions and tensions, with principals and more traditional teachers trying to implement the government's education programme facing off against younger teachers and learners determined to undermine that process. The weapons used were class boycotts, marches, general disobedience to school authority and the development of strong student organisations, most notably the Congress of South African Students (Cosas) formed in 1979 (Naidoo 1990). However, the boycotts and broader revolt worried many of those in the liberation movements who saw that student actions were dividing the opposition to apartheid and boycotts and weakening learner ability to organise in schools (Naidoo 1990); and the realisation that if anarchy took over in schools a post-independence government would inherit an under-educated 'lost generation'.

The ANC undertook extensive research to inform its education election platform or 'yellow book' (ANC 1994) for the 1994 election. This document presented a vision of an integrated education and training system where the focus was on universal access, equity and quality. This right to education was further embodied in Section 29 of the Constitution.

Education transformation

The first few years after 1994 saw intensive change in the South African school system or, as the Organisation for Economic Cooperation and Development (OECD 2008:37) says, 'since 1994, the government has worked to transform all facets of the education system'. The main focus was on consolidating seventeen education departments (for different race groups and Bantustans) into one national and nine provincial departments and putting in place a plethora of new legislation and policies. These have been detailed elsewhere (OECD 2008; Prew 2013). The important point is that these policies on language, religion, governance and management in education, as well as the funding of schools, time on task, educator salaries and so on, affected schools in a relatively unplanned manner, and were mediated by provincial education departments which often misinterpreted or only partially implemented the policies.

The decision to introduce a decentralised, multilevel system had an impact on school functionality and the effectiveness of the transformation process at school level. Most education district offices were too weak and under-resourced to offer any real support and guidance to schools in how to manage new policy demands. Generally, schools which deliberately took ownership of new policies affecting their school managed to keep on top of the situation, but those schools which failed to do so found that policies adversely affected their functioning. Ironically it was often the schools serving poorer communities, which these policies were most focused on assisting, that were most badly affected by these policies (Prew 2003b).

Early problems of system management

The first post-apartheid minister of education, Professor Sibusiso Bengu, had no struggle record and was not an ANC cadre. His appointment was related to reinforcing the government coalition. Compounding his political weakness he suffered a stroke early on in his five years in office which left considerable power in the hands of some of the old guard still in the Department and new ANC-aligned appointees. The result was weak management of the whirlwind of new legislation focused on the National Education Policy Act 1996 and the South African Schools Act (SASA) 1996. These cornerstone pieces of legislation were more political than educational in content and primarily focused on making sure that concurrent powers between provinces and national levels of government were clear and ensuring that governance in schools allowed considerable flexibility (a demand from the National Party in the Government of National Unity). The legislation was not adequate to establish a new school system and betrayed the progressive intentions of the Yellow Book.

SASA banned corporal punishment without warning and without preparing teachers. This was followed by the introduction of a completely new curriculum, Curriculum 2005, which was 'outcomes based' and aimed at ending rote learning. Curriculum 2005 was introduced with partial preparation of the teachers (South Africa Department of Education 2000) and without the required resourcing levels. Many teachers confessed to not understanding it. Since then, two further national curriculum changes have been made.

Parallel to these changes was a shedding of excess teachers. Attempting to reduce costs, meet new teacher learner ratio norms and transform the racial profile of the teaching profession, the Department allowed many 'anchor' teachers to leave, with a severe effect on many schools and the overall professionalism of the education sector. A few years later there was a teacher shortage, as all the teacher training colleges had been closed. The planning and modelling of the effect of this decision had been weak. The teacher training function was transferred from approximately 120 teacher training colleges generating 25 000 new teachers a year to reluctant universities with limited funding and the capacity to graduate 9 000 teachers each year (South African Council of Educators 2011). As a result far fewer new teachers were being trained than were being lost to the profession and in addition, as most universities were far from the rural areas, primary teacher training no longer attracted the high performing rural students who used to access the local rurally-based primary teacher training colleges. The unintended consequences of shedding teachers and closing the training colleges still plague the South African schooling system.

The new curriculum was implemented fairly well in the former white schools with their resources and graduate teachers, and very poorly in most black schools, where there was a lack of experience, training and resources. As it became clear that Curriculum

2005 was not being implemented as planned, the Department got into the habit of blaming teachers for this failure – a failure which the Chisholm Report lays squarely at the Department's door (South Africa Department of Education 2000). Not surprisingly, the 2000s saw the growth of private schools in reaction to the effect of declining morale and the state of flux and uncertainty dominating state schools faced with a barrage of curriculum and other policy changes.

South Africa, which like Zimbabwe had never had a large private schooling system, saw a burgeoning of private schools in the 2000s. Officially about 4.5 per cent of schools are private but a study found large numbers of unregistered low-cost private schools (Centre for Development and Enterprise 2010). It can be assumed that a higher percentage of learners are in private schools than official figures indicate. These children attend such schools because their parents have lost faith in state schools or struggle to gain access to them.

COMPARING THE TWO SYSTEMS

On the surface, the school systems are similar and therefore it can be legitimately claimed that they can be compared (Prew 2012a). They were both formed in a period of white minority rule based on restricting Africans to a subservient role in an economy which served white interests. The differentiated race-based schooling systems in both countries were built on providing very different levels of funding for schools serving the race groups. As apartheid in both countries became increasingly codified in the 1960s, there was a concerted attempt to take African education out of the hands of missionaries and put it under state control. However, while South Africa used this policy to expand access and attempt to control the minds of its black population and fit the products of the schooling system to particular jobs in the industrialising economy, in Rhodesia, where there were fewer resources, African schooling was largely left in the hands of missionaries, and black councils, who lacked the funds and will to adequately expand access and use schools to fit a particular political and economic model.

THE SCENE IS SET IN THE 1980S

In the 1980s, both systems opened up almost universal access to primary and, increasingly, secondary schooling. There was a fundamental difference between them in that the Zimbabwean expansion took place after independence and was based on access to schools where learners were meant to succeed – and in the first years after independence there were many extremely materially poor learners who got to university and into the professions (Prew 1993). Meanwhile, in South Africa the expansion was aimed at using schooling to extend the central state's ideological control over black youth and the needs of an expanding economy. The Zimbabwean process was planned nationally, was well organised and based on thousands of well-built schools. In South Africa the expansion was in townships, rural areas and Bantustans, and was not based on a national plan as there were eighteen departments of education all planning in parallel. The results were also very different. The Zimbabwean system started churning out well qualified artisans and professionals with 'O' and, increasingly, 'A' levels and university and nursing, teaching and technical college qualifications, while by the mid-1980s the South African system was mired in political action such as boycotts and strikes – and increasing levels of ill discipline by teachers and learners cloaked in anti-apartheid rhetoric. This culminated in the emergence of a powerful militant teachers' union, the South African Democratic Teachers' Union (Sadtu), while Zimbabwe's system spawned a 'sweetheart' association, the Zimbabwe Teachers' Association (Zimta).

The Zimbabwean government prided itself on its schools which, with their increasing quality of outcomes, were seen as a symbol of post-independence success, whereas the South African system was typified by plummeting performance indicated by falling matric pass rates and a common rejection of schools associated with the regime. It could be argued that even with the financial meltdown of the 2000s the Zimbabwean system has never completely lost the sound basis created in the 1980s – and inversely the South African system has never recovered from the chaos of the 1980s. The habits, which in both systems became entrenched in the 1980s, have been remarkably resilient to change. So, in the South African schooling system teacher absenteeism, union militancy, limited coverage of the curriculum each year and a generally low opinion of schools and schooling became entrenched and sustained into the post apartheid period; while, in contrast, in the Zimbabwean system teacher professionalism, discipline, and the expectation of high performance became normed.

POST INDEPENDENCE APPROACH TO EDUCATION

These tendencies in the 1980s were reinforced by the different approach each country took to its school system after independence. Both countries faced government by broadly left-wing liberation movement-led coalitions following the end of white suprem-acist settler rule. Zanu PF was overtly Marxist while the ANC shed most of its socialist leanings after independence and became a party where nationalistic neoliberal and social democratic tendencies flourished. The first minister of education in Zimbabwe, Dr Dzingai Mutumbuka, had been head of education in Zanla (Zanu's army) during the struggle against the Rhodesian regime, and had been instrumental in establishing the liberation schools in the camps (ZIMFEP 1991). He focused his attention on unifying and expanding school and curriculum provision, expanding the bureaucracy, bringing in overseas teachers to supplement the local teaching cadre, building new teacher training colleges and limited syllabus changes. He also ensured that Zimta was cooperative and compliant and supported his agenda. The most symbolic changes were to obnoxious parts of the curriculum – such as the history syllabus – and the introduction of EWP across all schools (Prew 2012b). The overall effect was to give teachers confidence in their knowledge and skills; to offer them many promotion opportunities; and to paint them as the core of the new society, critical to transformation. Teachers felt affirmed and their morale was high during the post-independence period. The profession attracted many relatively high performing school graduates, although it remained largely staffed by those without degrees. Access and success went hand in hand.

The post 1994 trajectory in South Africa was very different. The flood of policies, the closing of teacher training colleges, the shedding of 'excess' teachers, and radical curriculum changes left teachers feeling demoralised and confused: many left the profession or became more militant and uncooperative, with the support of Sadtu. Exam results improved, although not in all parts of the system, and not to a level where they reflected the high levels of investment in education. South Africa found itself coming at the bottom of international rankings in education comparability studies. In addition many schools remained largely segregated, with no South African equivalent of Zimbabwe's legal integration. This meant that a significant number of schools remain elitist and largely mono-ethnic, particularly those with an Afrikaans medium of instruction (Centre for Education Policy Development 2011). This combination of rapid transformation, declining results, pools of apartheid era status quo, and the negative image of teachers in the media have left teachers ever more demoralised. Reports that a large proportion of teachers wanted to leave the profession reinforced a downward spiral of low performance and low morale. Improving matric results, increased teachers' pay and the recruitment of more new teachers from universities and from outside the country have not halted the decline in morale.

MATHEMATICS AND SCIENCE TEACHING AND LEARNING

If we delve deeper into specific subjects and policies we find further differences between the way the two systems developed after independence. Zimbabwe never faced a crisis of confidence over the teaching and learning of Mathematics and Science, as has been experienced in South Africa and some other African countries. The introduction of a local, much-praised ZimSci syllabus for science in the 1980s supported that confidence and the general level of teaching in these subjects was relatively professional and successful. This seeking of local solutions typified the Zimbabwean school system and also helped to keep down the cost of textbooks, teacher training and the resourcing of new syllabuses. In South Africa it was the opposite. The under-training of Mathematics and Science teachers in black or 'bush' teacher training colleges has created a weak knowledge and skills base for these subjects, with each generation of teachers under-preparing the next. The result is a national crisis of belief that the South African schooling system can produce Mathematics and Science matriculants able to do university level courses, so many black schools offer Mathematics literacy, and arts subjects, rather than Mathematics and Science, to ensure that learners gain a matric certificate (EduAction 2013).

LANGUAGE POLICY AND PRACTICE

Another area of difference is that of language policy. If learners cannot understand their teachers they will not learn. In most township and rural schools Grades 1 to 3 are taught in the learners' mother tongue and then at Grade 4 English becomes the medium of instruction. However, no training and little direction was provided on how the transfer from home language to English should be effected in Grade 4, and how English should be taught in Grades 1 to 3 so that learners would be prepared for this changeover (CEPD 2011). Recent research (CEPD 2011) has indicated that many learners in black schools are in classes where the home language is not their own and is taught badly, while there is little or no teaching of English. These learners struggle in Grade 4 as they lack linguistic and conceptual grounding in their own language and in English, and a significant proportion of learners goes through school understanding little of what is being said by the teacher (CEPD 2011) and is unable to interpret questions set in class and exams.

The Zimbabwe rural schools generally teach to Grade 4 in home language and then in English, and urban schools often teach from Grade 1 in English supported by chiShona or siNdebele. As the linguistic composition of Zimbabwe is much simpler than that of South Africa, when a teacher uses chiShona or siNdebele all the children in her class will understand, as it will be their home language. In addition the quality of teaching of both home language and English is generally competent. The result is that most children are bilingual when they leave school. The Zimbabwean system seems to achieve competence in both home language and English, while South African schools generally fail to create competence in either language.

THE IMPACT OF CONFLICT

This section ends with a brief thought on the impact of conflict on both school systems. While much of Rhodesia suffered arbitrary rule under the minority regime, only the north east saw sustained fighting, and that for a fairly brief period in the late 1970s. However, many fighters from Zanla and Zipra (the two main resistance armies which fought for Zimbabwe's independence) returned home traumatised. School places were opened for those who needed them. At the same time, the stabilisation of the school system and strong family support systems meant that trauma was contained. Levels of violence in schools, and other symptoms of a traumatised system, were rarely obvious, and dissipated during the 1980s.

South African township and rural schools, which had often been wracked by violence during the 1980s, faced constant personnel and policy changes in the 1990s and, in some areas, saw gang violence replace political unrest. This destabilisation left them vulnerable and weak, such that any change hit them disproportionately hard. Such schools tend to see their matric results fluctuate dramatically. It also takes such schools months to recover momentum after any disruption such as teacher strike action, an accusation against a teacher or principal, a change of principal or a violent incident in the school. Although research has not proven this, it seems clear that the behaviour of these schools fits the pattern seen in post-conflict schools elsewhere in Africa and beyond (Nicolai 2009). Such schools require a stable environment where teachers and learners are affirmed and supported psychosocially, much as happened in Zimbabwe in the 1980s. In reality, such schools in South Africa are constantly criticised, poked and prodded. Until South Africa takes the level of trauma these schools have experienced (and in some localities are still facing) seriously, the country will make little headway in making these schools functional and high performing – as some of them were before the 1980s. In this situation, the defensive posturing of Sadtu in protecting teachers' rights may be deepening the crisis by preventing action to identify the problem and remedy it; such action tends to be seen by Sadtu as shaming teachers and unfairly exposing their weaknesses.

CONCLUSION

Much of the evidence presented in this article is circumstantial and I am sure there are other conditions that should be examined, but a case has been made for understanding why, comparatively, the South African school system is under-performing in relation to the Zimbabwean. The toxic combination of the poor state of the schooling system inherited in 1994 owing to apartheid and resistance to apartheid in the 1980s; to the legacy of poor work practices; and to student resistance and the trauma suffered, combined with teacher demoralisation as a result of policy changes after 1994, created a demotivated and poorly performing system. This situation was then compounded by closing the teacher training colleges and letting 'anchor teachers' leave the system, and by a language policy and practice which has deepened the poor performance.

REFERENCES

Centre for Development and Enterprise (2010) Hidden Assets: South Africa's Low-fee Private Schools. CDE In Depth no 10, August 2010. Johannesburg: CDE.
Centre for Education Policy Development (2011) Language in education policy in the context of Gauteng demographics: Report on policy and policy implementation in primary schools. Johannesburg: CEPD.
Chung F (1988) Education: Revolution or reform. In Stoneman C (ed.) Zimbabwe's Prospects: Issues of Race, Class, State, and Capital in Southern Africa. Basingstoke: Macmillan.
Coltart D (2012) Speech given at the Education World Forum, London, 11 January 2012.
EduAction (2013) Education Districts in South Africa: A Review. Pretoria: Department of Basic Education.
Fiske E and H Ladd (2004) Elusive Equity: Education Reform in Post-Apartheid South Africa. Washington DC: Brookings Institution Press.
Gultig J and M Hart (1990) 'The world is full of blood': Youth, schooling and conflict in Pietermaritzburg, 1987-1989. Perspectives in Education 11.

Harvey S (1998) Primary Science InSET in South Africa: An evaluation of classroom support. Unpublished PhD. Exeter University.

Jansen J (2003). Image-ining teachers: Policy images and teacher identity in South African classrooms. In Lewin K, M Samue and Y Sayed (eds) *Changing Patterns of Teacher Education in South Africa: Policy, Practice and Prospects*. Sandown: Heinemann.

Kahn M (1994) *Science and Technology Education and Training for Economic Development*. Braamfontein: CEPD.

Kallaway P (2002) *The History of Education under Apartheid 1948-1994*. Cape Town: Maskew Miller Longman.

Kallaway P (1984) *Apartheid and Education: The Education of Black South Africans*. Braamfontein: Ravan.

Katedza NH (1987) The contribution of education to development in Zimbabwe. Unpublished thesis. Georgia State University.

Makopa Z (2011) *The Provision of the Basic Classroom Teaching and Learning Resources in Zimbabwean Schools and their Relationship with Grade 6 Pupils' Achievements in the SACMEQ III Project*. Paris: IIEP.

Meldrum A (2004) *Where We Have Hope: A Memoire of Zimbabwe*. London: John Murray.

Molteno F (1984) The historical foundations of the schooling of black South Africans. In Kallaway P (ed.) *Apartheid and Education: The Education of Black South Africans*. Braamfontein: Ravan.

Motala S, V Dieltiens, N Carrim, P Kgobe, G Moyo and S Rembe (2007) *Educational Access in South Africa: Country Analytic Report*. Johannesburg: Create.

Mzamane MV (1990) Towards a pedagogy for liberation: Education for a national culture in South Africa. In Nkomo M (ed.) *Pedagogy of Domination*. Trenton NJ: Africa World Press.

Naidoo K (1990) The politics of student resistance in the 1980s. In Nkomo M (ed.) *Pedagogy of Domination*. Trenton NJ: Africa World Press.

Nicolai S (2009) *Opportunities for Change: Education Innovation and Reform During and After Conflict*. Paris: IIEP.

Nzimande B and S Thusi (1991) *'Children of War': The Impact of Political Violence on Schooling in Natal*. Durban: Education Projects Unit, University of Natal.

OECD (2008) *Reviews of National Policies for Education: South Africa*. Paris: OECD.

Prew M (2012a) Why is the Zimbabwean Schooling System Still Outscoring South Africa's? *Mail & Guardian* 20 January.

Prew M (2012b) People's education for people's power: The rise and fall of an idea in Southern Africa. In Griffiths TG and Z Millei (eds) *Logics of Socialist Education: Engaging with Crisis, Insecurity and Uncertainty*. New York: Springer.Prew M (2003a) Transformation and development of marginalised schools in South Africa: A school and district development model. Unpublished PhD thesis, Exeter University.

Prew M (2003b) Speech 'Best Practice for School Principals'. Presented to the Annual Conference of the South African Principals' Association in Durban, 3 May.

Prew M (1993) The effects of changes in the political-economy of a less developed country on the educational and occupational aspirations of peri-urban school students: A Zimbabwean case study. Unpublished M Ed dissertation. Institute of Education, University of London.

Riddell R (1980) *Education for Employment*. London: Catholic Institute for International Relations.

SACMEQ (2010) SACMEQ III Project Results: Pupil Achievement Levels in Reading and Mathematics. Working Document no 1. Paris: IIEP.

South African Council for Educators (2011) Teacher migration in South Africa: Advice to the ministers of basic and higher education. June 2011. Centurion: SACE.

South Africa Department of Education (2000) Report of the Review Committee on Curriculum 2005 (the Chisholm Report). Pretoria: DoE.

South African Institute of Race Relations (1983) *Survey of Race Relations in South Africa*. Johannesburg: SAIRR.

Suransky C (1995) 'Fundamental Pedagogics'. Presentation at University of Durban Westville, Education Department.

Unterhalter E, H Wolpe and T Botha (eds) (1991) *Apartheid Education and Popular Struggles*. Braamfontein: Ravan.

Zanu PF Central Committee (1980) Zanu PF Election Manifesto. Harare: Zanu PF.

Zimbabwe Ministry of Education (nd) *Codes and Allocations 1980-1996*. Harare: Ministry of Education.

ZIMFEP (1991) *Schools in the Struggle*. Harare: ZIMFEP.

Zvobgo RJ (1987) Education and the Challenge of Independence. In Mandaza I (ed.) *Zimbabwe: The Political Economy of Transition 1980- 1986*. Harare: Codesria and Jongwe Press.

NOTE

1   These statistics include all learners in school, however the vast majority of the increase in numbers was made up of black learners as white and Indian and to a lesser extent coloured children already had full access to schooling by 1970.

CHAPTER 12

Higher education in 2013:
At many crossroads

Ahmed Bawa

INTRODUCTION

In a recent survey carried out for a board meeting of Higher Education South Africa (HESA), Jeffrey Mabelebele, chief executive office (CEO) of HESA, noted that at the beginning of 2013 there existed an avalanche of more than thirty policy initiatives initiated by the Department of Higher Education and Training (DHET) and other government departments, each underway and each with important ramifications for the sector. On the one hand, these policy projects focused on broad vision-type enterprises such as the Green Paper and (soon to be released) White Paper on post-school education and training and the ministerial committee to study the possibility of 'free' higher education. On the other hand, there are policy projects meant to affect the sector at the more operational level: the ministerial review of the funding of universities; a review of the norms and standards for student accommodation; new reporting regulations ostensibly to bring the universities into line with the reporting requirements of government departments; the establishment of a transformation oversight committee; and the establishment of a national application and information service (NAIS). This is an ambitious policy programme by any measure. The question is: what drives it? Is it simply the passion and drive of an activist minister or are there deeper reasons and concerns that create the impetus?

In 2012-2013 the minister of higher education and training, Dr BE Nzimande, placed five universities (more than 20 per cent of the institutions in the public higher education system) under administration on the basis that they were, in some form or other, dysfunctional. This is equivalent to disbanding the councils of the institutions, in some cases suspending the vice-chancellors and appointing an administrator to act as one-person council/executive head. It would probably be accurate to estimate that about a third of the higher education system experiences poorly functioning university councils and/or poorly functioning administrative systems. This is seriously exacerbated (or even produced) by a weak national infrastructure including the National Student Financial Aid Scheme (NSFAS) and the lack of capacity at the national Department of Higher Education – an infrastructure that has yet to fathom the complexities of the context and the serious fragility of many of the institutions. The perennial issues are insufficient financial aid, insufficient or unsuitable student housing, poor infrastructure for teaching/learning, and instability in the dynamics of staff and student organisations. The older, more established, historically white universities escape much of this but they too experience levels of fragility – perhaps from other sources.

The higher education system remains deeply divided, with the historically white parts continuing to perform at a decent level, but there is serious concern in certain circles that none of these institutions appears in the top hundred in any of the international ranking systems. The deep imbalances that existed in the system in 1994 persist in 2013 and the trend of poor students going to the 'poor' universities continues.

A number of reviews of the performance of higher education as a system in terms of enrolments, throughput rates, graduation rates, dropout rates and so on have been completed or are under way (Council on Higher Education 2013, British Council 2012). This kind of review is not repeated in this chapter.

Higher education as a system is both intensely local and intensely global, publicly-funded and yet fiercely autonomous. As such it bears the characteristics of a social institution that floats uncomfortably on an ocean of spatial and temporal influences that are seldom broadly aligned; influences that are multifaceted, multilayered and often intensely non-linear. The older, stronger, more traditional universities are better able to navigate this often turbulent terrain but it will be argued below that these universities, too, have uncertain futures in South Africa. The relatively new, mainly historically disadvantaged institutions will find the future perilous. This review looks at some of the key influences on the system in terms of formal policy processes underway and in terms of other internal and external factors. Instability, together with the (not yet fully understood) high dropout rate in the system and the perception of the increasing unemployment of graduates, would indicate the need for major policy changes. A number of interesting questions arise. Why is there such a large slate of policy change underway? How are these changes likely to make an impact on the higher education system? And what do these policy changes portend in terms of the imagination of higher education by the current government?

UNIVERSITIES ARE INTENSELY GLOBAL

There are large and irreversible changes taking place in higher education globally. The universality of the institution of managerialism in higher education is complete, heralded either as the necessary development to improve the efficiency/effectiveness of higher education, or resisted – passively and actively – as a simple and natural outcome of the expansion of neoliberalism through all spheres of the socioeconomic fabric of society. This is exacerbated by numerous contemporary crises, an example of which is the economic downturn of 2008 that has resulted in massive budget cuts even at some of the world's most prestigious and outstanding public universities and university systems. On the other hand, there are more systemic changes that are contemporaneous with and reflective of the changes in the structure of the global organisation of economics, the new geopolitics and the globalising individual. We see for instance the creation of multinational systems of technology innovation; business-like higher education multi-nationals; new organisational systems of higher education with globalising tendencies – with rapidly increasing cross-border operations; the rapid and irreversible growth of the for-profit higher education sector; and changes in the structures of global trade in higher education. These are large irreversible changes and there are signatures of these on all South African campuses and in the system more generally.

Global organisation of higher education

Universities have always seen themselves as 'global' institutions and as being part of a family of institutions that occupy the broad knowledge production and knowledge dissemination stages. A new phenomenon, the emergence of new forms of international organisation of knowledge production systems, is beginning to take root. We are observing the early stages in the re-creation of a form of globally organised higher education with multinational/multilateral structures of university groupings and multinational operations of individual institutions and systems. One example of this is the creation of the Global Research Council involving fifty national funding agencies of research – and then there is the subsequent development of multinational aggregations of university systems, one of them involving the Association of American Universities, the League of European Research Universities (LERU), the China 9 League of Leading Universities and the Australian Group of Eight (Go8) research-intensive universities. They 'plan to join forces to tackle what the group sees as the challenges facing research institutions around the world' (Maslen 2013). These new groupings are likely to reshape global knowledge production in ways that have yet to be understood.

Globalisation and the purpose of higher education

Perhaps the most pressing issue is to ask what these changes mean to the question: what is the purpose of higher education? Bill Readings, in his challenging *The University in Ruins* (Readings 1999), which appeared posthumously, posed the key point that it is no longer clear what role the university as a social institution plays in society, especially in the face of globalisation. In his opinion the integrity of a university lies in its location in the nation-state and the idea of national culture. The purposeful expansion of universities into corporations that operate across borders undermines their role as shapers of nationhood.

Technology and higher education

There are other large forces operating on universities. The step-by-step incorporation of technologies into teaching/learning has been underway for more than two decades – to the extent that many universities now offer all their programmes via learning management systems, contributing vastly to more flexible learning paradigms and the opportunity for increased levels of self-pacing. South African universities have generally speaking responded positively to the technology challenge (the impetus for the massive expansion of for-profit higher education systems across the world) in different ways.

However, the impact of technology on higher education has shifted gear in the last two to three years with the development of a number of new delivery systems tapping into very large student markets. The development of massive open online courses (MOOCs) is one example of a (yet to mature) model of delivery, very likely either to place enormous pressures on universities or to present amazing opportunities to the higher education systems of the world. Companies like Coursera and Udacity that offer MOOCs have already amassed enrolments of the order of 2 to 3 million students each. The interview between Thomas Friedman, op-ed columnist with the *New York Times*, and the 12-year-old Pakistani prodigy, Khadija Niazi, is extraordinarily poignant (WiredAcademic 2013). At the age of ten she took an Artificial Intelligence course with Sebastian Thrun, a Stanford University computer science professor, via an MOOC. The course, at that time, had 160 000 students from around the world. She has since completed a Physics programme via a set of MOOCs taken through Udacity. This storm coming down the track has yet to register in most universities. A report in a recent issue of *The Ticker* pointed out that: 'California's public universities and colleges may soon be required to grant students credit for online courses, including massive open online courses, or MOOCs – a move that could radically alter the higher education landscape' (Huckabee 2013).

Massification and its roots

Massification of higher education is a global phenomenon, deeply and powerfully influential in the shaping of higher education systems. There are two major influences that drive this imperative: the human resource capacity needs of various kinds of economic transformation of societies on the one hand and the democratisation imperative on the other. This is very much (successfully or unsuccessfully) on the agenda in most societies and reflects the desire to build knowledge economies. The World Bank and other multilateral organisations advise the governments of sub-Saharan Africa to massify (World Bank 2002) – notwithstanding its imposition in the 1980s of structural adjustment programmes that decimated higher education on the continent. This is supported by other global multilateral organisations. In South Korea, the participation rate of eighteen to twenty-four year-olds grew from 11 per cent in 1980 to 71 per cent in 2008. By 2008, 53 per cent of Koreans between the ages of twenty-five and thirty-four held a higher education qualification. Between 1990 and 2012 the number of students participating in higher education globally grew by 160 per cent (Sharma 2012). While the economic arguments for growing the participation rate are made regularly and vigorously, the passionate demand by the youth for higher education grows at a furious pace in developing countries. These two impetuses, the top-down and the bottom-up, are powerful drivers of the transformation of higher education. Massification has had an enormous effect on the organisation of higher education, its labour market and its labour relations, its knowledge enterprises and – perhaps more importantly – on its expected roles in society.

Budget cuts

Another force acting on higher education internationally are the budgetary cuts that have flowed in earnest since the economic meltdown in 2008. Some of the most iconic models of higher education over the last fifty years, such as the University of California, are not exempt. It experienced a budgetary cut of some US$900 million in 2012 alone. According to Andy Kroll:

> The numbers tell the story. In 2011, public colleges and universities received 13 per cent less in state money than they had in 1980 (when adjusted for inflation). In 1980, 15 per cent of the state budget had gone to higher education; by 2011, that number had dropped to 9 per cent. Between the 2010-11 and 2011-12 state budgets, lawmakers sliced away another $1.5 billion in funding, the largest such reduction in any high-population state in the country (Kroll 2013).

The iconic institution of the late twentieth century is the American research university. The Ivy League institutions have large endowments but the public research universities do not. The Crisis of the Publics, a meeting convened in November 2007 by the Center for Studies of Higher Education at UC Berkeley presciently addressed exactly this issue. And much earlier the Rand Corporation in Santa Monica produced a report on how these universities were *Breaking the Social Contract* by pricing themselves out of reach of the middle class. There were earlier warnings that went unheeded (Benjamin 1997). These beacons of higher education of the twentieth century are in various states of stress. The State University of New York (SUNY) system has similarly experienced a cut of US$700 million in 2013. It is not at all clear whether any these institutions will be resilient enough to withstand the pressures brought to bear on them. How higher education responds to this form of pressure will determine the future of higher education in the USA and else-where. Are the universities of the future recognisable to us today?

UNIVERSITIES ARE INTENSELY LOCAL

Universities are global institutions but they are also intensely local. South African universities are public universities and are funded predominantly from the public purse (through state subsidies and student fees). How are these institutions shaped (or not shaped) by the context in which they find themselves? How are they perceived to make an impact (or not) on South African society? In the rest of this paper we explore the dynamics of and pressures on the South African higher education system. How does the slate of policy changes referred to above affect these pressures?

Higher education in a cauldron of national imaginations

South African higher education is a system on multi-angular, multi-axial roller skates as it attempted to work with the intricate hurly-burly of political imagination as we sped uncontrollably from 1994 to 2013. As the Reconstruction and Development Programme (RDP) gave rise to new directions in the RDP White Paper, then the Growth, Employment and Redistribution (GEAR) programme, then the African Renaissance, then the two tiered economy, then the second revolution and now the National Development Plan (NDP), the higher education system struggled to keep pace with these imaginations of South Africa. Perhaps more importantly, the National Commission on Higher Education (NCHE), signed into existence by President Nelson Mandela in 1995, sought to establish a new framework for higher education in South Africa that was to deal with some of the legacies of apartheid and the challenges of producing a system that was resonant with the needs of the new economy and the new sociopolitical challenges, including those of nation building. The NCHE's report did address many of these issues but it did not produce a framework that was transformative. There are expectations that the higher education system will align with the favoured national development strategies that emerge from time to time. The publishing of the NDP represents one such attempt and there will now be compulsory attempts to understand how to align higher education with it and how to shape its core activities to support its validation and its implementation.

To massify or not to massify

The participation rate in 1994 of 18 to 24-year olds in higher education was 14 per cent. In 2012, this figure has grown somewhat to about 17 per cent. In the meantime, between 1990 and 2012 the global participation rate grew by 160 per cent with the addition of some 170 million students to higher education institutions internationally. The NCHE did indeed consider the possibility of expanding the system with the aim of massification, but copped out at the end – notwithstanding the deliberate and sustained policy directives aimed at constructing a knowledge economy which would have required deliberate strategies to grow participation in the sector. Why did the NCHE eschew the idea of massification? The primary reason was that it was unaffordable. Well, this may have been true but no serious study was done to determine the feasibility of other models of organising higher education. Nor, for that matter was serious attention paid to the absorptive scope and capacity of private higher education, both not-for-profit and for-profit. The correct question to ask is: *what would the cost be of not massifying the post-school and higher education systems* (Bawa 2009).

There may be other more plausible reasons for the NCHE's conclusions on this matter. The Commission was a part of the negotiated settlement in which massification would have been seen as a threat to the existing order in the higher education system, specifically to the historically white institutions; the NCHE project was hamstrung at the very outset and unable to address many of the burning issues. Another reason – not unrelated to the first – is that the NCHE and a host of other policy initiatives at the time were flying on the wings of the unfolding but yet to be defined GEAR, underpinned by its neoliberalism.

Notwithstanding the complexities of attempting to understand the human capacity and research and development (R&D) needs of a growing knowledge economy, let's be sure to understand that there is a perfect storm brewing, likely to cause mayhem: a socio-political storm. In 2011, 2012 and 2013, the Durban University of Technology (DUT) received some 75 000 applications each year for the 6 500 places available to first entry students. The demand for post-school education by far exceeds the supply – and this is obviously a major challenge (or threat) that faces the state and the sector. We shall return to this question in a discussion on the Green Paper on post-school education and train-ing. Does South Africa have any option but to move towards a massified system?

The legitimacy deficit

Twenty years on from 1994, the South African higher education system is still seen by many as rather elitist, divorced from the realities of most South Africans, exclusionary (or at least alienating) of the poor, exclusionary of African students, and disarticulated from the many challenges of this society. Meetings between the universities and the Parliamentary Portfolio Committee on Higher Education and Training, the Ministry and Department of Higher Education and Training, some of the political parties, student organisations and the trade unions are very often spiked by distrust, antagonism and power-play. Issues at the edge are the lack of 'transformation', the use of selection and admission processes that are deemed to be unfair and discriminatory, the financial and academic exclusion of students, the unacceptably high dropout rates and the alienation of university research from a developmental agenda. There is a legitimacy deficit, and it places enormous and close to unbearable strains on the proper functioning of the provi-sions of institutional autonomy and academic freedom.

The South African Constitution and the Higher Education Act of 1997 protect the institutional autonomy of higher education institutions and the right to academic free-dom. It is very much the construction of these rights that are under scrutiny in these conversations and contestations. The question is: who owns the public universities? The model of cooperative governance that has taken shape over the last twenty years is very much at risk in this type of tensioned discourse – as is explored to some extent by Ihron Rensburg in *Business Day* (Rensburg 2013). The councils and executives of universities understand and accept the notion that the allocation of these rights to universities and academics are to be counterbalanced by responsibilities that must be borne by the institutions, and especially the responsibility of accountability. The use of the 'administrator' provisions of the Higher Education Act of 1997 by the minister where there has been a breakdown of the governance of institutions has not been contested where it has been deemed to be fairly implemented and where circumstances required such interventions. What then is the problem?

The legitimacy deficit is at the very heart of the threat to institutional autonomy. The defence of institutional autonomy and academic freedom is a role that every university and every academic must play. It is a responsibility to society. Any defence against an attack on institutional autonomy will require three kinds of protective shield. The first is simple: the universities must be able to generate popular support so that local communities, industry, the community of artists, its alumni and so on may speak voluntarily and with passion as they leap to the defence of the university. The second is for the university to demonstrate its willingness to be fully accountable for the public funds that it expends. And the third is for the institution to demonstrate its full and undivided understanding of the responsibilities that attach to the right of institutional autonomy.

Arguments have been made for the development of a social contract between the sector, the state and stakeholders that would provide the basis for sufficient consensus and alignment on the role of the sector in society and the nature of its governance (Bawa 2001). This would be an interesting exercise, and not without risk. The NCHE and more recently the Higher Education Transformation Summit held in April 2010 were *ad hoc*, unsatisfactory attempts at achieving a kind of consensus between the sector and stakeholders of all kinds. Neither achieved it.

The report of the Ministerial Committee on Transformation and Social Cohesion and the Elimination of Discrimination in Public Higher Education Institutions lays out serious challenges facing the sector in terms of deep cultural and social alienation faced by students and staff. There are strong (and correct) perceptions that South African universities do not do very well in serving young South Africans from the lower classes, the vast majority of whom attend the 'poorer' universities. This is multidimensional. On the one hand it has to do with poor student accommodation and infrastructure, poor administrative services, and the lack of sufficient academic support and development. On the other hand it has to do with the prevailing dominant culture at institutions that has remained largely unchanged over the last twenty years.

There may be other, more contentious, reasons for the deficit. Many millions of South Africans do not yet see themselves, their lives and their cultures represented in the core of these institutions. To paraphrase this perhaps – with some edge of the controversial – *when will universities in South Africa become South African universities?* This is a complex question. It has partly to do with the fact that the intellectual culture of our higher education system (whether at the historically advantaged or disadvantaged institutions) is still very European – or, at least, Eurocentric. This is much deeper than the fact that our universities all have their roots in Europe; it has to do with the nature of the continuing knowledge project. Transformation in South Africa has usually meant addressing the race and gender imbalances in the system. This is not to say that there haven't been exciting changes taking place in the areas of curriculum, for example. Much of this has been left to academics excited by the challenges that they face. But there have been few, if any, approaches to forms of transformation that take as their core the question: what is the knowledge project of South African universities?

At the beginning of the 2011 academic year, addressing all first-year students, as vice-chancellor at the DUT, I asked whether any students had read any of the novels of Zakes Mda. Not a single hand went up. What does it mean to be a *South African* if one is not aware of the nation's literature? In a similar vein, it would be deemed to be unacceptable for young people anywhere in the world to have twelve years of schooling, then three to four years of higher education and not have had any serious South African history. And how is it possible that very nearly twenty years on from 1994 it is still possible for young South Africans not to have a functioning level of at least one of our indigenous languages. This would be unthinkable anywhere else in the world. It may, and should, be argued that these issues are largely as a result of the failing primary and secondary school systems. But this takes us back to a question raised by Bill Readings (1996) and notwithstanding his concerns about the future of the university in the West: in South Africa it must still be very much the mandate of the university to contribute to nation building, one of the founding purposes of the modern university. South African universities *do not* see nation building as one of their purposes of existence, their rhetoric to the contrary. It would seem critically important for higher education in South Africa to understand how it addresses nation building explicitly through expression in the curriculum (more specifically) and through their knowledge project (more generally). There are many models that may be adopted. One example – a common one in the USA and elsewhere – is the insistence on general education at the core of every curriculum that covers the important areas that contribute to the processes of nation building.

There is probably a more systematic way to address this issue of epistemological 'legitimacy' through the construction of the notion of a knowledge project. The South African knowledge system – which is much broader than the universities – is fundamentally a part of the global knowledge system. The question then is whether there is a need for us to be able to define the knowledge system in South Africa as a South African knowledge system. I would argue that in the circumstances there is such a vast imbalance in productivity and influence in the global knowledge system that it is important to understand what is meant by *a South African knowledge system*. One (controversial) way of thinking about this is that South Africa's universities and other knowledge-intensive institutions *must assume the responsibility to generate knowledge about the human, social and natural contexts within which they find themselves*. This should not preclude them from working in other contexts and it should not dissuade them from striking partnerships with institutions from other parts of the world to work on local projects. The responsibility for this knowledge project lies with these institutions.

Why is this important? The creation, transport and embedding of knowledge about the local context into the global knowledge system will allow the South African system to enter the global one *on its own terms*. For South Africans to recognise, respect and see these institutions as their universities, they must first be recognised as universities within which they can see vibrant representations of their social, natural and human contexts. This may well be a necessary condition for the popular and political legitimacy of the system.

Towards a danger zone?

In 2008, the Council on Higher Education initiated a very substantial study of the state of academic freedom and institutional autonomy in South Africa's higher education system, following reports of deep disquiet amongst intellectuals and university leaders about a steady erosion of both rights. This study produced a substantial number of scholarly articles, a very interesting day of discussions and a final report by an independent task team titled *Academic Freedom, Institutional Autonomy and Public Accountability in South African Higher Education*. The Report focused on four governance underpinnings of the higher education system: co-operative governance, academic freedom, institutional autonomy and accountability. The Task Team found that:

> Amendments to the Higher Education Act since 1997 (Section 3.2.1) indicate to the Task Team a defensible intention by government to heighten the accountability of higher education institutions. Unfortunately, a preference for blanket application in these amendments, matched to inadequate consultation, has contributed to a sense amongst higher education institutions that government does not always strike a balance between principles of institutional autonomy and accountability and that government commitment to consultation is lacking (CHE 2008).

The Report goes on to say that steering through planning has highlighted the institutional autonomy-accountability terrain of contestation. While there appears to be a broad consensus that steering through planning is one way in which the state can ensure that the investment of public funds in higher education serves the interests of the national good, there is, more recently, deep concern about serious erosion to institutional autonomy.

Before embarking on a brief analysis of the current context, it is worthwhile recalling that the CHE Report contested the accepted notions of accountability in the South African higher education system. It points out

> The concept of *accountability* has received less attention in South African higher education than academic freedom or institutional autonomy. The Task Team finds that public accountability as formulated in South African higher education policy refers rather narrowly to the application of public funding to achieving public policy goals. In contrast, the Task Team views higher education accountability as multi-faceted, containing distinct but reciprocal elements of collegial, functional, fiduciary and public or social accountability. These dimensions in combination should ensure that academic endeavour serves the public good, as higher education's 'democratic

accountability' is not oriented around national goals of transformation only, but also inheres in an effective defence and practice of academic freedom and institutional autonomy (CHE 2008).

This presents a challenge to both universities and the state and assumes sufficient consensus on what the purpose of higher education is in its service to the public good; and it heeds the CHE's astute shaping of its study around the four underpinnings of governance mentioned above. Good governance of higher education occurs at the nexus of these four, each being required and each facilitating the others. The Higher Education Act of 1997 provides a framework for this, in terms of both the philosophical basis and the institutions of this cooperative governance model. The elastic adhesive (and there has to be some tension) in this nexus is a common understanding of what the CHE Report called *higher education's 'democratic responsibility'*. And the constituent chemicals of the adhesive are public legitimacy and trust which can only emerge as process and the product of a journey towards a social contract.

Not unexpectedly, concerns that gave rise to the 2008 CHE study have resurfaced in the wake of a number of new policies, amendments to existing policies and changes in practice. As an example, the promulgation of the Regulations for Reporting by Higher Education Institutions is obviously meant to produce a measure to tighten up the accountability reporting by universities by using a framework that focuses on a business model quite unhinged from a usual university cycle of activities. It is an attempt to align the reporting functions of universities with those of government departments and the Public Financial Management Act (PFMA). The methodology shifts the emphasis back to reporting on funding rather than reporting on the broader suite of metrics noted in the CHE Report. It would appear that the Bill, as it is currently formulated, undermines the fiduciary responsibility of the councils of universities and is a step towards the direct auditing of universities by the office of the auditor general of South Africa. The Bill uses a section of the Public Auditing of South Africa Act that trumps the provisions of other Acts passed by Parliament (including the Higher Education Act of 1997) to justify its erosion of council responsibility.

The Higher Education and Training Laws Amendment Act 23 of 2012 was passed into law at the end of 2012 notwithstanding strong objections from universities and from HESA to the Parliamentary Portfolio Committee on Higher Education and Training. Neither the CHE nor HESA were consulted by the DHET on the amendment to the Higher Education Act, which it is required to do in terms of the cooperative governance model set out in the Higher Education Act of 1997. What does the amendment to the Act do and why was it so rushed, without the necessary consultation? It extends the minister's power to intervene in the governance and management of higher education institutions. It gives the minister the power to issue instructions or directives to the council of a university if the minister is of the view that the council acted 'unfairly, discriminately or contrary to the public interests'. The failure of the affected council to comply with the instruction/directive requires the minister to remove the council and replace it with an administrator with powers to effectively replace the council and vice-chancellor. This automatically disbands the council. There are no counterbalancing provisions in the amendment to the Act even if the affected council is fully functional and compliant in every other respect. This is a new provision in the governance landscape of higher education in South Africa.

Should there be concern? There should be. Both of these examples (and there are others) pose threats to the independence of councils of institutions and therefore to institutional autonomy. The passage taken in the passing of the Higher Education Amendment Act provides irrevocable evidence that there has been a serious violation of the basic tenets of cooperative governance defined by the Higher Education Act of 1997. Why, when the infrastructure for good governance is in place?

Underlying these seemingly deliberate attacks on cooperative governance are three powerful forces. The first is that it would seem that there is a conflation on the part of the Ministry and the Department of Higher Education and Training of the imperatives of accountability with those of institutional autonomy. This confusion undermines both public accountability and institutional autonomy. The second is the legitimacy deficit and its effect, and its use by the state, underpinned by deep distrust of the sector; concerns about its inability to engage in organic transformation; and views of its disarticulation from the idea of the developmental state. It may be argued that the legitimacy deficit is a danger to the long-term sustainability of the sector and it is being 'helped to transform'. Or this attack on cooperative governance may be an attempt to change the terrain irreversibly through the erosion of institutional autonomy, academic freedom and other elements of good governance, and to deliberately shift the universities so that they are managed more directly by the state. The relationship between the state and the higher education – as sector, as individual institutions and as individual academics – will always be characterised by varying levels of tension. The key question is whether this tension can be managed so that it gives rise to creative rather than destructive outcomes.

THE GREEN PAPER ON POST-SCHOOL EDUCATION AND TRAINING

The Green Paper on post-school education and training will give rise to a White Paper. The Green Paper proposes the construction of a coherent post-school education and training system but it lacks new vision (this will, one hopes, be corrected in the White Paper). It does deal with a number of key issues through bringing together different parts of the post-school education and training complex to take the unification of education and training beyond the construction of a ministry and department.

The shortage of skills at all levels has been identified as an important impediment to the growth of the economy, and so there is a special emphasis in the Green Paper on what are currently called the further education and training colleges (FETC) – in the past regarded as technical colleges. There are large and substantial challenges relating to the administration of these colleges and to their capacity to deliver the kinds of skills development and education required.

The Green Paper is potentially path-breaking in its attempt to foster a serious engagement with the way to widen access to post-school learning within a system that includes all forms of post-school education and training. It envisages a growth in higher education enrolments from the existing 0.9 million to 1.5 million by 2030. More importantly, perhaps, it envisages very substantial growth in the FETC sector from its current enrolment of about 360 000 to 6 million during this same time-frame. This forms the basis of an extraordinary opportunity to construct a system that deals with massification, although much remains to be addressed. A key design element here is (or will have to be) the righting of the inverted pyramid and affordablity challenges in which the enrolments in the universities (the expensive part of the system) by far exceed the enrolments in the FET colleges.

OTHER CRITICAL ISSUES

The long-term sustainability of the higher education system depends on finding solutions to a number of other important problems at the more operational level. And unless these are dealt with the system will be placed under enormous strain in the near future.

The stability in FTE-unit subsidy funding that at least keeps pace with inflation is a fundamental requirement. The significant growth in the number of students in the system – notwithstanding the small growth in participation rates – has to be funded so that the subsidy per FTE does not slide backwards. This will be doubly important as we move towards the targets laid out in the Green Paper on post-school education and training. The recent tendency by the Ministry and Department to top-slice the overall higher education budget for 'special' projects is also likely to have dire consequences in the long term. Any lack of stability leads to inability of the individual institutions to plan with a sufficient level of certainty. Except for those institutions that operate large reserves and surpluses, long-term planning is absolutely crucial for their stability.

Second among these issues is the inability of the system to produce sufficient PhDs so that a new generation of academics and scholars is available to the system. This is a twofold problem. The South African system is simply not producing sufficient numbers of doctorates in fields such as engineering and computer science. Various comparative analyses indicate that South Africa ought to increase its output of doctorates by a factor of five. Among the challenges identified by a number of studies are the size of the pipeline, the quantity and quality of supervisory capacity, the funding of doctoral education and the match between supply and demand. But there is also some confusion about the supply-demand equation. If South Africa is successful in generating a fivefold increase in the output of PhDs, is there sufficient employment for them – especially when we know that there has been a significant contraction in the employment of high-level scientists in the science system since 1994 (Blankley 2004).

Third are the challenges that arise from the failing school system and the significant underpreparedness of students gaining access to higher education. On the one hand this has to be a national grand challenge – on the other hand it is a challenge to the universities to understand how to build the capacity of underprepared students and to ensure that they have a fair chance of success. The development of a four-year curriculum for the Bachelor's degree – yet another project of the DHET – is likely to be an important initiative in this regard.

SOME CONCLUDING THOUGHTS

These are challenging times for public higher education in most parts of the world. On the one hand there has been much pressure on the sector to be more 'useful', to have more instrumentalist imaginations, to be a part of the developmental state, to massify, to be more effective and efficient, to be more connected to society, to be more accountable. At the heart of it all is the question of the knowledge project, Bill Readings' question. As a product of such challenges there are developments which will bring as yet unpredictable changes to the sector – the growth of for-profit higher education and the way in which public higher education is being driven into the for-profit terrain is one of them. Another is the ramping up of the flexible delivery of programmes through the use of technology as a way of tackling massification. Is this all explicable within a neoliberal meta-narrative? This is an interesting question especially as there is still such heavy investment from the public purse (while the system is expected to do much more with less from it).

On the other hand, in the South African context the elephant in the room is the legitimacy deficit, the fact that the higher education system is perceived to be deeply embedded in the 'old South Africa' with little – if any – hope of undergoing transformations that are internally driven. This is an extraordinarily interesting challenge requiring new forms of engagement between universities and the societies in which they are embedded. The sector will have to take on the defence of institutional autonomy and academic freedom, the erosion of which began many years ago. The basic elements of good cooperative governance are well established and need to be reaffirmed and strengthened.

REFERENCES

Bawa AC (2010) A social contract between the public higher education sector and the people of South Africa. *South African Journal of Higher Education*, 105 (3), 2001.
Bawa AC and P Vale (2009) Education is expensive – but try ignorance. *Mail & Guardian*, 14 September.
Blankley W, R Maharajh, TE Pogue, V Reddy, M du Toit, G Cele and M Kahn (2004) Flight of the flamingoes: A study on the mobility of R&D workers. HSRC, Pretoria.
Benjamin RW and SJ Carroll (1997) *Breaking the Social Contract: The Fiscal Crisis in U.S. Higher Education*. RAND Corporation, Santa Monica. Carrim N and O Wangenge (2012) Higher education in South Africa. British Council, Johannesburg.
Council on Higher Education (2008) Report of the independent task team on Higher Education, Institutional Autonomy and Academic Freedom (HEIAAF): Academic Freedom, Institutional Autonomy and Public Accountability in South African Higher Education. CHE, Pretoria.
Council on Higher Education (2013) VitalStats.

Huckabee C (2013) 'California may require colleges to give credit for outside, online courses'. *The Ticker*, 13 March.

Kroll A (2013) The death of the golden dream of higher education. http://www.tomdispatch.com/blog/175600/.

Maslen G (2013) Research universities to establish global network. *World University News* 264. http://www.universityworldnews.com/article.php?story=20130321080356646.

Readings B (1996) *The University in Ruins*. Cambridge: Harvard University Press.

Rensburg I (2013) Regulatory overkill threatens academic autonomy in South Africa. *Business Day*, 31 January.

Sharma Yojana. 2012. Fast pace of higher education enrolment growth predicted to slow. *University World News*, 25 February.

WiredAcademic (2013). Davos: 12-year-old Pakistani prodigy girl talks about her online learning. http://www.wiredacademic.com/2013/01/davos-12-year-old-pakistani-prodigy-girl-talks-about-her-online-learning/#sthash.VVZjfqSi.dpuf.

World Bank (2002) *Constructing Knowledge Societies: New Challenges for Tertiary Education*. Washington, DC: World Bank.

CHAPTER 13

Democracy without economic emancipation: Household relations and policy in South Africa

Sarah Mosoetsa

INTRODUCTION

Almost two decades since South Africa celebrated its political freedom, unemployment, poverty and inequality remain undeniably high. The dominant narrative by most South Africans is '*awukho umsebenzi*' and '*asinamali*' – there is no work and we do not have money. Formal wage employment has been declining (Nattrass 2000; Makgetla 2010; Mohamed 2010). Using the 'narrow' definition of unemployment (only those who are willing to work and actively searching), South Africa's unemployment rate was 24 per cent in 2010; using the 'expanded' definition (which includes those who are willing to work but too discouraged to search) the country's unemployment rate was a staggering 35.8 per cent.[1] In Makgetla's (2010) analysis, which shows the gender, generational and racial profile of unemployment in South Africa, it is notably the African women and youth who are predominantly unemployed. The only work that has increased since 1994 is work in the informal economy (trading and manufacturing) and the unpaid work done at home, mostly by women. The most regular income has come from the state, through state social grants. The means-tested state income has, however, only benefitted a fraction of the poor and unemployed population of South Africa.

Unsurprisingly, then, economic emancipation for the majority has been elusive, with evidence of widening inequalities (Mbeki 2009; Seekings and Nattrass 2005; Terreblanche 2002). Using the gini-coefficient (to measure inequality), quantitative experts agree that between 1994 and 2010 there has been a steady rise of overall inequality in South Africa (Leibbrandt et al. 2009).[2] There is also consensus that poverty levels (head count) have declined since 1994, mainly because of government's social grants (Agüero et al. 2007). The General Household Survey of 2010 estimated that 21.9 per cent of households have 'inadequate or severely inadequate' access to food, with female-headed households more likely to experience hunger. The recent population census shows that income inequality is racially skewed, with black households' income far less than their white, coloured and Indian counterparts; for example, white households earned six times more than black households with more individuals per household (StatsSA Census 2012). Such a context presents challenges of thinking and theorising about gender identities, roles and dynamics in South Africa and especially for black households.

Historically, South African households have been racially classified (African, Indian, coloured and white) with the classification linked to households' economic wellbeing according to apartheid's legacy of racially skewed resource allocation. It is no coincidence then that the majority of poor households in South Africa are African households, even in the post-apartheid era. The apartheid and the post-apartheid state have both played a direct and indirect role in shaping the internal dynamics in African households in particular. The regulation of households by the state has often changed the structure, function and relationships within these households, with detrimental consequences for most.

During apartheid, the state regulated African households through repressive laws which dictated, for example, that men leave their households for long periods to work in the cities while their wives and families were expected to stay behind in rural areas. Through remittances, men's presence was felt and their contribution to the household became important for its survival. Women stayed behind and took major decisions for the household (given its absent 'head') such as how money would be spent and children raised (Murray 1981). That African men working in compound mines were earning low wages meant that the remittances were meagre, further undermining the long-term survival of the African household. Zolani Ngwane (2003:688) contends that because of apartheid's migrant labour system and the creation of Bantustans, African households were never a unit but, rather,

> … merely existed as a site of struggle over an imagined form of the household, a form whose realisation was perpetually deferred in practice owing to a combination of historical transformations (regional political instabilities in the nineteenth century, the rise of oscillating migrancy and the demographics of segregation) and attendant internal structural fluidities (for instance, constant movements of large sections of people, circulation of dependants across kin circles, and adaptation to new physical and cultural environments).

Men and women's positions and relationships with each other and with the state are shaped and reshaped by the context in which they happen. In South Africa, African men and women were subordinate to the apartheid state, albeit by varying degrees. White and African men have therefore experienced different forms of power and benefits of patriarchy because of their racial differences. An assumption and theorisation of masculinities as universally powerful misses the South African apartheid – and continued post-apartheid – reality. Sylvia Walby (1990:90) correctly cautions us to reject the 'notion that every individual man is in a dominant position and every woman in a subordinate one'. In the case of apartheid South Africa, race and class became the important signifiers.[3] Furthermore, not only are masculinities different; they are also 'subject to change' (Connell and Messerschmitt 2005:835). Economic, social, political and health transformation necessitate such changes in identity. Thus there are no universal hegemonic or subordinated masculinities (Connell 1995) or femininities.

In post-apartheid South Africa, the impact of such laws still reverberates but the pressure remains although it is a different one. The structure and survival of the African household is no longer undermined by repressive laws but, rather, by the unintended consequences of post-apartheid socioeconomic policies. While the post-apartheid state has extended social security protection to all, regardless of race, it has also introduced cost-recovery measures that undermine universal access to basic services such as water and electricity. There are also post-1994 challenges that have influenced the structure of households and the relationships within them. For example, health transformation associated with the prevalence of HIV and Aids and mortality rates has had a devastating impact on the structure and composition of households, particularly an increase in the number of orphaned and fostered children in poor households (Madhavan and Schatz, 2007).

This chapter draws on in-depth interviews with over a hundred men and women in the two communities of Enhlalakahle and Mpumalanga townships, in KwaZulu-Natal, South Africa, at selected intervals in 2002, 2003 and 2004. The research purposely sampled retrenched women and men workers of the clothing, textile and footwear industries. Snowball sampling was also used to identify further respondents. Face-to-face interviews formed the core of the research and all interviews were conducted in the local language, isiZulu. Pilot interviews, complemented by two focus group interviews, were undertaken initially in each of the research sites. Sixteen households in Enhlalakahle and thirteen households in Mpumalanga were selected for further study based on these initial interviews. Forty-four semi-structured interviews were then conducted with household members: adult women and men. This was followed by oral history interviews with older women from the twenty-nine selected households in the two townships and augmented by fifteen key informant interviews with members of local community organisations, local leaders and government officials. All household informants were guaranteed anonymity; accordingly, pseudonyms have been used for them and for those informants from the community who asked not to be named (community members are usually referred to in terms of their affiliation and/or role in the community). Follow-up interviews and informal conversations with seven unemployed (retrenched from the clothing, textile and footwear factories) women and men were also conducted in 2010 in Mpumalanga township. All interviews were thematically analysed.

In this chapter I will contend that unemployment and poverty adversely influence and shape the nature of intra-household gender dynamics. These are social consequences that quantitative data and labour market trends are unable to reveal, yet they have a profound influence on the functioning of society and the economy. The chapter presents the argument that in a context of high unemployment and rising income inequalities, household gender dynamics intensify and are characterised by gender-based and intergenerational conflict. Differences in the use, allocation and distribution of resources (income, time and space) and shifting gender identities influence both gender-based and intergenerational conflict. Five interrelated themes are discussed below.

THE CRISIS OF UNEMPLOYMENT AND EXPERIENCES OF PATRIARCHY

In a context of high unemployment, poverty and rising income inequalities, old definitions of patriarchy are challenged. The structural and ideological systems of racist and colonial South Africa that encouraged the privileging of masculinities are changing. Malehoko Tshoaedi (2008:13) correctly contends that in post-apartheid South Africa there are multiple patriarchies even in similar localities such as townships because: 'each local setting has its own particular culture, history and belief systems that will impact differently on its subjects.' For this research, such multiple patriarchies are informed by a narrow understanding of culture and tradition.

> Things have changed. We have forgotten our traditions and culture. As a man, I am told I cannot tell my wife what to do. I am told she has rights in my own house. When she does not cook for me, I am told to just keep quiet and not do anything about it. The police and the magistrate said that (Mr Mhlongo, Mpumalanga).

> Firstly, I am not supposed to discuss matters of my household with you, especially since you are a woman and so young. However, I will make an exception. Secondly, as a man and head of this household, I will not be told what to do. I will not be questioned by my wife as to where I have been and how I use my money. It is unheard of in my culture for a woman to raise her voice against her husband. Finally, I expect to find a clean house and a cooked meal every day (Mr Zwane, Mpumalanga).

Patterns of male domination and female subordination are reconfigured by the changing economic positions of men and women. Work has always played a major role in defining masculinities, and the absence of employment has led to a crisis in the ways in which men define themselves and their responsibilities in their households and communities. Many men experience feelings of powerlessness and shame, believing that the radical change in their economic position (unemployment) undermines their manhood. The weakening of their status in both the household and the community has resulted in a great sense of loss. Men frequently compensate for their sense of powerlessness by exerting power over women as they attempt to hold onto power in their households.

> As a man, I should provide for my family but circumstances do not allow me to do so. I cannot buy them bread or even pay their school fees ... [But] I am still the head of this household. I should be consulted about how money is spent in this house. My wife often uses money in her way, not my way. I want that to change. It has to change (Mr Mhlongo, Mpumalanga).

While the change in the relative economic positions of men and women has affected the balance of decision-making power in the majority of households, men have hung onto their traditional role as household heads to a significant degree. The tensions that this volatile situation produces lead to intense domestic conflict. Every factory closure represents diminishing power for men. A retreat by men to the household is also a search for lost power in the workplace and a need to assert their domination in new ways – with devastating results for women.

Power relations between men and women are also shaped by local histories and economic realities. The historical role of African working-class man as breadwinner and head of the household is seriously undermined by unemployment and retrenchment. The very identity of men comes into question when they lose their ability to earn an income and provide for their families. The apartheid military state with the booming mining industry and migrant labour system affirmed African men's power and status as economic providers in their households (Cock 1991). The gendered nature of the labour market guaranteed men higher wages than women.

Lack of income has made it impossible for many men to fulfil their social obligations and hence they experience feelings of shame and powerlessness (Hunter 2006). The Zulu tradition is inaccurately invoked to justify the subordination of women and to reassert the position of men as 'natural' heads of the household. Retrenchment and the defeat of men in the workplace has made men more determined to cling to their power in the household. Most women maintain that 'things were better' when their husbands were employed, for although their husbands exerted control over the way the household was run and the children taken care of, they allowed their wives to spend household money as they saw fit. Gender awareness has undoubtedly brought old forms of patriarchy into question, but the retreat to the household has also marked the return of traditional norms and values that have a strong patriarchal bias.

SHIFTING GENDER IDENTITIES AND ROLES: MOTHERHOOD AND FATHERHOOD

Gender identities and the roles of household members are also fluid, shaped and influenced by their changing socioeconomic contexts. Kandiyoti (1998) suggests that different forms of patriarchy present women with distinct 'rules of the game' and these, in turn, shape the terms of the 'conjugal contract' or what Kandiyoti terms a 'patriarchal bargain'. Sylvia Walby (1990) provides a useful definition of patriarchy where she contends that it is a 'system of social structures and practices in which men dominate, oppress and exploit women' (Walby, 1990:20); a system and process that manifests itself in six spheres of society: the household, the state, the workplace/factory, male violence, sexuality and cultural institutions (ibid.). It is these spheres of patriarchy (with the exception of the workplace or factory) that this chapter seeks to engage. The factory is not considered for the reason that all those who were interviewed were unemployed or worked in the informal economy, and no longer in a factory.

Traditional notions of fatherhood and masculinity, motherhood and femininity, are closely associated with patriarchy and the economic position of men and women which, in turn, shape their identities and relations with each other and society more broadly. A new political and economic context either affirms or undermines traditional identities of fatherhood and masculinity, motherhood and femininity. The problem does not arise when these identities are equally affirmed, but when they are unequally affirmed, or undermined. Inequity, subordination and domination often result. The consequence is gender and generational conflict.

In contemporary South Africa, gendered identities are indeed shifting and contradicting traditional notions of fatherhood. Motherhood has taken on new significance but not power, role reversal or an elevation in women's status. In comparison, in Russia since the collapse of the Soviet Union in 1991 changes to households meant changes in traditional, cultural norms and values and a rise in the status of women (Burawoy, Krotov and Lytkina 2001). In South Africa, men may have lost their status as breadwinners but they have remained heads of their households although their inability to provide financially has challenged old definitions of fatherhood and masculinity (Morrell and Lichter 2006). For example, Mr Mhlongo sadly remarked:

> When I lost my job, my manhood was taken away from me. I became useless to my family, as I was unable to provide for them. My position as the authority in this house was seriously undermined. I try to enforce rules in this house but they do not listen to me anymore; hence, you see my daughters having children out of wedlock. It is not acceptable in my culture. I am the head of the household and they have to listen to me. I am also not taken seriously and respected in my community. I am unemployed. (Mr Mhlongo, Mpumalanga).

Motherhood and femininity, on the other hand, is always defined around the household and the unpaid work (social reproduction) that women do with or without employment.

> I am a woman, a mother and community member. All my time in this world has to be spent taking care of those who are less fortunate than I am (Nonjabulo Mazibuko, Enhlalakahle).

Unemployment has not precipitated a crisis of identity for women in the way that it has for men. Many have started small businesses (mostly survivalist) or taken on jobs in the informal economy. They are also accessing income from the state through pensions or child support grants. Unemployment has made women's role as caregivers even more important than before. With high unemployment, poverty and AIDS, older women are important as mothers of the community and of their households, of which they are *de facto* heads and breadwinners. This echoes the role that women played during apartheid when their husbands were in racialised spaces such as mine compounds, or in jail. As the economic and social situation deteriorates, women take on more and more responsibility for caring for households and communities.

A process of 'feminisation of survival' (Sassen 2000), where the responsibility and burden of survival is placed on women, has had adverse social consequences for women and men, but for different reasons. Women's roles as economic providers in the informal economy, accessing income through state grants and caregivers in their households and communities through community-based organisations that take care of the sick and elderly do not necessarily translate into the acquisition of more power in the household. In many cases, husbands, sons and brothers dictate how the money that women earn should be spent. Several women reported that their 'new' role in the household seemed to threaten their husbands and brothers.

Cultural tradition tends to keep women subordinate to their husbands, brothers and uncles. Therefore, older women's selflessness in carrying the burden of social reproduction should be cautiously celebrated. They carry an enormous burden: mostly the primary caregivers for those infected and affected by HIV and AIDS, they have to make ends meet in a time of high unemployment and poverty – and often when they question their husbands', brothers' and uncles' power, they become victims.

During the days of the migrant labour system, men temporarily lost their role as head of the household when they were away from home but they regained this role as soon as they returned and their status as household head was never called into question. The remittances that they sent home affirmed their status. Today, however, an unemployed man's role as head of household is challenged by his failure to make an economic contribution, and his loss of status only changes when he finds a new job or becomes old enough to receive a state pension. Fatherhood, as defined in economic terms, ceases to exist where there is unemployment or no regular income. The importance of women in the survival of households and community is perceived as a threat to many men. While the link between being a breadwinner and head of household has been severed, this has not yet effected a significant role reversal in the household.

HOUSEHOLD CONFLICT: 'REAL ZULU MEN DO NOT BEAT THEIR WIVES, GIRLFRIENDS AND SISTERS'

> Not all men are abusers but there are those who do it to vent their frustrations. It has nothing to do with respect because if it did, these men would also be respecting their wives and not beating them or calling them names. It also has nothing to do with Zulu culture (Vusi, Mpumalanga).

Contrary to neoclassical economic theory, households are also social institutions where both gender and intergenerational relationships occur, through diverse power relations. The outcome is differentiated gender and generational responsibilities, entitlements and choices. These gender-age effects determine how tasks are shared and resources allocated within the household and they shape the opportunities and rights available to individuals (Kabeer 1994; Folbre 1994). Such age and gender variables also reveal often-overlooked inequalities and negotiations over household assets and resources. Kabeer (1994:103) concludes: 'The gender of the person owning wealth or earning income appears to have a systematic effect on patterns of resource allocation within the household.' Folbre (1994:23) also states that inequality within the family reflects 'inequality in individual power related to age and gender'. This is because household bargaining also takes place between parents and children. Children's bargaining powers are increased by their economic independence or decreased by their dependence. (This argument will be taken up later, where evidence reveals strained household relations between young mothers who receive state child grants and their elders who disagree with how these young mothers use the grants.) Gender as a socially defined role plays a significant part in our understanding of intra-household dynamics and bargaining. The argument that how a household allocates and distributes resources often has to do with the gendered division of labour (Pahl 1984).

The findings of this research suggest that domestic conflict and violence are influenced by both contextual and changing social realities of patriarchy and socioeconomic and structural reality (Vetten 2000a) influenced by unequal gender dynamics in the household, domination, power and control of men over women. Unemployment, loss or limited income, age and culture also shape gender and generational conflict. For women, being poor or unemployed may make them 'very vulnerable to harm or victimisation' (Vetten 2000b). Cultural understanding of manhood and masculinity are used to rationalise men's power and control and when their source of power (employment and income) vanishes or diminishes, men cling to their ethnic culture and tradition. Feelings of powerlessness and shame produce and contribute to the escalating incidence of gender conflict in many households. Most women interviewed stated that this gender and inter-generational conflict, abuse and violence is getting worse.

> When he was employed, I was happy and he was happy. He went to work in the morning and came back in the evening. He would go to his friends and drink there on weekends. Today he is unemployed and always at home telling me how to do my work. He tells me how to cook, how to clean and take care of the children (Veronica, Enhlalakahle).

> You know, you cannot do your work when they are around. They want to be directors as if they know what they are talking about. I wish he would get a job and stop interfering with mine here at home (Zanele, Mpumalanga).

A common source of conflict concerns alcohol abuse and the way in which it depletes household income. Often the very men who are 'heads of households' and take decisions about the allocation of household income are identified as the main culprits. Drug and alcohol abuse is rife among young, unemployed men and women. A retrenched mother of four experienced this directly.

> My husband and I worked for the same factory. We were retrenched at the same time. He was very angry and bitter about the retrenchment. That is when the fights started. He beat me up every day when he came home drunk and I asked him what he did with his retrenchment package. He chased us out of the house, and eventually I moved out with my children because he was threatening to kill me (Nonhlanhla, Mpumalanga).

Another form of household conflict associated with unemployment is that based on age. Older people are often victims in their own homes yet most are reluctant and embarrassed to report such cases to the police or to talk openly about such incidents (Wahl and Purdy 1991).

> Some of my friends also complain of being abused by their own children. They wait for them on pension day and take the little money that the government gives them (MaMkhize, Enhlalakahle).

It is precisely because the children are financially and emotionally dependent on their parents that such intergenerational conflicts ensue (Ward and Spitze 1992). Claims over this income often lead to intergenerational conflict and the resentment of parents.

Sometimes I wish I did not receive this money. Maybe then, there would not be any reason for such problems in my house. This one wants R100 and that one demands R400, but when there is no food in the house, they get angry (Sizakele, Mpumalanga).

They all demand my money. They wait the whole month for it. They do not even try to look for work. I do not give them a cent. They will have to wait until they are sixty or sixty-five to receive their grant. By then I will be dead (MaBhengu, Enhlalakahle).

Instead of households pooling resources together and sharing the little they have, conflict over income (including social grants), over time use, over space and over alcohol abuse often arise. Maria van Driel's (2009) survey of poor households in South Africa also confirms domestic conflicts in 83 per cent of respondents, including over money (34 per cent), unemployment (28 per cent), housework (17 per cent), food (10 per cent), alcohol (6 per cent) and childcare (5 per cent).

'WE ARE NOT PASSIVE VICTIMS': YOUNG WOMEN'S RESPONSES

Scholars have shown how women and men's perceptions, experiences and responses to patriarchy are shaped by their gender, race and class (Lorde 1984; Hooks 2000; Collins 2000). This research contends, however, that age or generational differences also shape perceptions and experiences of patriarchy. In this case, young men challenge notions of male control and domination based on culture and tradition, arguing that 'not all Zulu men beat their wives'. Young women in the two studied communities have different patriarchal views and reactions to those of their mothers and grandmothers. While experiences of patriarchy are the same between young and old women, it is their responses that place the two generations apart.[4] Young women were happy to remind me and their mothers: 'This is the new South Africa'; 'It is our democracy too'; and 'We are all equal'. The idea of sisterhood (the need and desire to help, support and work together as women) in this context is undermined by generational differences. As Audre Lorde (1984:116) puts it, 'There is a pretence to homogeneity of experience covered by the word sisterhood that in fact does not exist.'

The dynamics between young women and their mothers are often based on income, especially on how young women are using their child grants. The research reveals that the contestations are also about social roles and gender expectations. A second moment of the crisis of social reproduction arises when young women refuse to take on the social reproduction responsibilities that their mothers and grandmothers continue to embrace. In that case, who then will take care of the vulnerable, the aged and sick? It seems that in the absence of willing young women and of state failure to provide adequately for all poor households, the crisis of social reproduction in many poor communities will intensify (Mosoetsa 2011) Grandmothers' and mothers' narratives of femininity seem incongruent with their daughters' beliefs.

> I am both a mother and a wife in my household. These two roles are linked and I take them seriously. See, when I got married, my in-laws told me about my roles. I also grew up in a family where my mother cared for us. I was expected to help and my brothers were not. As a mother, I have to take care of my own children but also my neighbours' children as well. See, being a mother does not just end in this household; it goes beyond these four walls. As a wife, I have a responsibility to my husband. I have to clean and cook for him (Senethemba, Mpumalanga).

In contrast, young women are saying:

> I cannot be expected to clean the house alone, just because I am a woman. S'fiso, my brother, does not do anything around the house. He just sits the whole day but expects food on the table every day. I have a problem with a culture that expects women to be slaves for men. I am not anyone's slave. I know that my mother did that with her brothers and my father. I am not my mother. Times have changed (Nomagugu, Mpumalanga).

There is research that shows how intergenerational conflict arises because children with time and income do not want to emotionally and financially support their parents or grandparents (Katz et al. 2004; Bengtson et al. 2002). This research suggests the opposite: that intergenerational conflict arises because parents (with regular state income) refuse to financially support their adult children who are unemployed and have limited or no regular income. There is reversal of roles in the household (parents taking care of adult children, not vice versa) because of the socioeconomic and structural changes in South Africa that negatively influence intergenerational relationships.

Young women are seeking to redefine their identities in ways that differ from what their mothers and society expect. They often state that they are not care-givers, and indirectly challenge the state to take the responsibility of caring for the elderly, the sick and the vulnerable. Such resistance against gendered societal roles is often criticised by the older women. There are also other responses by young women that are arguably 'un-emancipatory' or do not seem to challenges traditional gender roles and patriarchy. For example:

> Yes, I have two children and I receive government money for both children but I do not feel the need to use my money for everyone in the house. Why should I do that if my brother is not expected to do the same? He works at the local taxi rank washing taxis and he gets paid more money than I get from the government. I do not remember a day when my mother shouted at him for not buying this or that for the house. She

shouts at me every day for not being 'responsible'. When I question her about my brother, the response is always the same – I am a woman, I should be more responsible. It is even worse with household chores. He just wakes up in the morning and does nothing in the house and I am expected to clean, cook and take care of the children (Nomagugu, Mpumalanga).

Another response is exemplified by the story of a young woman who no longer wants to accept sole responsibility for looking after her children:

I was tired of taking care of my children while my boyfriend did nothing for them. So one day I decided to take my children to his house. I left them there. It's been a year now. I wanted him to raise the children and feel the pain that I was feeling. I thought that my own mother would support me but instead she became one of those people who called me names. They say that the only reason I abandoned my children was that I wanted to be young again and free for all men to see me … *unondidwa* [isiZulu word that means a prostitute] (Khanyisile, Enhlalakahle).

Both examples challenge notions of mothers as always altruistic, self-sacrificing and morally good. The responsibility to preserve, care for and nurture children, especially, is often placed on women rather than men. The conceptualisation of motherhood in Zulu folklore stresses the importance of unselfish and self-sacrificing mothers. For example, an isiZulu expression '*intandane enhle ngumakhothwa ngunina*' (a good orphan is one that is licked by the mother) is taken to mean: 'A mother is capable of making great sacrifices for the welfare of the children, whereas a father may not care so much. Thus, a child without a father is generally in better circumstances than a child without a mother' (Nyembezi 1990:142).

There are many other sayings placing most of the responsibility on women, but while many women happily accepted such responsibilities the current socioeconomic context seems to force some into unorthodox responses. Motherhood and femininity for these young women is different from what is expected by their society. Mothers such as Nomagugu and Khanyisile are redefining and reconceptualising motherhood and femininity even though social expectations are high and the community shuns a woman who refuses to conform to the image of women as nurturers and carers, gentle and always unselfish. Expectations for men's behaviour are different. A man could 'abandon' his children and not pay child maintenance but society does not define such acts as 'un-emancipatory'. It is not surprising that derogatory names are given to young women – but not to their male counterparts – when they have multiple partners (Hunter 2004).

Young black women in the two townships are challenging their subordination and control by men. These responses contradict assertions that black women lack agency and gender consciousness. Women in the two townships are renegotiating, contesting and shifting gender identities and their meanings, revealing both coherent and contradictory gendered subjectivities shaped by their responses to subordination. They are confirming that subjectivity is 'precarious, contradictory and in process, constantly being reconstituted in discourse in everyday life' and the 'conscious and unconscious thoughts and emotions of the individual, her sense of herself and her ways of understanding her relation to the world' (Weedon 1997: 32).

In the context of poverty and patriarchy it is understandable why older women would accept what Connell (1987) described as 'emphasised femininity' or 'conservative femininity'. These women surrender to power and subordination in order to meet cultural expectations of 'good women' whereas young women are exercising their agency by not surrendering to patriarchy and by continuing to negotiate and challenge defined roles and responsibilities in their households and communities.

THE SOUTH AFRICAN STATE: POLICIES AND INSTITUTIONS?

Progressive measures and policies put in place post-1994 have ignored the unequal gender power relations in many African households and have thus failed to make a lasting impact. The first problem lies in the conceptualisation of policies such as social grants. South Africa's social security and employment programmes are based on a consensual view of households and ignore the unequal power relations and conflict in households and communities. They assume that individual social grants or income will filter through and benefit every household equally, but when the money does reach households it is not always used for the benefit of all members. Money is often appropriated from vulnerable old people. The elderly recipients of the pension grants frequently become victims of violence and abuse. Unemployed men feel inadequate, especially when they compare themselves to their female counterparts who have access to child grants and their frustration is often expressed through alcohol abuse and domestic violence (Mosoetsa, 2011)

Beyond the conceptual problems of state welfare policies, there are also problems with implementation. First, although state social grants are a major tool used by the state to distribute income to the poor (and for many African households social grants are the only source of income and without them these households will not survive) the grants do not reach all the intended beneficiaries because of bureaucratic challenges (Case, Hosegood and Lund 2005). Some of these have to do with the maladministration and corruption that plagues some government departments.

> There are a lot of backlogs in the social department office. The local district surgeon is also known for refusing to sign documents that would allow people who are terminally ill because of AIDS to receive government grants. Magistrates have also refused to sign consent forms for AIDS orphans. There is general non-cooperation from government departments (Reverend Zondi, Enhlalakahle).

Second, young unemployed women and men do not access such regular income until they are pensioners. Young women can access social grants only if they have a child and those who choose not to have children are excluded. Third, most people interviewed, especially young women and men, want a job not a grant. Fourth, for young women the amount of the child grant barely covers monthly daycare fees, or even nappies.

> All we want are jobs for our children. I am too old to be working but my children are unemployed and have never worked before. We just depend on state grants, which do not give us enough money (MaDhlamini, Enhlalakahle).

> Yes, I receive a child support grant for my two children. The money is too little but it is better than nothing. I do this and that with it. It helps me just to survive (Phindile, Mpumalanga).

The argument that young women have children to access state grants is false and a conservative view which seeks to undermine the intelligence of many of these young women. Monde Makiwane (2010) also negates the correlation between young women having children and accessing state grants. Even though the amount of the state pension is significantly higher than the child support grant, the fact that it has to support many unemployed people makes it also too small. Finally, state social grants are also limited because they are not for unemployed youth.

State institutions and policies to foster gender equality have failed to have any meaningful effect in most of the studied households. For example, most of the victims of domestic violence do not report it, mainly because they do not trust the police and are reluctant to approach other state institutions because of perceived corruption. A grandmother complained:

> Many of my friends are scared of reporting their children to the police. Wives are also scared of reporting their husbands. They just sit at home and hope for the best (Nonjabulo Mazibuko, Enhlalakahle).

The reluctance of women, especially, to claim their citizenship rights often has to do with how the state has been viewed as hostile to women. Shireen Hassim (2005: 643) correctly points out that: 'The extent to which poor women have been able to access their citizenship rights has been limited by faltering political will to address poverty in a comprehensive manner,' and also by 'an overarching macroeconomic framework that prioritises fiscal restraint over redistribution, and by an administrative system and infrastructure that is unable to fulfil the basic tasks of service delivery.' Service delivery, measured not by the number of households with access to basic services but by the quality of these services, is a mounting problem in many communities. Challenges over access to service delivery continue despite the fact that in the South African Bill of Rights Article 25.1, and Section 26 and 27 of the Universal Declaration of Human Rights it is stated that every citizen has the right to adequate health care services, housing, sufficient food and water and social security. Communities have challenged the state, through formal and informal organisations, to fulfil its promises and its constitutional obligation. The state has taken a hostile stance towards many legitimate community protests.

State policies play a role is shaping gendered identities, thereby influencing household gender and generational relations. Economic and political transition does not only transform the relationship between the state and its citizens but also changes that between citizens – in this case between household members, and between men and women (Connell 1987; Collins 2000). As Shahra Razavi and Shireen Hassim (2006:8) correctly note: 'Contemporary state reforms in many contexts have carried enormous implications for what is expected of families'. Therefore, the socioeconomic and political context of gender identities, roles and relations becomes important in understanding household gender and generational relations.

CONCLUSIONS

The empirical evidence in this chapter contributes to the ways in which theories of patriarchy, gender relations and households shift in different economic and social contexts. The chapter provides evidence that such concepts, definitions and experiences are not static or universal. For South Africa, the crisis of unemployment or 'the end of the factory' and the changing economic context have implications for social relations (gender and generational) in households and communities. Gendered identities, experiences and subjectivities are changing. For men, unemployment represents a struggle for their lost status as economic providers, heads of households and decision makers. They consequently draw on tradition and culture to justify the continued subordination of women. Young women and men are questioning this continued subordination of women in different ways: older women are embracing their roles as mothers, caregivers and nurturers but the feminisation of survival has not meant a role reversal or the elevation of women's status. Women's, and especially older women's, experience of poverty is not only a struggle for scarce resources, inadequate basic services and ill health, but also a battle against domestic violence and abuse.

This chapter has argued that economic rights are just as important as political rights. High levels of poverty and growing inequality are threatening South Africa's political democracy. State pension grants remain the most important regular income for many poor households but on their own such examples of income redistribution by the state are limited instruments for economic transformation in a highly unequal society.

REFERENCES

Agüero J, MR Carter and J May (2007) Poverty and inequality in the first decade of South Africa's democracy: What can be learnt from panel data? *Journal of African Economies.*

Bengtson VL, R Giarrusso, JB Mabry and M Silverstein (2002) Solidarity, conflict and ambivalence: Complimentary or competing perspectives on intergenerational relationships. *Journal of Marriage and Family* 64: 568-576.

Boonzaier F and C de la Rey (2003) 'He is a man, and I'm a woman' Cultural constructions of masculinity and femininity in South African women's narratives of violence. *Violence Against Women* 9 (8):1003-1029.

Burawoy MP, P Krotov and T Lytkina (2001) Domestic involution: How women organise survival in a North Russian city. In Bonnell E and G Breslauer (eds) *Russia in the New Century: Stability or Disorder.* Boulder, CO: Westview.

Case A, V Hosegood and F Lund (2005) The reach and impact of child support grants: evidence from KwaZulu-Natal. *Development Southern Africa* 22(4).

Cock J (1991) *Colonels and Cadres: War and Gender in South Africa.* Cape Town: Oxford University Press.

Collins P (2000) *Black Feminist Thought: Knowledge, Consciousness, and the Politics of Empowerment.* New York: Routledge. Connell RW (1995) *Masculinities.* St Leonards, NSW: Allen & Unwin.

Connell RW (1987) *Gender and Power: Society, the Person and Sexual Politics.* Cambridge: Polity Press.

Connell RW and JW Messerschmitt (2005) Hegemonic masculinity: Rethinking the concept. *Gender & Society* 19(6), 829-859.

Folbre N (1994) *Who Pays for the Kids? Gender and the Structure of Constraints.* London and New York: Routledge.

Hassim S (2005) Turning gender rights into entitlements: Women and welfare provision in post-apartheid South Africa. *Social Research* 72(3): 621-46.

hooks b (2000) *Feminism is for Everybody: Passionate Politics.* London: Pluto.

Hunter M (2006) Fathers without amandla: Zulu-speaking men and fatherhood. In Richter L and R Morrell (eds) *Baba: Men and Fatherhood in South Africa.* Cape Town: HSRC Press.

Hunter M (2004) Masculinities, multiple-sexual partners, and AIDS: The making and unmaking of Isoka in KwaZulu-Natal. *Transformation,* 54: 123-153.

Kabeer N (1994) *Reversed Realities: Gender Hierarchies in Development Thought.* London and Delhi: Verso and Kali.

Kandiyoti D (1998) Gender, power and contestation: Rethinking bargaining with patriarchy. In Pearson R and C Jackson (eds) *Feminist Visions of Development.* London: Routledge.

Katz R, A Lowenstein, J Phillips and SO Daatland (2004) Theorising intergenerational family relations: Solidarity, conflict and ambivalence in cross-national contexts. in V. L. Bengtson A, C Acock, KR Allen, P Dilworth-Anderson and DM Klein (eds) *Sourcebook of Family Theory and Research.* London: Sage.

Leibbrandt M, I Woolard and C Woolard (2009) Poverty and inequality dynamics in South Africa: Post-apartheid developments in the light of the long-run legacy. In Aron J, B Kahn and G Kingdom (eds) *South African Economic Policy Under Democracy.* Oxford: Oxford University Press.

Lorde A (ed.) 1984. *Sister Outsider.* California: Crossing Press.

Madhavan S and E Schatz (2007) Coping with change: Household structure and composition in rural South Africa 1992-2003. *Scandinavian Journal of Public Health,* 35(85) (Suppl. 69): 85-93.

Makgetla N (2010) The international economic crisis and employment in South Africa. In Daniels J, P Naidoo, D Pillay and R Southall (eds) *New South African Review 1: Development or Decline.* Johannesburg: Wits University Press.

Makiwane M (2010) The child support grant and teenage childbearing in South Africa. *Development Southern Africa,* 27(2): 193-204.

Mbeki M (2009) *Architects of Poverty: Why African Capitalism Needs Changing.* Johannesburg: Picador Africa.

Mohamed S (2010) 'The state of the South African economy'. In Daniels J, P Naidoo, D Pillay and R Southall (eds) *New South African Review 1: Development or Decline.* Johannesburg: Wits University Press.

Morrell R and L Lichter (2006) Introduction. In Richter L and R Morrell (eds) *Baba: Men and Fatherhood in South Africa.* Cape Town: HSRC Press.

Mosoetsa S (2011) *Eating From One Pot: Dynamics of Survival in Poor South African Households.* Johannesburg: Wits University Press.

Mosoetsa S (2005) The consequences of South Africa's economic transition: The remnants of the footwear industry. In Webster E and K von Holdt (eds) *Beyond the Apartheid Workplace: Studies in Transition.* Scottsville: Natal University Press.

Mosoetsa S (2001) The Manchester Road: Women and the informalisation of work in South Africa's footwear industry. *Labour, Capital and Society*, 34(2):184-206.

Murray C (1981) *Families Divided: The Impact of Migrant Labour in Lesotho.* Johannesburg: Ravan.

Nattrass N (2000) Inequality, unemployment and wage-setting institutions in South Africa. *Studies in Economics and Econometrics* 24 (3): 129-142, November.

Ngwane N (2003) 'Christmas Time' and the struggles for the household in the countryside: Rethinking the cultural geography of migrant labour in South Africa. *Journal of Southern African Studies* 29(3): 681-699.

Nyembezi CL (1990) *Zulu Proverbs.* Johannesburg: Wits University Press (revised edition).

Pahl R (1984) *Divisions of Labour.* Oxford: Blackwell.

Razavi S and S Hassim (2006) Gender and social policy in a global context: Uncovering the gendered structure of 'the social'. *News from the Nordic Africa Institute* 3.

Salo E (2007) Social construction of masculinity on the racial and gendered margins of Cape Town. In Shefer T, K Ratele, A Strebel, N Shabalala and R Buikema (eds) *From Boys to Men: Social Constructions of Masculinity in Contemporary Society.* Cape Town: Juta.

Sassen S (2000) Women's burden: Counter-geographies of globalisation and the feminisation of survival. *Journal of International Affairs* 53(2).

Seekings J and N Nattrass (2005) *Class, Race, and Inequality in South Africa.* Yale University Press.

Statistics South Africa. *National Census 2012.* Pretoria: StatsSA.

Statistics South Africa. *General Household Survey 2010.* Pretoria: StatsSA.

Statistics South Africa. *Labour Force Survey 2010.* Pretoria: StatsSA.

Terreblanche S (2002) *A History of Inequality in South Africa.* Scottsville and Johannesburg: University of Natal Press and KMM Publishing.

Tshoaedi M (2008) Roots of Women's Union Activism: South Africa 1973-2003. Unpublished doctoral thesis, University of Leiden, Netherlands.

Van der Berg S and M Louw (2003) Changing patterns of SA income distribution: Towards time series estimates of distribution and poverty. Paper delivered to the Conference of the Economic Society of SA. 17-19 September 2003, Stellenbosch.

Van Driel M (2009) The social grants and black women in South Africa: A case study of Bophelong Township in Gauteng. *Journal of International Women's Studies* 10: 127-133.

Vetten L (2000a) Gender, race and power dynamics in the face of social change: Deconstructing violence against women in South Africa. In Park YJ, J Fedler and Z Dangor (eds) *Reclaiming Women's Spaces: New Perspectives on Violence Against Women and Sheltering in South Africa.* Johannesburg: Nisaa Institute for Women's Development.

Vetten L (2000b) 'The economics of domestic violence'. *Sunday Independent*, 12 March.

Walby S (1990) *Theorising Patriarchy.* Oxford: Blackwell.

Ward R and G Spitze (1992) Consequences of parent-child co-residence: A review and research agenda. *Journal of Family Issues* 13: 553-572.

Weedon C (1997) *Feminist Practice and Poststructuralist Theory*. Oxford: Blackwell.

NOTES

1   Statistics South Africa, Labour Force Survey (LFS) for Q4 2010.
2   The level of rising inequality will vary depending on dataset or statistical technique used.
3   Elaine Salo (2007) makes a similar point in her study of the making and unmaking of masculinities for coloured boys in Cape Town, South Africa.
4   For example, Walby (1997) notes that young women are able to respond to the challenge of gender discrimination because of their improved levels of education.

CHAPTER 14

Prisons, the law and overcrowding

Clare Ballard

———

'Going to prison is like dying with your eyes open.'
Bernard Kerik, former New York City police commissioner

INTRODUCTION

This chapter is about a long-standing problem in the South African criminal justice sector that, despite an overhaul of the prison legislation after the enactment of the final Constitution, continues, twenty years on, to plague the Department of Correctional Services and, of course, those who are incarcerated in the country's prisons. I examine both the causes and the effects of overcrowding as well as the constitutional implications, and argue that currently the rights of inmates detained in overcrowded prisons are being infringed and that curative measures on the part of the state are needed urgently. I discuss what remedial measures are, or could be, available, some of which could be employed immediately, and others over the medium to long term.

A FEW PRELIMINARY POINTS

I use the term 'inmates' to refer to both sentenced offenders and those awaiting trial. The latter, to whom I shall refer as 'remand detainees', are detainees who have already been formally charged before a court, are awaiting trial, or who have not yet been sentenced and who are being detained in a prison. Approximately one-third of the prison population is composed of these remand detainees and they are thus a significant element in the problem of overcrowding (Judicial Inspectorate 2010/11). The term 'overcrowding' is used in this chapter as a description only of the ratio of inmates to rated capacity. Haney (2006) makes the important point that the term could include the extent to which a prison accommodates more inmates than its infrastructure can 'humanely accommodate, meaning a prison without adequate medical facilities for its population could be "overcrowded" even though, technically, it is not accommodating more inmates than that for which it was designed'. Although it is likely that South African prisons are overcrowded in the broader sense, the statistical information available is not sophisticated enough to support an argument along such lines. So, in this chapter, we consider only the numbers of inmates.

PRISON LAW AND THE CONSTITUTION

Since the advent of South African democracy the law in respect of prisons and punishment has been reformed in significant ways. Reform was prompted, of course, by the interim and then final Constitutions, the latter adopted in 1996. The value-laden text of the Bill of Rights makes it quite clear that all detainees, awaiting trial or sentenced, are entitled to a certain standard of treatment – 'conditions of detention consistent with human dignity' – and a set of specific rights (the Constitution). The relevant legislation giving effect to these rights, the Correctional Services Act 111 of 1998, came into force during 2004. The Act and its regulations include precise requirements for all aspects of the treatment of prisoners: accommodation, nutrition, clothing, medical treatment, discipline and methods of restraint. At the core of the Act is an acknowledgment that the prison system should ensure the safety and the protection and fulfilment of the rights of inmates, and promote the 'social responsibility and human development' of all sentenced inmates. Given the history of corrections in South Africa, the Act represents a fundamental shift in focus from its predecessor, the Correctional Services Act of 1959, which spoke little of the rights of inmates and dealt primarily with the administration of the prison system (Van Zyl Smit 2001). Five months after the final promulgation of the Act, the Department of Correctional Services released the White Paper on Corrections in South Africa which made it clear that one of the central purposes of the Department was the rehabilitation of prisoners (Muntingh 2005). In addition, as Muntingh states, it is in part a 'confession on the part of the Department for previous practices and policies'. Indeed, in his foreword to the White Paper the then minister of correctional services said:

> The White Paper on Corrections in South Africa presents the final fundamental break
> with a past archaic penal system and ushers in a start to our second decade of freedom
> where prisons become correctional centres of rehabilitation and offenders are given

new hope and encouragement to adopt a lifestyle that will result in a second chance
towards becoming the ideal South African citizen.

Prior to the enactment of the final Constitution and the legislation and policy
described above, the common law had made great strides towards the protection of the
rights of inmates. In 1993, the Appellate Division, in the matter of *Minister of Justice v
Hofmeyr* 1993 (3) SA 131 (A), held that all the fundamental rights of prisoners survived
incarceration – a notion known as the residuum principle.[1] This was an important
moment in the history of prisoners' rights, for the Appellate Division had effectively
reinstated a principle set down in a 1911 decision[2] which had been systematically eroded
over the years through draconian apartheid-era detention legislation and judicial decisions favourable to the executive. The *Hofmeyr* judgment has continued to form the basis
of South African jurisprudence on prisoners' rights which, since the advent of the final
Constitution, have 'been given fresh impetus by a number of our constitutional values
such as dignity, equality and humanity' (Van Zyl Smit 2005). Perhaps one of the most
important decisions on prisoners' rights was the first judgment of the Constitutional
Court, *S v Makwanyane* 1995 (3) SA 391 (CC), renowned for having declared the death
penalty unconstitutional. In doing so, the court adopted the Kantian notion that '[the
right to] human dignity precludes treating individuals as mere objects or means to an
end' (Botha 2009). The *Makwanyane* court stated:

> The death penalty ... instrumentalises the offender for the objectives of state policy.
> That is dehumanising. It is degrading and it violates the rights to respect for and
> protection of human dignity embodied in Section 10 of the Constitution.

Several years later, this idea was repeated by the Constitutional Court in *S v Dodo* 2001 (3)
SA 382 (CC), which considered the constitutionality of minimum sentencing legislation
(Criminal Law Amendment Act 1997). The Court stated that the imposition of a disproportionately severe sentence without sufficient inquiry into whether such a sentence was
a measure justified by the severity of the offence would be:

> ... to ignore, if not to deny, that which lies at the very heart of human dignity. Human
> beings are not commodities to which a price can be attached; they are creatures with
> inherent and infinite worth; they ought to be treated as ends in themselves, never
> merely as means to an end.

The Constitutional Court's emphasis on the value of self-actualisation cemented, so to
speak, the idea that the penal system should be a restorative and rehabilitative institution,
no longer defined by the retributive and punitive policies of its past.

CAUSES OF PRISON OVERCROWDING

Crime, policing and policy – looking back

Although the legislature and judiciary appeared to bear down in favour of prisoners' rights when they did, the opposite was true of policing and crime control. During the 1990s the levels of crime went up quite dramatically in South Africa,[3] and the criminal justice system did little to assuage the perception that the government was failing to respond to the problem effectively. In 2000, only 610 000 of the 2.6 million crimes recorded by the police were referred to the National Prosecuting Authority (NPA); although the NPA achieved convictions in the majority of cases they prosecuted, this represented only 8 per cent of the 2.6 million reported crimes (Schonteich 2003). Accordingly, the notion that the criminal justice system was no longer a capable guardian of public safety and security became more pervasive, as did 'community policing' (vigilante or otherwise) among poorer communities, and a wholesale movement towards a reliance on the private security sector among the middle classes (Van der Spuy 2000). In addition, according to the Independent Complaints Directorate, there was a 'growing, popular perception that constitutional rights for criminals [were] being protected above those of their victims' (Schonteich 2003).

The government responded with a surge in militarised police force. There was a marked increase in police clampdowns, as well as saturation policing, which required that certain areas be sealed off and people and property searched (Van der Spuy 2000). In one operation named Sword and Shield, more than 300 000 suspects were arrested during 1996 and 1997 (Matthews 2000). Unfortunately, as Subramanian (2013) notes, there were no efforts to equip the courts and remand detention facilities in the face of the inevitable rise in the number of people arrested and detained. The consequence, of course, was the flooding of an already over-burdened court system and of poorly equipped prisons.

The legislature responded with a spate of statutory amendments to the bail provisions of the Criminal Procedure Act. These resulted in the controversial reverse onus provisions which stipulate that a suspect must be denied bail when charged with certain serious offences unless able to prove that 'exceptional circumstances' exist, satisfying the presiding officer that it is in the interests of justice to release him or her. Unsurprisingly, the prison population escalated substantially: in 1995 it was just under 120 000; in 2002, it was approximately 190 000. From 2005 onwards the prison population tapered off somewhat, and in March 2013 it was 158 165.

A rehabilitative prison environment, responsive to the needs of individuals, cannot exist when prisons are overburdened, which is why the contrast in response on the part of the state and judiciary towards arrested suspects, and the treatment of prisoners, is rather bizarre. But it illustrates, perhaps, that legislation or legislative intent cannot change the status quo if political sentiment is lacking.

Remand detention

The crime rate in South Africa began to drop steadily from 1999-2000, which may explain the softening of policing tactics around this time and the consequent reduction of the prison population (Crime Stats SA). In 2012-2013, however, the crime rate was the lowest it has been in the last ten years, yet the prison population is still far greater than it was in 1995. Importantly, sentenced admissions do not appear to be a driving force in the general prison population – on the contrary, the sentencing rate dropped significantly between 2001 and 2007-2008 (from more than 200 000 total sentenced admissions per year to approximately 80 000 in 2010-2011), and, after increasing slightly during the years 2008-2010, reached an all-time low in 2010-2011 (Redpath 2013). This happened despite the introduction of a more punitive sentencing framework[4] and the fact that the rate of prosecutorial referrals from the police to the NPA did not decline during this period (Redpath 2012). The number of yearly admissions into remand detention fluctuated between 250 000 and 300 000 during the same period (dropping just below 250 000 in 2010-2011). The number of remand detention admissions per sentenced admissions, however, grew considerably between 2000-2001 and 2007-2008, from just below 1.5 to more than three (Redpath: 2013). This explains the more or less constant number of the total inmate population from 2005-2006 to 2012-2013 and also suggests that the remand detention numbers are indeed a significant driving factor in the prison population even though they constitute only 30 per cent of it, far below most other African and Middle East countries (World Prison Brief).

PRISON OVERCROWDING – SOME CONTEXT

Despite the legal and policy developments within the penal framework that have taken place since the advent of democracy, conditions in South African prisons have remained poor, and they are overcrowded.

Several African countries are classed as having some of the world's most overcrowded prisons (World Prison Brief). Benin, for example, has the second highest occupancy rate in the world – 307.1 per cent. The country reports of Special Rapporteur for Prisons and Conditions of Detention have revealed some alarming statistics on African prisons over the years. In Côte d'Ivoire, in 2006, a prison designed to accommodate 1 500 prisoners was actually accommodating 4 034. In 2004, the Special Rapporteur, on a mission to Ethiopia, noted that 'apart from [one prison] all detention facilities visited were overcrowded, some holding inmates more than thrice their capacity' (Dankwa 2008).

South Africa, at 133 per cent occupancy, is well below the startling figures representing the world's ten most overcrowded prisons, four of which belong to African countries according to the World Prison Brief. Averages can be misleading, however. The occupancy rates of individual prisons paint a far clearer picture of the conditions of detention to which inmates are subjected. The Judicial Inspectorate for Correctional Services acknowledges this in its 2011-2012 report when it states: 'Although overcrowding on a national level is reflected in an occupancy level of 133 per cent, there is a vast difference between overcrowding in individual centres, with some centres extremely overcrowded and some operating below capacity.'

It is therefore unsurprising that the provinces with the highest occupancy rates have the country's most overcrowded prisons, which range between 200 and 250 per cent capacity (Judicial Inspectorate 2010/11). It is important to mention at this stage that the Department of Correctional Services's own standing orders stipulate that the minimum permissible cell area per prisoner, excluding areas taken up by ablution facilities, walls and pillars and personal lockers (not built-in) in the cell, must be 3.344m^2 in respect of ordinary communal cells. Capacity is determined according to the Department's own space norm of 3.334m^2 per prisoner in a communal cell and 5.5m^2 in ordinary single cells. This regulation is just below the Committee for the Prevention of Torture's recommended minimum of 4m^2 per prisoner in a communal cell.[5]

Despite the existence of legislative measures intended to alleviate the burden on correctional facilities and the Judicial Inspectorate having consistently raised the problem of prison overcrowding since its first published Annual Report in 2000, the Department of Correctional Services itself admits that 'overcrowding remains high' (Department Annual Report: 2009/2010).

THE EFFECTS OF PRISON OVERCROWDING

The effects of prison overcrowding, which go far beyond simple discomfort, are crucial to the case in favour of the reduction of the prison population. Simply put, overcrowding hinders the realisation of inmates' other rights of nutrition, medical treatment and exercise. The case of *Lee v Minister of Correctional Services* 2011 (2) SACR 603 (WCC) illustrates this well. The plaintiff was detained for four and a half years while awaiting trial, during which time he contracted tuberculosis. The judgment relates the evidence of expert witnesses describing the conditions of detention:

> The average overcrowding in 2003 was around 234 per cent to 236 per cent. Overcrowding meant that disease could be spread more easily, and, as far as TB was concerned, the more people were packed into a cell, the greater the prospects that bacteria which were coughed up would infect other inmates. [The medical expert] regularly saw overcrowded cells in the maximum security prison and testified that his first impression was one of dinginess and squalor, because blankets are often used to protect or cover up places within a cell. He described the situation as dehumanising.

The effects of overcrowding also include less obvious consequences, and empirical research, although somewhat dated, has shown that 'crowding significantly worsens the quality of institutional life and increases the destructive potential of imprisonment' (Haney 2006). A brief summary of some of this empirical research, which originates, for the most part, in the United States, is as follows:

i. The nature of the stress and degree of uncertainty with which inmates in situations of
    overcrowding must cope can result in physical and psychological harm. Haney (2006)
    states:

    > Crowded conditions heighten the level of cognitive strain that prisoners experience by
    > introducing social complexity, turnover, and interpersonal instability into an already
    > dangerous prison world in which interpersonal mistakes or errors in social judgments
    > can be fatal. [O]f course, overcrowding also raises collective frustration levels inside
    > prisons by generally decreasing the resources available to prisoners confined in them.
    > The amount of things prisoners can accomplish on a day-to-day basis is compromised
    > by the sheer number of people in between them and their goals and destinations.

ii. Studies have shown an association between poorly regulated and overcrowded prisons
    and the occurrence of disciplinary infractions as well as higher rates of assault, rape
    and sexual violence (Haney 2006). Linked to this is the organisational strain that over-
    crowded prisons experience. Congested prisons lead to the 'less careful classification,
    monitoring and managing of inmates with psychological problems or who pose a
    threat of violence' (Haney 2006). The correlation between overcrowding and reduced
    management efficiency and increased recidivism is unsurprising.

Although there is very little South African empirical research on prison overcrowding, it
is notable that the most recent reported incidents of prison violence occurred in some
of the country's most overcrowded prisons.[6] One cannot escape the conclusion that, for
sentenced inmates, prison overcrowding, in addition to its adverse effects on the rights
enumerated in section 35(2)(e) of the Constitution, frustrates an important purpose of a
sentence of imprisonment: namely, as the Act states, to promote the 'social responsibility
and human development of all sentenced offenders' and ensure that the offender leads a
'crime free life in the future'.

There has not yet been a direct court challenge to prison overcrowding, although the
issue has arisen indirectly. In fact, there are a limited number of cases directly involving
section 35(2)(e) of the Constitution.[7] Prisoners' rights litigation has generally involved
the alleged infringement of certain discrete rights such as the right to education, privacy,
health and the right to vote.

THE CONSTITUTION AND THE LAW REDUX

Section 35(2)(e) of the Constitution, which applies to both sentenced and awaiting trial
prisoners, states that: 'Everyone who is detained, including every sentenced prisoner, has
the right to conditions of detention that are consistent with human dignity, including at
least exercise, and the provision, at state expense, of adequate accommodation, nutrition,
reading material and medical treatment.'

Chapter Three of the Correctional Services Act, entitled 'custody of all inmates under conditions of human dignity', gives effect – so to speak – to section 35(2)(e) of the Constitution. Put differently, it sets out in greater detail the requirements of the Constitution. Accordingly, prison conditions which fall below the requirements of Chapter Three are a violation of the standards expressed in section 35(2)(e) and may well amount to 'inhuman or degrading' treatment or punishment, a violation of section 12(1)(e) of the Constitution. The Act and its regulations require the following in respect of accommodation:

i.   Cell accommodation must have sufficient floor and cubic space to enable the prisoner to move freely and sleep comfortably within the confines of the cell;

ii. All accommodation must be ventilated according to regulation;

iii. Cells must be sufficiently lit by natural and artificial light so as to enable the prisoner to read and write;

iv. There must be sufficient ablution facilities available to prisoners at all times which include hot and cold water, and such facilities must be partitioned-off from sleeping areas; and

v.   Each prisoner must have his or her own separate bed.

Based on the current occupation rate, this means that prisoners at the most crowded facilities have between $1.3m^2$ and $1.7m^2$ of floor space. Although adjudicatory bodies around the world have expressed a range of acceptable floor space standards, as Steinberg (2005) notes: 'When floor space drops to as little as $2.1m^2$ per prisoner the grey areas in international jurisprudence narrow considerably.' Admittedly, measurements like these will never be an entirely accurate reflection of prison conditions, even at the most crowded facilities. The nature of prison accommodation varies considerably, not only between prisons, but also within each prison itself. For example, for security or disciplinary reasons, a number of prisoners may be grouped together in a communal cell, rendering it severely overcrowded, whereas the remainder of the prison population remains well below maximum capacity. A situation like this would not reflect, statistically, as problematic. Nevertheless, it is safe to assume, at the very least, that correctional facilities accommodating inmates at more than 200 per cent capacity are overcrowded to the point where it is almost certainly a violation of section 35(2)(e) of the Constitution and, in more extreme circumstances, section 12(1)(d), the 'right not to be treated or punished in a cruel, inhuman or degrading way'.

International tribunals have made such findings. The European Court of Human Rights (ECHR), for example, has found that cell size and overcrowding were indeed issues relevant to its determination that such conditions amounted to a violation of article 3 of the European Convention on Human Rights, which prohibits torture and inhuman or degrading treatment or punishment.[8] In *Kalashnikov v Russia* (No. 47095/99), the ECHR considered the effect of overcrowding on the applicant at a certain Russian prison in which he had been detained. At any given time, the ECHR observed: 'There was 0.9-1.9 square metres of space per inmate in the applicant's cell.' It found that the severely overcrowded and unsanitary environment and its detrimental effect on the applicant's health and well-being amounted to degrading treatment, a violation of article 3 of the Convention. It noted, too, that poor sleeping conditions as well as the 'general commotion and noise from the large number of inmates' – all of which were caused by acute overcrowding – constituted a heavy physical and psychological burden on the applicant.

REMEDIAL MEASURES

There are currently 55 038 prisoners accommodated in thirty-four prisons that are 175 per cent or more full. These prisons have an average capacity of 773 beds (the median being 557 beds). Of the prisoners, 49.9 per cent are sentenced and 50.1 per cent are unsentenced. If the capacity of all prisons with an occupancy rate of 175 per cent and more were to be added and spread over the entire group, the occupation rate would be 206 per cent. If releases were to be targeted at prisons that were 175 per cent or more full, it would require the release of 27 976 prisoners to bring them to 100 per cent occupancy. If the aim were to bring the occupancy rate down to 175 per cent, it would require the release of 8 253 prisoners. Occupancy of 150 per cent would require the release of 14 828 prisoners, and 125 per cent would require the release of 21 402 prisoners.

As I have explained above, the remand detention population is an important driving factor and, indeed, many of the country's prisons are overcrowded as a result of it (Judicial Inspectorate 2012). In some correctional facilities where overcrowding has reached a 'critical level' remand detainees account for 52 per cent of the inmate population (Judicial Inspectorate 2009/2010). On 31 March 2012, the awaiting trial detainee population in South Africa was 46 351, approximately 30 per cent of the total inmate population and almost double the Department of Correctional Services's proposed benchmark figure of 25 000. As with many human rights concerns, the poor, who cannot afford bail or the services of a lawyer, will suffer the worst of the effects of remand detention: exposure to torture, extortion, disease and the arbitrary actions of police and corrupt officials (Berry 2011).

There are legislative and policy provisions that could be used to alleviate overcrowding in remand detention facilities. First, the Criminal Procedure Act provides for the release of an accused on bail if a magistrate is satisfied that 'the prison population of a particular prison is reaching such proportions that it constitutes a material and imminent threat to … human dignity, physical health or safety…'. The provision only applies, however, to remand detainees who have been granted bail but cannot afford it and are incarcerated pending trial – they account for about 24 per cent of the remand detainee population (Damons 2008) and so this provision could certainly prove to be effective.

Second, the Criminal Procedure Act states that a magistrate or judge before whom criminal proceedings are pending '… shall investigate any delay in the completion of proceedings which appears to the court to be unreasonable and which could cause substantial prejudice to the … accused'. That an accused has been incarcerated in over-crowded conditions for an unnecessarily long period would certainly have an effect on the 'personal circumstances of the accused', one of the factors the court must take into account in carrying out such an inquiry.

Third, as required by the NPA's awaiting trial detainees (ATD) guidelines, prosecutors should reconsider bail if an accused has been in custody for longer than six months and ensure that the investigations and presentation of the state's evidence are fast-tracked.[9] These processes could be made more efficient if the prosecutorial agents referred to the information tabled before Parliament in terms of section 342A(7) of the Criminal Procedure Act. This stipulates that the National Director of Public Prosecutions must submit, within fourteen days after the end of January and of July of each year, a report to the cabinet member responsible for the administration of justice, in respect of each accused whose trial has not yet started with the leading of evidence and who, by the end of the month in question, has been in custody for a continuous period exceeding eigh-teen months from the date of arrest (where the trial is to be conducted in a High Court); or twelve months from date of arrest (if it is to be conducted in a regional court); or six months from date of arrest (if it is to be conducted in a magistrate's court). Ultimately, however, the successful reduction of the remand detention population depends on the implementation of effective backlog-reduction programmes and the Department of Justice and Constitutional Development should prioritise such initiatives.[10]

For sentenced prisoners, there is, admittedly, not much by way of legislative assistance. Nevertheless, given the extent to which sentenced facilities are overcrowded, the state of affairs is undoubtedly unconstitutional. The solution is not necessarily the building of more prisons, nor is it the transferring of prisoners from overcrowded prisons to other prisons in areas far from their own communities and visitors. Rather, the Department should add the necessary capacity to those prisons that simply require more bed space – far easier and cheaper than building new prisons from scratch (as was shown in the most recent Inspectorate's report); and with the level of overcrowding and constitutional urgency as they are it is remarkable that this has not yet been done to a sufficient stan-dard. Failing the Department's action, however, there is reason to believe that litigation may be successful although success is likely to turn on the potential effectiveness of the available remedies. Given the courts' understandable reluctance to quantify constitu-tional minimum standards,[11] the most probable and the best remedy would be a decla-ration, in broad terms, that the current state of prison overcrowding is a violation of constitutional standards and amounts to a violation of the right to be detained in condi-tions consistent with human dignity. A court, ideally, could grant a supervisory order directing the relevant government departments to remedy the problem within a certain time-frame, failing which a certain number of suitable prisoners would be released to bring the accommodation capacity within an acceptable range.[12] An 'acceptable range' could even be the Department's own benchmark of $3.344m^2$ per prisoner – at least as a start. A targeted release programme may provide some immediate relief to the problem of overcrowding, but it would make little sense to release prisoners only to let the prison population numbers rise all over again, and it is essential to propose policy measures that will be applied consistently so that the prisoner population remains stable (Giffard 2006). To the extent that overcrowding is driven by the sentenced population, it is perhaps apposite to revisit the mandatory minimum sentences legislation, especially in light of the fact that it was intended to operate as a temporary two-year measure.

Given the 'progressive content of the law', the state of South African prisons is inexcusable (Jansen 2011). And for too long now penal reform does not seem to have been made a priority either by government or by society at large. The solutions to the problem of overcrowding are not simple. Its causes are systemic and vary across the backlogs, poor management and maladministration of a range of government departments. An informed and meaningful effort by stakeholders would go a long way towards alleviating the numerous and severe effects suffered by thousands of inmates. But surely, twenty years after the enactment of the Constitution, the rights of inmates can no longer be ignored.

REFERENCES

Ballard C and R Subramanian (2013) Remand detention and pretrial services: A few lessons from the past. *South African Crime Quarterly* 44.

Berry D (2011) The socioeconomic impact of pre-trial detention: A global campaign for pre-trial justice. Report, Open Society Foundation and United Nations Development Programme.

Dankwa V (2008) Overcrowding in African prisons. In Sarkin J (ed.) *Human Rights in African Prisons.* Athens, OH: Ohio University Press.

Haney C (2006) The wages of prison overcrowding: Harmful psychological consequences and dysfunctional correctional reactions. *Washington University Journal of Law and Policy* 22: 265-294.

Jansen R and T Achiume (2011) Prison conditions in South Africa and the role of public interest litigation since 1994. *South African Journal of Human Rights* 218: 183-191.

Karth V, M O'Donovan and J Redpath (2008) Between a rock and a hard place: Bail decisions in three South African courts. Open Society Foundation for South Africa report.

Matthews I (2000) Government responses in South Africa: Policy and implementation (2000). Crime and Policing in Transitional Societies, 30 August-1 September 2000, Jan Smuts House, University of the Witwatersrand, Johannesburg.

Muntingh L (2005) Offender rehabilitation and reintegration: Taking the White Paper on corrections forward. Civil Society Prison Reform Initiative Research Paper No. 10.

Muntingh L and C Giffard (2006) The effect of sentencing on the size of the South African prison population, Open Society Foundation for South Africa report.

Paschke R (1999) Process and impact assessment of the pre-trial services demonstration project. Bureau of Justice Assistance Report No. 3.

Redpath J (2013) Presentation on Remand Detention in South Africa, delivered at CSPRI round-table event on 23 May 2013.

Redpath J (2012) Failing to prosecute? Assessing the state of the National Prosecuting Authority in South Africa. *Institute for Security Studies Monograph* 186.

Rodley N and M Pollard (2011) *The Treatment of Prisoners under International Law.* Third ed. Oxford: Oxford University Press.

Sarkin J, E Steyn, D Van Zyl Smit and R Paschke R (2000) The Constitutional Court's bail decision: Individual liberty in crisis? *South African Journal of Human Rights* 16: 292-312.

Schonteich M (2003) Criminal justice policy and human rights in the new South Africa. *Queensland University of Technology Law and Justice Journal* 3(2): 333-348.

Sekhonyane M and A Louw (2002) Violent justice, vigilantism and the state's response. Institute for Security Studies, Monograph 72.

Steinberg J (2005) Prison overcrowding and the constitutional right to adequate accommodation in South Africa. Centre for the Study of Violence and Reconciliation publication, available at http://www.csvr.org.za/wits/papers/papjonn2.htm3.

Van der Spuy E (2000) Crime and its discontent: Recent South African responses and policies. Crime and Policing in Transitional Societies, 30 August-1 September 2000, Jan Smuts House, University of the Witwatersrand, Johannesburg.

Van Zyl Smit D (2005) Sentencing. In Woolman S and M Bishop M (eds) *Constitutional Law of South Africa* OS 2005.

World Prison Brief, International Centre for Prison Studies. Available at http://www.prisonstudies.org/info/worldbrief/wpb_stats.php?area=all&category=wb_occupancy.

Zysk K, F Dunkel and D van Zyl Smit (2001) *Imprisonment Today and Tomorrow: International Perspectives on Prisoners' Rights and Prison Conditions.* Second ed. Leiden: Brill Academic Publishers.

Case law

Minister of Justice v Hofmeyr 1993 (3) SA 131 (A)

S v Makwanyane 1995 (3) SA 391 (CC)

S v Dodo 2001 (3) SA 382 (CC)

Lee v Minister of Correctional Services 2011 (2) SACR 603 (WCC)

Kalashnikov v Russia (No. 47095/99) 2002-VI

Masangano v Attorney General & Others [2009] MWHC 31 (9 November 2009)

Whittaker v Roos and Bateman; Morant v Roos and Bateman 1912 AD 92

Rossouw v Sachs 1964 (2) SA 551(A)

Strydom v Minister of Correctional Services 1999 (3) BCLR 342 (W)

Kudta v Poland No 30210/96) ECHR 2000-XI

Mazibuko and Others v City of Johannesburg and Others 2010 (3) BCLR 239 (CC); 2010 (4) SA 1 (CC)

Brown v Plata 563 U.S. (2011)

NOTES

1   The residuum principle is now captured in section 4(b) of the Correctional Services Act, which states that: 'the duties and restrictions imposed on inmates to ensure safe custody by maintaining security and good order must be applied in a manner that conforms with their purpose and which does not affect the inmate to a greater degree or for a longer period than necessary.' The Act also requires that the 'minimum rights of inmates entrenched in the Act must not be violated or restricted for disciplinary or any other purpose …'.

2   *Whittaker v Roos and Bateman; Morant v Roos and Bateman* 1912 AD 92. In that matter, the newly constituted Appellate Division of the Union of South Africa held that prisoners of all kinds were entitled to 'all the personal rights and personal dignity not temporarily taken away by law, or necessarily inconsistent with the circumstances in which they had been placed.'

3   In 1998 the South African Police Service (SAPS) reported crime figures included: 88 319 instances of aggravated robbery, 24 875 murders, 49 754 rapes, 256 434 assaults with intent to inflict grievous bodily harm, and 360 919 burglaries.

4   The Criminal Law Amendment Act 105 of 1997, which came into effect in 1998, created a range of minimum sentences for a long list of 'serious offences', despite the South African Law Reform Commission having recommended a thorough debate before a new sentencing regime be introduced. The swiftness with which this legislation was passed can be attributed largely to the government's aspiration to be seen as 'tough on crime', at a time when crime was reportedly on the increase

and public tension high. The minimum sentences range from life imprisonment for specified aggravated forms of murder and rape to set numbers of years for first offenders and recidivists for offences listed in the schedules to the Act. The sentences have to be imposed on adult offenders unless substantial and compelling circumstances exist which justify the imposition of lesser sentences.

5   The European Committee for the Prevention of Torture and Inhuman or Degrading Treatment or Punishment (CPT) is the torture prevention committee of the Council of Europe. The CPT was founded on the basis of the European Convention for the Prevention of Torture and Inhuman or Degrading Treatment or Punishment (1987). It allows the CPT to visit all 'places of detention' of the member states of the Council of Europe. The CPT has stated that $10m^2$ of floor space per prisoner is a desirable standard and that that anything below $4m^2$ per prisoner in a communal cell and $6m^2$ for a single cell is 'not a satisfactory amount of living space'. See Report to the Polish Government on the visit to Poland carried out by CPT from 30 June to 12 July 1996, Council of Europe, CPT/Inf (1998) 13; Report to the Albanian government on the visit to Albania carried out by the CPT from 9 to 19 December 1997, Council of Europe, CPT/Inf (2003) 6.

6   See 'Police called in to contain protest at Grootvlei prison' City Press 8 November 2011; 'Stampede at Groenpunt prison after riot and fires' Business Day 8 January 2013; 'Gang fight at Pollsmoor, 10 injured' News24 25 January 2013. Groenpunt, Gootvlei and Pollsmoor are all on the list referred to above.

7   One of these cases was Strydom v Minister of Correctional Services 1999 (3) BCLR 342 (W). The High Court was called to determine whether long-term maximum security prisoners had a right of access to electricity where the Department of Correctional Services had allowed the privilege of having electrical appliances in their cells. Schwartzman J stated (para 15):

> To deprive them entirely and in perpetuity of this prospect could also result in their being 'treated and punished in a cruel or degrading manner' (section 12(1)(c) of the Constitution) or their being detained in conditions that are inconsistent with human dignity (section 35(2) of the Constitution).

8   Unlike the International Convention on Civil and Political Rights (ICCPR) and the similarly-themed African and Inter-American regional charters, the European Convention for the Protection of Human Rights and Fundamental Freedoms (the Convention) does not contain two provisions separating the prohibition of torture (torture provision) from the right of detained persons to be treated with respect for their inherent dignity (dignity provision). The Convention contains only the former provision, article three. Perhaps this is why it is only in the last thirteen years or so that the European Court of Human Rights (ECHR) has found that certain conditions of detention amount to a violation of article three (Rodley: 2011). In the first of these cases, a Grand Chamber of the ECHR, in Kudta v Poland No 30210/96) ECHR 2000-XI quite clearly found that article three includes a 'dignity provision' element:

> The state must ensure that a person is detained in conditions which are compatible with respect for his human dignity, that the manner and method of the execution of the measure do not subject him to distress or hardship of an intensity exceeding the unavoidable level of suffering inherent in detention and that, given the practical demands of imprisonment, his health and wellbeing are adequately secured by, among other things, providing him with the requisite medical assistance.

9   In 2005 the NPA published a set of guidelines (ATD Guidelines) intended to sensitise prosecutors as to the various options available to try to reduce the number of awaiting-trial detainees. For the most part they are a condensed version of the statutory bail provisions but do offer a couple of meaningful recommendations. It is worth noting, however, that as early as 1999 the NPA was making a concerted effort to combat case backlogs, including the institution of Saturday courts and the deployment of more experienced magistrates and court officials to the busier court centres in the country

10   A number of backlog programmes have been shown to have been effective. See generally Paschke R (1999).

11   See for example *Mazibuko and Others v City of Johannesburg and Others* 2010 (3) BCLR 239 (CC); 2010 (4) SA 1 (CC). There is, however, international precedent for this approach. As Steinberg (supra) notes:

> The Council of Europe's CTP has established four square metres per prisoner as a minimum in a communal cell, six square metres in single cells. In the United States, both the American Correctional Association and the American Public Health Association have set standards requiring a minimum of 60 square feet (18.18 square metres) per prisoner. These latter standards have found their way into United States federal regulations; the Bureau of Prisons has used them to establish the rated capacity of its prisons.(In the United States, rated capacity reflects the number of inmates that can be housed safely in a facility.) Courts have used these standards to establish judicially enforceable minima. In the state of Florida, for instance, it is illegal for a prison to exceed its rated capacity. A similar situation prevails in Norway and Holland. In these jurisdictions, the size of the prison population is directly determined by available space.'

12   In *Brown v Plata* 563 U.S. (2011) the United States Supreme Court, in a 5-4 opinion, ruled that California's prisons were so overcrowded that they violated the Constitution's ban on cruel and unusual punishment. The majority decision describes a prison system failing to deliver minimal care to prisoners with serious health needs, and producing 'needless suffering and death'. Justice Kennedy states:

> Overcrowding has overtaken the limited resources of prison staff; imposed demands well beyond the capacity of medical and mental health facilities; and created unsanitary and unsafe conditions that make progress in the provision of care difficult or impossible to achieve. The overcrowding is the primary cause of the violation of [the ban against cruel and unusual punishment].

The remedy, in brief, was an order directing that approximately 36 000 prisoners be released or relocated within a two-year period. Put differently, the order required a reduction in prison occupation from 200 per cent to 137.5 per cent. Closer to home, in 2009 the High Court of Malawi handed down *Masangano v Attorney General & Others* [2009] MWHC 31 (9 November 2009). The Court insisted that overcrowding – which was, according to official figures, at approximately 200 per cent at the time of the court case – coupled with poor ventilation, had contributed to the deaths of 259 inmates in a space of about eighteen months. It held consequently that the severely overcrowded conditions of detention in certain Malawian prisons amounted to a violation of the right to be free from inhuman and degrading treatment. The Court directed the state to reduce overcrowding by half within eighteen months of the judgment and, with time, to eliminate overcrowding altogether. Notably, there was no supervisory element to the Court's order, making it difficult to determine how well the order was implemented.

SOUTH AFRICA
AT LARGE

4

INTRODUCTION

South Africa at large

Gilbert M Khadiagala

The last twenty years of South Africa's democracy have been accompanied by bids to reorder its place in the world to conform to domestic changes. Twenty years is not a long time to inaugurate fundamental alterations to the lives of nations or people. The drama, expectations and fanfare that greeted the birth of South Africa's democracy produced momentous events around its transition that have endured. More accurately, the past two decades have been largely a long and extended transition in which South Africa has tried to overcome its troubled past and has forged new ways of managing multiple foreign policy challenges. The recent demise of former president Nelson Mandela marks a major milestone in the conclusion of the transition, ending an era in which South Africa has refined, redefined and experimented with various approaches to dealing with the rest of the world. Widespread outpourings of grief and celebrations following Mandela's death in large measure underscored South Africa's indelible imprint on the global stage. In death, as in life, Mandela continued to exemplify the deep moral imagination and triumph against adversity that post-apartheid leaders and generations have invoked as templates for the present and future. By the same token, however, Mandela's departure ends the protracted transition, the triumphalism, and the optimism that have dominated South Africa's global dalliance. Foreign policy makers can now operate in normalised circum-stances of framing national and international priorities without being too encumbered by the past. In the normalcy of the post-Mandela era South Africa will probably continue to find new ways of projecting power and realigning national and global interests.

Despite the absence of significant shifts in foreign policy, the pattern of South Africa's engagement with the world witnessed small steps for furnishing leadership on African affairs, particularly in the construction of continental institutions: broadening alliances with new actors in the global North and South and jettisoning some of the commitments established by the apartheid government. These opportunities were, however, overshadowed at times by South Africa's inability to remake the world in its own image and by the constraints arising from partnerships with countries having questionable democratic and human rights credentials. Over the years, the combination of opportunities and constraints invariably yielded foreign policy pragmatism translated into toning down its global reach, reducing overexposure to some issues, and stepping down from the moral pedestal.

Leadership has shaped the parameters of foreign policy, helping to set priorities and navigate the competing claims of actors and constituencies that converge around policy making. But leaders have also responded to immense pressures that have restricted their actions and latitude. Mandela reclaimed South Africa's place in the world by his presence and stature, and equally sought to redefine South Africa's allies and friends, mending diplomatic fences with Cuba, China, Libya, Palestine and Myanmar. Thabo Mbeki's presidency exemplified the profound activism of deepening South Africa's diplomatic re-entry and economic reach into Africa through the African agenda of renewal. Mbeki also tried to revise and contest the asymmetrical rules and institutions that underpin the global order, leading moves to democratise both the UN Security Council and international financial institutions. Under Mbeki, attempts to reinvigorate the Non-Aligned Movement (NAM) as the centrepiece of South-South relations were, however, abandoned for a more focused and productive Southern alliance of Brazil, India and South Africa (IBSA). Equally vital, in a short space of time Mbeki downplayed the global revisionist crusade when he started to negotiate economic concessions from the G8 group of countries and socialised annually with the global glitterati at the Davos conclaves. Jacob Zuma stepped into a changing world in which South Africa was steadily learning to appreciate the limits of its leverage and moral suasion in Africa and elsewhere. But although there were low expectations about his interest in advancing foreign policy objectives, Zuma has innovated a great deal by taking a leadership role in Africa, cultivating close ties with the Brazil, Russia, India, China and South Africa (BRICS) group of nations, and participating actively in the G20 forum.

The chapters in this section speak to the changing roles of South Africa from the perspective of key actors and processes. My chapter addresses Zuma's Africa's policy against the backdrop of the patterns established by Mandela and Mbeki, contending that the twenty-year period was one of continuity rather than radical change. While the Zuma administration has attempted to adopt unilateral policies in Africa, the complexities of managing African affairs have forced the return to collective approaches. Similarly, Justin van der Merwe's perceptive analysis of South Africa's parastatals traces the demise of the extravagant expectations about South Africa's economic role in Africa articulated in

Mbeki's African renaissance. This decline is part of the broad collapse of the government-business-media complex, a set of ideas and practices that shaped South Africa's immediate post-apartheid engagement with Africa. This chapter dovetails nicely with Mopeli Moshoeshoe's analysis that probes the inability of South Africa to set the rules on trade in the Southern African Development Community (SADC) despite popular invocations of its hegemonic credentials. The two chapters ascribe the few successes in foreign policy to the abiding constraints in South Africa's domestic sphere. Outside Africa, South Africa has developed new alliances and partnerships that have influenced domestic politics. Ran Greenstein traces the rise and fall of Israel in South Africa foreign policy – a change that coincided with the end of apartheid and inevitably diminished the 'special relationship'. But the transition to a new South Africa-Israel order has not been smooth, as illustrated by the divisive and polarising debates over Israel and Palestine in domestic discourse. In the chapter on South Africa in north-east Asia, Scarlett Cornelissen departs from the conventional China-centred analyses by providing a comprehensive picture of commercial and trade relations with Japan and Korea. This chapter adds a refreshing depth to the wide-ranging links at the heart of South Africa's Asia's policy, but also demonstrates how China has increasingly sidelined Japan.

CHAPTER 15

South Africa in Africa: Groping for leadership and muddling through

Gilbert M Khadiagala

INTRODUCTION

Ideas and practices of South Africa's post-apartheid leadership role in Africa pivot around two perspectives. First, there is the triumphalist position that invokes South Africa's hegemony during the apartheid era, squandered in the regional destabilisation wars; proponents suggest that this hegemony should be recaptured for noble leadership purposes. This perspective posits leadership as the reclamation of place and space in articulating and shaping Africa's destiny. As a hegemon endowed with the economic and military muscle, South Africa is bound to lead in setting the norms and rules that would undergird security and economic cooperation in Africa (McGowan and Ahwiren-Obeng 1998; Habib and Nthakeng 2006; Alden and Le Pere 2009). The second perspective is less sanguine about hegemonic pretensions, proposing that years of isolation alongside the escalating demands on the South Africa economy furnish profound limits to Pretoria's capabilities for projecting soft and hard power in Africa. Besides, these limits to hegemony are compounded by the complexities of African conditions, particularly the geographical and cultural diversities, and the problems of galvanising leadership in African issues. Given these constraints, South Africa's role in promoting security, prosperity and stability has always proceeded cautiously and modestly through multilateral rather than unilateral approaches (Bischoff 2003; Schoeman 2003; Daniel et al. 2003; Barber 2005).

This chapter examines South Africa's policies in Africa on the basis of vigorous debates about the depth and breadth of its leadership in Africa, and proposes that South Africa's recent role in Africa has amounted to a frantic search for leadership that balances unilateral and multilateral perspectives. In a departure from Thabo Mbeki's penchant for collective and multilateral policies, Jacob Zuma has veered toward unilateralism that amounts to a quest for effective roles in Africa. Zuma has groped for leadership in Africa because of two major factors. First, since the mid-1990s, South Africa's ability to project itself in Africa hinged primarily on issues that galvanised the coalescence of collective leadership captured in the alliance of Mbeki, Nigeria's Olusegun Obasanjo, Algeria's Mohammed Bouteflika, and Senegal's Abdoulaye Wade. This coalition exercised leadership in the reconstruction of African political and economic institutions including the African Union (AU) and the New Partnership for Africa's Development (NEPAD). Toward the late 2000s, as these issues declined in salience and with the waning of the coalition, there were few vistas for leadership on continental affairs. Coinciding with these events has been the loss of a coherent African constituency in the foreign policy establishment, and the weakened role of the Department of International Relations and Cooperation (Dirco) as a foreign policy actor. As a result, South Africa has struggled to remain relevant in Africa, muddling through modest engagements.

Second, groping for leadership is illustrative of policy improvisation on African issues against the backdrop of limited room and resources for manoeuvrability, especially in light of growing domestic cynicism about South Africa in Africa. The existential crisis of finding meaningful engagement roles in Africa may not dissipate until the emergence of new overarching issues that would anchor the parameters of leadership. After a brief description of the pillars of Mbeki's African policy, the chapter will focus on major events that have defined Zuma's policies in African crises: notably, Côte d'Ivoire, Libya, the sponsorship of Nkosazana Dlamini-Zuma to chairperson of the AU, the crisis in Central African Republic, (CAR) and engagement in the Democratic Republic of the Congo (DRC). The chapter concludes that whereas the Zuma administration has in recent times resorted to unilateral positions, the most realistic long-term approaches will gravitate toward the recreation of collective leaderships in geographical and/or functional terms.

SOUTH AFRICA'S AFRICA POLICY UNDER MBEKI

Leadership on African issues has traditionally been driven by core concerns that animate debate and scramble the rise of individuals with the stamina and charisma to propel these concern. African experiences reveal that issue-based leaderships have arisen with strong charismatic personalities (Khadiagala 2010: 375-386). In most of the late 1950s and early 1960s, the agenda of pan-Africanism, African dignity and self-determination permitted the rise of Kwame Nkrumah in Ghana as the most spirited advocate of continental imperatives. While Nkrumah had challengers, forcing him to search for allies, the power of his convictions left a remarkable mark on the shape of post-colonial institution-building in Africa, notably the Organisation of African Unity (OAU) (Williams 2007; Powell and Tieku 2005). Emerging from the shadow of Nelson Mandela in the late 1990s, Mbeki was to lend an equally indelible imprint on the pace and shape of African institutions in a new ideological iteration of the African renaissance.

The Mbeki period marks the golden age of South Africa's engagement with Africa because it tapped into expectations of a new South Africa giving voice on critical African issues. The moral dividends occasioned by the successful transition to majority rule provided a powerful normative framework for leadership in Africa, which was steadily emerging from the legacy of anti-democratic regimes and human rights abuses. Mbeki's leadership lay in seizing the moment of continental political resurgence witnessed by the end of civil wars; the expansion of pluralism; and measures to revive African economies. These opportunities became the building blocks of a South African policy anchored on the premise of African renewal and regeneration. But Mbeki also adroitly crafted the African agenda to dovetail with the domestic transformation in South Africa and, furthermore, he optimistically defined this agenda as the antidote to Africa's growing international marginalisation (Vale and Maseko 1998; Schoeman 2003; Barber 2005; Bischoff 2003).

More than Nkrumah before him, Mbeki was alert to the significance of collective leadership in the search for African solutions to African problems. Mbeki abjured Nkrumah's messianic pretensions, recognised the multiplicity of African challenges, and emphasised the necessity of burden-sharing. This is how the coalition of Algeria, Nigeria, Senegal and South Africa became the key player in forging consensus on African issues (Landsberg 2010). In essence, building the African coalition stemmed from the conviction that despite the enormous expectations surrounding South Africa's leadership, Pretoria could not afford to go it alone in Africa. As a new player on the African scene, South Africa had to proceed cautiously and collectively because years of isolation had created a wide gulf between South Africa and the rest of Africa; in addition, the post-apartheid state was buffeted by vast weaknesses of inequities and poverty that precluded extravagant foreign policy engagements in Africa (Bischoff 2003).

At the height of Mbeki's engagement with Africa, South Africa had to provide leadership by example, expending considerable resources in the stabilisation of the Great Lakes region. Mbeki prodded the fractious Congolese parties in 1999-2002 through countless peace negotiations to reach a settlement that restored political stability to the Democratic Republic of the Congo (DRC). Similarly, through relentless diplomatic initiatives in Burundi, the Mbeki administration (at times using Zuma, who was then deputy president) steered the protagonists toward implementing the Arusha peace agreement of 2002 that Mandela had helped to negotiate. South Africa's major contribution to the stabilisation of Burundi was the deployment of a small military force that protected the rebels returning to Bujumbura, a force that built confidence around the transitional institutions and paved the way for the deployment of the AU and United Nation peace-keeping missions. As Landsberg has indicated:

> South Africa's peacemaking policy towards conflicts in the Great Lakes region has been based on broad georegional tactics and strategies, as Pretoria located them within the framework of a broader African policy of continental renewal and development vision called African renaissance. The policy toward Burundi and the Democratic Republic of the Congo forms a part of South Africa's attempts to help develop a New Partnership for Africa's Development (NEPAD) and the African Union, which are seen as key for development (Landsberg 2006: 121).

Despite the determination to play a leading role in peace-making and conflict resolution in the Great Lakes region, the limits of South Africa's role in Africa were demonstrated in the failure to resolve the intractable civil war that engulfed Côte d'Ivoire from the late 1990s. At the invitation of the AU, Mbeki mediated the conflict in 2004, but these efforts foundered because of intransigence of the parties and the disproportionate role of the French in the conflict. On the eve of the mediation, French President Jacques Chirac, annoyed by Mbeki's intrusion into his own backyard, remarked that Mbeki should first 'immerse himself in West Africa so as to understand the mentality and the soul of West Africa, because in times of crisis, you have to really know people's mentalities and what is in people's souls' (cited *in BBC News* 4 February 2004; see also Lamin 2005).[1] Mbeki was no less successful in Darfur, where the mobilisation of the AU Mission in Darfur peace keeping failed to stem the genocide committed by the Sudanese government of Al-Bashir against defenceless civilians seeking autonomy for the region. Closer to home, diplomatic efforts to resolve the Zimbabwe political crisis consumed most of Mbeki's term in office, culminating in an uneasy settlement in October 2008 between Robert Mugabe and his political opponents. Throughout this period, Mbeki resisted Western entreaties to sanction Zimbabwe and instead opted for quiet prodding and persuasion in a bid to break the political deadlock. South Africa's anti-Western stance on Zimbabwe mirrored the policy during its first term as a non-permanent member of the UN Security Council where Pretoria was criticised for indifference to human rights violations globally (Thipanyane 2011; Taljaard 2008).

Leadership on Africa's rejuvenation dovetailed with the forging of a collective engagement on global economic and governance issues. This multilateralism led to the selective invitation by Mbeki and his coalition partners to various G8 summits to spearhead new global partnerships with Africa. While these invitations potentially fragmented African voices on multiple global issues and, in the end, did not dramatically alter Africa's economic fortunes, the diplomacy around the G8 was significant in erecting the foundations for South Africa's leadership in the revamped G20 multilateral framework and the more recent partnership centred on the Brazil, Russia, China, South Africa (BRICS) group of nations (Qobo 2010, Kornegay and Landsberg 2009).

The political demise of Mbeki in September 2008 raised misgivings about South Africa's drift from the African agenda, often depicted as the 'absence of leadership' on African issues. Sudden leadership changes always produce anxiety about the direction of foreign policy, particularly when strong individuals such as Mbeki dominate foreign policy. More accurately, the concerns about the absence of leadership on African issues after Mbeki concealed the waning of the issues that had inspired the building of the continental institutions. The halcyon days of the African renaissance steadily gave way to a more normalised Africa where the age-old diversities and complexities reappeared and started to compromise coherent South African leadership. The inconclusive conflicts in far-flung places such as Côte d'Ivoire, North Africa and Central Africa were to test the diplomatic skills of the Zuma administration as it defined its place in Africa. The puzzle was whether Zuma would manage these conflicts, unilaterally or multilaterally.

ZUMA'S POLICY TOWARDS AFRICA

In circumstances where foreign policy remains essentially the domain of the presidency, debates about a leadership vacuum on African issues under Zuma were not entirely accurate. As head of intelligence under the exiled ANC, Zuma had been exposed to the African political and security scene and was familiar with most of the actors. Besides, Zuma's role as the chief mediator in Burundi in the early 2000s had endowed him with vital knowledge on African affairs. As Habib (2008: 13) observed, despite expectations of fundamental changes, it is 'worth bearing in mind that Jacob Zuma and many of those in his administration are second generation African nationalists. Also, many in the Zuma camp were integral to the foreign policy apparatus of the Mbeki administration.' Signalling the continued dominance of the presidency in foreign affairs, Zuma appointed the little known, Maite Nkoana-Mashabane as minister at Dirco, but he promised to incorporate multiple voices in decision-making (Landsberg 2012; Masters 2012). To allay fears about Africa's decline, Nkoana-Mashabane noted that Zuma would consolidate the African agenda by continuing 'to work towards achieving a vision of Africa which is united, peaceful, and prosperous' (Nkoana-Mashabane 2009). But there was also an attempt to shift from Mbeki's policies; as Landsberg has accurately observed, the attempts by the Zuma administration to make a break with the Mbeki past 'led South Africa into lots of costly and awkward policy U-turns' (Landsberg 2011: 71).

The initial thrust of the Zuma administration policies in Africa was focused on commercial and economic diplomacy. Although Mbeki's policy had a strong component of economic diplomacy and had been criticised for hiding commercial interests around humanitarian and conflict resolution goals, Zuma gave a new slant to economic diplomacy by highlighting the importance of building strategic economic relationships with a select group of countries. The projection of economic interests soon opened opportunities for the conflation of national and party interests as the ANC elites and Zuma's family members joined in the scramble for economic opportunities in the DRC,

Uganda, the CAR and elsewhere (*Mail & Guardian* 15 January 2012; Sturman 2011; *Mail & Guardian* 30 July 2010; *Business Day* 10 September 2010).[2] The privileging of these interests invariably produced confusion between the promotion of national economic and commercial goals and economic and the business interests of the party and private individuals, and this predatory dimension of commercial diplomacy was to compromise South Africa's military engagement in the CAR. The opening salvo in commercial diplomacy was Zuma's state visit to oil-rich Angola soon after his inauguration in May 2009, with the largest delegation of ministers and businessmen. Although a member of SADC, Angola under Eduardo dos Santos epitomises corruption, authoritarianism, human rights abuses and economic impoverishment – profound problems of governance that have made it a regional semi-pariah; Mbeki had avoided any bilateral engagement with Angola. Zuma's embrace of dos Santos in the name of commercial interests seemed to be an early sign that economic self-interests would trump the observance of human rights and democracy promotion in Africa.

The re-orientation of policy occurred against the background of radical changes at the continental level. Zuma took power when Mbeki's institutional compromises around the AU were under severe strain, with increasing divisions over the ideal approach to continental integration. Reminiscent of the late 1990s, Libya's Muammar Gaddafi challenged the pace of integration and advocated for the speedier formation of a 'United States of Africa' under a more powerful and reconstituted AU. His critics, however, preferred an incremental integration through regional economic communities (RECs). Zuma took a clear line in favour of the gradualists, as stated by Minister Nkoana-Mashabane: 'South Africa would continue to advocate for a gradual and incremental approach, focusing on the regional organisations, as building blocks toward the Union Government. South Africa's approach continues to be premised on the understanding that the African Union is a union of independent and sovereign states' (Nkoana-Mashabane 2009).

One year into the Zuma presidency, South Africa's response to the electoral conflict in Côte d'Ivoire signalled the start of unilateral initiatives on Africa. Following the run-off of the presidential elections in November 2010, a stalemate ensued between President Laurent Gbagbo and his challenger, Alassane Ouattara, when Gbagbo refused to concede defeat and relinquish power. As regional and international actors scrambled to find a solution to the standoff, the Economic Community of West African States (ECOWAS) emerged as the key actor because of its involvement in the conflict since 2002. From the outset, ECOWAS took the position of the Ivorian electoral commission and UN observers that recognised Ouattara's victory; as the conflict unfolded, the ECOWAS position became the dominant voice on the electoral outcome. Given his previous mediation in the conflict, Mbeki was one of the first external actors the AU appointed to launch a mediation initiative in early December 2010, but these efforts failed to convince Gbagbo to step down. Probably on the basis of Mbeki's report to the AU questioning Ouattara's win, South Africa teamed with Angola and Uganda to question the ECOWAS stance on the elections, angering Nigeria and sparking a strong rebuke from Victor Gbeho, the ECOWAS commission president:

African Union leaders publicly criticising ECOWAS on Ivory Coast are breaking with a tradition of regional responsibility. West African leaders yielded to the Southern African Development Community on political crises in Zimbabwe and Madagascar. So why are others not prepared to respect this tradition when it comes to Ivory Coast? They are making statements openly disagreeing and calling for the marginalisation of ECOWAS. The concern we have is that if we go like this, we will destroy the solidarity that has always existed on our continent, the solidarity that has brought us this far (cited in *Voice of America* 9 February 2011).

To pre-empt these rifts from widening, the AU peace and Security Council opted for an AU high level panel consisting of the presidents of Chad, Burkina Faso, Mauritania, Tanzania and South Africa. Although the panel arrived at a roadmap that included the recognition of Ouattara's victory, attempts to implement the recommendations failed because of Gbagbo's intransigence. In April 2011, French forces, working with the UN, forcibly removed Gbagbo from power, ending the crisis. In a subsequent scathing criticism of the 2010 elections, Mbeki argued that the country had not been ready for the elections and blamed the UN and France for the outcome:

The United Nations elected to abandon its neutrality as a peacemaker, deciding to be a partisan belligerent in the Ivorian conflict. France used its privileged place in the Security Council to position itself to play an important role in determining the future of Côte d'Ivoire, its former colony in which, *inter alia*, it has significant economic interests. It joined the United Nations to ensure that Ouattara emerged as the victor in the Ivorian conflict. The United Nations is yet another casualty. It has severely undermined its acceptability as a neutral force in the resolution of internal conflicts, such as the one in Côte d'Ivoire. It will now be difficult for the United Nations to convince Africa and the rest of the developing world that it is not a mere instrument in the hands of the world's major powers. This has confirmed the urgency of the need to restructure the organisation, based on the view that as presently structured the United Nations has no ability to act as a truly democratic representative of its member states (Mbeki 2011).

The crisis in Côte d'Ivoire was resolved amid another looming confrontation in early 2011 between South Africa and the United Nations following the Libyan civil war that pitted the Gaddafi government against rebels based in Benghazi organised as the National Transitional Council (NTC). Seeking to avoid the previous unilateralism in Côte d'Ivoire, Zuma joined four other presidents in an AU high level ad-hoc committee on Libya (AHCL) that was established in March 2011 to resolve the conflict. As part of the efforts to own the Libyan crisis through an African-led initiative, the AHCL unveiled a roadmap on 10 March 2011 with four points: an immediate ceasefire; the unimpeded delivery of humanitarian aid; the protection of foreign nationals (including African migrant workers); and an 'inclusive transitional period' and political reforms which 'meet the aspirations of the Libyan people' (Finnan 2011; Cornish 2011). But the prospects for a negotiated settlement were overshadowed by the UN Security Council Resolution 1973 of 17 March which authorised a no-fly zone over Libya to protect civilians. Alongside Gabon and Nigeria, South Africa voted for Resolution 1973, but soon repudiated it when NATO militarily intervened on the side of the rebels. Defying protests from South Africa and the AU, Arab and Western countries met in London at the end of March 2011 to endorse NATO's military action and proposed an alternative three-point plan to settle the Libyan crisis: that Gaddafi and his regime had completely lost legitimacy; the need to continue military action until Gaddafi met all UN conditions; and Gaddafi's departure from Libya (Campbell 2012: 77).

Zuma's about-turn on the Libyan vote presented dilemmas for South Africa's policy, raising questions about consistency and convictions. Even as South Africa condemned NATO's military campaign, critics charged that it had the option of abstaining from the resolution and should have known that Resolution 1973 would lead to the destruction of Gaddafi's army as part of the enforcement of the no-fly zone. Some critics in the AU complained that South Africa complicated the negotiations for the Libya roadmap by voting in favour of the UN resolution and then leading opposition to it (*Mail & Guardian* 14 June 2011; Wehmhoerner 2011: 2). The perception that the West had hoodwinked and marginalised Africa on Libya dominated South Africa's reaction to the death of Gaddafi and the victory of the NTC in August 2011. Thus South Africa vigorously opposed UN Security Council efforts to unfreeze US$1.5 billion in Libyan money to assist with recon-struction and only relented when the United Nations Security Council resolution omitted the name of NTC. Equally vital, South Africa led efforts in the AHCL to deny recognition to the NTC on the grounds that the new government had violated the AU's doctrine of unconstitutional change of government. South Africa changed course in September 2011 only after several African countries, including Nigeria, recognised the NTC. Reflecting on the Libyan crisis, Zuma observed: 'The AU was not given space to implement its roadmap and to ensure an African solution to the Libyan question. The UN undermined AU's work (*The Star* 13October 2011).

Foreign policy embarrassments in Libya and Côte d'Ivoire in part spurred South Africa's decision to support the candidature of the former minister of home affairs, Nkosazana Dlamini-Zuma, to challenge Gabon's Jean Ping for the position of chairperson of the AU Commission. In a high-profile and bitterly fought race, South Africa broke with the long-standing tradition whereby the chairperson position goes to smaller African countries to prevent vesting too much power in one country. In proposing Dlamini-Zuma, South Africa argued that, unlike other African sub-regions, SADC had never had the chance to lead the AU. While proclaiming that South Africa had no intention of dominating the continent or of 'bully[ing] any country or structure', Zuma reiterated that the campaign was motivated 'by the principle of strengthening the AU and improving its functioning and operations. In addition, we also believe in the principle of giving all regions of the AU an opportunity to serve the organisation' (*The Star* 17 May 2012).

At the first round of voting in January 2012 neither of the candidates garnered the two-thirds majority, partly because Nigeria led a group of states that opposed Dlamini-Zuma. Subsequently, the AU appointed an ad hoc committee of eight heads of state, including Zuma, to reach an amicable compromise. When diplomatic efforts to end the deadlock failed, South Africa embarked on a well-publicised campaign to oust Ping, accusing him of being pro-France and providing indecisive leadership during the Libyan crisis. In the words of one observer, South Africa's campaign entailed 'strategic vote-trading, some rough exchanges, and shuttle diplomacy and the utilisation of significant amounts of funding for horse-trading and 'envelope diplomacy.' Smear tactics and mudslinging and disinformation were also employed as part of the election campaign' (Maru 2012: 70). Ping responded to these criticisms in the lead-up to the final vote in July 2012:

> Just before the January election, it was maliciously alleged that I am under the influence of France and that France tele-guides the affairs of the Commission by remote control. No evidence has been provided to support this allegation and there is nothing in my conduct at the AU that remotely supports that allegation . . . It was further suggested that my country, Gabon, was not supportive of my candidature. When these two lies were debunked, attention was then shifted to my supposed inability to handle the situations in Côte d'Ivoire and Libya, when it is well known that it is the government of South Africa which impeded ECOWAS efforts to settle the Côte d'Ivoire crisis timeously and the same government that voted in favour of Resolution 1973 that authorised the bombing of Libya (African Union 10 July 2011).

Dlamini-Zuma's election gave South Africa a crucial strategic position at the AU with promises to focus on a policy that prevents inordinate Western – mainly French – interference in continental affairs. In what seemed like a bid to regain some of its radical credentials that were lost in its support for the UN resolution on Libya, South Africa couched the victory for the AU chairperson position as an anti-Western crusade. In a briefing before the AU vote, Nkoane-Mashabane stated that South Africa had been very clear that 'we want very good cordial relations with our cooperating partners, not based on colonial relations, or who colonised who' (Nkoane-Mashabane 2012). The ANC secretary general, Gwede Mantashe, was more explicit, noting that: 'We have shaken the AU because we have disorganised the French who always had a stronghold on the continent' (SABC 1 February 2012). But because of the high-handed manner of her election Dlamini-Zuma proceeded with caution to mend rifts arising out of her candidature, particularly when it emerged that Egypt, Ethiopia, Kenya, Nigeria, and Senegal had voted against her. Healing the wounds occasioned by South Africa's single-minded quest for AU's leadership has forced Dlamini-Zuma to downplay the image of being a South African candidate because her effectiveness hinges on carving an independent and autonomous position from Pretoria.

THE BATTLE OF BANGUI AND BEYOND

South Africa's intervention in the CAR that culminated in the death of thirteen soldiers in March 2013 epitomised the unilateralism that has marked Zuma's assertiveness in Africa. There have also been questions about the tenuous nature of South Africa's national interests in the Central Africa region as a whole. In the absence of any vital national interests, foreign policy toward the CAR has revolved around two main strands that have emerged in recent postures in Africa: first, the fixation with asserting South Africa's political and economic muscle in Francophone Africa to check French dominance; and second, the growing significance of ANC-linked commercial interests in Africa (Leon 2013; Mataboge, Underhill and de Wet 2013; Dawes 2013; Fabricius 2013b). These objectives converged in a combustible context of a civil conflict in the CAR that placed South African foreign policy in a difficult position – and, like the previous precipitous actions in Côte d'Ivoire, the policy on the CAR has dramatised South Africa's inability to work with regional actors who may be more knowledgeable about the dynamics of such conflicts.

Zuma inherited a February 2007 bilateral military agreement between Mbeki and the CAR government of President Francois Bozize in which South African forces would provide military training and refurbish the military infrastructure. The Mbeki administration took this opportunity to gain entry into French-speaking Africa and promote South Africa's pan-Africanist credentials. This agreement was renewed in December 2012 at an inauspicious moment when President Bozize was under renewed military pressure from a rebel coalition, Seleka, contesting his authoritarian rule. Following the renewal of the agreement, 200 out of the 400 anticipated South African troops were dispatched to Bangui without parliamentary approval or coordination with Dirco (Heitman 2013; Smith 2013a). At the same time, the embattled Bozize entered into negotiations with Seleka rebels that led to a power-sharing agreement in Libreville, Gabon, in January 2013 that sought to establish a transitional government and stop the escalation of the civil war. The rebels predicated compliance with the power-sharing agreement on the departure of the SANDF contingent because they saw South African troops as propping up the Bozize regime. But, as Minister Nkoane-Mashabane later acknowledged in an interview, President Zuma had rejected rebel demands, telling the AU in January 2013 that 'this new phenomenon where you have mutineers, referred to as rebels,[who] then go and negotiate power with a legitimately-elected government, should be stopped …because this is just another way of bringing about unconstitutional changes on our continent which should never be tolerated' (cited in Fabricius 2013a: 1).

Claiming that Bozize had reneged on the power-sharing agreement, Seleka launched a military offensive that captured Bangui and forced Bozize out of power in March 2013. It was during this offensive that the small and lightly-equipped SANDForce confronted 3 000 armed rebels in the battle for Bangui (Heitman 2013). During the confrontation, a regional military force under the auspices of the Economic Community of Central African States (ECCAS) did not intervene. Neither did the contingent of French forces that was in the CAR as a result of a 2010 defence agreement between President Nicholas

Sarkozy and Bozize (Smith 2013a; Smith 2013b; Mataboge and Underhill 2013).[3] South Africa's humiliating defeat coincided with the summit of BRICS nations in Durban where Pretoria attempted to showcase its leadership in Africa. Domestic criticisms of the debacle in Bangui focused on the opacity that surrounded the troop deployment, inconsistencies in the explanations for the deployment, and the monumental intelligence failures.[4] Rebutting allegations that South African soldiers were defending mining companies with ties to the ANC, Zuma claimed that the servicemen died for a worthy cause. 'They died in defence of the country's foreign policy. They died defending our commitment to the renewal of the African continent, and to the promotion of peace and stability which would lead to sustainable development in Africa. Our foreign policy is premised on the vision of building a better Africa and a better world' (*SAPA News* 3 April 2013). Defending the secrecy around the engagement, Zuma further noted:

> There must be an appreciation that matters of military tactics and strategy are not to be discussed in public … No country reveals and discusses its military strategies in the manner that South Africa is being expected to do. Those who are engaging in this game should be careful not to endanger both the national interest and the security of the republic. The problem with South Africa is that everybody wants to govern (*SAPA News* 3 April 2013).

In the aftermath of the imbroglio in the CAR, South Africa made veiled threats of reinforcing its military in the CAR to deal with the 'bandits in Bangui', but it soon bowed to domestic and regional pressures and withdrew its remaining forces in April 2013. In belated efforts to build bridges with regional leaders at an ECCAS summit in Chad, Zuma pledged to be 'guided by the continent as to next steps'(*News 24* 22 April 2013). But there was an appreciation of the limits of South Africa's role when ECCAS leaders made it clear that they preferred regional actors to take the lead on peace and security initiatives. Toward this end, ECCAS suggested the deployment of a regional multinational force of Central Africa (FOMAC) to help to stabilise the CAR but, in a measure to save South Africa's face, they promised to consider inviting South Africa to make a contribution to these efforts in future (Mataboge and Underhill 2013; Hartley and Kotch 2013). At the end of April 2013, amid the deterioration in security in the CAR, the Seleka government asked France and FOMAC to intervene to re-establish order. In early December 2013, as the CAR descended into further chaos, France pleaded with the UN Security Council to authorise the deployment of 3 600 African and French troops to restore stability. On a visit to South Africa in May 2013 to reach out to the Zuma administration, the prime minister of CAR warned against personalised relationships: 'We regret that the past relations with the former president (Bozize) were more personalised, and we are now aiming at improving these relations to be more at a state level. It was not the fault of President Zuma or the government of South Africa. It was because President Bozize was hiding the nature of the relationship between the two countries. We are convinced we have now entered a new chapter and that the relationship will be more transparent to both countries (*SAPA News* 28 April 2013).

Unlike the CAR engagement, South Africa's commitment to contribute a battalion to the Neutral Intervention Brigade (also known as the SADC Brigade) that would disarm and neutralise armed rebel groups in Eastern Congo is multilateral, above board, and has the endorsement of the United Nations and the AU. Yet it is also fraught with risks, primarily because of the size of the task and the obstacles of navigating the many actors and interests that continue to have stakes in the conflict. Moreover, although the Zuma government has reached out to Parliament on the engagement, there is still the formidable challenge of convincing a reluctant public about the wisdom of the deployment.

The stabilisation of Eastern Congo has proved difficult for the government of President Kabila of the DRC and remnants of the UN peacekeeping force, the UN Organisation and Stabilisation Mission in the DRC (MONUSCO) since the end of the civil war in the early 2000s. The combination of the prevalence of mineral resources and multiple militias has compounded the search for peace and security. In addition, armed rebel groups with strong links to Rwanda and Uganda have carved a strategic niche in the region to frustrate nation-building and state-building efforts. The security and humanitarian crisis in Eastern Congo deteriorated in October 2012 as a result of the military attacks on government forces by the March 23 Movement (M23), a movement linked to Rwanda and agitating for the rights of Tutsi-speaking Congolese. MONUSCO and government troops were outmanoeuvred by the M23 when it captured Goma in November 2012, presenting a grave danger to civilian lives and the credibility of international stabilisation efforts. New measures to resolve this crisis took two forms. First, through the mediation efforts of Uganda, leaders of M23 and the Kabila government began negotiations in Kampala starting in November 2012 to address rebel grievances. Second, the UN and regional actors converged around a new initiative of deploying a SADC force that would have the mandate to deal with the M23 and other rebel movements in Eastern DRC (Mataboge and De Wet 2013; Howden 2013).

South Africa was part of negotiations that led to the signing of the February 2013 Peace, Security, and Cooperation Framework for the DRC in which eleven states pledged to address the root causes of conflicts in Eastern Congo, including the establishment of the SADC brigade of 3 069 soldiers from South Africa, Malawi and Tanzania. Unlike MONUSCO, the SADC brigade has a stronger and independent mandate to conduct offensive operations against the armed groups. In mid-June 2013, South Africa announced the deployment of 1 300 soldiers as part of the SADC brigade (Fabricius 2013c). Given UN accusations of their complicity in funding M23 rebels, Rwanda and Uganda were not enthusiastic about the SADC brigade; instead, they preferred a stabilisation force under the auspices of the International Conference on the Great Lakes Region (ICGLR), an organisation that they can influence. The choice of a Tanzanian, rather than a South African commander to lead the SADC brigade was, in part, inspired by the need to address the perceptions that the brigade was a SADC imposition on the region. More ominously, in a propaganda campaign mailed to South African parliamentarians, the

M23 warned of 'continuous deadly combat' and 'high casualties' should SANDF engage them on their own turf. They further warned: 'President Zuma is meddling with affairs that do not concern him. South Africa's involvement in our problems is not going to benefit the region, so we have to wonder what motivations he has to send his troops to fight in the intervention force' (Myburgh and Sadiki 2013). In November 2013, South Africa achieved a major victory when the SADC Brigade routed the M23 out its strongholds in Eastern Congo, scattering its forces into Uganda and Rwanda. This was a remarkable show of force that may start to make a difference to the stabilisation of the region.

South Africa has accumulated wide experience in resolving conflicts in the Great Lakes that it can draw from in the SADC force for the Eastern DRC. But to avoid a long-drawn out and potentially open-ended involvement in the restoration of peace and stability, Pretoria would need to invest in diplomatic initiatives for comprehensive political solutions to the crises in the DRC and neighbouring countries. Even after the military defeat of the M23, finding a durable solution to the conflict will require political negotiations among all the groups involved in the conflict. Moreover, long-term solutions to instability in Eastern Congo depend on the resuscitation of functional security institutions that are locally owned. Similarly, diplomatic processes that assist Rwanda and Uganda to negotiate political settlements with rebel movements scattered across the Congo would be an important contribution to finding lasting political solutions to the instabilities that have engulfed the region since the mid-1990s.

CONCLUSION

There has never been any doubt about South Africa's leadership in Africa; the puzzle has always been the shape, content, and context of this leadership. Currently, South Africa contributes 15 per cent of the AU budget, and its chairperson has reinvigorated plans to establish a continental peacekeeping force. As in the Mbeki era, the Zuma administration is well placed to strengthen African institutions created in the last decade. These institutions remain saddled with weak mandates, few resources and unprofessional management. Yet effective leadership in Africa has often been collective and consensual, seizing small moments to make a difference while appreciating the constraints to leadership. South Africa has led well when it has scrambled sub-regional alliances anchored on the natural leaders within these domains. The creation of sub-regional coalitions recognises the imperative of subcontracting leadership roles in the circumstances of a fragmented and complex continent. A new momentum for the creation of functional African institutions needs to be recaptured through more consensus-building and collective arrangements. For South Africa, working with diverse African states is particularly pertinent because of the economic shifts that are producing some of the fastest growing economies in the world such as Ethiopia, Ghana, Tanzania and Nigeria. Flexing its muscles across Africa without a strategic vision is tantamount to squandered leadership; so is the projection of questionable power in the service of inchoate goals. Similarly, engagements on the continent that are ostensibly geared to counter Western designs – French, American, or otherwise – are not bound to be productive, especially when, as in the case of Mali and the CAR, African states ultimately turn to these countries for support.

REFERENCES

Alden C and G le Pere (2009) South Africa in Africa: Bound to lead? *Politikon* 36(1): 145-169.

Andreasson S (2011) Africa's prospects and South Africa's leadership potential in the emerging markets century. *Third World Quarterly* 32(6): 1165-1181.

Barber J (2005) The new South Africa's foreign policy principles and practice. *International Affairs* 81(5): 1079-1096.

Bischoff PH (2003) External and domestic source of foreign policy ambiguity: South African foreign policy and the projection of pluralist middle power. *Politikon* 30(2): 183-201.

Campbell H (2012) *NATO's Failure in Libya: Lessons for Africa.* Pretoria: Africa Institute of South Africa.

Cornish JJ (2011) 'AU leaders push for Libya "road map"'. *Business Day* 20 April.

Dawes N (2013) 'Central African Republic: How our leaders learned their lesson?' *Mail & Guardian* 15 April.

Habib A (2008) South Africa's Foreign Policy: Hegemonic Aspirations, Neoliberal Orientations and Global Transformation. Paper presented at the Regional Powers Network Conference at the German Institute of Global and Area Studies (CIGA), Hamburg, Germany, 15-16 September.

Habib A and N Selinyane (2006) Constraining the unconstrained: Civil society and South Africa's hegemonic obligation in Africa. In Carlsnaes W and P Nel (eds) *In Full Flight: South African Foreign Policy after Apartheid.* Midrand: Institute for Global Dialogue.

Heitman H (2013) 'How the deadly CAR battle unfolded' *Mail & Guardian.* 31March.

Howden D (2013) 'UN sanctions aggressive intervention in DRC'. *Mail & Guardian* 5 April.

Fabricius P (2013a) 'Are we seeing the emergence of a new 'Zuma doctrine' on Africa?' *The Star* 2 May.

Fabricius P (2013b) 'Is SA now big brother in Africa?' *The Star* 26 April.

Fabricius P (2013c) 'SA troops leave to fight rebels in Goma'. *The Sunday Independent* 16 June.

Finnan D (2011) 'Africa: AU mediators want Libya truce'. *AllAfrica.com* 10 April.

Hartley W and N Kotch (2013) 'Zuma Motlanthe march to different tunes on CAR'. *The Star* 25 April.

Kornegay F and C Landsberg (2009) Engaging emerging powers: Africa's Search for a common position. *Politikon* 36(1): 171-191.

Lamin AR (2005) *The Conflict in Cote d'Ivoire: South Africa's Diplomacy and Prospects for Peace.* Midrand: Institute for Global Dialogue Occasional Paper no. 49. August.

Landsberg C (2012) The Jacob Zuma government's foreign policy: Association or dissociation? *Austral: Brazilian Journal of Strategy and International Relations* 1(1): 75-102.

Landsberg C (2011) Transformation, continuity and diffusion. *Inroads* 29.

Landsberg C (2010) Thabo Mbeki's legacy of transformational diplomacy. In Glaser D (ed.) *Mbeki and After, Reflection on the Legacy of Thabo Mbeki.* Johannesburg: Wits University Press.

Landsberg C (2006) South Africa. In Khadiagala GM (ed.) *Security Dynamics in Africa's Great Lakes Region.* Boulder: Lynne Rienner.

Leon T (2013) 'CAR's Bozize is among the last of a dying breed. *Business Day* 2 April.

Maru MT (2012) Rethinking and reforming the African Union Commission elections. *African Security Review* 214(4): 64-78.

Masters L (2012) Opening the 'black box': South African foreign policymaking. In Landsberg C and J-A van Wyk (eds) *South African Foreign Policy Review, Volume 1.* Pretoria: Africa Institute.

Mataboge M and G Underhill (2013) 'Humiliated SA given its marching orders'. *Mail & Guardian* 5 April.

Mataboge M and P de Wet (2013) 'DRC rebels warn SA of massacre'. *Mail & Guardian* 12 April.

Mataboge M, G Underhill, and P de Wet (2013) 'SA, France battle for Africa'. *Mail & Guardian* 12 April.

Mbeki T (2011) What went wrong in Côte d'Ivoire. *Foreign Policy* 29 April.

McGowan P and F Ahwireng-Obeng (1998) Partner or hegemon? South Africa in Africa. *Journal of Contemporary African Studies* 16(2): 165-195.

Myburgh P-L and L Sadiki (2013) 'Zuma wants our oil'. *City Press* 28 April.

Nkoana-Mashabane M (2012) Press conference by the minister of international relations and cooperation following the election of AU Commission chairperson, 14 July.

Nkoana-Mashabane M (2009) Speech by the minister of international relations and cooperation to Heads of Mission Conference, 13 August.

Powell K and T Tieku (2005) The African Union's new security agenda: Is Africa closer to a Pax-Africana? *International Journal* 60(4): 937-952.

Presence C (2013) 'CAR attack should worry South Africa'. *The Star* 4 April.

Qobo M (2010) Refocusing South Africa's economic diplomacy: The 'African Agenda' and emerging powers. *South African Journal of International Affairs* 17(1): 13-28.

Schoeman M (2003) South Africa as an emerging power, 1994-2003. In *State of the Nation: South Africa 2003-2004*. Cape Town: HSRC Press.

Smith D (2013a) 'How Bozize lost his piece of Africa'. *Mail & Guardian* 28 March.

Smith D (2013b) 'Bangui is no stranger to armed revolt'. *Mail & Guardian* 28 March.

Sturman K (2011) 'Political intrigue undermines investments in the DRC'. *Mail & Guardian*.

Taljaard R (2008) 'South Africa lacks human rights based foreign policy'. *The Times* 13 July.

Thipanyane T (2011) South Africa's foreign policy under the Zuma government. Policy Brief. Pretoria: Africa Institute.

Vale P and S Maseko (1998) The African Renaissance. *International Affairs* 74(2).

Wehmhoerner A (2011) *South Africa's Foreign Policy: Quo Vadis?* Brussels: Foundation for European Progressive Studies.

Williams P (2011) From non-intervention to non-indifference: The origins and development of the African Union's security culture. *African Affairs* 106(423): 253-279.

Zuma on CAR: Decisions not SA's. *News 24*, 22 April 2013.

NOTES

1   Habib (2008:7) claims that 'Mbeki ... was humiliated in Côte d'Ivoire when his *bona fides* were questioned by Ivorian rebels.'

2   The involvement of Khulubuse Zuma's companies in oil exploration in the DRC surfaced soon after the new administration came to power. He is Jacob Zuma's nephew.

3   Amid reports that French troops were in control of the CAR international airport at the time the South African soldiers were attacked, a SANDF spokesperson, Brigadier Xolani Mabanga, noted: 'This implies that they [French forces] would go in and out of the airport. You have to ask what the role of the French was in that nation. We were in the CAR. They were in the CAR. The SANDF was attacked by the rebels. Were the French attacked by the rebels? One has to ask: Were the French on the side of the rebels, or were the rebels on the side of the French?' (Mataboge, Underhill and de Wet 2013:5).

4   Briefing Parliament's standing committee on defence, the minister of defence, Nosiviwe Mapisa-Nqakula, conceded the lack of preparedness by South African troops: 'We were not equipped in a way that will be able to repel that kind of battle. We were never deployed to the CAR to wage a battle. We never anticipated a battle' (Presence 2013).

CHAPTER 16

South Africa and Israel:
From alliance to enstrangement

Ran Greenstein

INTRODUCTION

A chapter on present-day relations between South Africa and Israel may not be an obvious component of a discussion of South Africa's position in the international arena. On the face of it, the current state of affairs between the two countries does not offer enough substance to justify paying it particular attention. If we look at South Africa's foreign policy with a view to examining its domestic and global economic and political implications, other countries may prove more rewarding. There is little doubt that the Brazil, Russia, India and China (BRIC) partners, as well as many big and medium-sized European, Asian and Latin American countries, have more extensive relations with South Africa than Israel has today.

But mere trading figures do not exhaust the story. We need to consider here the history of the relationship between the two countries, and questions of global diplomacy. These have been subject to intense political debates, both internal to South African society and external to it, becoming an issue of international concern. The extended notion of apartheid, taking it beyond its origins within South African borders, and its potential applicability to Israel/Palestine (in particular to the Arab territories occupied since 1967), has become a contested matter of interest to many in and outside these countries.

After a historical survey of the relations between the two countries, this chapter will examine the changing scene by focusing on political interventions and initiatives by South African forces, the implications of these for internal inter-communal relations between Jews and Muslims, and the analogy between apartheid South Africa and Israel.

HISTORICAL BACKGROUND

First, the history. For two decades, from the early 1970s to the early 1990s, Israel was apartheid South Africa's biggest partner for military and security-related exchanges: providing Israel with the raw materials necessary for the production of nuclear devices; joint programmes to develop advanced weapon systems, including artillery, aircraft and ballistic missiles (possibly with nuclear warheads) and training; and the more mundane trade in assault rifles, ammunition, military vehicles and other related security equipment. It is estimated that the military trade between the two countries amounted to US$10 billion over a period of twenty years (the most extensive discussion of this relationship is found in Polakow-Suransky 2010).

During that time, Israel's economic and military links with the USA were the only instance of an international relationship that eclipsed its South African partnership. At a crucial point in Israel's history, when it faced growing international isolation and big economic difficulties in the 1970s in the aftermath of the October 1973 war, meeting South Africa's military needs was a major factor in saving Israel from deep crisis. As for apartheid South Africa, because of the international campaign against it (and particularly the arms embargo imposed by the United Nations (UN)) it could not possibly have maintained such extensive relations with any other country.

It is important to keep in mind the international context. Until the late 1960s, Israel enjoyed diplomatic successes in sub-Saharan Africa. With the independence of many new countries, Israel managed to offer a range of training programmes and development projects in the agriculture, construction and military fields that were attractive to newly-formed elites on the continent. The Israeli-Arab conflict was off the global agenda at the time, and its specific Palestinian dimension was still largely dormant. With the end of the 1956 Sinai-Suez military campaign, relative calm on that front prevailed for about a decade. It did begin to acquire greater prominence with the formation of the Palestine Liberation Organisation (PLO) in 1964 (the first organised form of Palestinian national representation since the defeat of 1948) but at the time that step was seen more as a parochial intra-Arab affair than a major international development.

The lull in the Israel-Arab conflict, which coincided with the peak of African decolonisation, allowed Israel to offer a safe alternative to the continued dependence of African states on the old colonial powers, in areas in which it was willing and able to provide development aid. For this to become viable, Israel needed to create some distance between it and apartheid South Africa. When the prime minister, Hendrik Verwoerd, reportedly said in 1961: 'The Jews took Israel from the Arabs after the Arabs had lived there for a thousand years. Israel, like South Africa, is an apartheid state', it must have displeased Israeli officials. They did not appreciate the comparison, especially at a time when they sought to use access to the new Africa as a way to overcome the diplomatic exclusion they were facing in the Arab and Islamic worlds and large parts of Asia. But, for the time being at least, this did not interfere with Israel's position on the continent.

This relatively benign state of affairs began to change in 1967, when the Israeli-Arab conflict erupted again on the world stage in a spectacular fashion with the June war, in which Israel occupied the Egyptian Sinai, a territory technically in Asia but part of an African country. The resurgence of the Palestinian national movement after the war drew additional attention to questions of colonial rule, self-determination, and national liberation, in a way that re-positioned Israel within the same colonial camp that had dominated Africa before its independence. A gradual process of cooling off of relationships ensued, manifested in resolutions taken by African forums expressing solidarity with Arabs and Palestinians, and – from the early 1970s onward – the breaking off of diplomatic relations with Israel.

This trend started with a few cases only, but turned into a flood following the October 1973 war, in the course of which Israeli forces crossed the Suez Canal into Africa and took over Egyptian territory, albeit on a temporary basis. The combination of this breach of sovereignty with the intensifying Arab diplomatic campaign – backed up with new oil-based revenues – led to most African countries breaking off relations with Israel. Only South Africa and its satellite states (Swaziland, Lesotho and, further away, Malawi) did not follow suit. The shared position of diplomatic isolation brought these countries together.

South Africa was going through a somewhat similar process at the same time. From a position of powerful defiance of continental trends in the 1950s and 1960s, it started falling prey to growing internal dissent and external exclusion in the 1970s. The rise of the black consciousness movement and the workers' struggles in the early 1970s, combined with the victory of liberation movements in neighbouring countries (primarily Mozambique and Angola which gained their independence from Portugal in the mid-1970s) to undermine the position of the apartheid regime. The Soweto student uprising of 1976 gave further momentum to this development, followed by intensification of the international campaign of solidarity against apartheid. Diplomatically this was expressed in the suspension of South Africa from membership of the United Nations in 1974, and growing attempts to isolate the regime economically, militarily and diplomatically.

Israel and South Africa identified a common enemy responsible for their shared isolation: the emergence of a powerful alliance of Third World countries together with the Soviet Union and its satellites. This alliance was reinforced by political developments that affected the global scene in the 1970s, such as the defeat and retreat of US forces from Vietnam, the coup that saw the fall of Haile Selassie and the rise of the Mengistu regime in Ethiopia, the victory of the Sandinista Front in Nicaragua, and the popular uprising that led to the replacement of the Shah's regime with the Islamic Republic of Iran. That both Ethiopia and Iran had been close allies of Israel (and, in the case of Iran, of South Africa as well) was symbolically and materially important. It meant crucial regional political foundations were crumbling, and a new strategy was needed. This involved the domestic scene (local liberation movements), the regional scene (frontline states) and the global scene (the Soviet-led 'onslaught' as well as less than totally supportive US administrations).

This was the beginning of a 'beautiful friendship' that lasted for twenty years. The effective expulsion of South Africa from the UN coincided with the invitation of the Palestinian leader Yasser Arafat to address the General Assembly towards the end of 1974. These events were followed by the 1975 UN General Assembly Resolution 3379, which determined that Zionism was 'a form of racism and racial discrimination', recalling in the process a previous resolution (UNGA 3151) that condemned the 'unholy alliance between South African racism and Zionism'. All this left both countries with few other options if they wished to maintain their course of defiance of the growing international consensus against apartheid and in favour of the withdrawal of Israeli forces from the occupied Palestinian territories. An alliance based on a similar strategic position and a sense of being singled out and wronged by the world community was thus formed, but was kept secret for fear of giving more ammunition to critics and political opponents.

In a thorough review of the evolving relations, academic and journalist Sasha Polakow-Suransky (2010) outlined the dimensions of the alliance and the care its designers took to avoid public scrutiny. This was particularly the case with the Israeli side, which sought to retain its image as a Western liberal state deserving of support by fellow democratic regimes in Europe and North America. That image was already dented – but not yet severely so – by the prolonged occupation of 1967 and the ethnic cleansing of 1948, which made it possible for Israel to become a majority Jewish state and grant the remnant Palestinian population citizenship. It was, and still is, crucially important for the Israeli leadership to avoid being tainted by association with apartheid, as a concrete regime until the early 1990s and as a political-legal concept since then.

Historical events made this association stronger in the popular imagination. In particular, the Day of the Land uprising in March 1976, which saw tens of thousands of Palestinian citizens rising in protest against land confiscations, coincided with the Soweto uprising in June of that year; the first Intifada (popular uprising against the occupation) that erupted in the Palestinian territories in December 1987, and continued until the early 1990s, coincided with the last stage of the mass mobilisation of the anti-apartheid movement inside South Africa. Images of youths marching and throwing stones, facing heavily-armed security forces, tear gas and live bullets, were common in both cases. However, subsequent external events intervened to deflect attention from the Palestinian struggle: the process of negotiations and subsequent peace agreement between Israel and Egypt, which started in 1977, and the Gulf war of 1991, which saw Palestinians siding with the Iraqi regime, led to their losing much diplomatic support as a result.

Follow-up developments saw a change: the Oslo accords of 1993 gave the impression that a historical reconciliation between Israeli-Jewish and Palestinian-Arab nationalisms was being implemented. And, of course, it coincided with the political transition in South Africa which culminated in the 1994 inclusive democratic elections and the rise of the African National Congress (ANC) to political dominance. The change

in Israeli-Palestinian relations was too late to make much of a difference to the negative image of the Israeli state in southern Africa. Significantly, Israel was the only state
that was not invited to the Namibian independence celebrations and the inauguration of
President Nujoma in 1990. While it was invited to the inauguration of President Mandela
in 1994, its presence was clearly shadowed by the public enthusiasm expressed at that
event for its most vilified erstwhile opponent, Palestinian leader Yasser Arafat.

THE POST-1994 TRANSITION

For obvious reasons 1994 signalled the end of the close relationship between the two
countries. The new ANC-led government had no need for an exclusive partnership with
Israel. Its military needs – or rather such needs as defined by its political elites – were
different from those of the apartheid regime, and could be satisfied from other sources
(primarily western European countries and companies). The infamous arms deal of the
mid-late 1990s, which led to turmoil in the ruling party, and has had serious political
and economic implications, bypassed Israel completely. Despite the pragmatic attitude
adopted by the ANC government in its diplomatic efforts and international relations,
rewarding the apartheid state's most important military partner was not a priority, especially when South Africa became free from the isolation imposed by anti-apartheid sanctions. Even if the new government was not bent on revenge on Israel for its past collaboration with the apartheid regime, it clearly did not see any reason to provide it with
preferential treatment.

The Israeli military establishment also showed a more cautious attitude. South Africa
began to cultivate good relations with countries that were considered to be the Israeli
state's biggest enemies (Iran, Iraq, Libya, Syria), and the fear that imported technology
and weapons systems would find their way to those regimes acted as a break on the usual
zeal for selling Israeli military products. That South Africa itself became an important
arms manufacturer and exporter, and thus a competitor in overseas markets, made Israeli
state and military officials wary of having too close a relationship with their former partners. The simultaneous rise of new clients with an almost insatiable appetite for military
and technologically-driven security systems – China and India in particular – made the
South African market less important in Israeli eyes.

To appreciate the post-1994 circumstances, we need to go back to the question of why
Israel was the only country to have had such intensive military relations with apartheid
South Africa. Two main and related reasons for the military alliance can be advanced:

- A tactical reason: the similar position of the two countries in the relevant period
  (early 1970s to early 1990s), as pariah states on the international scene, and
- A strategic reason: their similar origins in prolonged conflict between indigenous
  people and settler political movements.

The first reason clearly is no longer relevant. It stemmed from a specific conjuncture that
passed away together with the Soviet bloc and the Cold War. Changing global relations

have extricated Israel from its diplomatic isolation and also opened the way to the deal that facilitated political transitions in southern Africa. The second reason, however, continues to shape the relationship between the two countries. Its consequences are visible in three areas:

- The historical similarities between the two conflict situations have made South African political forces particularly sensitive to the Israeli-Palestinian conflict. As a result, the South African government and independent activists have tried to play an interventionist role as mediators, generally without much success, as well as leaders in political initiatives. These include the imposition of a requirement by the Department of Trade and Industry (DTI) to mark products from Jewish settlements in the occupied Palestinian territories; the government-sponsored study by the HSRC to determine whether Israeli rule in the occupied territories is a form of colonialism and apartheid; and the recent support by the ANC for the sanctions campaign against Israel.
- The intense interest in the conflict has given rise to a clash between domestic constituencies identifying with different sides. This refers above all to elements within the Jewish and Muslim communities in the country, but also to other activists and solidarity movements. Although both ethnic/religious communities are fairly small and the clash has not affected the bulk of the population who belong to neither, it has become a topic of concern in some settings.
- The symbolic legacy of the anti-apartheid struggle has made analogies with Israel/Palestine powerful politically, both as an analysis of the situation and as a recipe for change. This use of the symbolism goes well beyond South African boundaries and has become an important issue in global solidarity politics and debates around them. The role some South African activists play in all this is visible – especially with regard to well-known and respected campaigners such as Desmond Tutu and Ronnie Kasrils – and they frequently draw on their expertise in being subject to oppression and struggling against it in South Africa (without necessarily demonstrating similar expertise on Israel/Palestine itself).

In contrast to these explicit political focus areas, ongoing economic relations between the two countries present an unremarkable picture. The only item that stands out is rough diamonds, which are sold by South African companies to Israel to be polished there and exported to other countries. The figures for this trade are difficult to establish since the diamonds are usually bought from international exchange centres in Europe (mainly Antwerp and London) rather than directly from South Africa. Israeli trade statistics normally exclude diamonds because the value added in Israel itself is relatively small in relation to the total value of the trade (it inflates both the import and export side of the balance of trade).

In what follows I focus on the three aspects mentioned above: steps taken as political intervention, domestic inter-communal involvement, and the role of the apartheid analogy in local and global solidarity campaigns.

INTERVENTIONS

Various initiatives in the last few years received extensive media attention. I deal with three such issues in particular: academic exchanges between the University of Johannesburg (UJ) and Ben-Gurion University (BGU) in Beersheba, Israel; the decision of the DTI to label goods originating in Jewish settlements in the occupied Palestinian territories; and the ANC's resolutions on Palestine. All these are related to the boycotts, divestment and sanctions campaign that is global in scope but serves as an organising framework for local activists.

The relations between UJ and BGU became subject to public debate in 2010, when a memorandum of understanding between the two institutions came up for renewal. The UJ Senate decided to form a committee that would study the issue and recommend how to proceed. The Committee could not decide whether BGU was complicit in discrimination against Palestinians, but established that the University conducted research and maintained other engagements that supported the Israeli military, in particular in its occupation of Gaza. It therefore found that 'as a university embedded in a highly militarised Israeli society, BGU's obligation to implement state policies, and its research and other relationships with the Israeli armed forces, does have a significant impact on the society, and therefore on the continued subjugation of the Palestinian population in Israel.'

The Committee recommended that UJ not continue the same relationship with BGU and that its policy should be guided by the following principles: 'In support of the principle of solidarity with any oppressed population (a defining principle emanating from our own history), we should take leadership on this matter from peer institutions among the Palestinian population', and this must be done to 'encourage reconciliation and the advancement of human dignity and human solidarity'.

On that basis the Senate was asked to endorse a process of consultation with Palestinian universities to include one or more of them chosen by agreement between the two original partners and ensure that the project 'will not entail any activity, including teaching and research, which has any direct or indirect military implications or contributes to the abuse of human rights'. Six months were given for the effort to put a new agreement in place. Subsequently, in March 2011, the Senate voted to allow the agreement with BGU to lapse, due to failure to meet the conditions set in the 2010 resolution, 'among them the inclusion of Palestinian university partners'. UJ made it clear that the vote did not call for a total boycott of BGU and did not preclude individual academics from proceeding with collaboration projects. Indeed, months later an agreement between researchers from the two universities was concluded, with no formal relationship between the two institutions.

This was hailed, inaccurately, by activists as a victory for the academic boycott campaign. UJ consciously avoided making such an overall decision and restricted itself to the question at hand: a specific agreement with a specific institution. Yet inevitably the issue became implicated in global solidarity politics. Several aspects of the story are of particular interest beyond the concrete details:

- It attracted considerable public attention which allowed it to escape the normal fate of scientific collaboration in a fairly obscure field of study which rarely receives media coverage. In fact, hardly any of the public intervention showed interest in the content of the collaboration or its possible academic outcomes (the project involved research in the field of water, but if it had been on poetry, banking systems or sports injuries, it would have made no difference to the debate). It was treated purely as a political issue.
- The identity of the specific institutions proved equally irrelevant: collaboration between South African and Israeli institutions was at issue, not the details of the partners. Attempts by the campaigners to present information about BGU and the collaborative research programme were met with indifference. It is likely that collaboration between, say, UKZN and Tel Aviv University would have met with exactly the same response.
- While the immediate stakes were clear – continued institutional collaboration or its termination – the concrete political outcomes desired by those involved in the debate (for and against the research agreement) were not. Was the campaign meant to apply pressure on the specific Israeli university or on the broad academic establishment in that country, on public opinion in general or on the Israeli government? And what concrete changes in policy could have been expected, given that the campaign targeted abuse by Israeli military forces rather than directly by academic institutions? In other words, the mechanisms of political pressure envisaged by the campaign were never made obvious.

These aspects of the UJ-BGU campaign were not unique to it; there were similarities in other academic and cultural boycott efforts in the last few years in Europe and North America. Of significance here is that the entire global solidarity campaign known as BDS (Boycotts, Divestment and Sanctions) is based on the notion that the anti-apartheid struggle in South Africa relied heavily on such tactics and was successful because of them. By implication, if the Palestinian movement which faces similar conditions uses similar methods, it will achieve similar results (restoration of rights and political liberation). The logic behind this assumption is not always presented in these explicit terms but it dominates the campaign.

South Africans are better positioned than solidarity activists elsewhere to set the record straight and identify the core strength of the anti-apartheid movement: its grounding in local conditions and its consequent reliance on mass action in the streets, factories, schools, townships and communities. Its ability to generate support overseas and enjoy the solidarity of thousands of committed activists was based on its widely-recognised claim to represent the South African masses and lead them in their struggle through the ANC, United Democratic Front (UDF), Congress of South African Trade Unions (Cosatu) and other mass organisations. The slogan 'one person, one vote' provided a banner behind which masses inside and outside the country could unify.

In contrast, the Palestinian solidarity movement in South Africa (and elsewhere) operates without an equivalent leadership and unifying slogans, and does not follow a local mass movement that enjoys broad support from grassroots activists. It seeks to replicate the achievements of the anti-apartheid solidarity movement with no substantive anti-apartheid mass movement of its own with which to be in solidarity. It acts as if the cart could pull the proverbial horses rather than the other way around. The absence of a mass movement on the ground in Israel/Palestine itself is not a result of a failure by solidarity activists, of course, but they must take this into account when aiming to develop strategies building on the South African experience. The crucial difference between the apartheid regime with its massive dependence on cheap and exploitable black labour power, and the Israeli regime which historically has relied on the labour power of immigrant Jews, is behind this contrast. Labour exploitation allowed for the creation of a mass movement of workers seeking to overturn the apartheid regime from within, while Palestinians have been restricted to a large extent to struggling against the oppressive regime from without. Uplifting but hollow slogans about similarity of conditions and strategies of struggle cannot hide this deep sociopolitical difference.

A recent and potentially more significant campaign involved the DTI in a debate over labelling products from Jewish settlements in the Occupied Palestinian Territories. These settlements are illegal under international law and are not recognised as falling within Israeli territory – yet products made in such settlements have been marketed overseas under the label of 'Made in Israel'. This has given rise to two related campaigns. The first calls for a boycott of products, in particular two items that are marketed globally and in South Africa: Ahava Dead Sea cosmetics and Sodastream. The second campaign calls to remove the 'Made in Israel' label, and no doubt many activists see it as a first step towards banning such products altogether. The campaigns are not unique to South Africa; calls for consumer boycotts of these products have been widespread.

Prompted by a campaign of local solidarity organisation, the DTI issued in 2011 a notice of its intention to prohibit the use of the label 'Made in Israel' for products made beyond the recognised Israeli boundaries (known as the 'Green Line'), which had existed before 5 June 1967. In the notice and press releases Minister Rob Davies reiterated the South African government's position which recognises the State of Israel only within these borders, excluding the territories occupied by Israel in the course of the June 1967 war.

Justified in terms of the Consumer Protection Act of 2008, the notice targeted inaccurate labelling as misleading South African consumers as to the origins of the products in question. Initially, the regulation sought to replace the label of Israel with that of 'Israeli Occupied Territory'. The intention to label the settlement products differently and, in particular, the choice of that new label raised serious concerns among Israeli state agencies and their local supporters. This was for two reasons: the notice made a distinction between legitimate Israeli boundaries and illegitimate conquests. It thus undermined Israel's stance that the territories were subject to negotiations and that some of them would become part of Israel in any future agreement. Although South Africa was following other countries in rejecting this claim, it was the first to enshrine it in its domestic legislation. In addition, the specific terminology used was blunt and broke away from the more diplomatic language used by European and American states. It asserted without qualifications that the territories were occupied rather than merely 'disputed' or 'administered', as is commonly claimed by Israel.

Local advocates for the Israeli state – the organised Jewish community as well as opposition parties (the Inkatha Freedom Party, the African Christian Democratic Party, the Shembe Church) – intervened in order to change the policy or at least moderate the language; it is likely that Israel exerted diplomatic pressure behind the scenes. These forces failed in their first goal: early in 2013 the regulation was formally endorsed and implemented. But they did succeed in the second goal: the reference to the occupation was removed. Instead, the new approved labels were 'Gaza: Israeli Goods', 'East Jerusalem: Israeli Goods', and 'West Bank: Israeli Goods'. In addition, the DTI clarified that it was not banning these products and not calling for a boycott but simply putting in place a technical correction.

This move to adopt a neutral language and depoliticise the debate is unlikely to settle the issue. The official Israeli position rejects any distinction between Israel proper and its post-1967 settlements (even with the use of such mild terms), and solidarity activists are not happy with the evasive solution, which avoids explicitly acknowledging the military occupation and the illegality of the Israeli settlements in the territories. As similar proposals to label settlement products are pending in the European Union, where many countries wish to use the South African example to bolster their own initiatives in this regard, the matter will not rest.

The third initiative involves the African National Congress. The question of Israel/ Palestine is a minor one on the international agenda of the ANC, but it does make a regular appearance in its conference resolutions, the latest of which were adopted in Mangaung in December 2012. These are consistent with the line taken by the ANC over the last three decades, which expresses solidarity with the struggle of the Palestinian people for freedom and independence. The conference supported statehood and UN membership for Palestine and was 'unequivocal in its support for the Palestinian people in their struggle for self-determination, and unapologetic in its view that the Palestinians are the victims and the oppressed in the conflict with Israel' (ANC 2012). With this in mind, it committed itself to 'solidarity efforts supporting a just solution including the strengthening of a sovereign independent state of Palestine, which will help to bring peace to the region and end conflict between Israelis and Palestinians'. It called for 'a united solidarity campaign' in South Africa, and support for 'the programmes and campaigns of the Palestinian civil society which seek to put pressure on Israel to engage with the Palestinian people to reach a just solution.'

The last call above could be a reference to the BDS campaign, which seeks to apply external pressure on Israel, including cultural and academic boycotts. No specific mention of the movement or of boycotts and sanctions as tactics in struggle and solidarity was made although the clause was interpreted in this way by some activists on both sides of the political divide, but it seems that the ANC was careful not to make an explicit commitment to the campaign. It is also necessary to distinguish here between the ANC as a party and as the South African government, whose policies are not determined by the conference resolutions.

INTRA-COMMUNITY RELATIONS

An important dimension of the debates over Israel/Palestine in South Africa is that they involve local people not only on the basis of their political positions and degree of identification with one side or another, but also as members of religious or ethnic communities that regard the issue as of particular concern; this means Jews and Muslims in particular but some Christian churches as well. Communities are internally divided on many grounds and not all of their members share the same political positions, but in this case each side – the State of Israel and the Palestinian national movement – enjoys a 'natural' constituency that expresses its solidarity predictably. The Jewish community is the smaller of the two, and relatively homogeneous, and therefore more directly affected by debates on Israel. South African Muslims share religion with the majority of Palestinians but not ethnicity, language or cultural heritage, and thus operate at a certain remove.

Another aspect of the issue – inevitable in the South African context – is race. Officially, Jews regarded as white under apartheid, while Muslims belonged to the Indian and coloured groups. Like many other white people, Jews, especially those who belong to the organised community, feel politically marginalised in the new South Africa. Even mild criticisms of Israeli policies voiced by government officials and civil society activists, and vague statements by ANC structures in support of Palestinians, give rise to angry, fearful and resentful sentiments in Jewish community media. They feel constantly on the defensive, as if the ANC/government were seriously targeting Israel rather than paying lip service to maintain their erstwhile international radical credentials.

Two recent incidents reinforced this sense of being under siege. An Israeli-born pianist, residing in Germany, performed at a musical event at the University of the Witwatersrand in March 2013. The event was organised with some financial sponsorship from the Israeli Embassy in Pretoria, and was disrupted by students organised by the Wits Students Representative Council. Although the concert was open to the public, many in the crowd were community members who must have regarded it almost as an internal event. They felt they were being attacked in their 'own' space, as responses in community media indicate, and were particularly incensed at the students' portrayal of the event as a propaganda device for the Israeli state. The gap between perceptions of the two sides was huge, and only partly mitigated by the response of university authorities who opened disciplinary procedures against the students involved. A subsequent concert featuring Israeli musicians at Wits in August 2013 intensified the acrimony amid accusations of 'racial profiling' by the concert organisers, and antisemitism expressed in chants of 'shoot the Jews' by some of the student protesters.

The other event was of a more clearly political character. A celebration of Israel's Independence Day at Gold Reef City in April 2013 was again disrupted by activists affiliated with a variety of movements including the ANC and Cosatu. Both the event itself and the protesters had a higher profile than the Wits music event. Physical altercations in the course of the protest heightened the tensions, and the legal procedures in its aftermath are still unfolding. Of interest here is that one of the organisations taking part in the protest was a dissident Jewish group that has adopted a critical attitude towards Israeli state policies and the complicity of Jewish community institutions in them. It had been active for while before the event and indicates a level of division internally that makes it impossible to speak of communities as if they were unified entities (although it clearly represents only a small minority of Jews in South Africa).

Operating under the name of Stop the JNF, this group of activists invoked Jewish memory of 'our own painful history of oppression' (BDS 2013) as a compelling reason for speaking out against human rights violations committed by the State of Israel 'in our name', against the Palestinian people. It directly distances itself from claims by the South African Jewish Board of Deputies and the South African Zionist Federation to be speaking on behalf of all South African Jews, particularly when it comes to the Israel/Palestine issue. The problem is not just blind support for Israeli policies, but neglect of 'one of the hallmarks of Judaism: respectful debate amongst those who hold divergent viewpoints', which leads to attempts to stifle opposing voices within the community.

Stop the JNF expresses support for the South African government in 'taking a clear stance against Israel's violations of international law and its acts of violence against the Palestinian people' (BDS 2013). This is expressed in the actions by the DTI, and the hope 'that the ANC and the SA government goes further and completely bans Israeli settlement products', as they are in violation of international law and undermine any chance of a just peace. These positions are adopted in the spirit of a 'proud Jewish tradition of respect for justice and human rights; regardless of race, religion or creed.'

The idea behind the campaign is to target the Jewish National Fund (JNF), historically and currently the main land settlement agency in Israel/Palestine. It has played a crucial role in acquiring land, using legal and financial means before 1948, and state power and military coercion afterwards, resulting in the ethnic cleansing and dispossession of hundreds of thousands of Palestinians. This was not just a once-off historical incident that took place in a period of war, but an ongoing process that continues to this day. In June 2013, the Israeli Parliament adopted a plan of resettlement of Arab Bedouins in the Negev, which would see the dispossession of tens of thousands from their ancestral land and their forcible relocation to new townships. The JNF is playing an important role in this process, as it does in supporting illegal settlements in the 1967 occupied Palestinian territories.

A specific South African involvement was highlighted in June 2013, in a documentary film produced by two local Jewish activists, telling the story of the South Africa Forest, planted with donations from the local Jewish community on the ruins of the Palestinian village of Lubya, whose residents were forced to flee the place in 1948. This took place in the framework of a systematic campaign by the JNF to disguise the traces of Palestinian existence in the country, by demolishing villages and other physical structures and then planting trees over the remains to make it appear as if the land had been empty and desolate until it was made to 'bloom' under the new State of Israel. An important part of mainstream Jewish education is to instil respect for the work of the JNF as an ecological and developmental agency while ignoring its role in entrenching exclusion and dispossession. Stop the JNF aims to counteract this effort from within the community, though it faces great difficulties in this endeavour.

THE APARTHEID ANALOGY

The various manifestations of Israeli/Palestinian solidarity politics discussed above would have been of marginal interest in a global context if it were not for the crucially symbolic role South Africa has come to play in them. This is not because of the inherent importance of South Africa in the global arena today but, rather, due to the historical resonance of the notion of apartheid and its applicability to the case of the Israeli regime and its mode of rule over Palestinian subjects.

Prodigious efforts have been made by Palestinians and their supporters to attach the label of apartheid to Israeli state practices, and by Israel and its supporters to reject its relevance. When affirmations and denials of the analogy come from South Africa they acquire additional weight – after all, who is better positioned to pronounce on the matter than South Africans, often regarded as the world specialists on the topic?

This logic is not unassailable, however. South Africans have experienced apartheid directly, but even informed statements about the suitability of the apartheid analogy need to demonstrate a level of knowledge of Israel/Palestine that goes beyond the superficial images presented by popular media. Whether we refer to Judge Richard Goldstone and journalist Benjamin Pogrund, who act as apologists for the Israeli state, or Archbishop Desmond Tutu and veteran activist Ronnie Kasrils, who condemn Israeli policies, there is a clear imbalance between their great expertise on South Africa and limited understanding of Israel/Palestine which makes them unreliable as experts on the topic. Of course, this is not to deny the value that the moral exhortations of Desmond Tutu bring to the solidarity campaign, or the power of the legal scholarship offered by John Dugard, special rapporteur to the UN Human Rights Council. Rather, it is to recognise that concerned South Africans are not necessarily authorities on historical questions related to Israel/Palestine, or on the appropriate political strategies that flow from them.

It is important, however, to recognise two useful contributions to the understanding of the Israeli regime and its oppressive policies made or inspired by South Africans. The first is the 2009 study by the state-funded Human Sciences Research Council (HSRC), which concluded that Israel was practising colonialism and apartheid in the occupied Palestinian territories. Having assembled an international team of scholars and practitioners of international law from South Africa, the UK, Israel and Palestine, the HSRC conducted a detailed investigation titled 'Occupation, Colonialism, Apartheid?' to assess Israel's practices in the occupied territories in light of international law.

The research team found that Israel's laws and policies in the Occupied Territories fit the definition of apartheid in the International Convention on the Suppression and Punishment of the Crime of Apartheid. These policies allocate or deny rights and privileges in a differentiated manner, on the basis of their ethnic-national identities, to Jewish settlers and indigenous Palestinians living in the same territory. They restrict Palestinians to 'reserves' in the West Bank, reserves which they cannot leave without a permit. In this sense these policies are similar to grand apartheid, which confined black South Africans to homelands whereas white South Africans enjoyed freedom of movement and full civil and political rights in the rest of the country. This system of domination is legitimised by the invocation of 'security' in order to 'validate sweeping restrictions on Palestinian freedom of opinion, expression, assembly, association and movement', and thereby to 'maintain control over Palestinians as a group' (HSRC 2009).

That such policies differentiate between people on the basis of ethnicity and religion rather than race – as was the case in apartheid South Africa – makes no difference to the substance of the discriminatory regime. It is important to note here that the study was restricted to Israeli policies in the Occupied Territories, and did not address other aspects of the Israeli-Palestinian conflict in the Palestinian Diaspora and in Israel in its pre-1967 boundaries.

A subsequent process took such analysis further. The Russell Tribunal on Palestine, which operated between 2010 and 2013, was an attempt by civil society and legal activists to examine critically various aspects of Israeli policies and practices vis-à-vis Palestinians more broadly, not just in the Occupied Territories. Several sessions were convened, that of most interest being the Cape Town session in November 2011 which tackled the apartheid question directly. Bringing together Palestinian, Israeli and South African witnesses, of diverse activist, legal and academic backgrounds, the Tribunal concluded that 'Israel subjects the Palestinian people to an institutionalised regime of domination amounting to apartheid as defined under international law. This discriminatory regime manifests in varying intensity and forms against different categories of Palestinians depending on their location', with those living under military rule in the Occupied Territories subject to 'a particularly aggravated form of apartheid'. Palestinian citizens of Israel have the right to vote but are 'excluded from the benefits of Jewish nationality and subject to systematic discrimination across the broad spectrum of recognised human rights.' Regardless of these differences, the Tribunal concluded, 'Israel's rule over the Palestinian people, wherever they reside, collectively amounts to a single integrated regime of apartheid' (Russell Tribunal 2011).

The Tribunal did not undertake a detailed historical study to examine the specific mechanisms of domination as they evolved over time, and the various social arrangements and political trajectories that became viable at different points in time. It did provide a legal framework that could be used to further our understanding of current conditions and potentially develop strategies to overturn them. While its operation was only partly based in South Africa and on the notion of apartheid, this specific focus was an important element of the process, and may open up additional avenues of investigation and activism in the future.

CONCLUSIONS

The discussion in this chapter should be seen in the context of a long-term shift in South Africa's global position and policies. Under apartheid its leadership sought in vain to be admitted to the Western club and was shunned by African and Third World states. The immediate post-apartheid era saw its return to international bodies and alliances, reflecting the glow of the 1994 transition and Nelson Mandela's iconic status as a global statesman. Over the years South Africa's quest to be seen as a modern democratic state, an integral part of the technologically advanced capitalist economies, declined in importance. Under Thabo Mbeki, alliances with alternative forces became a strategic goal of foreign policy. This stemmed partly from economic reasons – growing trade relations with China and India – and partly from an ideological orientation focused on challenging the global power structure by aligning South Africa with Russia, China, Brazil, and the Arab and Islamic worlds, all unified by desire to undermine Western hegemony.

In this environment relations with Israel have low priority. Economically it is more lucrative and diplomatically it is more fruitful to nurture alliances with other African countries (as markets for South African goods and reservoirs of diplomatic support for South African efforts to speak on behalf of Africa to the world), Middle Eastern countries (as markets, providers of oil, and partners in business deals), and emerging Asian powers – obviously China and India but also mid-level states such as Malaysia and Indonesia. This overall shift frames the issue of Israel. There is little to be gained from good relations with a country that is ostracised by many states in Africa and Asia and is a die-hard ally of the US and of Western powers in general. Israel and South Africa offer similar products to potential clients – arms, technical expertise, security systems – and thus are more competitors than potential partners.

Domestic politics also play a part. Catering to the sensitivities of the organised Jewish community brings no benefits to the ANC, and radical-sounding rhetoric of solidarity with Palestinians carries with it potential advantages (Muslim voters, especially in the Western Cape) with little cost. With such considerations in mind it is likely that the cold attitude towards Israel will continue and the erstwhile close partners will remain distant acquaintances. The response of the Israeli foreign minister, Avigdor Lieberman,[1] to the South African minister of international relations and cooperation, Maite Nkoana-Mashabane, may be an indicator of the future. When Nkoana-Mashabane announced in November 2013 that South African government officials will not visit Israel in solidarity with Palestinians, since 'the struggle of the people of Palestine is our struggle', Lieberman called on local Jews to flee the country because its government is creating a hostile atmosphere that would lead to pogroms against them. South African Jewish leaders rejected Lieberman's call as alarmist and inflammatory[2] but it is clear that open confrontation is not something of which the Israeli leadership is afraid. At the same time, it is unlikely that a sharp break between the two countries will take place. Calls by activists to break off diplomatic relations with Israel or to impose sanctions have little appeal to a South African government that is keen to boost its radical credentials locally and globally but stands to gain nothing from adopting a position that is at odds with its partners. We must remember that the critical diplomatic stance of China and Russia does not hinder them from engaging in lucrative economic and military deals with Israel, and South Africa has no reason to act differently. There will be no return to the close alliance of the years 1974 to 1994, and the cooling-off period from 1994 to 2014 can be expected to continue.

REFERENCES

ANC (2012) Recommendations from the 4th National Policy Conference June 2012. www.anc.org.za/docs/pol/2012/policy_conferencev.pdf.

BDS South Africa (2013) As Jews with our own painful history of oppression. http://www.bdssouth-africa.com/2011/12/as-jews-with-our-own-painful-history-of.html.

HSRC (2009) Occupation, Colonialism, Apartheid?: A Re-assessment of Israel's Practices in the Occupied Palestinian Territories Under International Law. http://electronicintifada.net/files/090608-hsrc.pdf

Polakow-Suransky S (2010) *The Unspoken Alliance: Israel's Secret Relationship with Apartheid South Africa*. New York: Vintage.

Russell Tribunal on Palestine (2011) Report of the Cape Town Session. http://www.russelltribuna-lonpalestine.com/en/sessions/south-africa/south-africa-session-%E2%80%94-full-findings/cape-town-session-summary-of-findings.

NOTES

1   Israeli parliamentarian Avigdor Lieberman was the former foreign minister at the time he made the statement, but was re-appointed foreign minister a few days later.

2   See for instance http://www.iol.co.za/news/south-africa/sa-jews-dismiss-call-to-flee-to-israel-1.1602699#.UoNpkt_FsUQ for details of the episode.

CHAPTER 17

South Africa's economic ties with north-east Asia

Scarlett Cornelissen

INTRODUCTION

Most present-day assessments of South Africa's ties with Asia focus on the country's relationship with the People's Republic of China (PRC). This is in the context of recent closer economic engagement between China and the wider African continent, and pronounced investments by China in some of South Africa's strategic sectors. Diplomatic interaction between the two countries has also deepened and become more distinctive, as signified by the conclusion of a Comprehensive Strategic Partnership Agreement in 2010.

Yet there are important dynamics in the economic and political relationships between South Africa and other Asian countries that are often disregarded. Connections between South Africa and India, Indonesia and Malaysia, for instance, have been forged through major processes of migration, settlement and cultural interlinkages that significantly shaped South Africa's political economy and sociocultural setting over the years, and that continue to be major influences in the relations among the countries. The Bandung spirit, further, has been a pervasive force in diplomatic ties between post-apartheid South Africa and those states.

There is also relatively little exploration of South Africa's links with other north-east Asian states beyond China, despite a lengthy and important history of economic and political interaction and, in the contemporary era, new types of engagement. Diplomatic ties between South Africa and Japan, for instance, date back more than a hundred years, and Japan has been an influential investor in South Africa's economy since the 1970s. After the end of apartheid, Japan continued to be one of South Africa's leading trade partners. Although its economic role has been smaller, South Korea has been another significant actor from the north-east Asian region. Outward expansion in recent years by Korean multinational enterprises such as Samsung, Hyundai and Kia has come to influence the corporate and consumer landscape in South Africa in important ways.

This chapter discusses the patterns and dynamics in South Africa's ties with north-east Asia, centring on the three major powers of that region: China, Japan and South Korea. First, the three countries are the principal economies in their region and they have large investment footprints in Asia and beyond; China and Japan are respectively the second and third largest economies in the world (with China's economic output originally eclipsing Japan's in 2010). Second, there is a history of political interlinkage and economic interdependence among the three that has shaped their engagements with other parties in Asia as well as with other regions. The last point is significant, thirdly, because in recent years all three countries have been fostering new types of ties with developing countries and have been positioning themselves as economic and political partners on the African continent as manifested in increased investments in African economies by the three Asian countries and the creation of multilateral aid and development platforms such as the Tokyo International Conference on African Development (TICAD), the Forum on China-Africa Cooperation (FOCAC), and the Korea-Africa Forum. There also appears to be growing rivalry as each of the three seeks to establish a stronger foothold on the continent.

Fourth, it is not only the nature, but also the substantive underpinnings of north-east Asia's relations with Africa that have seen significant shifts in recent years. Greater involvement by China, along with a change in international discourse about investment potentials on the continent, has spurred interest from the other north-east Asian players to explore growth opportunities. Fifth, within this setting, South Africa's relations with the north-east Asian states assume distinctive and strategic significance as the country is viewed variously as an entry point into the wider African economy, as an opportunity to enhance presence by the Asian countries in key industries in particular African sub-regions or, given South Africa's political standing, as an important diplomatic partner in Africa and with potential influence in other multilateral settings.

The chapter explores trajectories and tendencies in the relations between South Africa and the north-east Asian powers and contextualises and explains them against the way in which Asia's interests in Africa are shifting. It seeks to answer two analytical questions. What is the nature of the Asian countries' economic role in South Africa, and what are the primary drivers? How do these relate to South Africa's economic and industrial strategies and what are the attendant effects on political relationships with the Asian powers? In the next section, a historical contextualisation is provided of ties between South Africa, China, Japan and South Korea, and the pertinent features of interaction in the post-apartheid era are discussed. This is followed by a description of the north-east Asian countries' economic engagement with the African continent as backdrop to an analysis of the patterns and strategic dynamics in their involvement with South Africa.

There are structural similarities in the kinds of trade and investment links that the north-east Asian powers have with South Africa and the rest of Africa which see trade unevenly constructed on the exchange of primary resources from the continent, for capital and industrial goods from north-east Asia. South Africa is the focal point for the Asian powers' engagement with Africa, and although trade relations are asymmetrical there are distinctive dynamics in economic ties, conditioned by South Africa's industrial makeup and built around the country's strategic sectors. Trade patterns suggest key linkages between emergent industrial development priorities in South Africa and the Asian powers' economic interests. The chapter discusses how the changing landscape reflects and shapes economic diplomacy between South Africa and her north-east Asian counterparts, and concludes with a reflection on the implications for South Africa's industrial interests.

SOUTH AFRICA, CHINA, JAPAN AND KOREA: RELATIONS IN CONTEXT

In historical terms, relations between South Africa and north-east Asia have been distinctive, and were shaped for the bulk of the twentieth century by apartheid South Africa's fashioning of ties with states deemed part of the anti-communist Western bloc. This led to closer bilateral ties and extensive trade between South Africa and Japan, whose economic interests and diplomatic alliances overlapped; to more limited economic contact with South Korea, although there was some trade flow between the two; and, as an adversary of the apartheid state, to limited engagement with the PRC. Trade ties were maintained with Taiwan and, to a lesser extent, Hong Kong.

Official relations between South Africa and Japan are the longest, and started with the appointment of an honorary consul to look after Japanese citizens' interests in 1910, and the opening of a consulate in Cape Town eight years later. There is also a long history of trade between the two that dates back to the 1930s, although the volumes were relatively small and mainly comprised the export of textile goods from Japan. During the period of apartheid more meaningful ties between the two entities were forged as there was a significant increase in trade, and the development of strategic economic ties centred on the export of precious metals, in particular platinum, from South Africa. Indeed, South Africa became Japan's principal source of platinum after the 1960s (Ampiah 1997). The two countries also share a unique history as a result of the designation of Japanese residents as 'honorary whites' by the apartheid state, and the extension of business links during the period of international sanctions and disinvestment (Osada 2002).

By comparison, the history of engagement between South Africa, China and South Korea has taken on a less strategic character and has been moulded, in the case of South Africa's interaction with China, by the ideological considerations that underpinned the apartheid state's foreign policy objectives. As such, in the past, South Africa's relations with north-east Asia were largely fragmented and centred on Japan. As an illustration:

by the end of the 1980s, trade volumes between Japan and South Africa were around R9 billion, while the comparative figures for South Korea and the PRC were R1.9 billion and R0.5 billion respectively.[1]

The early post-apartheid period was the time when there was a change in South Africa's links with north-east Asia and a convergence of its interests in the region. Most significant was the country's establishing of diplomatic ties with the PRC in 1998, a decision partially motivated by signs that China would become a significant player in the world economy in the years ahead (Naidu 2008). Economic and foreign policy considerations also informed the way in which South Africa forged ties with South Korea, with the first exchange of diplomatic notes in 1992. In the same year South Africa opened an embassy in Tokyo. A visit by then president Nelson Mandela to Japan and South Korea in 1995 signalled an interest by the post-apartheid government to extend and deepen ties with north-east Asia (Cornelissen 2004).

Since that time there has been a progressive shift in South Africa's relations with the three north-east Asian powers. Ties with Japan evolved and became mediated by interactions with China and, to a lesser extent, South Korea. Mandela's visit to Japan was followed by visits by his successor, Thabo Mbeki, and the establishment of bilateral ministerial meetings. Japan provided two major aid packages to South Africa in 1995 and 1999 (termed respectively the 'Mandela' and 'Mbeki' packages), which by far exceeded the Asian country's aid disbursements to other parts of Africa. These were taken as signals of new partnerships between the two countries. A few years later, however, most of the elements of the packages were cancelled and observers cited tensions between South African and Japanese bureaucratic officials (see Alden 2002).

Diplomatic relations have also been less fervent than the re-establishment of ties in the late 1990s initially augured, although the two countries do maintain a ministerial-level 'partnership forum' which sees foreign ministers meet on an annual basis. In 2010 the two countries upgraded relations to a 'strategic cooperation partnership', a gesture of intentions to pursue common diplomatic objectives more energetically. Since establishing formal ties, Korea and South Africa have also signed various investment incentive, tax and science cooperation agreements.

At the same time exchanges with China escalated. A bi-national commission was established in 2001 which institutionalised regular high-level meetings, occasionally at executive level, between South Africa and China. Since the start of diplomatic relations fifteen years ago there have also been frequent reciprocal state visits and exchanges between the ruling African National Congress (ANC) and the Chinese Communist Party. Recent years have seen an even further intensification of diplomatic and political agreements, the most noteworthy being the upgrading of relations from 'strategic partnership' to 'comprehensive strategic partnership' in 2010, signalling intent to deepen relations across a wide spectrum of activities. In the same year South Africa became a member of the BRIC (Brazil, Russia India and China) alliance based on what has been assumed to be largely an outflow of Chinese support. Finally, following the fifth FOCAC summit in 2012 South Africa was selected as co-host for the next meeting.

Indeed, there seems to be a strategic orientation to China's engagement with South Africa that extends beyond bilateral relations and positions South Africa as a major partner for China's broader diplomatic and economic aims in Africa. Although there are some key differences, the same dynamic pertains to the way in which the other two Asian powers are fostering links with South Africa, as the next section shows.

NORTH-EAST ASIA'S ECONOMIC FOOTPRINT IN AFRICA

There has been a noticeable increase in economic ties between the north-east Asian and African regions in recent years that has been spearheaded by China. In Figures 1 and 2, comparative levels of trade between China, South Korea, Japan and the African continent are detailed. The charts reflect a clear growth in trade between China and Africa, with a doubling in export and import volumes over the past half-decade. Trade by Japan and South Korea has also seen some growth, although at much lower levels.

Importantly, while China has emerged as the major trade partner by value, its trade profile with the continent differs little from that of the other two north-east Asian players. Table 1 gives an overview of the proportion and nature of trade between Africa and the Asian countries.

The structure of trade between the two regions is significant, as it is anchored around the export of primary materials such as minerals and metals from Africa and the import to the continent of manufactured goods including machinery, transport, electrical and

Figure 1: Northeast Asian exports to Africa by value, 2007–2011 (US$bn)

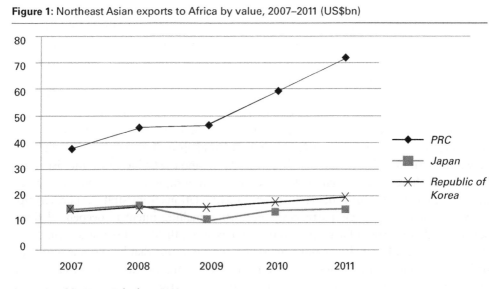

Source: UN COMTRADE database, 2012

Figure 2: Northeast Asian imports from Africa by value (US$bn)

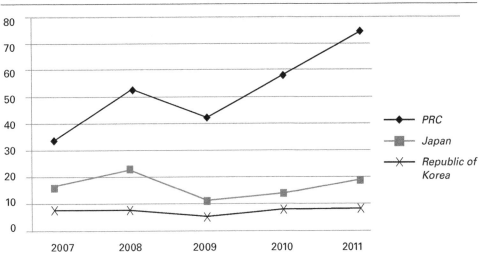

Source: UN COMTRADE database, 2012

Figure 3: Trends in Northeast Asian FDI flow to Africa (US$bn)

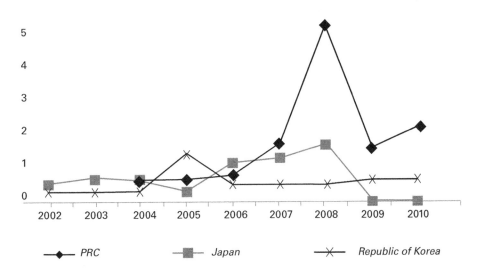

Source: MOFCOM, 2010; JETRO 2013a; AfDB 2011

electronic equipment, nuclear reactors and iron and steel articles. Further, while China captures a large proportion of Africa's exports and, in particular, imports (more than one-quarter of Africa's imports), the continent is a relatively minor destination for China's global exports, which in 2011 totalled US$ 1.9 trillion.[2] Based on these figures, China is clearly more important for African trade than the other way around. Finally, trade links are concentrated on a handful of African countries.

Investments by the three Asian countries in Africa exhibit similar patterns to those of the trade data. Figure 3 shows trends in foreign direct investment (FDI) flows to the African continent over the past decade. Most striking is the growth in Chinese FDI, with

Table 1: Profile of north-east Asian trade with Africa

	China	Japan	Republic of Korea
Exports to Africa as % of total exports (2011)	3.7	1.6	3.3
Share in Africa's total exports (2011)	13.3	3.1	1.3
Share in Africa's total imports (2011)	26.7	1.9	3.6
Principal export goods to Africa	Electrical and electronic equipment; Machinery and nuclear reactors; Vehicles; Ships, Iron and steel articles	Vehicles; Ships and boats; Machinery and nuclear reactors; Electrical and electronic equipment; Iron and steel	Ships, boats; Vehicles; Plastic and plastic articles; Machinery and nuclear reactors; Electrical and electronic equipment; Mineral fuels and oils
Principal imports from Africa	Mineral fuels and oils; Ores; Copper and copper articles; Iron and steel; Wood	Mineral fuels and oils; Pearls, precious stones; Ores; Iron and steel; Aluminium and aluminium articles; Fish	Mineral fuels and oils; Copper and copper articles; Ores; Pearls, precious stone; Iron and steel; Cereals
Main trading partners (based on exports to sub-Saharan Africa)	South Africa; Angola; Sudan; Congo; Democratic Republic of Congo; Zambia; Equatorial Guinea; Nigeria	South Africa; Liberia; Kenya; Nigeria; Algeria; Tanzania;	Liberia; Nigeria; South Africa; Central African Republic; Ghana

Derived from UN COMTRADE data

the increase most pronounced in 2008, when FDI flows reached about US$ 5.5 billion. Investment flows from Japan and South Korea have also risen over this period, although the volumes are considerably lower than from China.

When FDI to Africa is contextualised against the three Asian countries' overall investment profiles, it is clear that the continent still draws a marginal share of north-east Asian investment. As shown in Table 2, in 2010 just over 4 per cent of China's total FDI stock was held in Africa, and 3.5 per cent of total outward FDI flow from China went to the continent (MOFCOM 2010). The comparable figure for Japan in 2011 was less than one per cent (JETRO 2013a). On the measure of FDI flow, Africa captured 1.4 per cent of South Korea's overall investment flows for 2011. As discussed in greater detail below, the lion's share of FDI to Africa from the north-east Asian countries goes to South Africa.

Table 2 : Comparison of north-east Asian outward FDI

	China	Japan	Republic of Korea
Total FDI flow (US$bn)	68.8	108.8	26.4
Total FDI stock (US$bn)	317.2	957.7	171.5*
Value of FDI flow into Africa (US$bn)	2.11	0.46	0.37
Value of FDI stock in Africa (US$bn)	13.04	8.08	N/A
African FDI stock as proportion of total stock held (%)	4.11	0.84	N/A

Note: data for China are 2010 values; for Japan and South Korea 2011 values are shown
Source: MOFCOM 2010; JETRO 2013a; 2013b; Korea Exim Bank 2013
* Figure from OECD 2013a

These comparisons give some insight into the relative role of each of the Asian countries as investor in Africa. China's investment footprint on the continent is the largest and therefore most noteworthy. There is generally consensus among observers that the full scale of Chinese investments in Africa is unknown, in part because of varying estimates by the Chinese authorities of the country's outward FDI; in part because a large volume of China's overall investments are channelled through offshore locations such as the territory of Hong Kong and the Cayman Islands; and in part because of blurred lines between China's aid, trade and investments. A significant portion of what Chinese authorities define as aid to Africa, for instance, comprises both concessionary loans (usually for infrastructure and construction projects) and commercial deals (Renard

2011). The fact that entities such as private and small and medium-sized Chinese firms are arising alongside large state-owned enterprises as important investors on the continent, further obscures the picture and it is therefore assumed that Chinese FDI in Africa is both under- and over-reported (Bräutigam 2009). Nonetheless, the country has clearly emerged as the principal East Asian investor on the African continent.

A further issue of debate is the nature and size of China's corporate presence in Africa, although there is consensus that investments by the Chinese are starting to penetrate a diverse range of sectors on the continent that include mining, construction, agriculture, forestry, fisheries, manufacturing, information communication technology (ICT), the financial sector and tourism (see Alden 2007; Bräutigam 2009; and Huang and Wilkes 2011 for reviews and discussions). Japanese firms have had a notably longer presence in Africa, with investments in the manufacturing sector in a number of African countries starting in the 1960s. In 2012 the Japan External Trade Organisation reported 333 Japanese firms active on the African continent (JETRO 2012).

Like their Chinese counterparts, Japanese and South Korean firms operate in a variety of sectors, with enterprises such as Toyota, Nissan, Honda, Kawasaki, Sony, Hyundai, Kia, Daewoo, Ssanyong, LG and Samsung having left their mark in the automotive and ICT sectors of a number of African countries. However, a common feature of the investments by the north-east Asian players is that in terms of volume the bulk of investments are made in mining and resource extraction. From the Japanese side firms such as Mitsubishi, Sumitomo, Sojitz and Itochu have made substantial investments in the extraction and processing of minerals, metals, oil and gas in the Gulf of Guinea, Nigeria, Angola, Madagascar, Mozambique and South Africa (see Cornelissen 2012 and Hirano 2012 for discussions). The parastatal, Korea Resources Corporation (KORES) has also emerged as a significant new player in the continent's extractive industries. One of KORES's largest investments is a joint venture with Sumitomo and a consortium of Canadian companies to develop a major nickel mine and related infrastructure in Madagascar worth US$6.9 billion, which is known as the Ambatovy Project.

All three north-east Asian countries have started to structure their aid and multi-lateral relations with the African continent through flagship summits. Japan was the first to launch such a summit in 1993 with the inauguration of the five-yearly Tokyo International Conference on African Development, set up as a gathering drawing together African heads of state and a range of multilateral entities such as the United Nations Development Programme and the World Bank to discuss African development issues. In 2000, China launched the Forum on China-Africa Cooperation, a three-yearly meeting of Chinese leaders and African counterparts, and in 2006 South Korea held its first Korea-Africa Forum.

Although not initially intended as such, and even if it is not an explicit feature, the development summits have become a competitive platform for the three northeast Asian powers. It is typical that the summits are used by the respective Asian leaders to announce the disbursement of large aid and business packages to Africa and to signal major strategic focuses for multilateral relations. The FOCAC summits led the way, with voluminous pledges of loans and official development assistance. After the fifth FOCAC summit (FOCAC V) the Chinese government promised loans of around US$20bn and aid of nearly US$100m. At the latest two TICAD summits, held in 2009 and 2013, Japanese leaders announced aid disbursements of respectively US$1.8 billion and US$14 billion. Private sector support of around US$18 billion was pledged at TICAD V. For its part the South Korean government undertook to double development assistance to Africa to US$1.1 billion by 2015. There is even a measure of rivalry in how many African heads of state the summits can draw. A noteworthy aspect of the fifth TICAD summit, for instance, was the extensive public relations machinery that the Japanese government mounted around it, and their attempt to exceed the number of delegates at China's FOCAC V.

But beyond such showcasing the summits have also become occasions to discuss a wider set of issues that have led to deepened engagement between African countries and their north-east Asian counterparts. Agenda items at recent FOCAC meetings, for instance, have included discussion about scientific cooperation and scholarly exchange, the development of common interests in jurisprudence and the enhancement of corporate social responsibility. The fifth TICAD summit placed a notably strong accent on the extension of business links between Japan and Africa (MOFA 2013), while aspects such as the fostering of South-South economic links and the boosting of peacebuilding endeavours on the African continent have been features of the TICAD process since its inception (Cornelissen 2012). There has been some discussion between the three north-east Asian players about the possibility of collaborating and even coordinating aid activities on the African continent. These discussions have looked at how similarities in their modes of aid-giving, such as an emphasis on infrastructure development, could be enhanced, and how ideas about Asian lessons for African development – a theme underlying all of the north-east Asian countries' aid ties with Africa over the years – could be achieved. These discussions have not yet led to actual aid coordination.

Since the import, export and investment patterns with the African continent are broadly the same for the three north-east Asian countries, the question arises about whether they are likely to see themselves as competitors within the continent. There is an emerging discourse in the international arena about the expansion potential of the African market, resulting from the growth in the continent's GDP at an average of around 5 per cent over the past decade, and strong performance by individual economies such as Angola, Ethiopia and Zambia (see for example Mckinsey Global Institute 2010 and World Bank 2011). This discourse also appears to influence investment attitudes to the continent by the north-east Asian players. A recent report by JETRO (2012), for instance, suggests that the continent is viewed in a more positive light as an investment destination compared with a half-decade ago.

In interviews with representatives of Japanese firms, however, the continent is ranked behind the ten economies of the Association for Southeast Asian Nations (ASEAN), South Asia and, in particular, China as investment destination (Interview, manager JFE Steel, Tokyo, 28 February 2013; and Kojima 2013), and similar viewpoints appear to be held by Korean and Chinese counterparts (see for example AfDB 2011). Therefore, while Africa's growth potential is acknowledged, it is not overstated, and the focus for all three north-east Asian countries is on the continent's primary resources. The Asian powers' interest in resource extraction makes for asymmetrical trade relations, as demonstrated in Table 1.

There is the subsidiary issue of the impact that growing trade with Asia has on African economies. It is widely understood among observers that Africa's growth performance over the past years has been underpinned by boosts in commodity exports, particularly to China. At the same time a rise in imports from China has had detrimental effects on key economic sectors. This has been shown with respect to the textile sectors in a number of African countries (see Kaplinsky and Morris 2008).

Against the backdrop of rapidly changing interactions between Japan, China, Korea and the wider African continent, South Africa's economic relations with the three Asian countries are distinctive and significant. As evident in Table 3, South Africa features prominently in China and Japan's overall trade and investment relations with Africa, attracting more than half of the FDI from those countries since 2007. For Japan, further, out of a total of 333 enterprises active on the African continent, two-thirds are operational in South Africa (JETRO 2012). South Korea has started to invest greater volumes in South Africa, although most of the Asian country's FDI flows are to Madagascar (as part of KORES's involvement in the Ambatovy nickel mine), Morocco, Libya, Tunisia, Angola, Nigeria and the Democratic Republic of the Congo (see OECD 2013b). For all three Asian powers, South Africa is their principal trade partner on the continent.

Table 3: Trends in South African trade and investment with north-east Asia, 2007-2011

	China	Japan	Republic of Korea
FDI to South Africa as proportion of total FDI flow to Africa (%)	53.8*	59.6	6.9
Trade with South Africa as proportion of total African trade (%)	23.7	43.1	18.3

Source: MOFCOM 2010, JETRO 2013a; OECD 2013b; UN COMTRADE 2012
*Figures for China's FDI are for the years 2007-2010

It is also significant that South Africa is not a recipient of aid from the north-east Asian countries. This suggests a different type of relationship and places South Africa uniquely in terms of these countries' African engagements.

SOUTH AFRICA'S TRADE WITH NORTH-EAST ASIA: PATTERNS AND STRATEGIC DYNAMICS

The most significant aspect in South Africa's trade with the north-east Asian region has been the deepening of economic links with China. The rate of growth in trade between China and South Africa is striking. Based on data by South Africa's Department of Trade and Industry, since 2001 South Africa's imports from China increased tenfold, while exports to the Asian country grew by a factor of twenty-two.[3] China displaced Japan as South Africa's top bilateral trade partner for the first time in 2009. This surge in bilateral trade has underpinned the growing importance that north-east Asia has in South Africa's overall trade relations. As shown in Figure 4, north-east Asia accounts for nearly a quarter of all South African trade. Currently China draws more than half of South African trade with the north-east Asian region (Figure 5).

Figure 4: Northeast Asia trade as proportion of total South Africa trade, 2008-2011

Figure 5: Breakdown of South Africa's Northeast Asian trade partners*

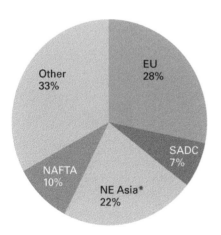

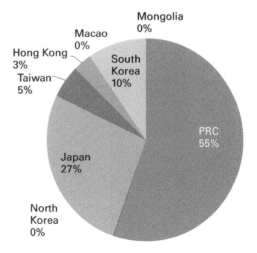

Source: Department of Trade and Industry 2013a
* Includes Hong Kong and Taiwan

Source: DTI 2013a
* Based on 2011 trade values

Figures 6 and 7 detail and compare recent trends in South Africa's trade with the three countries. The prominence of trade relations with China is clear. A breakdown of the composition of the trade, shown in Figures 8-10, reveals more interesting dynamics.

Figure 6: Value of South Africa's imports from principal Northeast Asian partners

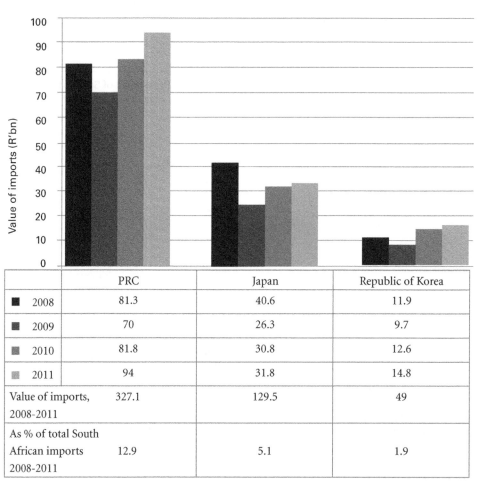

		PRC	Japan	Republic of Korea
■	2008	81.3	40.6	11.9
■	2009	70	26.3	9.7
■	2010	81.8	30.8	12.6
▦	2011	94	31.8	14.8
Value of imports, 2008-2011		327.1	129.5	49
As % of total South African imports 2008-2011		12.9	5.1	1.9

Source: Derived from DTI trade data, 2013

Figure 7: Value of South Africa's exports to principal Northeast Asian partners

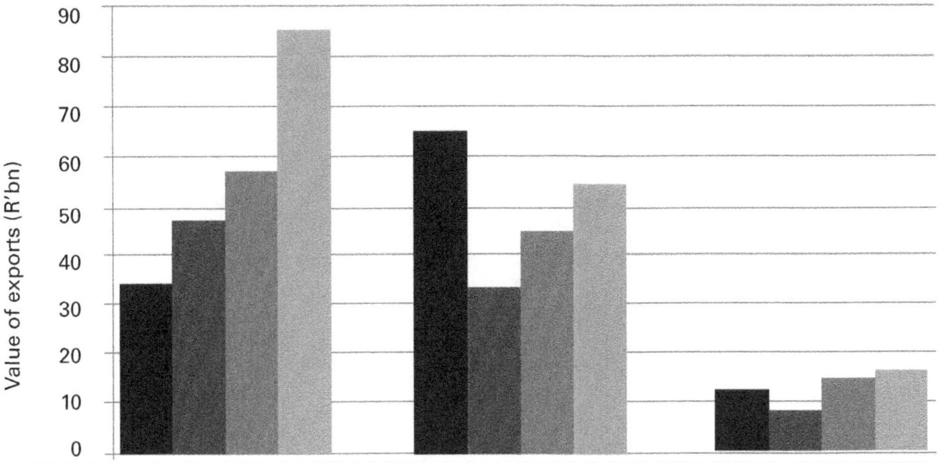

	PRC	Japan	Republic of Korea
■ 2008	34.4	65.7	12.5
■ 2009	48.7	34	7.7
■ 2010	58.6	46.3	13
■ 2011	85.1	54.8	15.8
Value of exports, 2008-2011 (R'bn)	226.8	200.8	49
As % of total South African exports 2008-2011	9.5	8.4	2.1

Source: Derived from DTI trade data, 2013

It is noteworthy that the nature of trade between South Africa and each of the three countries is broadly the same. This consists of the import of manufactured goods from north-east Asia and the export by South Africa of mining products such as base metals, precious metals, metal ores, and mineral fuels and oils. The structure of trade is therefore similar to north-east Asia's trade with the larger African continent, centred on the exchange of primary and secondary goods. The type of manufactured goods imported by South Africa is also quite similar, with a significant share comprising machinery, power equipment, transport goods and electrical and electronic equipment. About a quarter of South Africa's imports from China and Japan respectively consist of nuclear reactors and water boilers (that is, machinery used for power generation and in industrial research).

Figure 8: Breakdown of South Africa – China trade

Composition of South Africa's imports from China

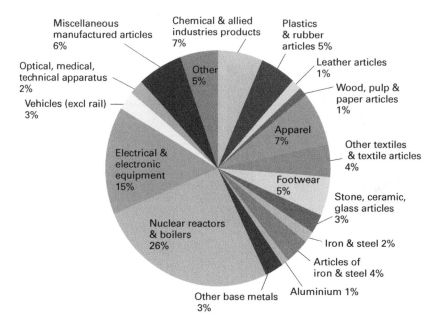

Composition of South Africa's exports to China

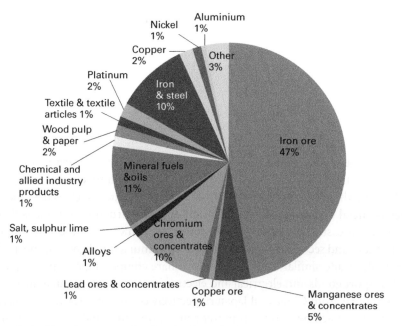

Source: Derived from Department of Trade and Industry data
Based on 2011 trade values

Figure 9: Breakdown of South Africa – Japan trade

Composition of South Africa's imports from Japan

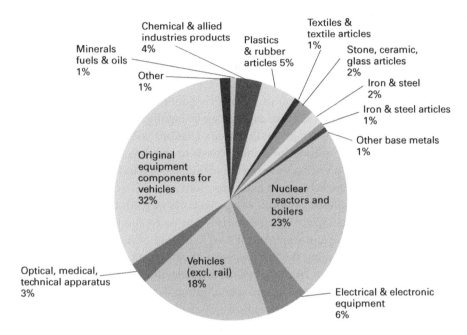

Composition of South Africa's exports to Japan

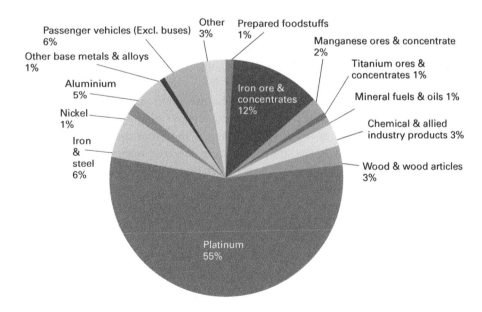

Source: Derived from Department of Trade and Industry data
Based on 2011 trade values

South Africa's imports from China are most diversified, and a significant share comprises textiles and related goods such as apparel, footwear, leather articles and fashion wear. Altogether, in 2011 textile and textile articles accounted for more than 10 per cent of the goods imported from China. Overall, South Africa's imports from all three Asian countries are roughly similar and include chemicals and related goods from the chemical industry; plastics and rubber articles; and optical, medical and technical apparatus. South Africa also imports some base metals, mineral fuels and oils, and iron and steel from all three countries.

A closer look at the composition of exports by South Africa gives a hint of specific industry and sectoral dynamics. Three aspects can be highlighted. The first concerns the primacy of the mining industry in South Africa's relations with north-east Asia. South Africa exports significant volumes of mining goods to the three Asian countries, and a range of base metals and metal ores used in the manufacturing industry, such as iron ore, manganese, aluminium, nickel, copper and chromium are sold to the Asian economies.

Most striking is the volume of South African exports of platinum to Japan which in 2011 comprised more than half of total exports to the Asian country, and was valued at R29.95 billion.[4] Platinum is a precious metal used in a range of manufacturing and high-technology industries including the automotive and construction sectors, the computer industry and in the production of electronics such as television, video recorders and MP3 players. Given its properties, the platinum metals group is also applied as a catalyst, and is widely used in the chemical, pharmaceutical and medical industries. Other applications include the production of catalytic converters and the development of fuel cells as alternative and environmentally friendlier sources of power, used in passenger vehicles and in manufacturing industries. Japan has been a global leader in all of these industries, and it has been reliant on platinum imports to sustain its domestic development of the industries. South Africa, which has 90 per cent of the world's platinum reserves (DTI 2012:6), has been one of Japan's main suppliers of the metal for several decades (Morikawa 1997). Long a feature of strategic links between the two, the export of platinum is still the mainstay of trade ties.

While China and South Korea import significantly lower volumes of platinum from South Africa – in 2011 the value of platinum exports to China was approximately R1.7 billion, while for South Korea it was R418 million[5] – they are major importers of other metals that play a similarly important role in their domestic manufacturing industries, such as aluminium and chromium. China is also an importer of alloys such as vanadium, zirconium, tantalum and niobium. These metals have wide industrial application, used *inter alia* in nuclear energy, aerospace, defence, medical, automotive, electrical and electronic, oil and gas and steel industries. At present these metals comprise about 1 per cent of China's imports from South Africa.

The second aspect to highlight concerns the links between the steel industries of South Africa and the three north-east Asian countries. South Africa exports to those countries both the raw materials used in steel production – in particular iron ore, copper, pig iron, copper ore and nickel – and the finished steel articles. Iron ore and steel exports are

Figure 10: Breakdown of South Africa – South Korea trade

Composition of South Africa's imports from South Korea

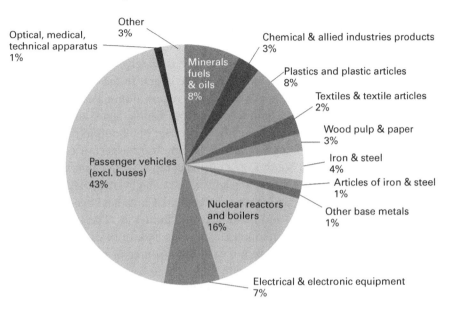

Composition of South Africa's exports to South Korea

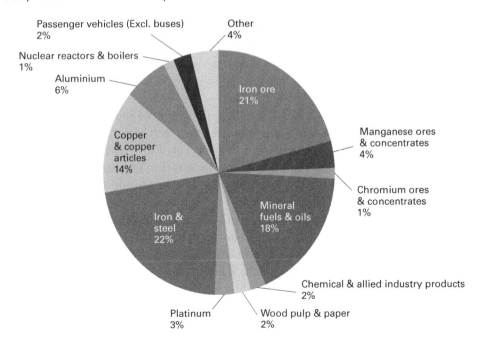

Source: Derived from Department of Trade and Industry data
Based on 2011 trade values

highest to China and South Korea, although a significant share of the country's steel products also finds its way to Japan. The steel industry is of strategic significance for the economies of the three north-east Asian powers, as it is the basis of domestic manufacturing and plays an important part in regional trade (Chan and Kuo 2005). The industry also links in important ways to ancillary sectors such as construction, the automotive sector, shipbuilding, mining, mechanised agriculture, and others.

China's economic expansion in recent years has underpinned the extensive development of its steel industry, which has become the largest in the world by output (World Steel Association 2012). The north-east Asian region dominates world steel production: nine of the top ten steel producers are from China, Japan and South Korea, and the three countries accounted for roughly 57 per cent of all output in 2011 (World Steel Association 2012). Steelmaking has become a significant aspect of economic rivalry in the region as Japanese and South Korean firms compete with China's large steel manufacturers. There is also competition to secure access to high-grade ores and raw materials, which influences trade links within Asia and beyond. China has large reserves of primary resources which feed its steel and manufacturing industries. The country however also imports significant volumes of resources from south and south-east Asia, South America, and various parts of Africa. The country is itself a source of metals and ores for Japan and, to a lesser extent, South Korea, although a large volume of Japan's imports arises from suppliers in Australia and Brazil (World Steel Association 2012, and interview with JFE Steel, Tokyo, 28 February 2013).

Given rising competition among the north-east Asian powers for stakes in global steel production, the nature of their trade ties with South Africa is significant. South Africa is the largest steelmaker on the African continent, responsible for about half of Africa's crude steel output (Research Channel Africa 2009) and the country exports to a wide range of markets that include North America, the Middle East and Europe. Its export to the rest of Africa is however largest, accounting for more than a third of its crude steel products. Around a quarter of exports find their way to China, South Korea and Japan (Research Channel Africa 2009). According to figures from the South African Iron and Steel Institute, the three north-east Asian countries are South Africa's primary suppliers of carbon, alloy and stainless steel, making up 50 per cent of the import of those goods.[6] Japanese firms also have a notably strong presence in ferrochrome, manganese and vanadium extraction in South Africa, with enterprises such as Mitsubishi and Sumitomo owning controlling equity in large mines.

These patterns indicate that the Asian powers have a prominent position in an industry of strategic importance for South Africa's economy. From discussions with stakeholders in the Japanese steel industry, it would seem that South Africa is regarded as an entry point into the larger African market for the delivery of both crude and finished steel goods. This potential is, however, influenced by a variety of factors, such as the stability of the South African industry, competition from other major domestic producers and external investors, and conditions within the Asian economies (interview, Nippon Steel and Sumitomo Metal Corporation, Chiba, Japan, 18 December 2012; interview, JFE Steel, Tokyo, 28 February 2013).

The third significant aspect relates to dynamics in the automotive sector, which is of relevance particularly for the trade between Japan and South Africa, and to a lesser extent, with South Korea. As evident in Figure 9, about a third of all imports from Japan are comprised of 'original equipment components for vehicles' and a further 18 per cent consist of vehicles other than rail, which are mostly passenger vehicles and cars. Six per cent of South Africa's exports to Japan consist of passenger vehicles. These trade figures point to an important economic relationship which had been built up over the past three decades between the two countries.

Japanese automobile manufacturers such as Toyota and Nissan had made large-scale investments in South Africa to establish assembly plants. Since the late 1990s, a number of auto component firms such as Bridgestone, NGK, Denso and others have entered the South African sector. Other firms such as Honda, Mitsubishi, Isuzu and Suzuki have a retail presence in the country. Currently three Japanese manufacturers have assembly plants in the country: Toyota South Africa Motors; Nissan (which has a partnership with Renault); and Mazda (which assembles branded vehicles in partnership with the Ford Motor Company of Southern Africa). These manufacturers have established a firm foothold in South Africa. For instance, Toyota South Africa Motors, whose roots date back to the 1960s and which became a full subsidiary of Toyota Motor Corporation in the early 2000s, is one of the biggest producers in the country, and accounts for a substantial share of domestic vehicle production. In total there are seven original equipment manufacturers (or vehicle assemblers) in South Africa. Alongside the three Japanese manufacturers these are BMW, Volkswagen, General Motors, Ford and Mercedes Benz.

The automotive sector is the largest manufacturing industry in South Africa and currently contributes just over 6 per cent to the country's GDP (DTI 2012). It is also the largest sector on the African continent. In 2012 vehicle output amounted to 540 000 units (DTI 2012:13), which is more than 90 per cent of all vehicles produced in Africa. About half of the vehicles assembled in South Africa are exported. Export destinations include African countries, the European Union, North America and Australasia (Moothilal 2012).[7]

Given its output, the automotive sector has an important position in South Africa's economy, and is a major employer and revenue earner. In the post-apartheid era the government had supported the sector's export-led growth through the Motor Industry Development Programme, introduced in 1995, which *inter alia* gave allowances to vehicle manufacturers and offered rebates on the import of components for vehicles assembled and sold in the domestic market. The aim of the programme was to help the South African sector re-integrate into the global sector (DTI 2012).

While the programme did help the local sector to expand and vehicle exports to substantially increase, it is dominated by manufacturers which are foreign subsidiaries. Local content in automobile assembly is low, and there is limited contribution by local component producers and suppliers. It is estimated, for instance, that 75 per cent of components are sourced from multinational firms outside South Africa. This is mainly a result of the inadequate quality of many locally produced components (DTI 2012:3). The high proportion of vehicle component imports from Japan shown in Figure 9 (which in

2011 constituted 32 per cent of all imports from the Asian country) is part of a general tendency by the automobile manufacturers to procure parts from other global suppliers. There has been a growing presence of Japanese component firms in the South African economy,[8] but existing trade patterns suggest that many of these firms import rather than produce automotive parts in the country.

Another dimension is the strong growth in vehicle imports into South Africa. Over the period of the Motor Industry Development Programme, car imports grew more than tenfold, and in 2011 amounted to 313 000 units. The sale of imported vehicles makes up the bulk of all vehicle sales in South Africa, constituting in 2011 around two-thirds of domestic sales (DTI 2012:14). Imports from north-east Asia make up a significant share of that with Japan and South Korea, in particular, as major sources for vehicle imports. The delivery of units from Japan still outnumbers that from South Korea, but as can be seen in Figure 10, passenger vehicles are South Korea's main export good to South Africa, making up 43 per cent of the Asian country's export profile. These are mainly composed of brands such as Hyundai, Kia and Ssanyong (Pather 2012). Vehicle imports from China are comparatively small, comprising in 2011 around 3 per cent of South Africa's total imports from the Asian country (Figure 8), but Chinese brands such as Chery, Chana, Foton and GWM have also gained entry into the South African market (Moothilal 2012).

EMERGENT DIMENSIONS IN ECONOMIC DIPLOMACY

There are a few points to be highlighted from the patterns detailed above. Most pertinent is that the three north-east Asian players (although their level of penetration varies) have cognate interests in the South African economy. They are also engaged in the same strategic sectors and display the same dynamics in how they seek to consolidate existing market presence, to build out compatibilities and shift into newer activities. Some of the major enterprises that have invested from north-east Asia have niche positions in key sectors that they utilise to enhance their foothold in the South African and African markets.

Given these overlaps, there is an element of competition in how the three Asian countries position themselves in their dealings with South African decision makers. This is significant because existing trade dynamics link to important aspects of South Africa's recent industrial and economic strategies, which aim to achieve growth and employment in key sectors through the upscaling of production activities and the expansion of local manufacturing. For instance, the Department of Trade and Industry's Industrial Action Plan, originally devised in 2007, highlights the need to increase domestic production in part through the expansion of labour-intensive industries and by building-out manufacturing capacities. The plan advocates the implementation of 'developmental trade policies' that benefit the country's economy, and suggests a sector-driven approach to skills, technology and innovation enhancement (DTI 2013b). Importantly, it places stress on value-adding activities that help to raise the overall worth of industrial output.

Three clusters of activities are promoted to achieve these goals: the development of new areas of focus (that include metals fabrication, agro-processing, transport equipment, green industries and boat-building, and oil and gas); the use of industrial financing and policies to increase domestic output in strategic sectors; and the longer-term development of capabilities in the nuclear and aerospace industries (DTI 2013b).

The sectors singled out for policy intervention by the DTI in the second cluster have implications for South Africa's economic links with the north-east Asian powers. The interventions include: growing economies of scale and local component input into the automotive sector; increasing downstream mineral beneficiation; developing the domestic chemical, pharmaceutical and plastics industries; re-establishing a stronger domestic presence in the country's clothing, textiles, leather and footwear industries; building-out the forestry and related paper and pulp industries; and, finally, developing the biofuels sector (DTI 2013b).

All of these sectors are important in the trade links between South Africa and the north-east Asian powers, as demonstrated in Figures 8-10, and they have played a role in recent economic diplomatic engagement. Political dialogue about trade issues has placed emphasis on the impact that goods imported from the Asian countries have on the South African economy, and in particular on sensitive or strategic sectors. It has also focused on how complementarities could be enhanced to benefit South African manufacturing, and how the Asian powers could contribute to the expansion of the country's infrastructure.

Discussions about sectors deemed sensitive have related to the effects of the growing presence of Chinese-origin textiles, clothing, footwear and apparel on South Africa's textile and garment industry. There has been some trade tension between the two countries about this issue in the past. Trade unions, in particular, contended that imports from China displaced domestic goods and forced the decline of the local sector. In a bid to protect the industry, the South African government imposed quotas on Chinese imports in 2006, a measure which has been shown to have mixed results. While the quotas led to lower direct textile imports from China, they did not prevent manufacturers sourcing textiles originating from China via third countries, nor did they help make the sector more competitive. There have been continuous job losses in the sector (see for example Fundira 2009; Nattrass and Seekings 2013; Wolmarans 2011).

In the years since the imposition of quotas, the approach has been to engage Chinese counterparts on this issue as part of wider diplomatic interaction. It is noteworthy that the Comprehensive Strategic Partnership Agreement between China and South Africa identifies textiles, along with chemicals, pharmaceuticals, wood pulp and steel – at present comprising significant shares of the country's imports from China – as goods that can be exported to China. Other goods identified for export are aluminium and capital and manufacturing equipment.

South African authorities' attempts to change the trade balance with the Asian powers also involve other strategic sectors, notably mining and the automotive sector. In political dialogues the focus has fallen on how local content in export goods could be enhanced and how, through that, value-adding could be achieved and the manufacturing industry expanded. South Africa's dealings with Japanese counterparts are instructive in this regard.

The issue of mineral beneficiation has become an important discussion point in engagement between South African and Japanese trade officials. South Africa's president, Jacob Zuma, addressed this matter in a first-time visit to Tokyo in June 2013 (MOFA 2013b). Recently, South Africa announced the intended establishment of two special economic zones aimed at mineral beneficiation in the platinum metals group with technical assistance from Japan. In a statement, the minister of trade and industry, Rob Davies, noted the importance of mineral beneficiation for South Africa's industrialisation (SAFPI 2013).

There has also been engagement with firms in the automotive sector as part of South Africa's attempt to develop local component production. The successor to the Motor Industry Development Programme, the Automotive Production and Development Programme (APDP), adopted in 2013, seeks to achieve greater local content in vehicle production through a range of incentives and allowances (see DTI 2012). There have also been initiatives between South African trade officials and industry stakeholders, and Japanese enterprises to explore component localisation opportunities (see for example Muthilal 2012). With Japan's prominence in South Africa's automotive sector it is clear why emphasis has been placed on Japanese firms. Over time, however, the introduction of the APDP can also have ramifications for the involvement in the sector by Chinese and Korean players.

Further, attempts have been made to involve firms in the expansion of infrastructure. In the energy sector, for instance, Japanese enterprises such as Hitachi have concluded agreements with the South African government to deliver boilers for the two new coal-fired power stations at Medupi and Kusile. Since there is a nascent presence by north-east Asian firms in South Africa's rail and heavy commercial vehicle (truck) sectors, there have also been efforts to have greater investments in transport. For example, Mitsui and Toshiba (from Japan) and China South Rail have established partnerships with Transnet to supply electric locomotives assembled at plants in South Africa. Overall, there has been a steady entry by various firms into South Africa's manufacturing, power and transport sectors, although this is small compared to concerns in mining, which is still of greatest interest for investors from north-east Asia.

The changing landscape, and efforts by South African authorities to steer the trade relationship towards the country's industrial and employment interests, will play a role in how the country fosters links with the Asian powers in the years ahead, as well as how firms from those countries might seek to position themselves in important sectors in South Africa. The interesting question is less about which of the powers wins the contest than about why. South Africa has concluded cooperation agreements with all three which, in their content, reflect the domestic development priorities spelled out in recent years. The country's partnership with China, although it has not been without controversy, is likely to be privileged because it relates to other aspects of South Africa's foreign policy interests, including their joint membership of the BRICS alliance. It remains to be seen, however, whether South Africa will be able to leverage its BRICS membership to gain more a favourable position vis-à-vis China on a bilateral basis.

Japanese officials have raised discussion with South Africa about the possibility of a free trade agreement (FTA), as part of the Asian power's attempts to give momentum to expanding trade links in various parts of Africa, and which has seen it negotiating with other African countries about the conclusion of economic partnership agreements (interview with the economic councillor, Embassy of Japan, Pretoria, 17 August 2011). South Africa has proved reticent, and in 2012 announced that it will not pursue an FTA with Japan since the conditions were not in South Africa's immediate economic interests. This suggests that while South Africa regards deeper economic links with north-east Asia to be important, the country is also cautious in its approach and that wider considerations shape economic commitments. On this count it is therefore probable that South Africa will continue to give greater priority to its engagement with China in order to serve broader foreign policy objectives.

CONCLUSION

The economic patterns detailed above developed out of various conditions over an extensive period of time. The nature of South Africa's trade with Japan, for instance, stems from the calculated fostering of ties at important junctures in the development of the economies and industries of both countries, and was built on considerations of the comparative advantage that each offered the other. The intensification of South Africa's interactions with China and South Korea, on the other hand, was part of the African country's re-integration into the global system and was largely motivated by an attempt to establish new partnerships that supported South Africa's changing economic priorities.

Against this setting, it is significant that there are similarities in the structure of trade between South Africa and the north-east Asian powers, focused on resource extraction. While involvement with north-east Asia has becoming increasingly important to South Africa, therefore, relations are still asymmetric.

In recent years these conditions have constituted the backdrop to a shift in momentum to South Africa's engagement with the north-east Asian powers. South Africa has been seeking to expand economic interaction with the region. The focus has fallen not only on drawing greater investments but, significantly, also on altering established trade patterns that help South Africa to achieve industrial objectives. This strategy has had mixed results so far. Nonetheless, given the north-east Asian powers' positioning in sectors of strategic significance for the South African economy, there are unique dynamics at play in the relationships that are now unfolding. These dynamics are mostly unexplored in analyses of South Africa's ties with Asia, but they are as important in determining South Africa's future global outlooks as they are in shaping Asia's role on the wider African continent in the years ahead.

REFERENCES

African Development Bank (AfDB) (2011) The Korea-Africa partnership: Beyond trade and investment. *AfDB Africa Economic Brief*, 2(9), www.afdb.org [Accessed 5 May 2013].

Alden C (2002) The chrysanthemum and the protea: Reinventing Japanese-South Africa relations after apartheid. *African Affairs* 101: 365-386.

Alden C (2007) *China and Africa*. London: Zed Books.

Ampiah K (1997) *The Dynamics of Japan's Relationship with Africa: South Africa, Tanzania and Nigeria*. London: Routledge.

Bräutigam D (2009) *The Dragon's Gift: The Real Story of China in Africa*. Oxford: Oxford University Press.

Chan S and C Kuo (2005) Trilateral trade relations among China, Japan and South Korea: Challenges and prospects of regional economic integration. *East Asia*, 22(1): 33-50.

Cornelissen S (2012) TICAD's directives for Southern Africa: Promises and pitfalls. *Japanese Studies* 32(2): 201-18.

Cornelissen S (2004) Japan-Africa relations: Patterns and prospects. In Taylor I and P Williams (eds) *Africa in International Politics: External Involvement on the Continent*. London: Routledge.

Department of Trade and Industry (DTI) (2013a). South Africa's annual exports by regions,www.dti. gov.za [Accessed 15 February 2013].

DTI (2013b) *Industrial Policy Action Plan 2013/14-2015/16*. Pretoria: DTI.

DTI (2012) *South African Automotive Industry Report 2012*. Pretoria: DTI.

Fundira T (2009) South African quotas on Chinese clothing and textile: 18 month economic review. Tralac Trade Brief, 23 April 2009, www.tralac.org/2009/04/23/south-african-quotas-on-chinese-clothing-and-textiles-18-month-economic-review/ [Accessed 17 January 2013].

Hirano K (2012) TICAD and the national interest of Japan. *Japanese Studies* 32(2): 183-99.

Huang W and A Wilkes (2011) Analysis of approvals for Chinese companies to invest in Africa's mining, agriculture and forestry sectors. Center for International Forestry Research (CIFOR) Working Paper 81, Bogor, Indonesia.

Japan External Trade Organization (JETRO) (2013a) Japan's outward FDI by country/region (Balance of payments basis, net and flow). www.jetro.go.jp [Accessed 23 April 2013].

JETRO (2013b) Japan's total outward FDI by country/region (International investment position). www. jetro.go.jp [Accessed 22 April 2013].

JETRO (2012). *Survey on Business Conditions of Japanese-Affiliated Firms in Africa*. Tokyo: JETRO.

Kaplinsky R and M Morris (2008) Do the Asian drivers undermine export-oriented industrialisation in sub-Saharan Africa? *World Development* 36(2): 254-273.

Kojima Y (2013) New trends in African business: Initiatives of Mitsubishi Corporation in Africa. Presentation to JETRO TICAD V Africa Symposium, Yokohama, Japan, 31 May 2013.

Korea Exim Bank (2013) Investment statistics by region, 2011. www.koreaexim.go.kr/en. [Accessed 5 May 2013].

McKinsey Global Institute (2010) *Lions on the Move: The Progress and Potential of African Economies*. www.mckinsey.com/mgi [Accessed 3 March 2011].

Ministry of Foreign Affairs of Japan (MOFA) (2013a). *Yokohama Declaration 2013 – Hand in Hand with a More Vibrant Africa*. Tokyo, MOFA, 3 June 2013.

MOFA (2013b) Joint Communique Between Japan and South Africa on the Occasion of the Working Visit of President Jacob Zuma to Japan. Tokyo, 4 June 2013.

Ministry of Commerce of China (MOFCOM) (2010). *2010 Statistical Bulletin of China's Outward Foreign Direct Investment*. Beijing: MOFCOM.

Moothilal R (2012) South Africa's automotive environment. Presentation at South Africa-Japan Suppliers Development Forum, Gordon Institute of Business Science, Johannesburg, 5 March 2012.

Morikawa J (1997) *Japan and Africa: Big Business and Diplomacy*. London: Hurst.

Naidu S (2008) Balancing a strategic partnership? South Africa-China relations. In Ampiah K and S Naidu (eds) *Crouching Tiger, Hidden Dragon? Africa and China*. Scottsville: University of Kwazulu-Natal Press.

Nattrass N and J Seekings (2013) Job destruction in the South African clothing industry: How an unholy alliance of organised labour, the state and some firms is undermining labour-intensive growth. University of Cape Town, Centre for Social Science Research Working Paper No. 323.

Organisation for Economic Cooperation and Development (OECD) (2013a). FDI in Figures, April 2013. www.oecd.org/investment/statistics.htm_ [Accessed 6 May 2013].

OECD (2013b) FDI flows by partner country: Korea. www.oecd.stat.org [Accessed 12 May 2013].

Osada M (2002) *Sanctions and Honorary Whites: Diplomatic Policies and Economic Realities in Relations between Japan and South Africa*. Westport: Greenwood Press.

Pather A (2012) Localisation challenges facing the South African automotive market. Presentation at South Africa-Japan Suppliers Development Forum, Gordon Institute of Business Science, Johannesburg, 5 March.

Renard MF (2011) *China's Trade and FDI in Africa*. African Development Bank Working Paper Series No. 126. www.afdb.org [Accessed 21 May 2012].

Research Channel Africa (2009). *South Africa's Steel Industry 2009,*.www.researchchannel.co.za [Accessed 18 March 2013].

South African Foreign Policy Institute (SAFPI) (2013) Rob Davies: Beneficiation is critical for the industrialisation of South Africa. www.safpi.org/news/article/2013/rob-davies-beneficiation-critical-industrialisation-africa [Accessed 12 June 2013].

United Nations Commodity Trade Statistics Database (UN COMTRADE) (2012a). China's exports to the world. www.comtrade.un.org [Accessed 15 May 2012].

Wolmarans J (2011) The Impact of Trade Policies on the South African Clothing and Textile Industry: A Focus on Import Quotas on Chinese Goods. Unpublished MBA thesis, University of Stellenbosch.

World Bank (2011) *Global Development Horizons 2011*. Washington, DC: World Bank.

World Steel Association (2012) *World Steel in Figures 2012*. www.worldsteel.org.

NOTES

1   Derived from South Africa's Department of Trade and Industry annual trade statistics accessed at http://tradestats.thedti.gov.za/ReportFolders/reportFolders.aspx.

2   Derived from the United Nations Commodity Trade Statistics (UN COMTRADE) database, accessed at www.comtrade.un.org.

3   Derived from DTI annual trade statistics. At the same time there was a steady decline in trade with Taiwan, and political relations between South Africa and Taiwan have been downgraded. Taipei maintains a liaison office in South Africa and although there are political exchanges, this is at a bureaucratic level.

4   Calculated from DTI annual trade statistics.

5   Calculated from DTI annual trade statistics.

6   See South African Iron and Steel Institute, 'Trading partners – primary steel products', www.saisi.co.za/tradingpartners.php.

7   The two bigger Japanese manufacturers, Toyota and Nissan, export flagship commercial vehicles such as the Hilux, Corolla and Hardbody to the EU and African markets, while BMW's 3-series is exported to Australia, the United States and Japan.

8   At present there are seven auto component firms from Japan active in South Africa: Bridgestone, NGK, Yazaki, Toyota Boshoku, Denso, NSK and Sumitomo Wiring Systems.

CHAPTER 18

Regional parastatals within South Africa's system of accumulation[1]

Justin van der Merwe

The notion of a 'complex' has been used to identify related phenomena and how their interaction influences core functioning in a given society. Such 'complexes' have been described as theories or systems of accumulation. Globally, the most common 'complex' discussed by academics is undoubtedly the American military-industrial complex (MIC), or a variation thereof (Mills 1956). However, it will be argued that such an analysis need not be fixed to the military and industrial relations when it is clear that the relationships and agents in imperial societies (and regionally dominant states or sub-imperial states, in South Africa's case) span many more sectors and operate through more subtle means of persuasion and influence. In apartheid South Africa the military was once considered central in government's decision making and in the allocation of resources – achieved primarily through Armscor, the arms manufacturing parastatal, and its contracting of private industry. But today the military plays a far smaller role in policy making and in driving industry, greatly reducing the analytical use of the concept 'military-industrial enterprise' in explaining complex political and economic phenomena in post-apartheid South Africa (see Rogerson 1990).

Fine and Rustomjee's (1996) concept of the minerals-energy complex (MEC) is useful in understanding the history and primary site of accumulation in South Africa. The concept describes a concentration of public and private interests centered on mining and its related industries, notably manufacturing and finance. The historical and post-apartheid expansion of parastatals such as Eskom and Transnet, as state-created monopolies underpinning the functioning of the MEC and its extension into the region, is particularly illuminating (Daniel and Lutchman 2006). It appears, however, that a broader concept may be necessary to describe the myriad post-apartheid business actors and branches of the state. For example, although mining growth is still important to the economy, telecommunications and retail industries have been dominant in South Africa's post-apartheid business expansion (Miller et al. 2008; Simon 2001). 'Retail, wholesale, motor and hotel trade' has remained consistently around 14 per cent of gross domestic product (GDP) between 1995 and 2010. Both mining and manufacturing were less than 14 per cent in 2010, with mining substantially less (Van der Wath 2012: 56-57),[2] and both these sectors have shrunk significantly over the past thirty years, with manufacturing dropping off rapidly during democracy (see below). The historical gains of the mining sector have been complemented, strengthened and expanded through interlinking relationships to other sectors. These industries have affected the substance and style of the economy and its modes of accumulation within the region, suggesting both complementarity and competition. The 2008 energy crisis and subsequent high cost of energy have not aided the MEC. A political and trade unionist movement has also weakened the dominance of the MEC post-1994.

In addition to the intertwined relationship between the state and the private sector, the roles of academia, information systems and media also warrant attention in the functioning of the 'complex'. Peet's (2002) analysis of how globally constructed hegemonic discourses 'colonise' alternative ones, focuses on academic and media processes within the 'complex'. Peet wishes to demonstrate how these spheres, along with the influence of global and domestic financial institutions, influence the decisions and thinking of elite members and the general public. Peet develops what he calls the 'academic-institutional-media complex' through which he describes how a neoliberal discourse 'disciplined' the African National Congress (ANC) into adopting a neoliberal policy in the 1990s after the leftist Reconstruction and Development Programme (RDP) was effectively abandoned.

The broader point that should be made in respect of the existing literature is that 'complexes' should not be seen as mutually exclusive but, rather, complementary. Each concept highlights similar, yet slightly different, aspects of the functioning of a dominant society. However, by the same token, a broader, more integrated attempt at understanding South Africa's system of accumulation – as conceptualised through a 'complex' – could and should be made. Although the military, mining and information sectors are crucial to understanding patterns of accumulation, they would ostensibly benefit from a 'tying-up' and more systematic treatment of the core sectors of government, business and media – as well as a focus on the temporal-spatio assumptions of the exchanges between these spheres, and the actors involved. Such a model of accumulation would shed light on a complex web of interactions between the elite members spread across government, business and media.

This research note attempts to set out such a system of accumulation. The system, it is argued, is embodied in the concept of a 'government-business-media (GBM)' complex.

The concept draws from Harvey's (2005) reworking of Marx's primitive accumulation in his concept 'accumulation by dispossession' and Gramsci's (1971) notion of hegemony. The concept is further guided by the critical geopolitical literature focusing on discourse (Ó Tuathail and Agnew 1992).

Parastatals and other state-owned entities are crucial to understanding South Africa's broader system of accumulation. Parastatals play a decisive role in determining the tone and character of the relationship between business and the state. They are also a core site of interest promotion for the middle class through staffing and procurements practices, not to mention their facilitatory role in generating spatially-expanded rounds of accumulation (Southall 2007: 210, 222-23). Foregrounding the role of regionally-orientated parastatals in the functioning of such a 'complex' is therefore a good place from which to start, as they play an instrumental role in accumulation over space.

WHAT ARE THE GEOGRAPHIES OF THE GBM COMPLEX?

The GBM complex operates at national, regional and international levels but the focus of this chapter will be on the regional scale. Geographies of the GBM complex operate through networks established between government, business and media elite members, within the borders of South Africa but also through the transnational flows of information, capital and goods between elite members in the region and beyond. These networks play a defining role in the day-to-day decision making and executable functioning of the state; the type, nature and locations of business transactions and trade; and the role of the media in influencing citizens. Such geographies operate on trading floors, in boardrooms during high-level policy deliberations, and in newsrooms where editorial decisions are made.

The geographies of the GBM complex span both public and private spaces, and 'open' and 'hidden' spaces. Practices within the GBM complex are sometimes hidden from the public, occurring behind closed doors during meetings between state and members of the corporate elite. When such hidden practices between elite members are exposed they are often labelled as corruption, collusion or insider trading.

The GBM complex is maintained through 'experts' and their affective and infrastructural 'labour'. The 'experts' and 'workers' in the GBM complex are those who play a role in maintaining a discourse favouring neoliberalism and who are assumed to be following the lead of elite members. They could be journalists, marketers, advertisers, academics, managers or civil servants. They need not be powerful, but can play a small role in maintaining the discourses which support the GBM complex through funding patterns, recruitment and training, and the encouragement of certain lifestyle and consumption choices. They use corporate spaces and government-owned property and goods. They operate through the technologies of formal contracts; public-private partnerships (PPPs); 'revolving doors' between universities, commercial research, businesses and government; informal ties and favours based on race, ethnicity, nationality, familial relations or other forms of affiliation; kick-backs; patronage; tip-offs; and even bribery. Most obviously, the 'workers' gather around government tenders and other major construction projects or public works including the building of roads, railways, hotels, airports and stadiums. Less obviously, these 'workers' act as agents maintaining the GBM complex by seeking to inculcate sentiments in their support through the media, commercial research and other information systems.

The geographies of the GBM complex are therefore to be found not only in the 'everyday' activities of the working spaces, but are pervasive throughout popular culture and the domestic spheres. These geographies are modelled on a culture of conspicuous consumption and are evident throughout shopping malls (see Miller et al. 2008 for a discussion on South African shopping malls in Africa), magazines, newspapers, television and movies.

THE REGIONAL 'SPATIAL FIX' OF SOUTH AFRICA'S GBM COMPLEX

The underlying premise of the GBM complex is that the state works in tandem with business for purposes of accumulation over space. The state is not only an administrative and technical centre, but acts as a financial and institutional facilitator of capital accumulation. Class formations further reinforce these patterns of accumulation driving the interests of the dominant elite. Parastatals or state institutions are used to support capital accumulation through the development of monopolies, spatially selective policies, or industrial and manufacturing complexes that support and encourage the organic processes that adhere the state to regional processes of accumulation. By so doing, the state seeks to shut out competition in crucial areas such as energy, transport and communication. This is often achieved through the winning of tenders for major infrastructural projects in the region. From this flows the development of infrastructure and the creation of assets that are often literally fixed to the land in other countries to support business investments. The state thereby supports business in several ways. The state-driven projects serve as a way to award tenders to its corporates; here, there is often a high degree of collusion between state and members of the corporate elite. Ventures are assessed on their ability to benefit both sectors, and typically operate through PPPs. These impulses could also extend to peacemaking and the creation of diplomatic environments conducive to business expansion. This is often achieved through regular summit diplomacy in the region or attending and hosting high profile meetings, conferences or events pertaining to this locality. For example, it is now commonplace for state presidents to be accompanied by a large entourage of business representatives when on official duty or state visits, and the rise of pan-continental or regional summitry serves to drive this two-pronged agenda. The strong focus on infrastructure means that the state is seeking to make doing business transactions in the region easier. This has a snowball effect. The movement of commercial banks into the region further paves the way for other businesses to follow, and stimulates a sense of reliability in these markets. Securing one-sided trade relations is another way in which the state supports and promotes its industries. 'Multinational corporations' (MNCs) from the dominant state therefore seek to expand into the region in pursuit of maximising profits and can operate with or without the state's direct support, invariably benefiting (at least tacitly) from state discourses.

The state and business discourses are not always in harmony. Official state discourses emphasise 'development' and the reciprocity of regional integration. These are infused with a business discourse emphasising the benefits of a neoliberal, market-driven approach. Yet when business discourses become too prevalent, or business is guilty of unscrupulous behaviour, the state runs the risk of having its self-interest and exploitative practices laid bare.

The ideological power behind such expansion is driven by two key areas and institutions: the corporate-endowed research community and the more conventional state-linked and corporate media institutions. The former provides most of the impetus and 'intellectual' contributions behind the GBM complex through position papers, policy briefs, conferences, popular articles, expert interviews and public participation platforms. This group comprises the 'state intelligentsia' who, for better or worse, are compelled to chase government tenders linked to official state discourses. Although the commercial research environment typically receives some of its funds from nongovernmental sources, its major client is often government. Thus much public money will go into establishing centres, institutes and multi-year projects dedicated to exploring the regional role played by the dominant state. These forces also permeate the universities insofar as they are compelled to respond to market pressures or the demand for consultancy in research institutes. Universities also respond to state discourses through course design and content, and have at least a nominal duty to be 'society relevant' by conforming to market pressures facing graduates. They also play a role in educating the intellectual and financial elite from the region, often drawing them in as experts on their own countries and socialising them into the dominant state's values and ideals.

The role of the media is particularly important as a form of 'business through ideological means'. The media not only represents a form of 'non-neutral' business, but also acts as a mediator and often independent actor shaping the government-to-business informational flows. With its powerful role in shaping discourses and agendas, the media holds a privileged position in the GBM complex. Depending on its ownership, it can be critical of both spheres simultaneously, or represent the grievances of the one against the other, particularly when the state's capitalist interests are under threat.

The media, including newspapers, radio and television, plays a key role, through its expansion into the region, in developing a national identity for the dominant state. The movement of the state broadcaster into the region, often with its own regional news network, is the strongest form, with channels and programmes designed to capture a focus on the region for both entertainment and information. Satellite services providing for paid television services further carry programmes developed in the source country. Implicit in these forms of communication is socialisation into the dominant state's culture which includes aspects as diverse as movies, music and sport.

THE HISTORICAL DEVELOPMENT OF SOUTH AFRICA'S GBM COMPLEX AND THE ROLE OF REGIONALLY-ORIENTATED PARASTATALS

The historical development of South Africa's GBM complex evolved around capital accumulation premised on a spatially and commercially expanding state controlled by a ruling English and Afrikaans oligarchy. This oligarchy's power was premised on mining which gave rise to control of the commanding heights of the economy through conglomerates (centered on interlinking ownership in mining, manufacturing and finance), with strong links to the government and/or a capacity to influence politics. These conglomerates had a significant regional footprint through various holding companies or stakes in MNCs. They were able to exercise monopolistic control of the region by means of capital flows, labour and production. The ruling oligarchy therefore managed to concentrate capital accumulation in the region in the hands of a few, and did so by means corresponding closely to Harvey's (2005) accumulation by dispossession.

The relationship between the state and private capital in the region was reinforced through the state's investments in various sectors related to mining, such as energy and transport. This allowed the GBM complex to sustain the conditions for monopolistic control of the region and helped to consolidate and concentrate the wealth of the ruling oligarchy, with its roots in mining. Given the strong nexus between capital accumulation and energy provision, the regional expansion of South Africa's MNCs was premised on the steady and reliable flow of electricity. Eskom was therefore founded in 1928 and mandated to sell low-cost energy to South Africa's enterprises. It also serviced regional markets with its substantial surplus production. The regional railroad system was part of the legacy of the discovery of minerals; an efficient and low-cost transport system was vital to the competitiveness of South Africa's MNCs, especially over the long distances to the coast and with the costs involved in mineral extraction – and the South African Transport Services (SATS), the precursor to Transnet, was to further exploit this historical legacy. It was to establish a monopoly of regional transport (and therefore trade) spanning railways, harbours, airlines and some road transport. Butts and Thomas (1986: 24), drawing from data obtained from the Department of Foreign Affairs in 1982, observe that: '[In] the sub-continent (10 degrees south latitude and below), wherein most of the strategic minerals are located, one will find that South Africa accounts for 75 per cent (32 000km) of the total rail linkages.'

The monopolistic control exercised by the GBM complex was further apparent in respect of basic services and goods such as oil, coal, iron, steel, water and, later, telecommunications. Agencies such as Sasol (oil and coal), ISCOR (iron and steel), and vast water schemes such as the Lesotho Highlands Water Scheme were created to extract resources from neighbouring countries. Regional initiatives in these areas often took the form of large infrastructure projects based on PPPs; the state would collude with domestic and international capital on these major projects. Hanlon (1987: 14) states that on the level of state intervention in these industries, the role of government in the economy was 'closer to that in socialist countries than capitalist ones. Many of the largest corporations are parastatals, including SATS... ISCOR ... Sasol... and Escom [now Eskom] ... The private sector is tightly regulated.' The state industrial corporations were instrumental in lowering the costs of production for MNCs, enabling them to establish and retain regional markets. Sometimes Armscor, Eskom and Sasol would keep their prices fixed for years at a time, indirectly subsidising industrial development (Libby 1987: 70-75). These conditions further aided the perception of South Africa as the gateway to doing business in the region.

However, by the late 1980s splits within the GBM complex were irreparable. English and Afrikaner capital started realising the irreversibility of the political changes. Corporate elite members in the GBM complex understood that they needed to align themselves with the ambitions of the new ANC elite, and distance themselves from the National Party (NP). The relationship between English and Afrikaner capital, driven by a dominant Afrikaner state elite, and formed through decades – if not centuries – of a bizarre siege mentality and the defence of privilege and wealth, had all but crumbled. This happened under sustained international pressure, economic sanctions, internal instability and the increased need to create conditions *truly* favourable for an expanded round of capital accumulation in a post-Cold War era.

FULL ENGAGEMENT OF THE GBM COMPLEX

The democratic period opened up a new political and historical epoch for South Africa's capital accumulation and the continent availed itself as a 'fixed space' to absorb its excess capital. After apartheid, the state continued to support business in the region through monopolies established by its parastatals, cross-border spatial development initiatives (SDIs) and major infrastructural projects (Daniel, Naidoo and Naidu 2003; Rogerson 2001). These institutional arrangements of the state facilitated rapid business expansion into the continent. Between 1990 and 2000, South Africa was the largest investor in Africa, investing an average of US$1.4 billion of its annual foreign direct investment (FDI) in the continent (South African Foundation 2004). A new wave of regionally-orientated South African MNCs such as Shoprite, MTN and Multichoice was to emerge.

The first democratic dispensation under President Nelson Mandela was focused on allaying the fears of the English and Afrikaner elite in the GBM complex. It was centered on accommodation of the *old* GBM complex and gave the elite members, along with the public, a chance to embrace (or co-opt) the *new* black state elite members. However, once political stability had been secured, the man who was to significantly further the ambitions of the GBM complex was Mandela's successor as president, Thabo Mbeki, who had already started playing a decisive role as deputy president during Mandela's tenure.

Mbeki's presidency was the fulcrum of the post-apartheid GBM complex. In order to achieve this he surrounded himself with close allies. He also sought to centralise policy making in critical areas such as the economy and foreign policy. His close-allies were Essop Pahad, his life-long friend, general 'enforcer', spin-doctor and minister in the presidency;

Alec Erwin in charge of trade and industry; and Trevor Manuel, minister of finance, whom Mbeki could trust to implement his policies. Mbeki himself was to forge a close relationship with business and was to also provide the 'intellectual' substance behind the state and business expansion. Through an ambitious mix of continental neoliberal restructuring, multilateralism and inspirational speech writing, he was able to concentrate and widen the African 'spatial fix'.

Once the GBM complex had co-opted the new elite it sought to maintain and expand its dominance throughout the region. The desire and pressure by the GBM complex on the new state elite members to consolidate capital accumulation within its 'fixed space' eventually manifested in three crucial areas or actions instigated by Mbeki's presidency: the African Renaissance, the New Partnership for Africa's Development (NEPAD) and the broader 'multilateralism project' of government.

The African Renaissance was launched in 1998. It was effectively a vision of African economic and social rejuvenation. The post-apartheid GBM complex was held together by the 'rallying call' of the African Renaissance, which was to provide the motivation and ideational power behind its capital accumulation. The African Renaissance was the perfect foil for the GBM complex as it acted to allay fears concerning South Africa's hegemony, seeking to bridge the tension between regional resistance and capitalist expansion through an abstract notion of African renewal which was to transcend state boundaries.

The new ANC and corporate elite members were instrumental in laying the institutional environment for capital accumulation through the creation of the neoliberal macroeconomic project, the Growth, Employment and Redistribution programme (GEAR), in 1996, and through the creation of its continental equivalent, the New Partnership for Africa's Development (NEPAD) in 2001, the macroeconomic policy officially adopted by the reconstituted African Union in 2002, with Mbeki as chairman. Much of what the GBM complex was hoping to achieve was to be accomplished through NEPAD: a NEPAD investment council was established by Mbeki. South African and international capital colluded with state elite members, as PPPs were the primary vehicle of NEPAD.

Closely related to the neoliberal macroeconomic project was a broader 'multilateralism project'. A key feature of this was the South African-led restructuring of the Organisation of African Unity (OAU) into the African Union (AU). Mbeki himself was to play the leading role in this by acting as chairman of regional and international organisations. Mbeki was often termed a 'foreign policy president' and was certainly the most prominent, if not important, African leader of the early twenty-first century. The various organs created in the AU were of strategic importance for the GBM complex to wield its influence, such as the Pan African Parliament (PAP). South Africa was to host the PAP and used the opportunity to further signal its leadership role. As part of this 'multilateralism project' the South African government also took the lead in peacemaking throughout Africa. Inherent in the 'multilateralism project' was the idea of establishing South Africa as the foremost African power. The India, South Africa and Brazil (IBSA) trilateral initiative founded by Mbeki in 2003, and South Africa's joining of BRIC (Brazil, Russia, India, China) in 2010 cemented these aspirations. The move to a broader focus on the global South coincided with a broadening of its business expansion as its MNCs looked to expand into emerging markets beyond Africa.

The affective 'labour' enacted by state elite members through continental diplomacy and policy formulation was underpinned by the infrastructural 'labour' conducted through the parastatals. The dominant geopolitical script articulated through the post-apartheid GBM complex was centred on the mutual benefits of regional integration. It is because the success of South Africa's capital accumulation rests partly on its ability to persuade regional states that the expansion of its state-owned enterprises and businesses is also in their interests; South African state elite members stressed the benevolence of the expansionary measures of its parastatals in an apparent attempt to rejuvenate regional infrastructure. Spoornet, the railway division within Transnet, signed contracts in eighteen African countries to rehabilitate neglected rail networks, often agreeing to supply rolling stock and locomotives. In 2003 Spoornet won a US$5 billion contract to restore the entire Zambian railway network, and agreed to operate the railways for the next twenty years (Johnson 2008: 486). South African Airways (SAA) had increased its number of flights into Africa and bought existing African airlines. Eskom had gone into the continent with a rhetorical claim to 'power the region' and is the strongest example of South African parastatal expansion into the continent.

Eskom had networks in thirty-four of the fifty-four African countries in 2006, up from seven in 1997, giving it a presence in Africa unrivalled by any other private or state-owned company (Stephan et al. 2006: 313). All acquisitions by Eskom were made by Eskom Africa which was largely viewed as Eskom's vehicle to spearhead the drive into the continent. Much of this was achieved under the auspices of NEPAD – so much so that the then Eskom chief executive officer established a NEPAD unit in his office (Greenberg 2008: 93).

Most estimates suggested that Eskom was the seventh-largest power utility in the world at the time South Africa attained democracy, and Eskom emerged as the leading player in setting up the Southern African Power Pool (SAPP), a twelve-nation consortium of regional power utilities created in 1995 in an effort to foster the growth of the southern African electricity market. It achieves this through interconnectors allowing states to export and import electricity within the region (Horvei 1998). In 2008 South Africa generated 80.4 per cent of electricity in the SAPP with Mozambique generating 5 per cent, Zambia 3.6 per cent, Zimbabwe 4.1 per cent and the Democratic Republic of Congo (DRC) 2.6 per cent (Sibeene 2008). Botswana and Namibia were insignificant players in power generation, falling among the few countries that made up the remaining 4.3 per cent of power generation in the region (ibid.). Although the regional countries benefited from the creation of the SAPP, as building their own power-generating infrastructure was prohibitively expensive, Eskom had effectively secured a 'fixed market' through the SAPP to sustain its regional monopoly. Eskom also entered into a fixed, long-term contract with BHP Billiton's Mozal Aluminium Smelter in Mozambique and was to make a series of overtures throughout the continent and beyond, often in a joint capacity.

One of the regional megaprojects which Eskom was to lead was the Grand Inga Project in the DRC. The Grand Inga Project was devised as a NEPAD initiative. Eskom was to work with four other power utilities on the project as part of the company Westcor, short for 'Western Corridor'. It would be the world's largest hydropower scheme, deriving its power from the world's second biggest river, the Congo. Although it was planned in four phases, of which the first two were completed in 1972 and 1982 respectively, when they are all finished it will have the potential to produce 40,000 MW. Inga 3 alone will cost US$5.2 billion (Kavanagh 2010). The drive by South African state elite members to secure peace in the DRC, and the abundance of the DRC's natural resources (in this instance, its pumping rivers with vast hydroelectricity potential) is surely more than mere coincidence.

With the post-apartheid expansion of South African capital into the region, the image of the country needed to be changed and the 'white', supposedly 'exceptionalist', image of the apartheid government had to be overcome. The media played a crucial role in this. South Africa's capital accumulation needed a new face; and after the initial transitional phase overseen by Mandela, the GBM complex needed to create a positive spin on capital accumulation in the region. The ideological power was primarily driven by the extension of the state broadcaster, the South African Broadcasting Corporation (SABC), into the region. The SABC's official slogan was 'The pulse of Africa's creative spirit' and the news division branded itself as 'Africa's news leader' (Teer-Tomaseli 2008: 93). In 2003, the SABC launched SABC Africa, an external service which was carried by Digital Satellite Television (DSTV), a Multichoice service. SABC Africa was beamed to forty-nine African countries. The weekdays were dominated by news and topical shows and the weekends featured entertainment content developed in Africa (Teer-Tomaseli 2008: 94). The regionally-focused MNCs would advertise on SABC Africa. In 2007, the SABC launched a twenty-four hour news network, SABC International to fulfill the role of what Al Jazeera does for the Middle East and the Arab states, but for Africa, effectively telling an African story. The marketers and branders played their role and an International Marketing Council (IMC) was established to promote the country as a tourist and business destination. Tourism was to be generated from the slogan: 'Alive with possibility'.

One of the most persuasive means through which the GBM complex was to bolster the legitimacy of its capital accumulation, was through the policy research and think tank community. South Africa has a well-developed commercial research environment and a history of research into its foreign affairs. In the immediate post-apartheid era these organisations provided much of the 'intellectual' drive behind the GBM complex and were to become persuasive purveyors of Mbeki's message of a South African-led 'African Renaissance'. Realising its strength, the ANC government transformed state-linked research institutions to institutions promoting the development of a black intellectual elite and African renewal. The Human Sciences Research Council (HSRC), a tool of the former apartheid regime, is an example of such transformation. The Africa Institute of South Africa (AISA) had been established in 1960. It changed its mandate drastically after the end of apartheid, becoming a statutory body in 2001, and has a particular focus on South Africa's 'new' role in the region. Throughout the commercial research sector many large-scale and multi-year projects were created, investigating aspects of South Africa's relationship with the continent, often leading to a series of annually-produced publications and keenly aware of the importance of this research topic. A naturally 'lubricating' relationship was to develop between government, local and international donors, and commercial research. The universities, also dependent on government funds, sought through their links to commercial research to drive a similar agenda by the establishment of African Studies centres, African institutes and projects aimed at investigating aspects of South Africa's foreign policy in Africa. This was supported by a 'conference industry' consisting mainly of academics, civil servants and business representatives. A new 'state intelligentsia' and 'organic intellectual' were to emerge in the universities, trade unions, civil society and state-owned enterprises, and were rapidly promoted, often because of their ability to fundraise through their links to government and other donors. South African universities also attracted some of the brightest scholars from Africa and provided a sound and more affordable alternative for African students than did European and American universities.

The GBM complex was fully engaged.

TRANSITION FROM THE 'OLD' TO THE 'NEW ORDER' POST-APARTHEID GBM COMPLEX: A LACK OF STRATEGIC DIRECTION FOR PARASTATALS?

The GBM complex attained its highpoint in the first ten years after 1994. Then, the carefully-crafted confluence of interests spanning government, business and media, and driven by expanded rounds of capital accumulation, started to come undone. By 2008 the 'African agenda', as it was later derisively called, was in disarray and Mbeki made an ignominious (forced) exit from politics. The year 2008 therefore signalled the rapid unravelling of the network of relationships which had its nerve centre in the Mbeki presidency. It also led to the rise of what may be called a 'new order' post-apartheid GBM complex under a Zuma presidency (whose *true* character and key actors are still emerging). The slow but steady shift from the old to the new order GBM complex gained momentum in the build-up to, and aftermath of, the ANC's elective conference in Polokwane in December 2007 where Mbeki was replaced by Jacob Zuma as the party leader. A forceful overthrow of the old order elite members through a powerful and rebellious confluence of populist and disgruntled elite interests ushered in the new.

There was a sequence of dramatic political events in 2008 – many with an explicit regional slant. The electricity crisis, the xenophobia attacks, the ongoing service delivery protests and the nature of the leadership struggle – with Mbeki's legacy arguably in tatters – had led to uncertainty over the country's regional role. South Africa's expanded rounds of accumulation on the continent, a hallmark of its engagement with the continent throughout the 1990s and early twenty-first century, had started to level out (Daniel et al. 2007) particularly with the onset of the global financial crisis and with expansion projects and new businesses having to be put on hold or closed owing to a lack of energy. There was a tacit expectation that South Africa would have to pull back regionally because of its domestic problems. Initiatives such as the African Renaissance and NEPAD were likely to fade fast and the resources devoted to the continent to fulfill Mbeki's vision of the

'African century', likely to have been squandered. NEPAD was unable to gain widespread support and raise the funds it badly required and had mostly faded from national and continental political discourse.

Parastatals operating in the region had run into difficulty – seemingly through over-stretch. The idealistic nature and subsequent detrimental nature of these expansionary measures by the parastatals as a cornerstone of foreign policy can be seen in the case of Spoornet. Although Spoornet had agreed to supply rolling stock and locomotives else-where in Africa, in reality it needed all it had back home. The absurdities and competing domestic and regional priorities were apparent when Spoornet was running at a R2 billion loss in 1999, yet paid US$77.7 million in 2002 for the opportunity to restore and run a major Mozambican rail line (Johnson 2008: 486). Spoornet's handling of its project in Zambia had also run into difficulty by 2004 over charges of alleged mismanagement and reckless conduct relating to two top officials. The idea that Spoornet would be able to operate the Zambian network for twenty years was clearly implausible (ibid.). The expansion of Spoornet in Africa and its imperialist ambitions were stopped after the appointment of Maria Ramos as CEO in 2004. She decided to focus on the local railway instead (Johnson 2008: 491).

The biggest setback for the GBM complex was the energy crisis. As a result of this crisis, regional energy security and the competence of Eskom as the sole and major energy provider underpinning the capitalist expansion, were seriously questioned. The business and media informational networks provided a significant pressure point in lobbying the government. Specifically, the costs incurred by South African mines – the main driving force of the country's economy – and the effects on the country's regionally-orientated telecommunications and retail monopolies, provided a significant tipping point in the policy and lobbying processes concerning energy. As a result of the crisis, South African mining companies in the region suffered lowered output. Expansion projects had to be put on hold. Regional projects such as the Mozal Aluminium Smelter in Mozambique were affected. In May 2008 the National Energy Regulator of South Africa (Nersa) esti-mated that the total cost to the economy of the energy crisis was R50 billion (Nersa 2008: 36). The long-term costs and lost opportunities are unquantifiable. The energy crisis also led to a slipping of Eskom's monopoly. When regional countries realised that they needed to take urgent steps to break the cycle of dependency on Eskom, rehabilitation projects and new projects were fast-tracked.

In 2010 the DRC claimed that it wanted to develop the Grand Inga Project alone. Westcor closed as there was no need for its existence (Khanyile 2010). However, negotia-tions with the DRC government have resumed, a draft treaty has been approved and R200 billion had been allocated to the project in South Africa's 2013 budget (Maake 2013). It remains to be seen whether the project will commence on schedule given the DRC government's fickleness in the matter, not to mention the potential for rampant corrup-tion by DRC government officials and through collusion within the GBM complex.

SABC Africa was pulled from the air in 2006 owing to lack of funds. Its successor, SABC International, was scaled down considerably after a limited viewing on the government-owned Sentech satellite service. It then had limited broadcasts in Washington DC and after 1 am on SABC 2 (Davie 2009). A 24-hour SABC news channel carried on the DSTV satellite service was re-launched in 2013. However, the Minister of Finance, Pravin Gordhan, had shown serious reluctance to support such an initiative, having earlier referred to the idea as a 'vanity project' – questioning, to some extent, the financial sustainability of the channel (Underhill 2013). The global financial situation had led to a decline in private international funds for research, and placed further strain on declining public funds for research. Many of the organisations, institutes and projects focusing on Africa in commercial research have closed or downsized.

The vision of a South African-led African renewal had been discredited by the manner in which Mbeki had to leave office and the extent of the problems facing the country. The persuasive state intelligentsia and organic intellectuals of the old order were left with a discredited vision of African renewal that was no longer lucrative or relevant. The Mbeki legacy, idealistic and visionary as it was, had overstretched the South African state. The long-term trajectory of South Africa's African involvement was clearly unsustainable.

Serious questions had arisen concerning the suitability or stature of South Africa as the 'gateway' to the continent. The UN index on FDI flows into African countries indicated that Egypt and Nigeria attracted more FDI in 2010 than did South Africa, which was ranked tenth out of the African countries in terms of the amount of FDI attracted in 2010. Other African countries were growing far more quickly than South Africa, with some countries attaining growth rates of between 5.9 per cent and 7 per cent, while South Africa was struggling to attain more than 3 per cent (Lefifi 2011). It has been estimated, somewhat optimistically, that by 2014 Egypt will overtake South Africa as Africa's largest economy, and that by 2026 Nigeria will also outstrip South Africa (Cilliers et al. 2011: 82).

Historical records suggest that some of the core productive sectors of the economy have been on a steady decline over the past thirty years as part of a broader de-industrialisation of the country. Mining peaked at 20.6 per cent of GDP in 1980. In 2010, 9.41 per cent was attributed to mining (Van der Wath 2012: 56), and in 2013 most estimates suggested that mining contributed 6 per cent or less to GDP. Manufacturing peaked at 24 per cent of GDP in 1981. In 2010 it was 13.78 per cent (Van der Wath 2012: 56). Capital flight has also been on the steady increase. As a percentage of GDP, capital flight had increased from an average of 9.2 per cent between 1994 and 2000, and averaged 12 per cent between 2001 and 2007, finally reaching 20 per cent in 2007 (Ashman et al. 2011: 7).

The new order GBM complex was modelled on increased state intervention in the economy to appease the left and a growing restlessness among the poor. Yet paradoxically its ultimate goal was to secure expanded rounds of accumulation for the state-linked bourgeoisie and elite, to be achieved through tightened state control of patronage networks and increased pressure on, and direct involvement in, private enterprise. Although the Polokwane conference and the rise of Zuma to the presidency were hailed as a victory for the left, this did not in reality translate into the wholesale economic policy shift that the left had hoped for.

In the new order, personal wealth and political connections are likely to be more unashamedly linked: the 'revolving door' between the public and private spheres was wide open, giving rise to what some have called the 'predatory elite'. Not least of all is the influence of the Gupta family over the Zuma family, government ministers and leaders of parastatals (see Southall 2011). It is likely that elite formation will be concentrated around large infrastructure projects involving PPPs and a more interventionist role played by parastatals. The minister of public enterprises, Malusi Gigaba, has emerged as a key broker in the new order as he will oversee most of the R300 billion awarded to Transnet as outlined in the 2012 State of the Nation address. As part of the drive to re-industrialise the country, Transnet will extend and renew the existing railways and upgrade ports in an attempt to unblock bottlenecks in the export of minerals. The region is included insofar as railways running through Swaziland and to Mozambique can be used to export coal and other minerals. Collectively, the integrated infrastructure programme, which is spread over several years and was revealed in earnest during Zuma's 2012 State of the Nation address, is estimated to be worth R3.2 trillion (Kgosana 2012). It is centred on selected corridors identified as key areas to unlocking the country's mining and manufacturing potential. A centralised Presidential Infrastructure Coordinating Committee (PICC) was established to manage the infrastructure rollout, paving the way for a few well-connected companies to reap the benefits. Since the unveiling of these plans, concerns have arisen regarding the implementation and feasibility of these projects, particularly in respect of a lack of funds and a shortage of technical skills.

On a trip to Ghana in October 2012, Gigaba indicated that parastatals were once again looking to expand into Africa to boost their flagging profits, although the competition from China and India will be severe this time – something which was not really the case under the old order. These expansionary plans could include the creation of a transport hub in West Africa to facilitate trade between the BRICS (Pillay 2012). Yet the feasibility of such ventures seems unrealistic with the financial and management problems plaguing the state-owned transport and energy utilities. SAA has struggled since late 2012 after a fallout between Gigaba and its former board followed by a succession of poor financial results leading to state bailouts (Donnelly 2013a). Despite declaring to Parliament that SAA is expanding its routes into Africa, the former board was criticised by Gigaba for providing no long-term vision for the airline (Donnelly 2013b). Transnet should consider such expansionary plans carefully given the extent of its domestic commitments. Eskom is building new power-generating capacity in the form of Medupi and Kusile and has neither the capacity nor the money to invest elsewhere.

There is no overall abiding vision or overarching ideological drive behind the Zuma administration. 'Ubuntu' is seldom heard and does not have the same ideological 'reach' for civil servants, academics, businesses and the media as the African Renaissance. South Africa appears to have fragmented into a collection of private interests. The policy and think tank community has adopted a more blatantly oppositional stance to govern-ment. Large sections of commercial research have also been co-opted by government in the compilation of the National Development Plan (NDP), headed by Trevor Manuel's

National Planning Commission. Whether the NDP will provide the direction the country needs remains to be seen. Trust between government and business had broken down towards the end of the 'old order', primarily because of the energy crisis and conflicting signals over nationalisation. These problems have intensified significantly in 2012 after the Marikana tragedy and the state's inability to gain control of the subsequent rolling strikes in the mining and farming sectors.

CONCLUSION

A new sense of realism towards the region has taken root under the new order. This is part of a more pragmatic, trade-focused foreign policy dictated by the interests of China, and a closer linking of South Africa's interests to infrastructure projects in the region. In line with its inclusion in BRICS, South Africa's 'spatial fix' has broadened to include emerging markets and its aspirations to be a major player in the global South, and is therefore less focused on the region. Paradoxically, the viewpoint that South Africa is a gateway to Africa is slowly giving way to 'Africa' as a competitor. The final draft of the White Paper on foreign policy (Department of International Relations and Cooperation 2011: 19) notes: 'A number of regional trends could combine to result in challenges to [South Africa's] regional leadership position. High energy prices and rapid growth rates could see the emergence of other regional economic centres, with aspirations for regional influence and leadership.' The industrialisation drive should have been ongoing over the past twenty years of democracy, giving South Africa time to build and maintain a competitive edge; but the country is now in a position where it is effectively playing 'catch up' in an altogether more competitive African environment.

REFERENCES

Ashman S, B Fine and S Newman (2011) Amnesty international? The nature, scale and impact of capital flight from South Africa. *Journal of Southern African Studies* 37(1): 7-25.

Butts K and H Thomas (1986) *The Geopolitics of Southern Africa: South Africa as a Regional Superpower.* Westview Special Studies on Africa. Boulder and London: Westview.

Cilliers J, B Hughes and J Moyer (2011) *African Futures: The Next Forty Years.* Institute for Security Studies. January.

Daniel J and J Lutchman (2006) South Africa in Africa: Scrambling for energy. In Buhlungu, S, J Daniel, R Southall and J Lutchman (eds) *State of the Nation: South Africa 2005-2006.* Cape Town: HSRC Press.

Daniel J, J Lutchman and A Comninos (2007) South Africa in Africa: Trends and forecasts in a changing African political economy. In Buhlungu, S, J Daniel, R Southall and J Lutchman (eds) *State of the Nation: South Africa 2007.* Cape Town: HSRC Press.

Daniel J, V Naidoo and S Naidu (2003) The South Africans have arrived: Post-apartheid corporate expansion into Africa. In Daniel J, A Habib and R Southall (eds) *State of the Nation: South Africa 2003-2004.* Cape Town: HSRC Press.

Davie K (2009) 'SABC International goes down the tube'. *Mail & Guardian.* 11 August.

Department of International Relations and Cooperation (2011) Building a Better World: The Diplomacy of Ubuntu. White paper on South Africa's foreign policy. Final draft. 13 May.

Donnelly L (2013a) 'Could the Chinese provide a model for SA's 'developmental state'?' *Mail & Guardian* 24 January.

Donnelly L (2013b) 'What is causing SAA's turbulence?' *Mail & Guardian* 5 October.

Fine B and Z Rustomjee (1996) *The Political Economy of South Africa: From Minerals-Energy Complex to Industrialisation.* Johannesburg: Witwatersrand University Press.

Gramsci A (1971) Prison notebooks. In Hoare Q and G Smith (eds) *Selections from the Prison Notebooks of Antonio Gramsci.* London: Lawrence and Wishart.

Greenberg S (2008) Market liberalisation and continental expansion: The repositioning of Eskom in post-apartheid South Africa. In MacDonald DA (ed.) *Electric Capitalism: Recolonising Africa on the Power Grid.* Cape Town: HSRC Press.

Hanlon J (1987) *Beggar Your Neighbours: Apartheid Power in Southern Africa.* London and Indiana: Catholic Institute for International Relations, James Currey, Indiana University Press.

Harvey D (2005) *The New Imperialism.* New York: Oxford University Press.

Horvei T (1998) Powering the region: South Africa in the southern African power pool. In Simon D (ed.) *South Africa in Southern Africa: Reconfiguring the Region.* Oxford: James Currey. Athens OH: Ohio State University Press.

Johnson RW (2008) *A Brave New World: The Beloved Country Since the End of Apartheid.* London: Allen Lane.

Kavanagh M (2010) 'DRC in power play as it scraps Inga 3 venture'. *Sunday Independent* 28 February.

Kgosana C (2012) 'Lack of capacity retarding SA'. *Sunday Times* 25 February.

Khanyile S (2010) 'DRC to go solo on 5000MW Inga project'. *The Star* 1 March.

Lefifi T (2011) 'Threat to SA's gateway status'. *Sunday Times* 22 October.

Libby R (1987) *The Politics of Economic Power in Southern Africa.* New Jersey: Princeton University Press.

Maake M (2013) 'Concern over SA's billions in DRC Inga project'. *Business Day* 24 March.

Miller D, R Saunders and O Oloyede (2008) South African corporations and post-apartheid expansion in Africa – Creating a new regional space. *African Sociological Review* 12(1): 1-19.

Mills C (1956) *The Power Elite.* New York: Oxford University Press.

Molele C, L Donnelly and M Mataboge (2013) 'Zuma's mixed bag of State of the Nation promises'. *Mail & Guardian* 8 February.

Nersa (2008) Inquiry into the National Electricity Shortage and Load Shedding: Report by the National Energy Regulator. 12 May.

Ó Tuathail G and J Agnew (1992) Geopolitics and discourse: Practical geopolitical reasoning in American foreign policy. *Political Geography Quarterly* 11(2): 151-166.

Peet R (2002) Ideology, discourse, and the geography of hegemony: From socialist to neoliberal development in postapartheid South Africa. *Antipode* 34(1): 54-84.

Pillay V (2012) 'Troubled parastatals look to Africa for growth'. *Mail & Guardian* 2 October.

Rogerson C (2001) Spatial development initiatives in Southern Africa: The Maputo Development Corridor. *Tijdschrift voor Economische en Sociale Geografie* 92(3): 324-346.

Rogerson C (1990) Defending apartheid: Armscor and the geography of military production in South Africa. *Geojournal* 22(3): 241-250.

Sibeene P (2008) 'Energy projects to gobble N$10bn'. *New Era.* 12 May.

Simon D (2001) Trading spaces: Imagining the 'new' South Africa within the regional and global economies. *International Affairs* 77(2): 377-405.

South African Foundation (2004) South Africa's Business Presence in Africa. Occasional paper 3. Johannesburg: The South African Foundation.

Southall R (2011) Family and favour at the court of Jacob Zuma. *Review of African Political Economy* 38(130): 617-626.

Southall R (2007) The ANC, black economic empowerment and state-owned enterprises: A recycling of history? In Buhlunga S, J Daniel, R Southall and J Lutchman (eds) *State of the Nation: South Africa 2007*. Cape Town: HSRC Press.

Teer-Tomaseli R (2008) 'National' public service broadcasting: Contradictions and dilemmas. In Hadland A, E Louw, S Sesanti and H Wasserman (eds) *Power, Politics and Identity in South African Media*. Selected Seminar Papers. Cape Town: HSRC Press.

Stephan H, M Power, A Hervey and R Fonseca (2006) *The Scramble for Africa in the 21ˢᵗ Century: A View from the South*. Cape Town: Renaissance Press.

Underhill G (2013) 'SABC gambles millions on two new channels'. *Mail & Guardian*. 26 July.

Van der Wath WN (2012) Trends 34(4). Bureau for Economic Research. Stellenbosch University.

NOTES

1   Some of this material appears in the author's DPhil thesis at Oxford University.
2   The GDP figures were recorded at 'basic prices', that is, before taxes and subsidies were subtracted.

CHAPTER 19

The leadership challenge in Southern Africa

Mopeli L Moshoeshoe

INTRODUCTION

The history of Southern Africa has been one of cooperation and conflict. The late 1940s saw the rapid cooling of relations as apartheid became the official policy of the Republic of South Africa, and from 1948 the apartheid system became the paramount factor around which sub-regional relations evolved. As successive National Party governments worked tirelessly to defend apartheid, the neighbours endeavoured to defeat the hated and unjust system. However, given South Africa's economic and military domination of the region and the history of deep interdependence, South Africa's relations with its neighbours – while tense and hostile – remained remarkably close, and although efforts to isolate South Africa politically and culturally were relatively successful they were not matched by similar successes at the economic level. South Africa's relations with its neighbours have paradoxically been characterised by moments of tension, even intermittent wars, and by relative stability and cooperation.

With the demise of apartheid in the early 1990s, many anticipated a thawing in sub-regional relations with peaceful coexistence and cooperation for mutual gains replacing old tensions. The new South Africa, led by a popular democratically elected govern-ment, was expected to use its proven capabilities and its democratic credentials to play a pivotal leadership role on the African continent in general and the Southern African region in particular. It is against this backdrop that South Africa's relations with the newly revamped SADC came into sharp focus. Analysts and scholars expected South Africa's membership to the regional body to bring about qualitative difference and to substantially strengthen the organisation (Biswas 2004: 8). President Robert Mugabe of Zimbabwe vividly captured this sentiment and hope in 1994, when he said: 'Given its level and size of economic development, South Africa will have a positive and major role to play in enhancing the efficacy of SADC as a regional organisation' (Conradie 2001: 47).

South Africa was perceived as a 'natural leader' in Southern Africa (King 1994:8). And with its economic and financial resources, its democratic dispensation and substantial military capabilities, South Africa was considered an unchallenged political, economic and strategic heavyweight in Southern Africa. Its accession to the SADC Windhoek Treaty of 1992 was generally perceived as something of a 'shot in the arm' for the sub-regional organisation, which would give it an edge in enhancing performance and driving progress (Seymour 1996:1).

A decade and a half later, the performance of SADC indicates that significant challenges remain in the way of regional progress despite the presence of a cooperative regional hegemon. Reviews about South Africa's role in SADC do not reflect the initial optimism (Nathan 2012:7). Many reports on SADC are rather gloomy, and observers note that while the sub-region has indeed made some progress in terms of signing numerous protocols, the implementation of these protocols is generally poor, not leading to significant improvement in SADC's general performance. Interestingly, some pundits argue that since joining SADC South Africa has failed to emulate Nigeria's leadership in the Economic Community of West African States (ECOWAS) where the deployment of Nigerian resources has ensured a credible and effective operation of the sub-regional organisation (De Coning 2005:102-3). South Africa's membership in SADC has not resulted in a 'great leap forward' towards a more integrated sub-region (Biswas 2004:54). This raises the question of why South Africa has struggled to perform an effective leadership role in SADC, given its relative resource advantages.

This chapter aims to make a contribution to the ongoing debates on this important question. I start by re-assessing the position of South Africa in Southern Africa, examining South Africa-SADC relations with the explicit aim of illuminating the constraints that affect its performance as a regional leader. To achieve this, I present an overview of the main debates on the leadership challenges in SADC. Insights from assessing negotiations on specific aspects of the recently implemented SADC Protocol on Trade – in particular examining the role played by South Africa in resolving the difficult issues in these sectors – inform subsequent analysis of the broader question of South Africa's leadership. I do not seek to replace the existing explanations but, rather, to make a contribution to the debates, even if only by augmenting one or other of the prevailing arguments.

UNDERSTANDING SOUTH AFRICA IN SADC: POWER, OPPORTUNITIES AND CONSTRAINTS

South Africa's performance as a regional leader has been a subject of vigorous debates among scholars and regional observers in recent years. While some have sought to explain South Africa's performance as a middle power, two more interesting camps have risen to prominence. One camp invokes South Africa's 'exceptionalism' which, they argue, confers some advantages but also imposes major constraints in South Africa's relations with its highly unequal neighbours. Sidiropoulos (2007:2) has argued that South Africa's engagement with Southern Africa 'is both consciously and unconsciously coloured by its gigantism'. This, coupled with lingering perceptions of South Africa as a regional bully of yesteryear, is a significant constraint (based on moral dimensions) on South Africa's regional policy.

South Africa's exceptionalism is perceived as a double-edged sword. Relative economic and political successes simultaneously impose a constraint on South Africa's ability to exercise full leverage in regional relations. According to this view, a paradox is that South Africa's advanced and sophisticated economy, coupled with military capabilities that are massive in relation to those of its neighbours, put it in a position to play an effective leadership role, but these advantages simultaneously create fear and suspicion in its vulnerable neighbours, thus imposing a limit to South Africa's regional policy options. Despite South Africa's objective strengths and real leverage, its sub-regional policies have to navigate around being a driver of regional cooperation and integration and the reluctance to project power that could entrench the negative perceptions of its hegemony. Therefore, South Africa's unassailable position of power and dominance paradoxically imposes, in practice, significant limitations for effective regional leadership (Chimanikire 1992).

Acceptance of Pretoria's leadership today continues to be constrained by the historical legacy of apartheid (Flemes 2007:12). South Africa's ability to exercise effective regional influence has been undercut by the fact that since the 1970s the apartheid government had utilised its economic power position and its military capabilities to the detriment of its neighbours (Ajulu 1985:119). In the words of Chris Landsberg, effective leadership by the post-apartheid government has been limited or hamstrung by government's efforts to dispel notions of a regional big brother, pursuing self-interest or hegemonic ambitions (Landsberg 2004: 230).

The second view looks to the type of policies pursued and embraced by South Africa since 1994 which do not sit easily with the interests of many developing countries, including its neighbours in Southern Africa. In comparison to its neighbours, South Africa is a relatively developed country with a sophisticated economic infrastructure and an economy that is well integrated into the global economic system. The argument is that South Africa's interests markedly diverge from those of the rest of the continent, which leaves it in an isolated and unpopular position (Muller 2001: 89) because superior economic strength and better integration into the global economy translates into differences in the key interests, or priorities, between South Africa and other poorer counterparts in sub-Saharan Africa. Patrick Bond argues that South Africa is associated with the same global capitalist system which some decry as exploitative and unfair. He posits that South Africa's role on the continent is viewed rather negatively and he notes that this view is shared by some countries in Southern Africa as well (Bond 2006: 68).

South Africa's intra-SADC investments are concentrated in the service industries and seldom in the manufacturing sectors, which aggravates the import-export imbalances and contributes little to economic development in these countries (Schoeman 2001: 80). In spite of the huge surpluses in its trade with SADC, Pretoria is often perceived as defensive and protective in its sub-regional trade relations (Moshoeshoe 2012: 58). This feeds into suspicions by fellow regional countries that South Africa does not really have their national interests at heart (Bond 2006: 59). The fact is that, as a relatively developed country, South Africa's interests are not entirely in tune with the national self-interest of its neighbours. In practical policy terms, South Africa is isolated, not merely in terms of its economic status but also in terms of its strategy choices and the ideological positions it tends to adopt. Perceived shortfalls in South Africa's leadership in the region partly reflect real opposition by regional countries resisting what they deem as unfavourable policies supported by South Africa.

The foregoing arguments make a meaningful contribution to understanding intra-regional relations in SADC but although these views are partially helpful they are certainly not sufficient to account for perceived and real shortfalls in South Africa's leadership performance in SADC because they are not exhaustive in explaining why an undisputable regional hegemon is struggling to play an effective leadership role in a sub-region which it so substantially dominates. For example, the first argument, which emphasises moral considerations and lack of trust as one of the main constraints on South Africa's regional policy, makes a valid and informative point given the unique historical circumstances of Southern Africa – however, it is also true that hegemonic domination or lack of trust does not in itself preclude discharge of effective leadership or cooperation.

The second view revolves around questions of exceptionalism and self-interest based on incompatible ideological positions as a challenge for consensual leadership between South Africa and its neighbours. Again, this is a valid argument, and well supported in the literature. However, the counter argument is also true: that even where there is consensus, one would still expect collective action problems to constrain regional cooperation and thus affect the leadership performance by the hegemon.

Therefore, since both explanations are generally valid, the aim is not to dismiss or falsify them but to complement them.

TOWARDS THE SADC FTA: THE NEED FOR HEGEMONIC LEADERSHIP?

In 1992, SADC moved away from the simple coordination structure of its predecessor to a new organisation capable of facilitating deeper forms of political and economic cooperation. On the political front, SADC aimed to forge a shared identity by nurturing, evolving or propagating common political values, systems and institutions. The stated objectives on the economic front include the achievement of economic growth through deeper forms of integration (SADC 1995). Early efforts by SADC were to deepen intra-regional ties by forging meaningful and mutually beneficial relations through trade cooperation. Political and military stability being imperative for regional economic development, SADC also prioritised the 'evolution of common political values and institutions as the basis for regional peace and security (SADC Secretariat 1992: 9-10). SADC aimed to 'develop a prosperous and balanced regional economy in Southern Africa based on the principles of equity and mutual benefit' and regional economic cooperation was seen as a pillar towards the achievement of an integrated regional economy in SADC (Landsberg 2004: 192).

When South Africa acceded to the SADC Treaty on 14 September 1994, integration was at the top of the regional agenda. With its peaceful political transition to multiparty democracy and its considerable economic and military resources, South Africa was well poised to assist SADC in realising these goals. Accession to the SADC Treaty conferred responsibilities on South Africa, and its performance in this role would be assessed in the context of the collective regional programmes as reflected by the goals and objectives of SADC. South Africa's commitment to the region was never in doubt. Mandela's government quickly acceded to the SADC Treaty and, in line with the official agenda, South Africa's main efforts focused on the development, operationalisation and implementation of the protocols in the complementary areas of trade, politics and security.

It was not a coincidence that South Africa, having joined SADC officially in 1994, hosted a SADC conference in 1995 in which the idea of forming a sub-regional trading block was first broached. Subsequent talks between member states led to the signing of the SADC Protocol on Trade on 24 August 1996 in Maseru, Lesotho, by all eleven heads of state and government of SADC, reflecting a unanimous declaration of intent to cooperate in liberalising respective national trade regimes and to form a sub-regional free trade agreement (FTA). The Protocol committed governments to resuming negotiations towards the gradual elimination of barriers to intra-regional trade as a step towards the FTA.

In theory, free trade arrangements can boost trade volumes, partly by reducing or eliminating the cost of intra-regional trade exchanges. Trade liberalisation arrangements can also facilitate national economic growth in various ways, including attracting foreign direct investments (FDIs), hence improving balance of payments prospects and attracting new technologies and requisite skills into national economies. Experiences from other parts of the world empirically support the logic of the free trade theory. Trade liberalisation in these regions has resulted in significant increases in cross-border economic activity from which all participating members benefited (Nahimana 2007: 14). For example, from 1990 to 2000, exports between Mercosur (Argentina, Brazil, Paraguay and Uruguay) members rose from US$ 4.1 billion to US$17.9 billion and imports also grew from US$4.2 billion to US$ 17.9 billion. In the same period, the general exports of every Mercosur member state to other members maintained a steady upward trend (Ruiz-Dana et al. 2009: 16).

In Southern Africa, the FTA presented an attractive prospect of a sub-regional market worth US$360 billion with a total population of 70 million. Angola and the Democratic Republic of Congo could add a further US$71 billion and 77 million people to the SADC market (SADC 2008: 2), the combined potential income of which was estimated at around US$431bn with a total population of 247 million people (TIPS 2008:2). In spite of huge economic and developmental disparities between SADC member countries, the FTA was deemed to be key in enhancing intra-regional trade and investment flows from which all countries in the region could benefit. Regional governments big and small expressed a common desire to 'liberalise intra-regional trade in goods and services on the basis of fair, mutually equitable and beneficial trade arrangements' (SADC 1996: 4). In the words of the then South African president Thabo Mbeki: 'Integration can create the basis for regional markets and industries to overcome the limits of small markets, to achieve economies of scale, and enhance competitiveness (Mbeki: 2008). Therefore, the idea of liberalising intra-SADC trade enjoyed support from all the member governments.

The SADC Trade Protocol proposed a gradualist approach to regional trade liberalisation. Member governments committed to realise the regional FTA over a period of eight years. The approach was that, subsequent to the signing of the Protocol in 1996, member governments would engage their respective national legislatures for ratification and immediate implementation. The then general secretary of SADC, Kaire Mbuende, expected members to ratify the Protocol, to resume implementation by early 1998, and to have an FTA in place by 2004 (Mbuende: 1997). Despite a strong theoretical rationale, widely acknowledged potential gains from free trade, strong traditions and support for regional cooperation within SADC, Mbuende's expectations proved too optimistic, and the 2004 deadline for the inauguration of the FTA proved to be over-ambitious. SADC trade negotiations were (with hindsight, perhaps not surprisingly) arduous, with a number of stalemates that resulted in a series of missed deadlines – which in turn delayed ratification and the coming into force of the Protocol.

While trade liberalisation has potential for mutual gains, it also carries short-term costs. The implementation of reciprocal trade liberalisation commitments might eventually benefit all participants in the future, but opening up one's market carries immediate costs, ranging from revenue losses and possible increases in national unemployment rates to curtailed autonomy on trade policy. When self-interested governments liberalise trade, unless various national interests are successfully reconciled, the trade agreement may never be reached – which can stall the realisation of a free trade area.

Trade negotiations between signatories of the SADC Protocol on Trade were not easy. The prominent stumbling blocks included the modalities of tariff reduction schedules and the rules of origin on textiles and apparel, and wheat/wheat products. The then minister of trade for Mozambique captured cogently some of his government's motives for delaying the ratification of the Protocol: 'We had to think of the losses and gains, and ratification was conditional or dependent on concluding the negotiations and this was also South Africa's position' (Baloi 1999). Despite SADC members' expressed desire to liberalise intra-regional trade and establish a mutually beneficial free trade area, the trade negotiations were drawn-out and difficult.

The next section focuses on some of the most intractable issues in these negotiations, examining the role South Africa played towards overcoming these hurdles.

TRADE IN SUGAR

Negotiations on trade in sugar were a great source of discord in the SADC negotiations. The negotiations split the members into two camps: the non-sugar producers comprising Botswana, Lesotho and Namibia, and the majority producers. The three wanted trade in sugar to be liberalised while the others pushed for exclusion of the sector from liberalisation. SADC sugar producers, including South Africa, raised concerns over cheap sugar imports adversely affecting their producers, while the non-sugar producers protested the high prices of sugar in the region.

Generally, sugar producing members faced strong domestic lobbies. For example, in 2000 investors in this sector threatened to pull out of Mozambique if the government yielded to pressure from the International Monetary Fund (IMF) and removed the existing protective measures for domestic sugar producers (Holm: 2007). Consequently, the government stood its ground against the IMF and Mozambique later defended this position in the SADC negotiations. Other SADC sugar producers faced similar domestic challenges, and declarations of self-interest were echoed in various ways. The majority of SADC members treated the sector as sensitive, and despite efforts by the regional sugar importers Botswana, Namibia and Lesotho, which wanted liberalisation and lower regional prices, there was resistance from the exporting countries. South Africa being one the major sugar producers, meant that even the Southern African Customs Union (SACU) was split on the issue. Eventually they agreed that sugar would not be liberalised under the terms of the Protocol but would be traded under a special arrangement. Exclusion of the sugar sector from the liberalisation process was to have consequences for the volume of trade occurring within SADC FTA and therefore its effectiveness.

TRADE IN WHEAT AND WHEAT PRODUCTS

It is notable that until the signing of the Protocol in 1996, the volume of intra-SADC trade in agricultural products was negligible, as post-independence restrictions were in most instances strengthened through a series of legislative amendments by governments. The majority of member states, with farm-based economies that employ the bulk of their populations, were quick to declare the agricultural sector politically sensitive. And sustained implementation of protectionist measures in this sector by individual governments stood in sharp contrast with free trade principles and put a strain on the regional trade liberalisation process.

For example, in the dying days of trade negotiations, Swaziland amended its Dairy Act of 1968 to give effect to new import levies on selected agricultural and dairy products. Lesotho retained bans and restrictions on several agricultural commodities, including poultry, bread, eggs, pulses, fruits, vegetables and milk. In 2002, and well into the implementation phase of the Protocol, Zambia imposed a six-month ban on imports of fourteen Zimbabwean products – following bans of Zimbabwean beef and poultry in 1993 and 1994 respectively. Malawi delayed free trade in a number of key products such as poultry, salt, maize and tobacco, by insisting on import licences. South Africa was accused of protectionism as its importers demanded strict processing standards and a consistent flow of fresh produce (Mopeli 2012: 65). Negotiations in the agricultural sector in general presented a challenge in SADC, but talks on wheat and wheat flour products were extremely difficult despite SADC's being the net importer of wheat, with only South Africa and Zimbabwe growing wheat on a meaningful scale. An example from Mozambique is instructive. Mozambique was importing subsidised wheat – from outside the region – to mill and sell wheat domestically and to export animal feed made from the residue. From these activities the national milling industry created thousands of jobs and paid more taxes to the state than the huge gas and petroleum project Mozal; it trained people from the banking industry and supplied other cereal-based industries such as pasta and cake factories with cheaper domestically milled wheat flour. Liberalisation in this sector alone threatened approximately 1 500 direct layoffs and about 10 000 indirect (Holm 2007).

Mozambique's situation was by no means unique, and edifies the underlying motives of many regional governments in the negotiations on trade in wheat and sugar if not all agricultural products. Interestingly, South Africa, one of the key producers but still a net importer of wheat, was also a regional net exporter of wheat flour. Therefore, any liberalisation in the sector would effectively raise a dilemma for the biggest economy, as it would mean that South African millers could import wheat at prices lower than the local cost, which would adversely affect the local producers. South Africa faced a paradox, because as a net exporter of wheat flour it was logical to support liberalisation of trade in the sector. However South Africa was also the main producer of wheat in SADC, with about 6 000 commercial wheat farmers sustaining no less than 28 000 jobs (NAMC 2004). Liberalisation of trade in the sector might benefit the millers, but it was going to negatively affect the wheat growers and surely aggravate unemployment in the country.

TEXTILES: THE RULES OF ORIGIN

The 19th Annual Summit of SADC held in Maputo, Mozambique on 18 August 1999 was expected to conclude the SADC trade talks and to secure ratifications to get the protocol into force. But any such hopes were dashed when Zambia, 'expressing the need to protect local industry' and, with support from South Africa and Mauritius, asked for further postponement for the implementation of the Protocol until the agreement on the rules of origin on clothing and textiles was reached (Harrington 2006). The SADC trade negotiations had reached a deadlock, and according to the South African trade official, the proposed rules were 'simply too lax' (Ngwenya 2000). It was a strong view of the SACU block led by South Africa that liberalisation was linked to a 'process of viable regional development' and that regional arrangements should not undermine the viability of the sector in the region (SADC 1996). One South Africa/SACU trade negotiating team member, Angus September, pointed out in a 2006 interview that '…it wasn't liberalisation for its own sake, we had to maintain growth and create jobs for our own.'

Thus, SACU proposed a more tedious double transformation rule which required that two stages of production process – from yarn to fabric and from fabric to finished product – take place within the region. Non-SACU members preferred to import fabric from cheaper global sources, produce finished product and sell it into a lucrative SACU market at a profit. Smaller regional economies with weak production bases and without the ability to produce their own fabric protested that the double transformation rule of origin effectively barred them from benefiting from the trade liberalisation.

It was not surprising that fears and concerns about integrating extremely heterogeneous economies had permeated SADC trade negotiations since the signing of the Trade Protocol in 1996. There was perennial fear that firms in smaller countries might not survive competition from South African firms. While these 'shut-offs' might be desirable in principle, in practice any such displacements are undesirable as they aggravate domestic unemployment levels and can lead to political instability if displaced workers fail to get alternative employment. Smaller countries feared reinforcement of 'spoke and hub' relations between South Africa/SACU and the rest of the region through de-industrialising smaller economies while increasing the concentration of industry in South Africa (Mutambara 2007).

The flipside of this argument found expression from the labour sector in South Africa itself. The Congress of South African Trade Unions (Cosatu) expressed fear that liberalisation might lead to the influx of cheap imports from lower-wage economies in the region and that firms in South Africa might relocate to these countries – with devastating effects on domestic production and employment levels (Cosatu: 1999). A compromise was eventually reached in September 1999, when tailor-made provisions were adopted to mitigate polarisation effects. Firstly, LDCs were granted extended liberalisation periods, as well as non-reciprocal SACU market access in specific commodities and more relaxed rules of origin in textiles for a limited period. Secondly, members also invoked the principle of asymmetry in tariff differentiation in return for the adoption of the new double transformation rule of origin demanded by South Africa.

REVENUE IMPLICATIONS AS A CHALLENGE FOR REGIONAL TRADE LIBERALISATION

The prospect of revenue concerns featured strongly in the trade negotiations and also significantly influenced trade policy decisions during the implementation of the protocol, as regional governments were not equally predisposed to revenue losses as a result of liberalisation. For example, prior to implementation, trade tariffs accounted for about 10 per cent of total government revenue for Tanzania and Zimbabwe, 30 per cent for Mauritius, Namibia and Zambia and for more than 50 per cent of government revenues in Lesotho and Swaziland. At full implementation in 2008, Zambia and Malawi were expected to forfeit between 66 and 50 per cent respectively in total trade duty collections. Zimbabwe and Mozambique were expected to experience 42 and 34 per cent duty reductions respectively (Kandelwal 2004).

To appreciate the seriousness of revenue concerns on policy decision making, one must consider what proportion of national revenues these duty losses represented. In Zambia, Malawi and Zimbabwe full implementation of the SADC free trade commitments were estimated at 9, 8 and 7 per cent respectively of total government revenues; and predictions were 8, 9 and 1.6 for Mauritius, Mozambique and Tanzania respectively. South Africa/SACU faced a lesser revenue loss prospect at about 0.1 per cent. Fears of revenue loss were mostly legitimate and they had a bearing on how governments behaved towards their liberalisation commitments. For example, in February 2004 the Zambian government informed the SADC Committee of Ministers of Trade that implementation of the tariff reductions seriously threatened the fiscal stability of the government (Ministry of Finance 2004). This report further warned that implementation of the 2004 tariff reduction schedule alone was going to cost the Zambian government about 41 billion kwacha (US$8.6 million).

For some of the member states, liberalisation represented the loss of a crucial policy instrument. South Africa, for example, has historically used trade tariff as an instrument of industrial policy to protect selected home industries. South African law still does not allow the importation of second-hand clothing and vehicles, partly to protect the key programmes and sectors such as the Motor Industry Development Programme (MIDP) and the clothing and textile sector.

On 1 January 2008 the SADC FTA came into being, officially inaugurated at the 28th summit meeting of SADC heads of state and governments, held on 16-17 August 2008 in Johannesburg. The inauguration of the FTA signalled not only progress but also commitment to deeper integration by SADC member governments. From the onset, however, it was clear that the new SADC FTA had very limited impact and was failing to deliver the predicted mutual free trade gains that motivated the liberalisation in the first place, as the bulk of intra-SADC trade continued to take place outside the free trade arrangement, leaving only about 25 per cent to go through the FTA. In his speech at the inauguration of the FTA, Thabo Mbeki blamed supply-side constraints as obstacles that inhibit SADC members from taking full advantage of the 'increasingly open and freer regional market' (Mbeki 2008). But while the supply-side argument may hold to some extent, it is also true that poor implementation of the Trade Protocol and growing use of non-tariff barriers (NTBs) had substantial counter-effects. Self-interest by individual governments led to poor rates of compliance and the re-introduction of non-tariff measures undermined the regional goal of achieving a functional FTA.

THE SADC EXPERIENCE: A ROLE FOR A REGIONAL HEGEMON?

The South African economy is not only the biggest in Southern Africa, it is also the biggest and most advanced economy on the African continent. Its gross national product (GNP) constitutes over 60 per cent of that of the entire SADC region. And because of its advanced infrastructure the South African economy is well-integrated into the global economy – hence it is often touted as a gateway into Africa. The extent of its global integration means that South Africa's economic policy options go well beyond Africa and Southern Africa.

When it acceded to office in 1994, the ANC government had to respond speedily to pressures from the previously disadvantaged majority in the country. Aiming for swift delivery on socioeconomic objectives such as job creation and poverty reduction, the government adopted Growth, Employment and Redistribution Programme (GEAR) in 1996. Central to GEAR was the promotion of South Africa's exports to the global markets and the attraction of foreign direct investments needed to sustain required economic growth rates. South Africa therefore had to play by global rules, hence its choice to drop the Reconstruction and Development Programme (RDP) strategy for a neoliberal policy as reflected by the GEAR strategy. However, adoption of neoliberal policies left South Africa in an awkward position and cast doubts on its leadership role on a continent that is generally opposed to these policies. Patrick Bond observes that South Africa has been gradually diverging from the rest of the African continent and has even contested some African positions in World Trade Organisation (WTO) negotiations (Bond 2006).

Bond and others argue that the differences in policy perspectives between South Africa and its poor and least-developed African counterparts has negative implications for its ability to exercise leadership on the continent. But while this view is generally valid, it does not satisfactorily explain South Africa's leadership challenges in Southern Africa. Firstly, the majority of Southern African states had already been put on a neoliberal path by the structural adjustment reforms implemented throughout the 1980s and 90s and there was not much resistance to neoliberalism per se among SADC member states. South Africa's leadership performance may not be understood exclusively in terms of ideological differences. Normally, any situation involving self-interested governments working towards a mutually beneficial end raises collective action problems regardless of whether the governments involved share similar ideological notions.

A review of the regional trade liberalisation process suggests that South Africa's domestic challenges of widespread poverty, inequality, high unemployment and service delivery problems place severe constraints on its role in the region despite its obvious economic dominance. South Africa's insistence on a double transformation rule of origin for the textile and clothing sector, its ban on second-hand motor vehicles and its failure to facilitate consensus on trade in sugar and in wheat and wheat flour products show that, faced with chronic unemployment levels and pressure from the trade union movement, South Africa's options were not that much better than those of its counterparts. It is actually fair to question whether South Africa has the capacity to act as an economic growth pole in Southern Africa.

The other view explains South Africa's leadership shortfalls by correctly drawing attention to the manner in which its relative economic and military preponderances had been utilised in the past. The gist of this argument is that although the post 1994 dispensation may be new, South Africa is not a brand new country. The negative manner in which apartheid South Africa used its military and economic power continues to have a limiting effect on the country's regional policy today, for acceptance of its leadership is constrained by the historical legacy of apartheid (Flemes 2007). Therefore, how South Africa engages the sub-region is shaped, and usually limited, by concerns of not entrenching perceptions of domination associated with the hated minority regime.

South Africa's aim of avoiding a 'bully-boy' image is a valid foreign policy limitation as it militates against the use of power. However, moral considerations alone cannot explain South Africa's regional leadership performance in Southern Africa and they should not obscure the objective realities that constrain it. For example, the military intervention into Lesotho in September 1998, even though it stands in contrast to other interventions (such as in Zimbabwe), is significant as it illustrates that, where it has real leverage, South Africa is willing to use power, including military force. Greg Mills (2001:2) makes the point that, by Mbeki's own admission, South Africa's policy position was informed by its own lack of leverage over Zimbabwe and its leadership.

The SADC FTA, if successfully implemented, was expected to improve regional GDP and assist members to achieve growth rates of between 6.8 and 7.2 per cent (Ramsamy 1996). Therefore, trade liberalisation represented a mutually beneficial arrangement that could improve prospects for advancing national development programmes, alleviate poverty and reduce unemployment. For South Africa in particular, a fully-functional FTA would contribute to fast-tracking socioeconomic transformation.

The widely acknowledged potential gains from the FTA notwithstanding, SADC trade negotiations showed that South Africa, like its smaller regional counterparts, faced challenges that severely limited its own options – which partly explains why, despite being a major manufacturing economy and facing potential gains from a regional FTA, South Africa did not assume responsibility either to facilitate the negotiations or to ease the implementation of the Protocol. The disparities that exist between South Africa and its partners clearly complicated the trade negotiation process, and without clear assistance or support mechanisms for the weakest economies, it is not surprising that the negotiations were so difficult and subsequent implementation so poor. As one of the poorest member states in SADC, Malawi failed to implement its trade liberalisation commitments despite having ratified the trade protocol and, as a result, remains outside the FTA. Because of poor implementation and no clear leadership, in particularly in the form of concessions or financial support to the weakest members, SADC inaugurated an FTA whose credibility and functionality were already in question in 2008. The experience of SADC in trying to realise a regional free trade area, the challenges encountered (particularly by weaker states), and the lack of clear interventions to mitigate these problems does not bode well for current and future regional initiatives. Even more importantly, it raises questions about South Africa's capacity to lead the Southern African region into deeper integration.

CONCLUSION

The end of the Cold War in the 1990s and the demise of the hated apartheid system was a game changer in South Africa, necessitating a radical shift from hostile political relations of isolation to friendly regional relations based on solidarity and cooperation within the sub-region. This period also ushered in a whole new paradigm that gave hope to new regional aspirations, presenting new opportunities. The role of the new South Africa in the region quickly became a talking point, with the general feeling that, given South Africa's economic, financial and military resources, plus sound democratic credentials and stability, the country was going to pull the region along a strongly developmental path by supporting mutually beneficial cooperation initiatives.

The expectations of South Africa's role in the sub-region were either simplistic or based on questionable assumptions, generally ignoring the fact that foreign policy is the function of how policy makers conceive of their own domestic circumstances – which means that performance of the new South Africa in influencing the regional development processes would depend primarily on South Africa's internal political and economic realities. These expectations also failed to recognise that the same hegemonic strengths of South Africa also impose constraints that limit its foreign policy options, as is illustrated by trade negotiations pursued for wealth creation by South Africa but with the potential to damage or stunt the economic development of its neighbours and increase insecurity in these countries. Contrary to its predecessor, the democratic South Africa does not have all policy instruments – carrots and sticks – available for dealing with the region. It is confined primarily to those options that are sufficiently attractive to its neighbours to solicit voluntary consent to cooperate.

This discussion on SADC trade liberalisation illuminates some of the objective internal socioeconomic conditions that afflict South Africa, and illustrates how – despite apparent domination – South Africa falls short of expectations as a hegemonic leader. Lack of leverage has been cited by South African officials as a limitation to its interventions in the region. In concluding, I argue that despite the resources and its hegemonic poise, South Africa faces a number of internal constraints that limit its leadership ability in Southern Africa. Typical hegemonic responsibility would entail acting as a paymaster to secure cooperation or to facilitate regional agreements and the biggest economy, South Africa, would have been expected to offer 'sweeteners' in the form of concessions to the poorer member states as a way of smoothing the SADC trade liberalisation process. But South Africa did not seem to have the political will to facilitate trade negotiations or ensure good implementation in order to secure a credible FTA in Southern Africa.

REFERENCES

Baloi O (1999) 'Mozambique to ratify SADC trade protocol before 1999.' *Midweek Sun*. www.online-newspapers.com/botswana.htm [Accessed March 2006].

Barber J (2004) *Mandela's World: The International Dimension of South Africa's Political Revolution 1990-99*. Oxford: James Currey.

Biswas A (2007) *Post-Apartheid South Africa: Its Relations With the Neighbouring Countries*. New Delhi: Asian Books.

Bond P (2006) *TALK Left, Walk Right: South Africa's Frustrated Global Reforms*. 2nd edition. http://ccs.ukzn.ac.za/files/BondTalkLeftWalkRight2ndedn.pdf [Accessed 26 July 2013].

Chetty L (2013) 'SA a key player in regional trade and development'. *Mail & Guardian*. http://www.thoughtleader.co.za/leeroychetty/2013/0312sa-a-key-player-in-regional-trade [Accessed 12 March 2013].

Chilala B (2008) SADC trade capacity and compliance mechanism. *Southern Africa Global Competitiveness Hub*. www.satrahub.org/index.php [Accessed 11 February 2009].

Chimanikire DP (1992) *South Africa's Destabilization Policy: The Zimbabwean Experience: Part 1. ISAS Working Paper Series, No. 1*. Institute of Southern African Studies. Roma NUL.

Cosatu (1999) Submission on the SADC Protocol on Trade (presentation to a joint sitting of the Portfolio Committees on Trade and Industry, Foreign Affairs, Agriculture and Land Affairs and the NCOP Select Committee on Economic Affairs, 25 October, Cape Town.

De Coning C (2005) Peacekeeping stand-by-system for SADC: Implementing the African Standby Force framework in Southern Africa. In Hammerstad A (ed.) *People, States and Regions: Building a Collaborative Security Regime in Southern Africa*. Johannesburg: SAIIA.

Department of International Relations and Cooperation (2012) The National Development Plan. Pretoria: SA Government.

Erwin A (1998) South Africa and the SADC Trade Protocol. Paper presented at a conference on regional integration in Southern Africa, 27 October. Johannesburg: SAIIA.

Flemes D (2007) Conceptualizing Regional power in international relations: lessons from South African case. GIGA Working Papers No. 53, German Institute of Global and Area Studies.

Hamlyn M (2006) It would take a miracle for SADC to integrate South Africa and Zimbabwean Economies. http://www.busrep.co.za [Accessed 13 September 2006].

Hangi A M (2012) Is the SADC Suitable for a Monetary Union? ESRF Discussion Paper, No. 44, Dar es Salaam: The Economic and Research Foundation. http://www.policy.org.zaarticle/sa-mbeki-launch-of-free-trade-area-at-sadc-summit-17082008-2008-08-17 [Accessed 21 July 2013].

Harrington W (2006) quoted in *The Times of Zambia*, Lusaka, 3 January. http://www.africanews.org/south/stories20000103/20000103_feat1.html.

King A (1994) Paper delivered to the Seminar on The Image of the United Nations on South Africa. UN Department of Information and the Centre for Southern African Studies. University of the Western Cape, 8-10 February, Somerset West.

Krister H (2007) Impact of EPAs on Mozambique: The Case of Wheat, Wheat Flour and Rice. www.tradescentre.org.zw/newsletter/2004/december/article5.html [Accessed 23 April 2009].

Landsberg C (2004) *The Quiet Diplomacy of Liberation: International Politics and South Africa's Transition*. Johannesburg: Jacana.

Lewis DJ, S Robison and K Thierfelder (2003) Free trade agreements and the SADC economies. *Journal of African Economies* 12: 156-206.

Mabuza Z (2006) Presentation on SADC Finance and Investment Protocol. Maseru.

Makumare J (1998) 'SADC Trade Protocol Lies in Limbo'. *The Zambian Mirror*, Lusaka.

Mills G (2001) The dilemma of representing South Africa's foreign policy: In *The South African Yearbook of International Affairs 2001/2002*. Johannesburg: SAIIA.

Mbeki MT (2008) Speech at the launching of the SADC FTA. Midrand, South Africa.

Mbuende K (1997) SADC trade protocol to be ratified early 1998.' *Zimbabwe Independent*,12 September, Harare.

Moshoeshoe LM (2012) Multiple Logics of Collective Action: A comparative Study of Cooperation in the Southern African Development Community. PhD dissertation, University of the Witwatersrand.

Mudzonga E (2008) Implementation Challenges for the SADC FTA: Tariff and Non Tariff Barriers. Paper presented at the Southern African Forum on Trade, 6-7 August, Pretoria.

Muller M (2001) South Africa's economic diplomacy and its role in multilateral fora. *In South African Yearbook of International Affairs 2001/2002*. Johannesburg: SAIIA.

Mutambara TE (2007) Regional cross border investment between the Southern Africa Development Community member states and the expected potential benefits. *Studies in Economics and Econometrics* 31: 53-77.

Nahimana G (2006) Can Regional Integration Save Africa? A world of ideas. http://www.project-syndicate.org/commentary/nahimana1/English [Accessed 17 January 2010].

Nathan L (2012) *Community of Insecurity: SADC's Struggle for Peace and Security in Southern Africa.* Surrey: Ashgate.

National Agricultural Marketing Council (2004) Final report of the food pricing monitoring committee. Pretoria, NAMC.

Ngwenya S (2000) quoted in the *Zimbabwe Mirror*, Harare, 20 January.

Oosthuizen G (2006) *The Southern African Community: The Organisation, Its Policies and Prospects.* Johannesburg: Institute of Global Dialogue, 255-256.

Padamja K (2004) COMESA and SADC: Prospects and challenges for regional trade integration. International Monetary Fund: IMF Working Paper, WP/04/227. Washington.

Ruiz-Dana A, P Goldschagg, E Claro and H Blanco (2009) Regional Integration, Trade and Conflicts in Latin America. In Khan SR (ed.) *Regional Trade Integration and Conflict Resolution.* London and New York: Routledge and IRDC.

SADC Secretariat (2009) Activity Report of the SADC Secretariat: August 2007 to July 2008. Gaborone

SADC (2008) *SADC Free Trade Area: Growth Development and Wealth Creation.* SADC Handbook.

SADC Secretariat (1992) Towards the Southern African Development Community: A Declaration by Heads of State and Government of Southern Africa. Windhoek.

Schoeman M (2001) Objectives, structures and strategies: South Africa's foreign policy. In *South African Yearbook of International Affairs 2001/2002*. Johannesburg: SAIIA.

Seymour V (1996) Global Dialogue, human rights and foreign policy: will South Africa please lead. *Southern African Perspectives, 55,* Centre for Southern African Studies, University of the Western Cape. Cape Town.

Sidiropoulos E (2007) South Africa's regional engagement for peace and security.' FRIDE Comment, October.

TIPS (2008) SADC free trade area: growth development and wealth creation. http://www.oecd.org/dev/emea/0401475 [Accessed 3 January 2009].

World Bank (2013) The World Development Indicators database [online]. http://www.siteresources.worldbank.org/DATASTATISTICS/Resources/GDP.pdf [Accessed 23 March 2013].

Zambian Ministry of Finance (2004) The Revenue Implications of the SADC Free Trade Area for Zambia – Baseline Revenue Loss. Lusaka: Ministry of Finance.

Contributors

Clare Ballard: Researcher, Community Law Centre, University of the Western Cape.

Ahmed Bawa: Vice-Chancellor, Durban University of Technology.

Aninka Claassens: Chief Researcher, Rural Women's Action Research Programme, Centre for Law and Society, University of Cape Town.

John GI Clarke: freelance writer, social work practitioner and lay Catholic theologian.

Scarlett Cornelissen: Professor, Department of Political Science, Stellenbosch University.

Miriam Di Paola: Researcher, Centre for Education Rights and Transformation, University of Johannesburg.

Keith Gottschalk: Fulbright Scholar, Department of Political Studies, University of the Western Cape.

Ran Greenstein: Associate Professor, Department of Sociology, University of the Witwatersrand.

Bridget Kenny: Associate Professor, Department of Sociology, University of the Witwatersrand.

Gilbert M Khadiagala: Jan Smuts Professor of International Relations, University of the Witwatersrand.

Ian Macun: Director Collective Bargaining, Department of Labour.

Xolela Mangcu: Associate Professor, Department of Sociology, University of Cape Town.

Zethu Matebeni: Researcher, Institute for Humanities in Africa, University of Cape Town.

Boitumelo Matlala: Researcher, Rural Women's Action Research Programme, Centre for Law and Society, University of Cape Town.

Dale T McKinley: Independent researcher and activist.

Mopeli L Moshoeshoe: Lecturer, Department of International Relations, University of the Witwatersrand.

Sarah Mosoetsa: Senior Lecturer, Department of Sociology, University of the Witwatersrand.

Prishani Naidoo: Lecturer, Department of Sociology, University of the Witwatersrand.

Devan Pillay: Associate Professor, Department of Sociology, University of the Witwatersrand.

Nicolas Pons-Vignon: Senior Researcher, Corporate Strategy and Industrial Development Programme, University of the Witwatersrand.

Martin Prew: Visiting Fellow, School of Education, University of the Witwatersrand.

Roger Southall: Professor Emeritus, Department of Sociology, University of the Witwatersrand.

Justin van der Merwe: Researcher, Centre for Military Studies, Military Academy, Stellenbosch University.

Jeremy Wakeford: Senior Lecturer Extraordinary, School of Public Leadership, University of Stellenbosch.

Index

Printed and bound by CPI Group (UK) Ltd, Croydon, CR0 4YY

16/04/2025

14658447-0003